Financial
Accounting

Financial Accounting

A spreadsheet approach

N. Marriott and J. Simon

PRENTICE HALL
New York · London · Toronto · Sydney · Tokyo · Singapore

First published 1990 by
Prentice Hall International (UK) Ltd
66 Wood Lane End, Hemel Hempstead
Hertfordshire HP2 4RG
A division of
Simon & Schuster International Group

Typeset in $10\frac{1}{2}/12$ pt Times
by APS Ltd., Salisbury, Wiltshire, UK.

Printed and bound in Great Britain at the
University Press, Cambridge

British Library Cataloguing in Publication Data

Marriott, N.
    Financial accounting.
    1.   Financial accounting
    I.   Title   II.   Simon, J.
    657'.48

ISBN 0-13-315334-7

1   2   3   4   5   94   93   92   91   90

To Dee, Pru, Eunice, Arthur and May

Contents

Preface   xv

Acknowledgements   xix

Part A   Introduction: The changing world of accountancy   1

1   **The history of modern accountancy**   3
   1.1 What is accounting?   3
   1.2 The accountant and the computer   4
   1.3 The changing world of business education   6
   1.4 Financial accounting: an approach for the future   7
   1.5 The rudiments of accountancy   8

2   **The spreadsheet**   10
   2.1 Introduction   10
   2.2 What is a spreadsheet?   10
   2.3 How a spreadsheet works   11
   2.4 Common features of spreadsheets   11
   2.5 Spreadsheet convergence   14
   2.6 A few tips   16
   2.7 Good housekeeping   17
      Checklist   17
      Appendix   18

PART B   Basic financial accounting practice   19

3   **Balance sheet transactions**   21
   3.1 The accounting equation   22
   3.2 Double-entry accounting   23
   3.3 The concept of wealth   24
   3.4 Recording business transactions   24

3.5	What transactions is a business likely to make?	24
	Checklist	36
	'What if?' problems	36
	Answers	37
	Selected questions and exercises	37
4	**Profit and loss transactions**	**39**
	4.1 What is profit?	39
	4.2 Profit and the balance sheet equation	40
	4.3 Using the spreadsheet to calculate profit	41
	Checklist	47
	Workshop 4.1	47
	'What if?' problems	49
	Answers	50
	Selected questions and exercises	51
5	**Accruals and prepayments**	**54**
	5.1 Introduction	54
	5.2 Accrued expenses	54
	5.3 Prepaid expenses	56
	5.4 Accrued revenues	57
	5.5 Prepaid revenue	58
	Checklist	62
	Workshop 5.1	63
	Workshop guide	63
	'What if?' problems	66
	Answers	66
	Selected questions and exercises	66
6	**Provisions and debtors**	**69**
	6.1 Introduction: accruals and provisions	69
	6.2 Accounting for bad and doubtful debts	70
	Checklist	75
	Workshop 6.1	75
	Workshop guide	79
	'What if?' problems	79
	Answers	80
	Selected questions and exercises	80
7	**Depreciation and the disposal of fixed assets**	**83**
	7.1 The concept of depreciation	83
	7.2 Methods of calculating depreciation	84
	7.3 Accounting for depreciation	88

7.4 The disposal of fixed assets 93
7.5 Statement of standard accounting practice on depreciation 95
Checklist 96
Workshop 7.1 96
Workshop guide 97
'What if?' problems 97
Answers 100
Selected questions and exercises 100

8 Stock valuation **105**
8.1 Manufacturing companies 105
8.2 Basic cost accounting 105
8.3 Stock valuation 108
8.4 Accounting for stocks 113
Checklist 118
Workshop 8.1 118
Workshop guide 119
'What if?' problems 124
Answers 125
Selected questions and exercises 126

**9 The trading, profit and loss and appropriation account and
balance sheet** **132**
9.1 The trading and profit and loss account 132
9.2 Capital and revenue expenditure 134
9.3 Some additional transactions 135
9.4 The appropriation account 139
9.5 The balance sheet 147
Checklist 150
Workshop 9.1 150
Workshop guide 151
'What if?' problems 157
Answers 157
Selected questions and exercises 157

**10 Errors in the spreadsheet: the use of a trial balance, suspense
accounts and journals** **165**
10.1 Introduction 165
10.2 Using the spreadsheet for error detection 165
10.3 Errors revealed by the spreadsheet 167
10.4 Errors not revealed by the spreadsheet 168
10.5 Suspense columns 170
10.6 Journal entries 170

10.7	A worked example	170
	Checklist	175
	Workshop 10.1	176
	Workshop guide	176
	Selected questions and exercises	178

11 Accounting ledger systems — **183**
11.1	Introduction	183
11.2	Books of prime entry	184
11.3	The ledger system	188
11.4	Control accounts	191
	Checklist	197
	Selected questions and exercises	198

12 Reconciliation statements — **200**
12.1	Introduction	200
12.2	Debtors control account reconciliation statements	201
12.3	Creditors control account reconciliation statements	203
12.4	Bank reconciliation statements	206
	Checklist	212
	Selected questions and exercises	212

PART C Application of basic financial accounting practice to different types of organisation — **217**

13 The accounts of the sole trader: incomplete records — **219**
13.1	Introduction	219
13.2	The advantages and disadvantages of being a sole trader	219
13.3	The accounts of the sole trader	220
	Checklist	224
	Workshop 13.1	225
	Workshop guide	228
	'What if?' problems	234
	Answers	235
	Selected questions and exercises	235

14 Club and society accounts — **241**
14.1	Introduction	241
14.2	Receipts and payments account	241
14.3	Income and expenditure accounts	244
	Checklist	246
	Workshop 14.1	250
	Workshop guide	252
	'What if?' problems	252
	Answers	256
	Selected questions and exercises	257

15 Partnership accounts   **259**
    15.1 Introduction   259
    15.2 Accounting for partners   260
         Workshop 15.1   267
         Workshop guide   270
         'What if?' problems   270
         Answers   270
    15.3 Accounting for changes in partners   270
    15.4 Dissolution of a partnership   278
         Checklist   283
         Workshop 15.2   288
         Workshop guide   288
         'What if?' problems   290
         Answers   296
         Selected questions and exercises   297

16 Introduction to company accounts   **304**
    16.1 Limited liability and other legal requirements   304
    16.2 Appropriations of profit   306
         Checklist   308
         Selected questions and exercises   308

17 Sources of finance   **311**
    17.1 Introduction   311
    17.2 Types of finance   312
    17.3 How to account for the sources of finance   318
         Checklist   334
         Workshop 17.1   334
         Workshop guide   335
         'What if?' problems   338
         Answers   338
         Selected questions and exercises   338

18 Taxation in company financial statements   **339**
    18.1 Introduction   339
    18.2 Value added tax   340
    18.3 Corporation tax (CT)   341
    18.4 Advanced corporation tax   344
    18.5 The imputation system   346
    18.6 Income tax   346
    18.7 Deferred taxation   349
    18.8 A worked example   356
    18.9 Notes   359
         Checklist   360
         Workshop 18.1   360
         Workshop guide   361
         Selected questions and exercises   362

19 Accounting standards   **368**
    19.1   The need for accounting standards   368
    19.2   The standard setting process   369
    19.3   Individual accounting standards   370
    19.4   SSAP 3-earnings per share   371
    19.5   SSAP 4-accounting for government grants   371
    19.6   SSAP 6-extraordinary and exceptional items   374
    19.7   SSAP 6-prior year adjustments   374
    19.8   SSAP 9-long-term contract work in progress   375
    19.9   SSAP 13-research and development expenditure   377
    19.10 SSAP 17-post balance sheet events   378
    19.11 SSAP 18-contingencies   379
    19.12 SSAP 21-leases and hire purchase   379
    19.13 SSAP 24-pension costs   380
    19.14 Note   380
           Checklist   380
           Selected questions and exercises   381

20 Final accounts of companies   **387**
    20.1   Introduction   387
    20.2   Profit and loss account layouts   388
    20.3   Balance sheet layouts   389
    20.4   Notes to the accounts   390
    20.5   Small and medium-sized companies   395
    20.6   Abridged accounts   396
    20.7   Directors report   396
    20.8   Chairman's statement   397
    20.9   A worked example   398
           Checklist   398
           Selected questions and exercises   402

PART D   Interpretation and comparison of financial statements   **409**

21 Funds flow statements   **411**
    21.1   Introduction   411
    21.2   The cash flow statement   413
    21.3   Working capital flow of funds statement   414
    21.4   Source and application of funds statement   425
           Checklist   427
           Workshop 21.1   427
           Workshop guide   427
           'What if?' problems   429
           Answers   429
           Selected questions and exercises   435

22 Interpretation of financial statements: The use of ratios   **440**
   22.1 Introduction   440
   22.2 What is a ratio?   440
   22.3 Liquidity ratios   442
   22.4 Profitability ratios   444
   22.5 Long-term growth ratios   445
   22.6 An example using ratio analysis   446
   22.7 Problems encountered in ratio analysis   446
          Checklist   451
          Workshop 22.1   451
          Workshop guide   454
          'What if?' problems   455
          Answers   456
          Selected questions and exercises   456

23 The corporate report and value added statements   **463**
   23.1 Introduction   463
   23.2 The corporate report   463
   23.3 The value added statement (VAS)   465
          Checklist   468
          Workshop 23.1   468
          Workshop guide   468
          'What if?' problems   469
          Answers   470
          Selected questions and exercises   470

24 Introduction to inflation accounting   **473**
   24.1 Problems of historic cost accounting   473
   24.2 Systems of current value accounting   479
   24.3 Current accounting financial statements   481
          Checklist   490
          Workshop 24.1   491
          Answers   491
          Selected questions and exercises   493

25 Auditing   **495**
   25.1 What is an audit?   495
   25.2 Stages of an audit   500
   25.3 Examples of audit reports   502
   25.4 Notes   503
          Checklist   503
          Selected questions and exercises   503

PART E   Solutions to selected questions and exercises   **505**

   Index   571

Preface

We are living in changing times. Information technology is now permeating many areas of our lives, and accounting education and training is no exception. Accountants are using the relevant elements of the new information technology in their jobs and potential trainee accountants are being taught at school to use this technology. This text takes some of these skills (the ability to use a microcomputer and any spreadsheet package) and utilises them to assist in the learning of financial accounting.

This is an introductory financial accounting text, which takes an innovative approach in that spreadsheet packages are used to record and analyse financial information. The text is based on UK financial accounting practice, but the skills are relevant to all countries in which financial accounts are prepared. Accounting conventions are dealt with in the chapters in which they are introduced (e.g. entity concept in the chapter on recording business transactions). The text is innovative in that spreadsheets are integrated in the teaching approach. As with all innovations, criticism is easy, but adoption requires determination and foresight to appreciate the benefits that will surely result from this computer-based approach.

The text is underpinned by a sound theoretical framework; we have tried to explain not only how to perform an aspect of accounting, but also why it is necessary, and why it is tackled in that particular way. In this way a critical approach is adopted. Later in the book, many of the underlying asumptions of financial accounting, as it is practised today, are assessed.

In learning and applying any skill a student proceeds through a number of stages. The first stage is the acquisition of knowledge. In this text this role is fulfilled by the chapter content. The next stages are ones of comprehension and application. This is the function of the workshop sessions which are designed to be completed with the student working at the computer, with or without the help of the tutor. It is assumed that students will be motivated not merely to input the model spreadsheet answer, but also to work their way through the example (which is based on material already covered in the text), turning to the relevant pages of the chapter or workshop guide when in difficulty, or consulting the tutor if present.

A range of skills is tested in the 'what if?' scenarios. The early questions involve changing the cell values with the student attempting to predict the consequences. This reinforces knowledge and comprehension, the correct answer immediately being given by the spreadsheet model that the student has constructed. Later 'what if?' questions ask the student to alter the nature of the transaction by changing cell contents or even the cell references. This can then be used to test higher levels of cognitive ability such as analysis, synthesis and evaluation. The end-of-chapter exercises are designed to achieve these more advanced learning goals as the students are required to apply their knowledge-base and skills to new and different applications.

Questions are provided at the end of the chapters to give further practice. Many questions are taken from the professional examinations of the various accounting and examining institutes. Answers are provided for some of these questions in the fifth section, Part E.

The main text is divided into four parts:

Part A: An introduction: the changing world of accounting
Part B: Basic financial accounting practice
Part C: Application of basic financial accounting practice to different types of organisation
Part D: Interpretation and comparison of financial statements

In Part A we discuss the development of accounting and provide some introductory assistance for students who have not previously used a spreadsheet, or whose spreadsheet skills need developing.

In Part B we show how to prepare a set of financial statements, starting with fairly straightforward situations and introducing more involved business problems in later chapters. The identification and correction of errors which might arise in the preparation of financial statements are then examined, followed by an exploration of accounting systems.

In Part C we examine how to prepare financial statements for a range of different organisations; these organisations include one-person businesses, clubs, societies, partnerships and companies.

In Part D we evaluate financial statements and discuss their uses. We explain how to interpret the statements prepared in Parts B and C and introduce two new statements to aid this interpretation: the funds flow statement and the value added statement. The historical cost statements are evaluated and their limitations examined; some solutions to counter these limitations are developed. Finally, the audit process is outlined.

We consider this book suitable for:

● university, polytechnic and college of further and higher education, first-year and second-year financial accounting courses;

- professional examinations;
- MBA courses in financial management;
- practising accountants who might use a spreadsheet package to assist in the preparation of financial statements.

N. M.
J. S.

Acknowledgements

We would like to express our thanks to friends, colleagues and students for their help, advice and support over the years in developing, writing and testing this text. In particular we are grateful to:

- Dee and Pru who have provided invaluable support, assistance and understanding;
- Ellis Jenkins, our much respected colleague at the Polytechnic of Wales, for his advice and constructive criticism;
- Paul Taylor of Lancaster University who introduced us to the approach through the many useful articles he has written;
- The examining bodies of the accounting institutes including the Association of Accounting Technicians, the Institute of Cost and Management Accountants, the Chartered Institute of Public Finance and Accountancy, the Joint Matriculation Board, the London Chamber of Commerce and Industry and the Royal Society of Arts, for their permission to use questions from their examinations.
- Cathy Peck, Maggie MacDougal and all those at Prentice Hall who have worked on the text.

Part A

Introduction
The changing world
of accountancy

1 ‖ *The history of modern accountancy*

1.1 What is accounting?

Accounting, at its most basic, is the term given to the provision and interpretation of financial information. Its history is as old as civilised man. Even our Neanderthal ancestors needed to know information of a numeric nature. The first accounting may have been on a cave wall in Lascaux in France, where nameless hunters attempted to record how many wild animals were available in the region. Apart from lacking a computer, our forebears lacked even the concept of numbers, so they drew a portrait of each beast. This was 16,000 years ago, but it was not until the Phoenicians that the symbol 'aleph' was invented, a triangle with two horns, to represent a cow. Once inverted, aleph became the Greek alpha and eventually the Roman letter A.

The concept of 'number' was, of course, introduced far sooner, but it is difficult to date. The earliest adding machines, possibly 30,000 years old, were in the form of notched bones or sticks, but the first counting board dates back some 3,000 years. The counting board was an early form of abacus, with ten stones arranged in rows. The first real abacus, that is, with beads on wire, appeared some time later, with contesting claims of origin: it could have been Chinese, Arabic or possibly even European.

As the adding machines developed, so we find records kept of stocks of goods and transactions, i.e. 'ins' and 'outs' of these stocks. These records were kept in Crete and Egypt, among other ancient civilisations, but the introduction of money measurement was left to classical Greece.

The accounts for the Parthenon building would probably have been just two lists of items, as follows:

1. Charges – consisting of balances arising at the beginning of the period plus any receipts.

2. Discharges – consisting of goods sold and consumed during the period plus the closing balances remaining.

The aim of this form of accounting was to prevent fraud and error. This principle still remains important today. However, the information produced was not used for performance appraisal, that is, to see how successful (or unsuccessful) the business had been, which is one of the functions of modern accountancy.

The passing centuries saw a growth in international commerce, accompanied by the rise of an influential merchant class in Europe. The origins of the system of accounting known as 'double-entry book-keeping' was in Renaissance Italy in the thirteenth and fourteenth centuries. The earliest text on the subject was by the Venetian, Luca Pacioli, whose book, *Summa de Arithmetica, Geometria, Proportioni et Proportionalita* was published in 1494. The work attempts to summarise the mathematical state of play of the times, but contains reference to a system of accountancy for ventures. Some of the principles he recorded are the cornerstones of modern accountancy theory, for example the use of a profit and loss account to take the difference between selling price and cost price, and the use of capital accounts to take capital introduced and profit.

The first explicit manual of accountancy appeared in 1543, and by the end of the seventeenth century, the double-entry system was in widespread use throughout Europe. By 1800 'accountants' were extracting balance sheets and profit and loss accounts on a regular basis. However, it was ignored, even looked down upon, by universities and other academic institutions.

Modern accountancy developed for a number of reasons. The growth of large scale corporate enterprises such as railways meant that many individuals had invested money in the business. These individuals wished to limit their liability to the amount invested in the enterprise, and as owners they appointed managers to run the company's day to day affairs. This divorce of ownership from control led to a requirement of accountability on the part of managers. The owners wanted information on how well their company was performing, but the current, very basic, financial information was insufficient in its preparation. For example, managers were able to manipulate the profit figure to the desired level and pay 'dividends' to the owners out of funds the business could not afford to lose.

In the United Kingdom, there were many legal requirements to regulate accounting information. There were Companies Acts passed in 1844 and 1862, along with acts to deal with the appointment of auditors (individuals employed by owners to check that managers were acting in the owners' best interests) and to deal with groups of companies (1948). The Companies Acts provide a framework for disclosure and require that financial statements such as a balance sheet and profit and loss account are periodically produced, with certain items specifically identified.

This legislative framework gave credence and quality to the providers of this financial information and the first professional body was established in 1880 in England by Royal Charter. This is now the largest of the accountancy institutes – the Institute of Chartered Accountants in England and Wales.

1.2   The accountant and the computer

The year 1642 is an important one in history. Galileo died, Newton was born and in France, Blaise Pascal built the first gear-driven mechanical calculator. Pascal's father was a tax official, albeit a mathematically gifted one, and Blaise would spend long hours helping his father to add columns of figures. He invented the Pascaline to help in the process of addition and subtraction of figures, to assist in the provision of basic financial information.

Gottfried von Leibniz's 'calculator', invented later in the seventeenth century, was able to perform multiplication and subtraction. It worked on a primitive base, for example to multiply twelve by ten, it added twelve to itself, and then added twelve to twenty-four, and so on, until it had performed the sum ten times. This is still the basis behind modern computers, although the current process is much quicker and more informed.

Charles Babbage's analytical engine of the eighteenth century had a memory capability which avoided the need to copy calculated results onto paper and so reduced the errors caused by this manual transposition process.

In 1886, William Burroughs invented the first adding machine that could be described as a commercial success, with over one million sold by 1926.

Dr Herman Hollerith developed a tabulating machine to assist in the compilation of the 1890 census in the United States. This machine used punched cards and was able to sort them. In 1914, Hollerith's company was renamed the International Business Machines Corporation (IBM) by his successor at the helm, Thomas Watson.

So far, the provision of financial information and the need to develop machines to speed up the process has been closely linked with the world of business and hence the accountant. Perhaps the most significant step, however, was taken by John von Neumann who helped to solve one of the major problems in computer development. The decimal system was causing problems of data manipulation and storage. Computers do not think in terms of 'hundreds, tens and units'. They respond to electrical impulses which are either off or on. Von Neumann abandoned the decimal system and began to think in terms of binary notation. The term 'byte' in computer jargon comes from 'by eight'. This in turn refers to the eight bits of information needed to make a byte. The computer recognises an impulse (notated by 1) or no impulse (notated by 0). Therefore:

Zone bits	Data bits
0010	0001

is neatly handled by the *electronic* computer. The zone bits determine the fact that it is a number that needs to be produced, while the data bits produce the figure, in this case 1. The series 0010 0101 would produce the figure 5, etc. The binary system, whose two digits represent the on or off state of the switch, is the basis of modern computer arithmetic and logic.

Many advances in technology, primarily military-led, have resulted in the widespread use of computers in society today. At heart, however, computers are basically just adding machines, machines to help in the provision of financial information, and to make the process of information provision more error free and much quicker. Just as Von Neumann used lateral thought to take a step 'back to basics', so this book will take accounting theory back to its simplest roots to enable the modern student of accounting to use this new sophisticated adding machine for one of its most useful purposes – to assist in the provision of financial information.

Just like the calculator of the 1970s, today's microcomputer spreadsheet will become as common as the abacus, and as easy to operate for the modern accountant.

1.3   The changing world of business education

Information technology has been the growth area of the 1980s. The adoption of the microprocessor in computer design has led to the production of increasingly small and cheap computers. Computers are no longer the domain of the big company: a large growth area has been found in education and home ownership. However, as with many new industries, its adoption has been hampered by a fragmented market, supplying different hardware and software. An analogy is the railways development of the industrial revolution: railway companies cornered the market in various regions by deploying different gauge sizes, with the result that it was impossible to travel the length and breadth of the country without changing trains, and hence, company.

Market leaders have emerged in the computer field, with **IBM** the current front runner, but the diversity of hardware and software ownership remains rather chaotic.

This has presented problems for teaching and learning through the medium of computers. In many educational establishments, information technology has been taught as a discrete subject, with students learning the skills of three main types of software: spreadsheets, word processing and databases. If education is to develop further, then these skills must be incorporated into the way in which other subjects are taught.

Accountancy is one subject where the skills of using spreadsheets are widely deployed. In April 1986, the ICAEW estimated that 70 per cent of practising accountants used some form of computer. A recent study commissioned by the CACA and DTI found that the impact of new technology has been in the use of spreadsheet and word processing packages. This surely implies that in the learning of accountancy, the student should be using the skills of information technology.

Many publishers have recognised the need for an integrated approach to the teaching of accounting, but they have tended to link the textbook to a specific spreadsheet package. This is fine if you own the software deployed, but can be very limiting and expensive if you currently operate a different spreadsheet.

One answer to the problem is to wait until a market leader of spreadsheets emerges, and use the accountancy textbook that integrates it into its examples.

However, this is an inadequate strategy for the present time and a market leader may take many years to emerge, if it does emerge at all.

A spreadsheet package is a tool for the completion of a task involving figures. Many spreadsheets use the same commands, and when differences occur they tend to be minor. Once you have a 'transferable skill', you will be able to pick up another spreadsheet package relatively easily. It is like driving a car: you may learn to drive in a Mini, but once you have passed your test you can drive a Ferrari, or even a small truck. The controls and capabilities of the vehicles will vary enormously, but you are still able to travel from A to B. The ignition switch may be in a different place, the clutch a bit more fierce (it may even be an automatic); the car may move faster or slower than you are used to, but after a brief settling-in period you soon become comfortable: the skill is in driving, not the vehicle you drive. So your spreadsheet skills can be used to operate unfamiliar spreadsheets, and they can be used to perform a variety of tasks. Many new spreadsheet packages allow you to import data from another package.

The ability to drive is almost taken for granted these days, as in the future the ability to use a spreadsheet will also be a prerequisite of many occupations. The skill requirement of the modern accountant is changing. An ability to use computers is becoming a necessity, rather than just a desirable weapon in the accountant's armoury. The students of the 1990s will be the accountants of the twenty-first century, so the time has come to rethink the teaching approach so that they are able fully to utilise the tools available to them.

1.4 Financial accounting: an approach for the future

This book is not about computers. The authors are not computer experts or specialists, but mere accountancy lecturers who have developed their teaching approach to meet the needs of this changing environment.

The future for accounting will be dominated by information technology. To shy away from the computer is to ignore the enormous advantages that the new science brings with it.

This does not mean that accountants and the students of accountancy have to rethink the basic concepts. The knowledge base remains unaltered. The principles are as familiar as those of Luca Pacioli in 1494, so those readers wishing to seek the sanctuary of debits and credits will be relieved to find that they still survive the test of time.

The approach taken involves using a computer spreadsheet to learn accountancy. It is envisaged that as you open the book, you have a computer switched on in front of you ready to help you learn.

We assume a basic understanding of a computer spreadsheet. The type of computer, the type of spreadsheet and the size of disks is irrelevant, but you must be capable of using the basic commands quite readily.

If you haven't yet attained this level of skill, do not close this book in frustration. Chapter 2 outlines how to use a spreadsheet. It is a new skill that you will find extremely useful and, like anything else, needs a lot of practice. There are a number of hurdles to overcome: the first is using the computer and the second is using the spreadsheet. The use of the computer is normally quickly learned, requiring the basic skills of loading the program, etc. A major barrier, however, can be the use of the keyboard, and slow progress is to be expected while you acquaint yourself with the position of various letters and numbers. Learning to use the spreadsheet correctly may well involve frustrating sessions overcoming what seem to be basic hurdles, but remember that once you have cleared a hurdle, you don't have to jump it again.

An accountant's skills represent the application of his knowledge base to the tackling of business problems. It is these skills that need to change. Skills are subject to a continual process of evolution, reflecting the demands of the changing environment faced by the accountant.

In the mid-1970s, the calculator was a relatively expensive commodity. To perform some mathematical functions a slide rule was used. In order to multiply and divide large numbers, 'log tables' were taught to students. In the space of just over ten years, calculators are almost a disposable commodity, even incorporated into the watch you wear. Just as with the development of the calculator, computers have become cheaper, smaller and are selling in large numbers. Who would be without one? At the time of writing, the latest growth market is laptop computers, with the same capabilities as their desktop brothers, only smaller and in some instances, cheaper.

This book is an attempt to integrate newly acquired computer spreadsheet skills into the learning of accountancy. It is based on the authors' own teaching programmes and is necessarily innovative in its approach. Traditionalists may well find it too radical, but it is an attempt to change the way in which accounting is taught, so that the student is able to work as readily with a computer as current students work with a calculator.

1.5   The rudiments of accountancy

A great deal of the terminology or jargon of modern accountancy can be traced to the Middle Ages. Many landowners, noblemen and merchants had estates to run, but being busy individuals they often had to appoint a third person to handle their affairs. Lines of communication were imperfect and small journeys by today's standards would have taken weeks, if not months. A knight in the Crusades would not have any contact with his estate, and hence his affairs, for a number of years! Consequently, agents or stewards were appointed to act for their masters and report to them what had happened during their absence. Indeed, they were called to account, that is, to present a statement of money (and other chattels) received and expended with a balance. This reporting role is today still referred to as the function of financial accounting.

However, how was our absentee landlord going to be able to trust his steward? His serf could not read, let alone add up, so our wily land-owner would make his steward present his account in the presence of his master, serfs and other interested parties. The Latin noun *auditus* means hearing, and this is the origin of audit. An auditor is a listener. The gathered assembly were all auditors, who could tell if the steward was in fact presenting a true and fair interpretation of what had happened; e.g. if the steward claimed to have sold sheep for twopence each to a neighbouring tenant, then the tenant would be able to verify that fact immediately. In fact, the origin of the word 'credit' (as per double-entry book-keeping's debit and credit) is 'believe' or 'trust'. Indeed, even today a businessman needs to trust the information and advice that his accountant gives him.

As the years progressed, so this stewardship role of accounting developed, until today it has a legal place in the financial reports of a limited company. This stewardship function has developed into the division of accounting called 'financial accounting'.

The principles have not altered. The information presented is still essentially historic, i.e. it is telling the owner what happened. Therefore speed in the provision of this information is a key element if the owners of the business wish to act upon it. Computers are very quick at handling numerical data. Their operating speed is measured in nanoseconds, i.e. 1 second $\times 10^{-9}$. To give an indication of how fast this is, some computers are able to perform as many mathematical computations in the time it takes for your coffee cup to drop from your desk to the floor, as a man could perform in his entire lifetime.

Information, however, is not just numbers. Information is data that is gathered, collated, summarised and presented in an aggregated form that the user can understand. So computers can assist in this aggregation and enhance the presentation of this information.

There is a phrase in computing – 'garbage in, garbage out'. A computer acts only on what is input. If the data is input incorrectly then the output is likely to be incorrect. However, if the data is correctly input then the *accuracy* of the aggregated information is assured.

Even accurate, well-presented and timely financial information can be confusing to the user. The information needs to be *interpreted* into a form that the recipient can act upon. Interpreting this information can mean even more calculations, e.g. by how much has profit risen in the past year? Why has profit risen? Has the business sold more items, or sold less but at a higher price? These mathematical manipulations are easier to perform with computer power at the accountant's fingertips.

In summary, financial accounting is based on the stewardship function, which means presenting the owners of the business with timely, accurate, well-presented, summarised financial information, together with any necessary interpretation. Today's financial accountant has his computer to assist him in this role.

2 ‖ *The spreadsheet*

AIMS OF CHAPTER _____

- to introduce the idea of the spreadsheet to the student;
- to identify key concepts and terms;
- to present some of the common features of spreadsheets used in the remainder of this text;
- to mention, where appropriate, the main differences between the major spreadsheets on the market.

2.1 Introduction

If you have had previous experience of a spreadsheet package then this chapter can be skipped over. On the other hand, if it has been some time since you've used a spreadsheet or you would like to refresh your memory, then you would benefit from reading the next few pages.

This chapter is not designed to teach you spreadsheets. This task is best performed by the manual accompanying the spreadsheet you are using, which may include a series of 'teach yourself' lessons. Before you start, read through the next few pages, which are designed to give you a general overview of spreadsheets and will indicate areas that you may choose to concentrate on in the manual. The features isolated are fairly universal and should be present in the package that you are using no matter how basic it is. Be aware of differences in command structures and, possibly, terminology. This is not an attempt to isolate *all* differences and eventualities, merely an indication of where these differences may be.

2.2 What is a spreadsheet?

A spreadsheet is an electronic worksheet that has grown in popularity since the late 1970s, when microcomputer sales started to boom. A typical spreadsheet is

10

shown on page 12. In fact, the spreadsheet application has sometimes been credited as selling more micros than any other application, possibly more than the word processor. It is a computer program that permits arithmetic manipulations of columns of rows and figures in what is best described as a matrix format. Once a spreadsheet has been developed it can be stored on disk and the data updated or amended. The data need not be purely numeric. Alphanumeric data, i.e. containing letters of the alphabet as well as numbers, and special characters (e.g. *, !, ?) can also be manipulated by most spreadsheets.

2.3   How a spreadsheet works

The first point to note is that the screen only views part of the spreadsheet, and you start at the top left-hand corner with the first eight columns and twenty or so rows as in Spreadsheet 2.1.

The remainder of the spreadsheet is stored in the computer's memory and can easily be accessed by moving the cursor keys to the right or down. Most spreadsheets allow much quicker movements, either by jumping or using the special function keys labelled **Home**, **PgUp**, **PgDn** or **End**. These allow the entire spreadsheet to be viewed one screen at a time, similar to browsing through a book. The prefix **Pg** means page, although this is a misnomer as the spreadsheet is one large page on a two-dimensional plane.

The columns are labelled at the top of the screen with the rows labelled on the left-hand side. This grid is divided into cells, i.e. where each column and row intersect, and positions on the grid are referred to by co-ordinates, e.g. cell A1 is the first cell on the spreadsheet in the top left-hand corner.

A cell can typically hold ten characters of data, either numeric or alphanumeric, but the column width can be varied to enable more data to be contained if necessary. The row width cannot be altered.

The spreadsheet works by making use of the grid reference to permit mathematical functions to take place at the will of the user. Data is entered into the cursor cell, e.g. a figure of 10 in cell A1 and 5 in A2. Formulae can then be entered in other cells, e.g. in cell A3 place A1 + A2. In cell A3 the figure 15 is displayed, i.e. 10 + 5. By varying the data contents of cells A1 and A2, the result of the formula in cell A3 automatically recalculates.

2.4   Common features of spreadsheets

2.4.1   Arithmetic operations

Even unsophisticated packages permit the basic arithmetic functions, but the keys chosen may be unusual. The + and − keys hold no surprises, but multiplication is achieved by * and division by /. More complex operations are for the most part

Spreadsheet 2.1   The top left-hand corner

```
            A         B         C         D         E         F         G         H
1          10
2           5
3          15
4
5
6
7
8
9
10
11
12
13
14
15
16
17
18
19
20
 A3                    Form=SUM(A1:A2)
Width:  9  Memory: 187   Last Col/Row:A3
   1>
READY F1:Help   F3:Names   Ctrl-Break:Cancel
```

```
         A        B        C        D        E        F        G        H
1        10
2         5
3        15
4
5
6
7
8
9
10
11
12
13
14
15
16
17
18
19
20
Arrange  Blank  Copy  Delete  Edit  Format  Global  Insert  Justify  Load  Move
Name  Output  Protect  Quit  Save  Title  Unprotect  View  Window  Zap  /more
   2>/
```

unnecessary for this text, other than the key ∧, which usually means 'to the power of'.

2.4.2 Formulae

A formula is the contents of a cell performing some sort of mathematical manipulation, e.g. B5 * C4, placing the result in the cell containing the formula. The formula can be a mixture of cell references and absolute values, e.g. F5 + 7 would add seven to the value in cell F5. You cannot perform mathematical manipulations with cells containing text or alphanumeric data (other than other formula cells). Sometimes a number of cells in a column or row need to be added up and this can be a long exercise, e.g. A1 + A2 + A3 + A4 ... A20. As this is a frequent demand most spreadsheets use a shorthand by utilising a sum command and specifying a range. On Supercalc derivitives this would be **Sum(A1:A20)**, while on Lotus lookalikes this would be @**Sum(A1 ... A20)**. This command is frequently referred to in later chapters so it is imperative that you know how to perform this function on your spreadsheet.

2.4.3 Copying and/or replication

The spreadsheet construction rests on grid references, but these references are only relative to the cell accessed. If the accessed cell is A5 and there is a reference to cell A1 in the formula contained therein, then this tells the spreadsheet to extract the data from the cell in the same column and four rows up. Most packages contain functions called **Replicate** or **Copy**. If the contents of cell A5 were replicated to cell B5 then the same *relative* relationships would hold true, i.e. the cell four rows up in the same column, but this time that would be cell B1. It is sometimes possible to copy the cell contents to another cell and to maintain the *absolute* relationships, i.e. still refer to cell A1 once copied to cell B5. These are concepts that you should be familiar with, as they will decrease the amount of inputting you perform in the spreadsheets you will construct later. You can usually copy a range or block of cells in one go with all relative relationships still holding. This is helpful when examples are repeated for later years. Remember, use the computer's capacity to work for you to reduce the monotony of constant inputting of cell references. Master this skill before you start and you will be rewarded with the ability to work through the examples in the text, workshops and exercises much more quickly.

2.4.4   Titles and windows

As most of the spreadsheet models you construct will be larger than the screen's capacity, the software writers have normally included the facility for some of the spreadsheet to remain static while the remainder passes underneath or to the side. This is a title facility and is used to keep headings at the top of the screen and narratives to the left so that you can see what you are doing. This is an important feature that we recommend you use extensively to enhance the learning process. If you are operating on some remote part of the spreadsheet model then you are unlikely to guess the column correctly and errors can easily be made. Where possible spreadsheets referred to in the text may be screen prints of much larger spreadsheets, concentrating on the accounting element under scrutiny. This is the way you should be able to work.

Windows resemble titles, but are used to split the spreadsheet horizontally or vertically to achieve the same result, i.e. you can see what you are doing. They can be used in conjunction with titles if necessary. An example of a spreadsheet utilising both these facilities is given in Spreadsheet 2.2.

2.4.5   Other facilities

There are too many features to mention in this overview, but commands such as **Blank**, **Delete**, **Edit** and **Insert** are all self explanatory and the usefulness of the basic tools is without question in constructing accounting models.

Blank is used to erase a cell's contents, while **Delete** removes either an entire row or column. **Edit** allows the contents of a cell to be accessed and amended and **Insert** refers to the addition of blank rows or columns within the spreadsheet work area.

One feature of the spreadsheet is that it permits 'what if' calculations to be performed quickly, without damaging any of the underlying relationships, to assess the outcome of various scenarios.

2.5   Spreadsheet convergence

As with developing products in a competitive market, the rivalry between software firms results in product improvement and refinement until most spreadsheets now look and 'feel' fairly similar. Command structures and layouts are following a consumer-acceptable norm, with more recent derivatives able to import spreadsheets developed using a different package or to export models to a form acceptable to a different package. (See the appendix on page 18 for a brief summary of spreadsheet commands.)

Spreadsheet 2.2 The title and window facilities (the use of compressed print is also shown)

	A	B	D		F	G
1	Income Statement			1		
2				2		
3		Q1	Q3	3	Year	
4		----------------------		4	------------	
5	Sales	25,000.00	35,000.00	5	105,000.00	
6	Costs	15,000.00	21,000.00	6	63,000.00	
7				7		
8	Profit	10,000.00	14,000.00	8	42,000.00	
9				9		
10				10		
11	EXPENSES			11		
12	General & Admin	3,750.00	5,250.00	12	15,750.00	
13	Consultant Fees	3,000.00	4,200.00	13	12,600.00	
14				14		
15	Total Expenses	6,750.00	9,450.00	15	28,350.00	
16	Net Before Tax	3,250.00	4,550.00	16	13,650.00	
17	Income Tax	650.00	910.00	17	2,730.00	
18				18		
19	Net Income	2,600.00	3,640.00	19	10,920.00	
20				20		

```
 F20
Width: 12   Memory: 251  Last Col/Row:G19      ? for HELP
  1>
F1=Help F2=Cancel F9=Plot F10=View
```

	A	B	C	D	E	F
1	Income Statement					
2						
3		Q1	Q2	Q3	Q4	Year
4		--				
5	Sales	25,000.00	20,000.00	35,000.00	25,000.00	105,000.00
6	Costs	15,000.00	12,000.00	21,000.00	15,000.00	63,000.00
7						
8	Profit	10,000.00	8,000.00	14,000.00	10,000.00	42,000.00
9						
10						
11	EXPENSES					
12	General & Admin	3,750.00	3,000.00	5,250.00	3,750.00	15,750.00
13	Consultant Fees	3,000.00	2,400.00	4,200.00	3,000.00	12,600.00
14						
15	Total Expenses	6,750.00	5,400.00	9,450.00	6,750.00	28,350.00
16	Net Before Tax	3,250.00	2,600.00	4,550.00	3,250.00	13,650.00
17	Income Tax	650.00	520.00	910.00	650.00	2,730.00
18						
19	Net Income	2,600.00	2,080.00	3,640.00	2,600.00	10,920.00
20						

```
 A1    TL     Text="Income Statement
Width: 15  Memory: 251  Last Col/Row:G19     ? for HELP
  1>
F1=Help F2=Cancel F9=Plot F10=View
```

Spreadsheet 2.3   Lotus 1–2–3™

```
A3: @SUM(A1..A2)                                                        MENU
Worksheet  Range  Copy  Move  File  Print  Graph  Data  System  Quit
Global,  Insert,  Delete,  Column,  Erase,  Titles,  Window,  Status,  Page
         A         B        C        D        E        F        G        H
 1        10
 2         5
 3        15
 4
 5
 6
 7
 8
 9
10
11
12
13
14
15
16
17
18
19
20
01-Jan-80  12:20 AM
```

Most packages have an identifiable status line giving the contents of the cell and the cursor position, and option lines giving the commands available to the user at that prompt. Spreadsheet 2.3 is a Lotus 1–2–3™ version of the Supercalc4™-based Spreadsheet 2.1, with these features indicated.

2.6   A few tips

Save your work at regular intervals rather than only at the end of the exercise, as mistakes do happen and can be costly. Always take back up copies of your important files, preferably on a different disk. Your back up disks should be rotated so that old back up files are overwritten when no longer required. This reduces the numbers of disks required and creates a good organisational discipline.

Use your printer to its best advantage, e.g. use compressed print modes if present. Your spreadsheet may have landscape print utilities, which are invaluable. If not, there are commercial packages available that will print most files landscape and give you a selection of font sizes, page lengths and print quality.

A golden rule is to ensure that the spreadsheet is doing as much work for you as possible. There may be some minor features available that can make life easier, e.g. the use of the repeat key ' can be used to draw lines across the entire spreadsheet width; for instance, '- or '_ produces lines of ---- or ____ as desired.

2.7 Good housekeeping

One last word concerns the development of good habits when working with computers. The care needed when using disks should be clear: they are not bits of paper and can be damaged by magnetic fields, heat, damp, pressure, bending or sticky misplaced fingers.

Your computer is the tool that you will use to help you. Treat it with respect, it is a delicate piece of machinery. If you are using the facilities of an institute of learning, think of other students who need to use the equipment. If something is not working, report it. Computers do not smoke cigarettes or drink coffee. They react badly to both.

When you start a session of study make sure that you have a formatted disk, with enough space on it to save your work at the end, or you will soon become frustrated. If you find a disk, do not be selfish and reformat it, it probably contains many hours of a fellow student's work and is worth far more to him or her than the blank is worth to you.

Put your name on the volume label to identify a disk. Taking the time to enter the date and time during the DOS prompts can also avoid confusion later on, especially when using similar filenames. It can also be used to prove that the file is your work and not someone else's.

CHECKLIST _____

Having completed Chapter 2, you should be able to:

■ understand what is meant by a spreadsheet;

■ identify the main concept, terms and common features associated with spreadsheets;

■ identify some of the main differences between major packages.

Appendix *Summary of spreadsheet commands*

Description	Supercalc	Lotus
Loading spreadsheet	sc3	123
Loading previously saved spreadsheet	/Load,b:FILENAME	/File,Retreive, FILENAME
Saving spreadsheet	/Save,b:FILENAME	/File,Save,FILENAME
Printing spreadsheet	/Output,Display,(RANGE),Print	/Print,RANGE,Go
Plus	+	+
Minus	−	−
Multiply	*	*
Divide	/	/
To the power –	^	^
Add a range of consecutive cells	Sum(__:__)	@Sum(__..__)

Erasing a cell's content –
    useful when you have
    made a mistake
	/Blank	/Range,Erase,__

Deleting a row/column	/Delete	/Range,Erase,(__..__)
Changing a cell's contents	/Edit	f2
Copying a block of cells	/Copy	/Copy
Replicating	/Replicate	/Copy,(__..__)
Putting a window into your spreadsheet	/Window	/Worksheet,Window
Putting in a title	/Titles	/Worksheet,Titles
Underlying	'-	\-, then copy for range

Notes
1. Where the spreadsheet program only requires you to input the first letter of the instruction, the first letter is marked with a capital letter
2. _ means you are required to input a number
3. __ means you are required to input a cell reference
4. FILENAME requires you to input the file name

Part B

Basic financial accounting practice

3 ‖ *Balance sheet transactions*

AIMS OF CHAPTER

- to introduce the accounting equation and the concept of wealth;
- to introduce you to a method of recording business transactions called double-entry book-keeping;
- to show you how to use your spreadsheet package to record these transactions, minimising the amount of effort on your part through the use of relative cell referencing;
- to introduce you to the concept of the business entity;
- to introduce you to the concept of duality and to give you experience of recording transactions in this way;
- to introduce you to the cost concept;
- to show you how to prepare a balance sheet at any point in time for a business.

All businesses buy goods and/or services (items to use in the business such as goods to resell, motor vehicles to transport these goods, and so on), pay wages, pay rent, sell goods and/or services in an attempt to make profit. It is necessary to record all these transactions to keep track of what has happened to the business and to work out the profit the business has made. This chapter will focus on the setting up of the business and the purchase of items used in the business. The next chapter will focus on the payment of expenses and the sale of goods to customers. A spreadsheet program will be used to record these business transactions.

The spreadsheet is used rather than pen and paper since it has many advantages, some of which are shown in Figure 3.1.

You will need to load your spreadsheet package in preparation to working through the examples in this text. However, before you do this it is necessary to understand some accounting theory. The theory sets the rules we will use to record all business transactions; it is not complicated and is quickly understood.

1.   A spreadsheet is far better at manipulating figures than the human brain and, despite popular belief, it does not make mistakes.
2.   The fact that you are using a spreadsheet forces you to structure your accounting knowledge, thus ensuring that you have a better grasp of the affairs of the business.
3.   The spreadsheet can calculate your accounting statements quickly, and can recalculate any statements if there is a necessary change to any of the original transactions. It can also produce figures based on changing assumptions. These are called 'what if' statements and are useful in planning the future of a business.

Figure 3.1   Some advantages of using a spreadsheet package for accounting purposes

3.1   The accounting equation

The central tenet of a financial accounting system is the accounting equation, which can be written as

Assets $=$ Capital $+$ Liabilities

Assets represent resources possessed by the firm such as cash, stock it has purchased for resale or a motor van used to transport these goods. These assets must have been supplied by someone; in fact they could have been financed by only two sources. Firstly from money invested in the firm by its owners; this is called capital. Secondly from money lent to the business from someone other than the owners, such as a bank loan or money owed to suppliers of goods; this is called liabilities.

Now it is immediately apparent that assets must equal capital plus liabilities, as all resources possessed by the firm must come from either the owners (i.e. capital) or someone else (i.e. liabilities). This equality holds good throughout all occurrences, so it provides the bedrock of the accounting system.

We can rewrite the equation as follows:

Assets $-$ Capital $-$ Liabilities $= 0$

As we can see, capital and liabilities are negative, reflecting the fact that the business owes money. It is this form of the equation we will use throughout the rest of this book, since in this form the accounting equation can be recorded on a spreadsheet program.

3.2 Double-entry accounting

When the business acquires assets they must be financed by either the owners (through capital) or by others (through liabilities). Therefore if assets increase then either capital or liabilities must increase by the same amount. For example, if assets increase by £100 then either capital or liabilities must also increase by £100 to ensure the accounting equation remains in balance, i.e.:

$$
\begin{array}{llllll}
 & \text{Assets} & - & \text{Capital} & - & \text{Liabilities} & = 0 \\
 & 100 & - & 100 & - & 0 & = 0 \\
\text{or} & 100 & - & 0 & - & 100 & = 0
\end{array}
$$

This is what accountants call double entry or the duality concept, since one part of the equation cannot change without another part changing by an equal amount; remember the equation must sum to zero. See Figure 3.2 for more about the duality concept and an explanation of the terms debit and credit.

In fact we can list all possible combinations of double entry which can be applied to the accounting equation. These possibilities are shown in Figure 3.3a, with examples of each transaction presented in Figure 3.3b.

Duality is the underlying concept of double-entry book-keeping, referring to the fact that there are two aspects to the balance sheet. On one side there are assets, which are equally matched by the claims against them, either the amount owing to the proprietor(s) of the business or to other suppliers of finance. This concept is clearly seen in the balance sheet equation written in its traditional form:

Assets = Liabilities + Captial

Double-entry book-keeping ensures that the principles of duality are always maintained. Accountants use the terms 'debit' and 'credit' to distinguish each part of the transaction. The relationship between debits and credits and the accounting equation is shown below:

	Assets =	Liabilities +	Capital
Debit	+	−	−
Credit	−	+	+

By following the fundamental rule of 'for every debit there must be a credit', the equation stays in balance. If an asset is purchased using cash, the asset account is debited while the cash account, another asset, is credited by the same amount. Thus the equilibrium is maintained. See Chapter 2 for the other permutations available.

Figure 3.2 The duality concept

1.	Increase in an asset	(i)	Increase in capital
		(ii)	Increase in liability
		(iii)	Decrease in another asset
2.	Decrease in an asset	(i)	Decrease in capital
		(ii)	Decrease in liability
		(iii)	Increase in another asset
3.	Increase in capital	(i)	Increase in an asset
		(ii)	Decrease in a liability
4.	Decrease in capital	(i)	Decrease in an asset
		(ii)	Increase in a liability
5.	Increase in a liability	(i)	Increase in an asset
		(ii)	Decrease in another liability
		(iii)	Decrease in capital
6.	Decrease in a liability	(i)	Decrease in an asset
		(ii)	Increase in another liability
		(iii)	Increase in capital

Figure 3.3a   Possible combinations of double-entry transactions

3.3   The concept of wealth

At this point it is interesting to ask, how much is the business worth, or put another way, what is the wealth of the business? This question can be answered in two ways. It is worth the amount of money the owners have invested, so it is worth the amount of capital invested. Alternatively, it is worth the amount of resources the business possesses less the amount owed to third parties (i.e. those people who have lent the business money). Therefore it is worth the amount of assets less liabilities.

3.4   Recording business transactions

You should now have a screen in front of you displaying a blank spreadsheet, as in Spreadsheet 3.1. Don't worry if your spreadsheet is not exactly the same, but remember to use the correct commands for your spreadsheet. The text will tell you what to do in broad terms so that you can adapt the instructions to your configuration of computer and software.

3.5   What transactions is a business likely to make?

We will look at a few typical transactions.

1(i)   When Mike Rowe, a sole trader, starts a business, investing his personal savings, he opens a bank account for his new venture. Mike puts £1,000 of his own money into the new account. The business now has an asset, i.e. £1,000 *increase* in the business bank balance, which is equally matched by the investment made by Mike, i.e. an *increase* in capital of £1,000.

(ii)   If Mike buys a van for £7,000 by borrowing money from the bank, i.e. by way of a loan, then the business has *increased* its assets, as it now owns a van worth £7,000, but it has also *increased* its liabilities, i.e. it owes the bank £7,000.

(iii)   Alternatively, if the van had been bought using the money already in the bank account, then while the assets of the business still *increase* by the value of the van, the asset of money in the bank must *decrease* by the amount paid for the van.

2(i)   Just as Mike invested his savings in 1(i) above, so he is entitled to take money from the business for his own personal use. Say he withdrew £500 for his holidays. The business bank account, i.e. an asset, would *decrease* by £500, but the capital invested in the business by Mike would also *decrease*.

(ii)   If Mike chose to pay off his loan for the van using money from the bank account, this would *decrease* the assets of the business, i.e. the bank balance would decrease by £7,000, but the liability of the loan would also *decrease* by £7,000.

(iii)   Eventually, Mike buys some stock to resell. Assume that the stock is paid for by cheque and he buys stock worth £1,500. This is an asset to the business, i.e. it is worth £1,500. Hence another asset has *increased*. However, this stock needs to be paid for from the bank account, thus *decreasing* the business asset of money by the same amount.

3(i)   Rather than take out a loan for the van, Mike could have used his existing vehicle for the business. He already owns an estate car worth approximately £4,000 which he intends to use solely for his new business venture. Just as in 1(i) above, he is *increasing* the capital he has invested in the business by £4,000, but instead of the bank account increasing, the asset of motor vehicles has *increased*.

(ii)   Mike could pay off the business's loan from his personal savings. This would *increase* the capital he has introduced, but it would also *decrease* the liabilities of the business by the amount of the loan.

4(i)   As 2(i).

(ii)   Mike does not have to use his own money to start the business. Many sole traders borrow money to launch a new venture. If Mike borrowed £3,000 at the start, then his capital could be *decreased* and his liabilities *increased*.

5(i)   As 1(ii).

(ii)   As you have seen, a liability can be a loan, e.g. to finance the purchase of a motor vehicle. However, many businesses buy stock on credit, owing the money to their suppliers or creditors. With a limited amount of money in the bank, Mike may have to become overdrawn in the bank to *decrease* the liability to his creditors. However, by so doing, he has *increased* his liability to the bank.

(iii)   As 4(ii).

6(i)   As 2(ii).

(ii)   As 5(ii).

(iii)   As 3(ii).

Figure 3.3b Examples of double-entry transactions

Spreadsheet 3.1   The spreadsheet

	A	B	C	D	E	F	G	H
1								
2								
3								
4								
5								
6								
7								
8								
9								
10								
11								
12								
13								
14								
15								
16								
17								
18								
19								
20								

```
 A1
Width:  9  Memory: 254  Last Col/Row:A1      ? for HELP
  1>
F1=Help F2=Cancel F9=Plot F10=View
```

3.5.1   Capital and the entity concept

What is likely to be the first thing that happens when a business is started?

The businessman will introduce some money into the business so that it can buy goods and/or services to sell to its customers. Capital is the accounting term which is widely accepted as the money the owner introduces into the business. This is the first of many words which accountants over the centuries have used to describe parts of the business. You need to learn these words, together with their meanings, as they form the language of accounting. Let's say £10,000 is introduced into the business on 1 January 19X7.

How do we record this capital on our spreadsheet?

Before we can answer this question we need to understand the first of a number of accounting concepts (the other concepts will be introduced at the appropriate time in the text). This concept is called the 'entity concept'. The entity concept states that we must record all transactions as they affect the business and ignore the effect they have upon the businessman. This an important distinction which we need to be clear about from the very beginning, as it underlays most of what we are going to say about recording business transactions.

1. By focusing on the business we are able to work out the profit made by the business. The inclusion of personal expenditures (for example holidays and the weekly shopping bill) and personal income (wins on the premium bonds) would mix up business profit or loss with personal profit or loss. Of course we could keep a separate set of records for these personal expenditures and revenues, in which case the individual would be the entity to be accounted for. Maybe you would like to record your own personal transactions after you have mastered this chapter.
2. Large organisations employ managers to run the business. These managers require financial information to run the business efficiently (this is produced by the business's management accounting system) and to report to the owners of the business; this reporting by the business's management to its owners is a stewardship function and is the problem to which most of this book is addressed.
3. Companies can have limited liability. This is a legal privilege granted to companies. It restricts the loss suffered by the owners should the business go into liquidation, to their investment in the business. That is, their personal possessions are not at risk. Sole traders and partnerships have no such insurance against bankruptcy.

The entity concept has a number of problems associated with it:

1. It can be difficult to separate transactions between those relating to the business and the owner, for small unincorporated businesses. For example, if the owner runs his business from home, then expenditures such as the cost of lighting and heating the premises will have to be divided between business and personal use.
2. For groups of companies (i.e. a holding company and its subsidiaries), the entity concept is extended to include all companies in the group. The problem is in deciding whether a company is a member of the group. This problem is discussed in most advanced financial accounting books.

Figure 3.4 The entity concept: advantages

The entity concept

The entity concept separates the business from its owners. Therefore we record transactions as they affect the business and ignore the effect they have on the owners directly. This dichotomy produces several advantages, which are shown in Figure 3.4.

The concept in practice

Let us show how this concept works by examining the effect upon the business of the owner introducing the £10,000 cash into the business. Spreadsheet 3.2 shows the recording of this transaction. The business now has resources of £10,000 cash (an asset), so we need to record this by opening up a column for the asset cash, labelling it **ASSET: Cash**, in D4, and recording the £10,000 as a positive entry (a

Spreadsheet 3.2   Starting the business using relative cell referencing

	A	B	C	D	E	F	G	H
1								
2	Trans.			ASSET				
3	Date	Description		Cash	CAPITAL			
4								
5	01/01/X7	Capital Introduced		10000	-10000			
6								
7								
8								
9								
10								
11								
12								
13								
14								
15								
16								
17								
18								
19								
20								

```
E5                Form=-D5
Width:  9  Memory: 253  Last Col/Row:E5      ? for HELP
   1>
F1=Help F2=Cancel F9=Plot F10=View
```

debit) in D5. We use column D to record this cash entry, leaving the first three columns for the date of the transaction, column A, and a narrative description to remind us of the transaction that we are recording, column B. (Note the narrative in column B is overlapping column C.) Your spreadsheet may be capable of formatting column B to make it large enough to take the narrative. Try duplicating this spreadsheet layout on the package you are using, ensuring that column D is formatted to a width large enough for five figures, and column E is large enough for six figures to account for the minus sign.

However, we have no record of where this £10,000 comes from. Since this would be a useful piece of information, we open up another column called **capital** in column E and record a second £10,000 on the same line as the cash £10,000. Since the business owes this £10,000 to the owner, we need to record it as a negative figure (a credit). To record this entry we could enter − **10000** in cell E5, but it is better if we make the computer do the work for us by telling it to place it in cell E5 minus the amount that is in cell D5. Spreadsheet 3.2 shows the current position and displays on the status line the fact that cell E5 contains the formula − **D5**. This is known as relative cell referencing.

It is a rule that we take a separate row for each transaction. Each row will tell us what the transaction is, when it took place and the double entry necessary to record its effects on the accounts of the business.

Remember we are recording the transaction from the point of view of the business and not the businessman; this is the entity concept.

Let us analyse what we have done. We have used the accounting equation to record this transaction. The introduction of £10,000 by the owner has led to two entries on the spreadsheet: a positive and a negative entry of equal size. This is the basis of the double-entry recording system used by accountants throughout the centuries and in most countries in the world. Note that when added together the two entries sum to zero; this is always the case and as we've used a relative cell reference to record the double entry this acts as a checking mechanism. This transaction is a type 1(i) transaction (see Figure 3.3).

All that remains to be done is to make a brief description of the transaction in the description column, to remind us of the transaction at a later date. Three columns are usually adequate for this purpose – one to record the date of the transaction, column A, and two to give some narrative information, column B; this is why we started with column D above. Spreadsheet 3.2 shows the spreadsheet after this transaction has been recorded.

3.5.2 Opening the business bank account

Until the businessman decides what to spend the £10,000 on, it is sensible to ensure this £10,000 is kept safe and secure. The usual way of ensuring this security is to deposit the money in a bank account, opened in the name of the business.

Let's say £9,900 is deposited into a business bank account (another type of asset) on 2 January 19X7, leaving £100 in cash to pay for any small items such as business lunches. How do we record this transfer of £9,900 from cash to the bank account? Cash has gone down by £9,900 so we need to record a negative (credit) £9,900 in the cash column of the spreadsheet. The other side to the transaction is the increase in the bank account; therefore we need to open up a new column, column F, called **bank**, and record £9,900 as a positive entry (debit). Again a brief description of the transaction is placed in the description columns. Spreadsheet 3.3 shows the new spreadsheet. Note that cell F7 is using relative cell referencing to insert the positive entry to match the negative entry of cell D7. (The fact that the figure in D7 is −9900 means that the formula −D7 will result in a positive figure in the **bank** column.) This transaction is a type 1(iii) transaction.

3.5.3 The balance sheet – Part 1

After each transaction is recorded onto the spreadsheet the columns can be summed to see the current position of the business as shown by the accounting equation. Let's do this on line 10 of the spreadsheet. For cell D10 enter the formula that will sum column D from line 5 to 7. Spreadsheet 3.4a shows the

Spreadsheet 3.3   Depositing cash into the bank

	A	B	C	D	E	F	G	H
1								
2	Trans.			ASSET		ASSET		
3	Date	Description		Cash	CAPITAL	Bank		
4								
5	01/01/X7	Capital Introduced		10000	-10000			
6								
7	02/01/X7	Depositing Cash		-9900		9900		
8								
9								
10								
11								
12								
13								
14								
15								
16								
17								
18								
19								
20								

```
 F7              Form=-D7
Width:  9  Memory: 253  Last Col/Row:F7      ? for HELP
    1>
F1=Help F2=Cancel F9=Plot F10=View
```

Spreadsheet 3.4a   a–c Summing the transactions

	A	B	C	D	E	F	G	H
1								
2	Trans.			ASSET		ASSET		
3	Date	Description		Cash	CAPITAL	Bank		
4								
5	01/01/X7	Capital Introduced		10000	-10000			
6								
7	02/01/X7	Depositing Cash		-9900		9900		
8								
9				-----------------------------------				
10				100				
11								
12								
13								
14								
15								
16								
17								
18								
19								
20								

```
 D10             Form=SUM(D5:D7)
Width:  9  Memory: 253  Last Col/Row:G10      ? for HELP
    1>
F1=Help F2=Cancel F9=Plot F10=View
```

Spreadsheet 3.4b

	A	B	C	D	E	F	G	H
1								
2	Trans.			ASSET		ASSET		
3	Date	Description		Cash	CAPITAL	Bank		
4								
5	01/01/X7	Capital Introduced		10000	-10000			
6								
7	02/01/X7	Depositing Cash		-9900		9900		
8								
9				------------------------------				
10				100				
11								
12								
13								
14								
15								
16								
17								
18								
19								
20								

```
 F10
To? (Enter Range), then <RETURN>; or <,> for Options
 23>/Replicate,D10,E10:F10
F1=Help F2=Cancel F9=Plot F10=View              POINT
```

Spreadsheet 3.4c

	A	B	C	D	E	F	G	H
1								
2	Trans.			ASSET		ASSET		
3	Date	Description		Cash	CAPITAL	Bank		
4								
5	01/01/X7	Capital Introduced		10000	-10000			
6								
7	02/01/X7	Depositing Cash		-9900		9900		
8								
9				------------------------------				
10	02/01/X7	Balance Sheet		100	-10000	9900		
11								
12								
13								
14								
15								
16								
17								
18								
19								
20								

```
 F10           Form=SUM(F5:F7)
Width:  9  Memory: 252  Last Col/Row:G10      ? for HELP
 1>
F1=Help F2=Cancel F9=Plot F10=View
```

status line necessary on our example. Repeat this formula for cells E10 and F10 using the replicate command (or its equivalent) as shown in Spreadsheet 3.4c. Notice that a dotted line has been inserted in row 9 to indicate that the figure in row 10 is the total of the columns above.

Once we have installed the transactions, we can see that the business has £100 in cash and £9,900 in the bank; these are the assets of the business. The remaining column total is the £10,000 capital; this shows how the assets have been financed. These column totals form a statement called the 'balance sheet', shown in Spreadsheet 3.4c. The balance sheet shows the position of the business at any moment of time and is prepared as often as is necessary. Our spreadsheet system shows how it is constantly updated after each transaction is recorded. However, it is usual to prepare it after a distinct period of time has elapsed, usually a year or a month. In the spreadsheet it is a good idea to draw a line to show the transactions that the balance sheet has accounted for.

Note from Spreadsheet 3.5 that we have only input two figures; the remainder have been calculated by the computer. This has distinct advantages over manual completion of accounts as, by changing any of the original entries, we can produce a new balance sheet and be confident that it will balance.

Spreadsheet 3.5   The use of relative cell referencing

	A	B	C	D	E	F	G
1							
2	Trans.			ASSET		ASSET	
3	Date	Description		Cash	CAPITAL	Bank	
4							
5	01/01/X7	Capital Introduced	10000		-D5		
6							
7	02/01/X7	Depositing Cash		-9900		-D7	
8							
9				-------------------------------------			
10	02/01/X7	Balance Sheet		SUM(D5:D7)	SUM(E5:E7)	SUM(F5:F7)	
11							
12							
13							
14							
15							
16							
17							
18							
19							
20							

A1
Width: 9   Memory: 252   Last Col/Row:G10   ? for HELP
    1>
F1=Help F2=Cancel F9=Plot F10=View

Spreadsheet 3.6 The purchase of a motor van

```
            A          B          C         D         E         F         G        H
 1
 2      Trans.                            ASSET               ASSET     ASSET
 3      Date      Description             Cash    CAPITAL     Bank      Van
 4
 5      01/01/X7  Capital Introduced      10000   -10000
 6
 7      02/01/X7  Depositing Cash         -9900               9900
 8
 9                                       --------------------------------
10      02/01/X7  Balance Sheet            100    -10000      9900
11
12      03/01/X7  Purchase of Van                            -3000     3000
13
14
15
16
17
18
19
20
 G12                   Form=F12*-1
Width:    9   Memory: 252   Last Col/Row:G12          ? for HELP
     1>
F1=Help F2=Cancel F9=Plot F10=View
```

3.5.4 Purchase of a motor van

A business needs a motor van (another type of asset) to transport its products; therefore let our business buy a van costing £3,000, paying by cheque on 3 January 19X7. We record this transaction by recording a negative entry (a credit) into the bank column of £3,000 and opening up a new column entitled **motor van**, recording the cost of the van as a positive entry (a debit) by inserting the formula $-F12$ in cell G12. The motor van is an asset of the business. Spreadsheet 3.6 shows the updated spreadsheet. This is another type 1(iii) transaction. The logic behind the choice of which cell is a value and what is a formula is open to your discretion. Here you would expect the money to leave your bank account before you took possession of the van. Therefore the value cell is in the bank account with the formula cell in the van account.

3.5.5 Purchase of goods on credit

Now our business buys £5,000 worth of goods from a supplier on 5 January 19X7, which it intends to resell at a profit. We need to record this purchase of goods in

When preparing a set of accounts, all assets are shown at the price that the business paid for them.. This is because accounts are based on historic cost. This concept is useful because it ensures objectivity, i.e. the asset will receive the same accounting treatment from any accountant preparing the accounts. The concept works in conjunction with other rules, e.g. prudence. If the asset is no longer worth its historic cost then a more representative valuation is used in the accounts preparation. Other systems of accounting which take account of the effects of inflation do not use this concept.

Example
A business bought some raw materials for £2,000 a year ago and has not used them in production yet, i.e. they are in stock. If the same items were purchased today they would cost £2,500, but the balance sheet value is still £2,000. If the items were worth £1,500 then this lower figure would be used. The prudence concept is said to be overriding the cost concept.

Figure 3.5 The cost concept

our spreadsheet. We now have a new asset called 'stock', so we open up a new column labelled **stock** and record a positive (a debit) £5,000 into that column. Where does the negative (a credit) £5,000 go? We cannot record it as a negative entry in the bank column as we have not yet paid for these goods. We need to reflect the fact that we owe this money to a supplier; this is a liability, remember. This is achieved by opening up a new column for this liability called **creditors** and recording the negative entry (credit) in that column. Creditors represent a liability of the business, since it will have to be paid in the future. If you use the same logic as above then it may be wise to make the value cell the amount in the creditor column and the formula cell the amount in the stock column. This is a type 1(ii) transaction. Have you realised that we are recording the assets (the motor van and stock) at the price we paid for them? This is the cost concept which is explained in Figure 3.5.

3.5.6 Raising a loan

Now our business raises a loan from a local finance house of £5,000 which is paid by cheque on 8 January 19X7. We record this loan as an increase in assets by entering a positive (a debit) £5,000 in the bank column and a negative (a credit) £5,000 in a new liability column, called **loan**. This is a type 1(ii) transation, presented in Spreadsheet 3.7.

3.5.7 The balance sheet – Part 2

Let's produce a new balance sheet for the business at this point in time. It's the same routine as before, just sum the columns to date, using the replicate command

Spreadsheet 3.7 The balance sheet as at 8 January 19X7

	A	B	C	D	E	F	G	H	I	J	K
1											
2	Trans.			ASSET		ASSET	ASSET	ASSET	LIABILITY	LIABILITY	
3	Date	Description		Cash	CAPITAL	Bank	Van	Stock	Creditor	Loan	
4											
5	01/01/X7	Capital Introduced		10000	-10000						
6											
7	02/01/X7	Depositing Cash		-9900		9900					
8											
9				------------------------------							
10	02/01/X7	Balance Sheet		100	-10000	9900					
11											
12	03/01/X7	Purchase of Van				-3000	3000				
13											
14	05/01/X7	Goods on Credit						5000	-5000		
15											
16	08/01/X7	Raising a Loan				5000				-5000	
17											
18				--							
19	08/01/X7	Balance Sheet		100	-10000	11900	3000	5000	-5000	-5000	

Spreadsheet 3.8 The balance sheet as at 8 January 19X7: the extent of relative cell referencing

	A	B	C	D	E	F	G	H	I	J
1										
2	Trans.			ASSET		ASSET	ASSET	ASSET	LIABILITY	LIABILITY
3	Date	Description		Cash	CAPITAL	Bank	Van	Stock	Creditor	Loan
4										
5	01/01/X7	Capital Introduced		10000	-D5					
6										
7	02/01/X7	Depositing Cash		-9900		-D7				
8										
9				---						
10	02/01/X7	Balance Sheet		SUM(D5:D7)	SUM(E5:E7)	SUM(F5:F7)				
11										
12	03/01/X7	Purchase of Van				-3000	-F12			
13										
14	05/01/X7	Goods on Credit						-I14	5000	
15										
16	08/01/X7	Raising a Loan				5000				-F16
17										
18				---						
19	08/01/X7	Balance Sheet		SUM(D10:D17)	SUM(E10:E17)	SUM(F10:F17)	SUM(G10:G17)	SUM(H10:H17)	SUM(I10:I17)	SUM(J10:J17)

to cut down the work that you have to do. Notice that you only need to sum from the previous balance sheet, i.e. rows 10 to 17, as the previous transactions have been accounted for. Also the total line itself sums to zero, i.e. the balance sheet balances! Try it for yourself by totalling columns D to J and placing the result in column K. No matter how much we alter our original figures the balance sheet remains perfectly in balance. Spreadsheets 3.7 and 3.8 show where you should be at this stage. Spreadsheet 3.8 shows you just how much work the computer is doing for you. Notice that you have only input five figures, but the computer has worked out eighteen. That's the way to do it!

Save your work at this point *before* you attempt the 'what if' problems – it will be required with the existing values at the start of Chapter 4.

CHECKLIST _____

Having completed Chapter 3, you should be able to:

- define the accounting equation and the concept of wealth;
- see how the balance sheet changes as transactions are entered;
- define, in your own words, the entity concept;
- define, in your own words, the duality concept;
- record business transactions on the spreadsheet in double-entry form and prepare a balance sheet at any moment in time;
- amend business transactions which you have entered on the spreadsheet;
- define, in your own words, the cost concept;
- understand the effect on the balance sheet of amendments you have made.

'What if?' problems

These problems examine the effect on wealth of changes in the original transactions.

Let's have a look at how the wealth of the business will alter if we change our transactions. Try to answer the following questions:

1. If the owner invests £12,000 cash into the business instead of £10,000, then the wealth of the business will increase by _____?

    Insert −12000 in cell D5 and see how the computer recalculates all the necessary double entries to produce a final capital figure of £_____?

2. If only £9,500 was lodged in the business bank account, wealth will be £_____?

Insert − 9500 in cell D7 and see what the new capital figure is. Why doesn't it change?

3. If the motor van cost £4,000 instead of £3,000, wealth will be £_____?

    Insert − 4000 into cell F12 and see what the new capital figure is. Why doesn't it change?

4. If the business purchases £7,500 of goods on credit, wealth will be £_____?

    Insert 7500 in cell H14 and see what the new capital figure is. Why doesn't it change?

5. If the business raises a loan of £3,000 instead of £5,000, wealth will be £_____?

    Insert 3000 into cell F16 and see what the new capital figure is. Why doesn't it change?

Answers

1. £2,000; £12,000.

2. £10,000 – it does not alter the amount of money invested in the business.

3. As above.

4. As above.

5. As above.

Selected questions and exercises

Question 3.1   You are required to enter the following transactions and prepare the closing balance sheet as at 31 January:

1 January	Started business with £2,000 cash
1 January	Put £1,500 cash in a bank account
4 January	Bought goods for £450 cash
5 January	Raised a loan of £1,000 from J. Smith
16 January	Bought goods on credit £500

Solution on page 507.

Question 3.2   You are required to enter the following transactions and prepare the closing balance sheet as at 31 January:

1 January	Started business with £10,000 cash
1 January	Put £4,000 of the cash in a bank account

4 January	Bought goods on credit for £5,000 from S. Jones
5 January	Bought a motor van for £5,000 on credit from Van Sales Ltd
16 January	Bought goods for £500 cash
18 January	Paid S. Jones £3,000 by cheque

Solution on page 507.

Question 3.3   You are required to enter the following transactions and prepare the closing balance sheet as at 31 January:

1 January	Started business with £250,000 cash
1 January	Put £200,000 of the cash in a bank account
4 January	Bought goods for £200,000 cash from ICI plc.
5 January	Bought vehicles for £105,000 credit from Grumpits Ltd
6 January	Bought three motor cars from AB Cars for £40,000 cash
16 January	Raised a bank loan of £100,000
18 January	Paid ICI plc. £180,000 by cheque

Solution on page 507.

4 || *Profit and loss transactions*

AIMS OF CHAPTER _____

- to familiarise you with the concept of profit;
- to enable you to use the spreadsheet approach to calculate profit for a given period;
- to increase the number of transactions you can deal with, enhancing the development of the skills learned in the previous chapter;
- to introduce the realisation concept;
- to introduce the accruals or matching concept;
- to prepare a profit and loss account using a spreadsheet;
- to introduce the profit and loss account as a period statement and the idea of the accounting period concept.

4.1   What is profit?

When assessing the performance of a business, the question of how much profit it has earned is one of the first indicators of its success or failure. The term 'profit' is in everyday use and yet the concept can be quite complicated to understand.

Profit is, in its simplest form, defined as net income for the period. When you talk of income you usually refer to a salary or grant or some other source of fairly regular cash. You can usually distinguish this from wealth (i.e. what resources you possess in terms of assets, for example your bank balance). If your income increases, and you spend less than you earn, then it stands to reason that you will have increased your bank balance; or, to put it another way, you have increased your wealth. In order to assess how well you are doing, you can look at your profit or change in wealth.

Just as you assess your performance in this manner (income and wealth), so a business tries to assess its own performance, for the benefit of the owners and other interested parties (such as the tax man!).

We will now see how to determine profit and how this fits into the balance sheet equation that we examined in Chapter 3.

4.2   Profit and the balance sheet equation

In the balance sheet equation we saw how the wealth of the business could be measured in terms of the accounting equation:

Wealth = Assets − Liabilities = Capital

Just as in your case, if the business earns more money than it spends, then its wealth will rise. The income of the business would be sales revenue, while the expenditure would be the expenses it incurred in earning the sales.

Net income = Sales − Expenses = Profit

For example, if the business sells items for £1,000 and incurs expenses of £600 in so doing, then the net income or profit on the transaction is £400.

If we, as individuals, make a profit, then our wealth increases, and this is also true of the wealth of the business (capital). Therefore capital is increased by the profit earned. Of course the converse is true of a loss (i.e. capital decreases).

Profit can be thought of as the difference between wealth at any two points in time. For example, if your wealth at the start of the year is £10,000 and you make a profit of £1,000 during the year, what is your wealth at the end of the year? Clearly it is £11,000 (i.e. opening capital + profit = closing capital).

	£
Opening capital	10,000
Profit for year	1,000
Closing capital	11,000

It can be difficult for a student new to accounting to view the idea of a negative entry in the profit column as being a good thing. The reality is that profit is a minus figure in the original equation, just like capital:

Assets − Liabilities − Capital − Profit = 0

If the profit figure rose, i.e. more minuses are placed in the column, then for the equation to remain in balance the business must have bought more assets or reduced its liabilities, both of which are good things as far as the business is concerned.

Figure 4.1   Explanation of profit

Profit for the period is therefore added to the capital balance, or wealth, that we had at the start of the period.

Assets = Liabilities + Capital at beginning + Profit of period

or

Assets − Liabilities − Capital at beginning of period − Profit = 0

Figure 4.1 summarises this concept of profit.

4.3   Using the spreadsheet to calculate profit

The spreadsheet example that you have been using has so far dealt with transactions affecting the balance sheet only. Now we will use the same example to record entries that make up profit.

First of all, load up your file and insert a column on the right (column K), and label it **profit**. Now we will look at a few typical transactions.

4.3.1   Rent

A business needs premises from which to operate. A new business such as ours will probably not have the resources to buy premises, so it will rent premises. Let us say the rent is £1,200 per year or £100 per month.

Once the business has occupied these premises for a month it will have incurred £100 rent, which it pays out of its bank account. This rent is payable on the tenth day of each month.

How do we record this payment of rent? The first entry is not too difficult, as the bank column will be reduced by recording a negative entry of £100. However, where are we to record the positive £100 (remember the duality concept: all transactions have two entries, a positive and a negative entry)?

So where does the positive entry go? Has the business got a new asset called rent? Surely not, as the rent is an expense of the business; that is, monies spent in running the business. Therefore this positive entry is recorded in the profit column. Remember that in our equation a negative figure in the **profit** column is a good thing; don't forget to use the appropriate relative cell reference, rather than the absolute value (i.e. a number).

Spreadsheet 4.1 shows how this transaction is recorded.

Spreadsheet 4.1   Paying rent using money from the bank

	A	B	C	F		I	J	K
1					1			
2	Trans.			ASSET	2	LIABILITY	LIABILITY	
3	Date	Description		Bank	3	Creditors	Loan	Profit
4					4			
5					5			
6	01/01/X7	Capital Introduced			6			
7					7			
8	02/01/X7	Depositing Cash		9900	8			
9				---------	9			
10	02/01/X7	Balance Sheet (1)		9900	10			
11					11			
12	03/01/X7	Purchase of Van		-3000	12			
13					13			
14	05/01/X7	Goods on Credit			14	-5000		
15					15			
16	08/01/X7	Raising a Loan		5000	16		-5000	
17				---------	17	---------------------		
18	08/01/X7	Balance Sheet (2)		11900	18	-5000	-5000	
19					19			
20	10/01/X7	Rent		-100	20			100

```
 K20              Form=-F20
Width:   9  Memory: 250  Last Col/Row:Q30      ? for HELP
    1>
F1=Help F2=Cancel F9=Plot F10=View
```

4.3.2   Payment of wages

In order to transport the goods and find a customer the business needs to have employees. Let us suppose our business has one employee, who is paid £600 every month. Towards the end of the month, on 27 January 19x7, the employee will receive a cheque for £600 drawn on the business bank account. This transaction is recorded by placing a negative entry of £600 in the bank column and a positive entry of £600 (i.e. $-$ F22) into the **profit** column, as these wages represent an expense of the business (in the same way as rent was an expense of the business).

This transaction is shown in Spreadsheet 4.2.

4.3.3   Sales and cost of sales

Now the business is ready to make a sale. A customer is willing to pay £3,000 for some goods which cost us £1,000. However, he is not prepared to pay £3,000 straight away; we agree that the £3,000 will be paid in two months' time.

To record this transaction we must record a positive and a negative entry on our spreadsheet. The positive entry is recorded in a column labelled **debtors** to tell us that someone owes the business money.

Spreadsheet 4.2 The balance sheet as at 29 January 19X7

	A	B	C	D	E	F	G	H	I	J	K	L	M
	Trans.		ASSET		ASSET	ASSET	ASSET	LIABILITY	LIABILITY			ASSET	
	Date	Description	Cash	CAPITAL	Bank	Motor Van	Stock	Creditors	Loan		Profit	Debtors	
	01/01/X7	Capital Introduced	10000	-10000									
	02/01/X7	Depositing Cash	-9900		9900								
	02/01/X7	Balance Sheet (1)	100	-10000	9900								
	03/01/X7	Purchase of Van			-3000	3000							
	05/01/X7	Goods on Credit					5000	-5000					
	08/01/X7	Raising a Loan			5000				-5000				
	08/01/X7	Balance Sheet (2)	100	-10000	11900	3000	5000	-5000	-5000				
	10/01/X7	Rent			-100						100		
	27/01X7	Wages			-600						600		
	29/01/X7	Sales									-3000	3000	
	29/01/X7	Cost of Sales					-1000				1000		
	29/01/X7	Profit			-1300						1300		Total
	29/01/X7	Balance Sheet (3)	100	-11300	11200	3000	4000	-5000	-5000		0	3000	0

Where does the negative entry go? It goes to the **profit** column. Notice that the transaction is dated on the day of the sale, in this case 29 January 19X7, and not on the day of payment, when a different transaction is recorded (i.e. the settlement of the debt). Accountants call this the 'realisation concept', which is explained in Figure 4.2.

However, this is not the end of the story, as we need to record the fact that stock has been reduced by £1,000. We do this by recording a negative £1,000 in the **stock** column and by recording a positive £1,000 in the **profit** column. The sale has cost the business £1,000. The accounting term for stock used up in this way is cost of sales. This matching of costs in the same accounting period as the sale is an illustration of the accruals concept. See Figure 4.3.

These transactions are shown in Spreadsheet 4.2.

Realisation in accounting terminology refers to the moment of time when profit is recognised. This point in time is usually when a business sells goods or services to a customer (usually when the goods change hands or, in the case of a service, when it is performed). It is important to note that there are other moments in time that we could use to recognise profit; some of these are as follows:

1. Payment is received by our firm. This would be a more cautious approach and is favoured by some accountants. However, it is not generally used, as the customer becomes liable once the goods are received or the service rendered. If, after this point, cash has not been handed over, then the customer becomes a debtor, i.e. legally liable to pay the debt in full. Therefore it is this concept that can lead to the dichotomy of a business being profitable (as it has made many sales at a good margin) while at the same time going bankrupt due to its customers not paying. The following paragraph tells an all too familiar story.
    A firm agrees to supply a customer with a large quantity of its output for the period. The customer agrees terms that entail payment within 28 days of the goods being delivered. The firm in the meantime has to pay its workforce, pay the suppliers of raw materials, and pay for delivery of the goods before any liability is incurred by the customer. While the order is profitable, the firm's bank balance is soon overdrawn and the bank have stopped payments of any further cheques. The firm's suppliers have filed legal proceedings and the workforce are refusing to complete the work necessary to finish the job until they receive their unpaid wages. The bank will not grant any further overdraft as the firm cannot recognise the profit on the sale, i.e. the customer has not received the goods and is therefore not liable to pay anything.
2. The goods are produced. This is rarely used, as the firm still has to sell its goods, so it would be imprudent. There may be an argument for using this point of time to recognise profit if there is a ready market for the goods and/or services of the firm.

Figure 4.2   The realisation concept

In accountancy, the term 'profit' is defined as revenue less expenses. The difference between money received and money expended is the bank balance. The company's profit is not the same as the company's bank balance; this is one of the early problems all students of accounting have to understand. The underlying methodology behind the profit calculation for an accounting period is that the revenue realised (see Figure 4.2) is matched (this concept is therefore often referred to as the matching concept) with the expenses incurred in producing it. The goods sold may not have been paid for by its customers, nor will our firm have paid for all the raw materials received from its suppliers. So the expenses (paid or not) are matched with the revenue they enable the firm to earn, so that profit can be calculated.
    See Chapter 5 for an in-depth analysis of this concept.

Figure 4.3   The accruals concept

4.3.4 Calculation of profit

If we look at the **profit** column we see a series of entries:

	£
	£
Rent	100
Wages	600
Sales	− 3000
Cost of sales	1000

If we summed the column we would have a total of £1,300 (negative). However, in accounting terms we would like to transfer the balance on this account into the **capital** column (remember closing capital = opening capital + profit), thereby making the sum of the **profit** column zero. This is shown in Spreadsheet 4.2.

We do this by summing column K between rows 20 and 26 and multiplying the sum by minus 1. The opposing entry we will place in the **capital** column, column E, again using our rule of relative cell referencing and multiplying by minus 1 (−1).

4.3.5 The balance sheet

We have now completed our series of transactions, so let's do a new balance sheet for the business at this point in time. By now you will know the routine: sum the columns from the opening balance sheet figures inclusive, using the replicate command to cut down the work that you have to do. To ensure that the balance sheet balances, sum the total line in the spreadsheet; if it sums to zero, it balances. Refer to Spreadsheet 4.2 for guidance. Spreadsheet 4.2a (see pp. 50–1) gives the formula back up, which is an important reference point. Ensure that you have used the appropriate cell references to achieve the same result.

The closing balance sheet is the bottom row (row 30) of the spreadsheet, and is the sum of the account balances to date. These should sum to zero on the spreadsheet, but it is usual to see the balance sheet written in a vertical format, as in Figure 4.4.

4.3.6 The profit and loss account

The balance sheet shows the position of the business after all transactions have been recorded. If we focus our attention upon the **capital** column (column E) we can see that it has increased from £10,000 to £11,300, indicating £1,300 profit has

	£	£	£
Fixed assets			
Motor van			3,000
Current assets			
Stock	4,000		
Debtor	3,000		
Bank	11,200		
Cash	100		
		18,300	
Less current liabilities			
Creditors		5,000	
Net current assets			13,300
NET ASSETS			16,300
Financed by:			
Capital introduced			10,000
Profit retained			1,300
Closing capital			11,300
Long-term liabilities:			
Loan			5,000
CAPITAL EMPLOYED			16,300

Figure 4.4   The balance sheet

been earned during the period of trading. How this profit has been earned is described by all the entries in the **profit** column. These entries are usually recorded in a statement called a 'trading and profit and loss account'. This statement is shown in Figure 4.5. A profit and loss account is a period statement, in that it explains how profit has been made from one date to the next. This is often called 'the accounting period concept'. This time period can be any period of time, but by convention is usually one year. Accountants distinguish between gross profit, which is the profit from trading, and the net profit, which takes account of any expenses incurred in earning the gross profit.

	£	£
Sales		3,000
Less cost of sales		1,000
GROSS PROFIT		2,000
Less expenses:		
Rent	100	
Wages	600	
		700
NET PROFIT		1,300

Figure 4.5   Trading and profit and loss account

CHECKLIST _____

Having completed Chapter 4, you should be able to:

■ define, in your own words, what is meant by profit;

■ understand the relationship between the profit and loss account and the balance sheet;

■ use the spreadsheet to calculate profit for a given period;

■ use the spreadsheet to record a large number of business transactions;

■ outline and apply the realisation concept;

■ outline and apply the accruals (or matching concept);

■ outline the accounting period concept.

Workshop sessions

Workshops are hands-on sessions that you should attempt after reading the corresponding chapter. The example given is similar to the one illustrated in each chapter. Try not to look at the answer, given in the accompanying spreadsheets, unless you have to. Make a note of any problems that you cannot understand to go over later with a colleague or your tutor. A workshop guide is given to talk you through some of the tricky transactions.

The cell references are the ones used by the authors; your references may well be different. To make sure that you've completed the spreadsheet model correctly, attempt the 'what if?' questions. These are progress questions, with the later one requiring some adjustment to the prepared model. Depending on the workshop and your spreadsheet skills, you should allow one to two hours to complete the task. Good luck!

Workshop 4.1

This workshop is based on the example in the text and is designed to:

1. consolidate the double-entry recording system you have learned in this chapter and

2. introduce some new transactions and the way they can be recorded. These new transactions are as follows:
   (i) sales to (and receipts from) specific customers. Businesses usually have more than one customer. In fact it makes good business sense not to rely exclusively upon one customer, since if they stop trading with you for some reason, you have other customers to sell your product to.

In this example Jason sells his product to C. Jones, T. Ellis and J. Brown. We record the credit sales Jason makes to these customers by having a separate column for each customer and recording a positive entry, the value of the sale in the relevant column.

The reason for having a separate column for each customer is that the business needs to know how much each customer owes so that these debts can be controlled. This information would be difficult to find if all sales were recorded in one column called **debtors**.

Receipts of money from the individual customers are recorded as negative entries in their columns; the positive entry goes to the **bank** or **cash** column, depending upon whether the receipt is in cheque or cash form
(ii) purchase from (and payments to) specific suppliers. In the same way that the business needs records of who owes it money, it needs records of who it owes money to.

Therefore a separate column is needed for each supplier the business buys goods on credit from. Since Jason buys goods on credit from three suppliers (A. Smith, L. Thomas and C. Vine), three columns are needed.

Purchases are recorded by entering a negative entry in the **suppliers** column and a positive entry in the **stock** column. Payment to these suppliers is recorded by entering a positive entry in the **suppliers** column (to cancel out the negative purchase entry) and a negative entry in the **cash** or **bank** column.

Transaction details

Date	Description of transaction
1 January 19X8	Jason started his business, investing £4,000 cash into the business
3 January 19X8	Deposited £3,800 into a newly opened business bank account
4 January 19X8	Bought goods on credit from A. Smith, a local supplier, for £3,000
10 January 19X8	Sold goods which cost £200 to C. Jones on credit for £400
11 January 19X8	Bought goods for cash costing £100
12 January 19X8	Bought a second-hand motor van for £1,200, paying by cheque
14 January 19X8	Paid a month's rent by writing a cheque for £200
18 January 19X8	Paid motor expenses of £50
19 January 19X8	Made a series of credit sales to:
	C. Jones £600
	T. Ellis £800
	J. Brown £600
	The cost of these goods sold amounted to £1,000

20 January 19X8	Received cheques from: C. Jones £600 T. Ellis £400 J. Brown £250
21 January 19X8	Paid A. Smith £2,000 by cheque
27 January 19X8	Purchased goods on credit from: L. Travis £600 C. Vine £800
29 January 19X8	Paid by cheque: L. Travis £600 C. Vine £400

Record the above transactions, showing the profit for the business for the month of January and the balance sheet at the end of the month.

Once you have completed Workshop 4.1 please check your logic with Spreadsheet 4.2a.

'What if?' problems

These problems examine the effect on profit of changes in the original transactions.

Let's have a look at how profit will alter if we change our transactions. Try to answer the following questions:

1. *Rent.* If the business pays £200 rent instead of £100, then profit will reduce by £_____?

    Insert −200 in cell F20 and see how the computer recalculates all the necessary double entries to produce a profit of £1,200.

    If this is not the case then maybe you've made an error in the relative cell referencing. Does your balance sheet balance, i.e. does it sum to zero? If not, then you possibly failed to make the double entry for a transaction.

2. *Purchase of goods on credit.* What if the business bought £4,000 worth of goods instead of £5,000? Will this alter profit?

    Try it; change the entry for cell I14 to £4,000. Did profit alter? No? Good! This is because this is a balance sheet transaction and it does not affect the profit column.

3. *Wages.* If we reduced the wages to £400, then what happens to profit? Alter cell F22 accordingly and your new profit figure is £1,400. As wages fall so profits rise. Try an increase in wages. Yes, profits fall. The evidence of this direct relationship explains why there is a lot of hard bargaining with unions each year!

Spreadsheet 4.2a   The balance sheet as at 29 January 19X7 (showing the use of relative cell references)

	A	B	C	D	E	F	G
1							
2	Trans.			ASSET		ASSET	ASSET
3	Date	Description		Cash	CAPITAL	Bank	Motor Van
4							
5							
6	01/01/X7	Capital Introduced	10000		-D6		
7							
8	02/01/X7	Depositing Cash		-9900		-D8	
9							
10	02/01/X7	Balance Sheet (1)	SUM(D6:D8)		SUM(E6:E8)	SUM(F6:F8)	
11							
12	03/01/X7	Purchase of Van				-3000	-F12
13							
14	05/01/X7	Goods on Credit					
15							
16	08/01/X7	Raising a Loan				5000	
17							
18	08/01/X7	Balance Sheet (2)	SUM(D10:D16)		SUM(E10:E16)	SUM(F10:F16)	SUM(G10:G16)
19							
20	10/01/X7	Rent				-100	
21							
22	27/01X7	Wages				-600	
23							
24	29/01/X7	Sales					
25							
26	29/01/X7	Cost of Sales					
27							
28	29/01/X7	Profit			-K28		
29							
30	29/01/X7	Balance Sheet (3)	SUM(D18:D28)		SUM(E18:E28)	SUM(F18:F28)	SUM(G18:G28)

4. *Sales.* If we sold the items for £4,000 instead of £3,000, then profit will be _____. What is your new profit figure?

Alter the debtors figure in K24 and see what happens to the profit total in column K.

So if we can increase the price of our products then we can make more money.

The balance sheet

If you only change the original value of your double entry, you should find that your balance sheet remains perfectly in balance. If it does not, then perhaps you have altered the referenced cell by mistake, rather than the cell of the original entry.

Once you feel you have understood the above transactions, attempt the workshop, which presents you with more, not more difficult, transactions.

Answers

1.   £100.

2.   Profit is unaffected by balance sheet transactions.

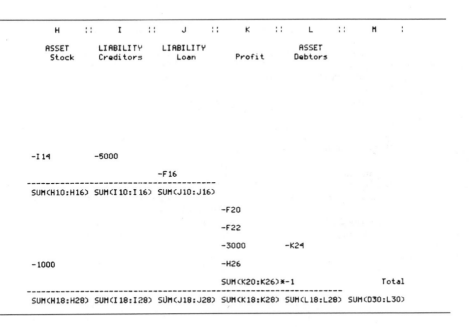

3. The profit figure is £1,400.

4. The profit figure is £2,400.

Selected questions and exercises

Question 4.1
Spreadsheet 4.3 shows the transactions which have occurred for Jones's business during the year ended 31 December 1990.

You are required to prepare the balance sheet and profit and loss account from the spreadsheet.

No solution provided.

Question 4.2
You are required to prepare a balance sheet as at 31 December 1990 and profit and loss account for the year then ended from the totals of Table 4.1.

No solution provided.

Spreadsheet 4.3   Jones's business, year ended 31 December 1990

	A	B	C	D	E	F	G	H	I
1	Description	Cash	Profit	Capital	Bank	J.Smith	A.Kile	Stock
2								
3	Capital Introduced	10000		-10000				
4								
5	Opened bank a/c	-7000			7000			
6								
7	Purchases					-5000		5000
8								
9	Sales		-7500				7500	
10								
11	Cost of Sales		4250					-4250
12								
13	Paid J.Smith				-2500	2500		
14								
15	Receipts from A. Kile				5000		-5000	
16	--
17	Balance Sheet	3000	-3250	-10000	9500	-2500	2500	750
18	==

Table 4.1 *Details of the accounts for question 4.1*

	Debit £	Credit £
Sales		45,789
Purchases	34,621	
Wages	5,670	
Sundry expenses	564	
Rent	680	
Rates	795	
Motor vans	12,250	
Debtors	5,680	
Creditors		9,800
Bank		890
Cash	56	
Stock	5,000	
Capital		44,527
Machines	6,790	
Land	8,900	
Buildings	20,000	
	101,006	101,006

Stock as at 31 December 1990 is £5,670

Question 4.3

You are required to record the following transactions and prepare a balance sheet
and profit and loss account.

Date	Description
1/1/90	Started business with £12,500 cash
2/1/90	Opened bank account paying in £10,000 cash
3/1/90	Bought goods on credit from T. Run for £900, D. Opal £5,600 and G. Lime £4,500
4/1/90	Bought van from T. Cooke for £8,790 on credit
5/1/90	Sold goods on credit to F. Smith £5,600 Cost of sale £3,000
8/1/90	Sold goods for cash £12,000 Cost of sale £8,000
9/1/90	Bought equipment for cash £5,431
10/1/90	Loan raised from J. Updike £10,000 by cash
11/1/90	Bought goods on credit from D. Opal £4,320, G. Lime £3,579 and K. Star £5,600
12/1/90	Bought goods for cash £4,376
15/1/90	Paid rent for month in cash £450
16/1/90	Sold goods on credit to F. Smith £4,500, G. Williams £12,980 and H. Herbert £13,000 Cost of sales £15,000
17/1/90	Received cheque from F. Smith £5,000
18/1/90	Paid T. Run £900, D. Opal £5,000 and G. Lime £4,250 by cheque
19/1/90	Paid T. Cooke £8,790 by cheque
22/1/90	Received cheques from F. Smith £4,400, G. Williams £11,000
23/1/90	Bought machine from K. Kelly £4,500 on credit

Solution on page 508–10.

5 | *Accruals and prepayments*

- to examine the limitations of cash accounting in financial reporting and the need to incorporate accruals and prepayments;
- to account for accruals and prepayments.

5.1 Introduction

In Chapters 3 and 4 we looked at the fundamental mathematics of accountancy – the basics of double-entry accounting. As we found, accountancy is not just simple arithmetic as in the real world business transactions do not always relate to neat definable periods of time. For example, in Chapter 3 we found fixed assets are used over a number of periods and goods purchased for resale are not always sold or paid for in the accounting period in which they are purchased. In Chapter 3 we found that customers do not always pay for goods by the business's year end, which results in debtors. Therefore, if we just used the receipts and payments of the cash/bank column to form the basis of the profit and loss account and balance sheet then we may omit some vital transactions that relate to the period in question. In this chapter we introduce more of these real-life business situations which need to be accounted for.

5.2 Accrued expenses

Expenses are often incurred (which provide the business with benefits) which do not coincide with its accounting periods. For example, consider the situation of electricity used by a business. Just as with a domestic household, businesses buy electricity on credit terms (i.e. they receive the product before they pay for it). These unpaid expenses are called 'accruals' (see Figure 5.1).

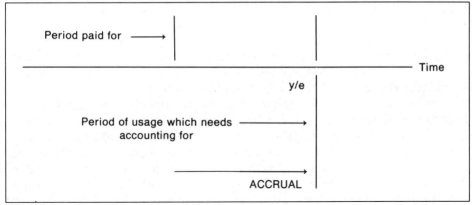

Figure 5.1 Accrued expenses

Spreadsheet 5.1 Accruals and prepayments

```
              !  A  !!  B  !!  C  !!  D  !!  E  !
     1
     2
     3   (a) Accruals
     4
     5   Description    Bank    Elect-  Profit
     6                          ricity  and
     7                                  Loss
     8
     9   Payment                -900    900
    10
    11   Usage                          -1200   1200
    12   ------------------------------------------
    13   Balance Sheet          -900    -300    1200
    14   ==========================================
    15
    16
    17   (b) Prepayments
    18
    19   Description    Bank    Elect-  Profit
    20                          ricity  and
    21                                  Loss
    22
    23   Payment                -1500   1500
    24
    25   Usage                          -1200   1200
    26   ------------------------------------------
    27   Balance Sheet          -1500   300     1200
    28   ==========================================
```

Unlike a domestic consumer's bill, the electricity bill can be substantial so it is necessary to reflect in the accounts that electricity has been used but not yet paid for. How is this done? The accountant includes an estimate for the amount outstanding. This estimate is called an accrual. Accruals are basically goods and services that the business has received on credit and are classified as liabilities to the business as it will have to pay for them in the future.

How do we account for accruals? Let's put amounts and dates to our electricity example and see how it is done. Suppose the business has paid for its electricity up to 30 September 1990; these payments come to £900. Its year end is 31 December 1990, so it needs to include in its accounts an accrual for the electricity used from 1 October 1990 to 31 December 1990, which is estimated as £300. Spreadsheet 5.1a shows how the accrual is accounted for. The payment is recorded by crediting the **bank** column (it could just as well have been the **cash** column). A newly opened column is used to record the debit entry (called **electricity**). It is necessary to have a separate column for electricity, as the value of electricity *used* does not equate to the amount *paid* for during the period being accounted, and the column is used to house the accrual. It is then necessary to work out the amount of electricity *used* during the period (i.e. the amount *paid* for the nine months to 30 September 1990 and an estimate of the usage for the three months to 31 December 1990). In this case the annual usage is £1,200. This amount is recorded as a credit to the **electricity** column and a debit to the **profit and loss** column. The total in the electricity column represents the accrual which is recorded in the balance sheet under current liabilities, as it will have to be paid within the next twelve months.

5.3   Prepaid expenses

You may be asking yourself what happens if the business pays in advance of the goods being received or the service rendered. These prepaid expenses are called 'prepayments'. Examples of such prepayments are rent, rates and insurance payments. Rent on a business premises is normally payable in advance, say during the first week of the month, while rates and insurance premiums are often paid yearly in advance (see Figure 5.2).

It is necessary to reflect this prepayment in the accounts. Let us assume that instead of paying for electricity in arrears, the business pays in advance. For example, suppose £1,500 is paid for the 15 months up to 31 March 1991 and we are preparing the accounts up to 31 December 1990, when the usage was £1,200. The accounting entries are shown in Spreadsheet 5.1(b). The payment is recorded as a credit to the **bank** column and a debit to an **electricity** column. The usage is recorded as with the accrual. The total in the **electricity** column represents the prepayment, which is recorded in the balance sheet under current assets, as it will be used up with in the next 12 months.

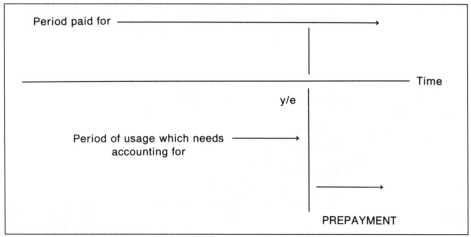

Figure 5.2 Prepaid expenses

5.4 Accrued revenues

In the same way that expenses can be paid in one accounting period and be used up in another accounting period, revenues can be received in one accounting period and relate to another.

Let us consider the situation where a business owns a few houses and receives rent from letting these properties; the annual rental is £1,200. If at the end of the year only £900 has been received (say the rent is payable in arrears), clearly £300 is still owed. This is illustrated in Figure 5.3.

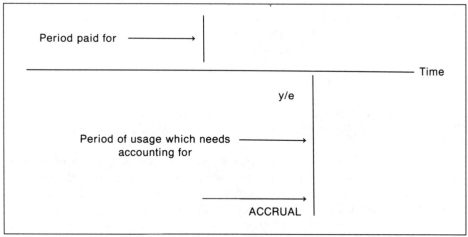

Figure 5.3 Accrued revenue

Spreadsheet 5.2   Accrued and prepaid revenue

```
              :  A  ::  B  ::  C  ::  D  ::  E  ::  F  :
    1
    2
    3        (a) Accrued Revenue
    4
    5   Descriptions           Bank    Rent    Profit
    6                                          and
    7                                          Loss
    8
    9   Cash received                   900    -900
   10
   11   Rent for period                        1200   -1200
   12   ----------------------------------------------------
   13   Balance Sheet                   900    300    -1200
   14   ====================================================
   15
   16        (b) Prepaid Revenue
   17
   18   Descriptions           Bank    Rent    Profit
   19                                          and
   20                                          Loss
   21
   22   Cash received                  1500   -1500
   23
   24   Rent for period                        1200   -1200
   25   ----------------------------------------------------
   26   Balance Sheet                  1500   -300   -1200
   27   ====================================================
```

Spreadsheet 5.2a shows how we can account for this accrued revenue. The rent received is recorded as a debit to the **bank** column and a credit to a **rent** column. The annual rent is recorded as a debit to the **rent** column and a credit to the **profit and loss** column. The columns are summed and we find a positive figure in the rent column of £300; this is accrued revenue and is a debtor of the business. It is a current asset as it is expected to be received within twelve months.

5.5   Prepaid revenue

On the other hand rent may be required to be paid in advance; say £1,500 for fifteen months. As £300 relates to next year, this is classified as prepaid revenue (see Figure 5.4).

Spreadsheet 5.2b shows how we can account for this prepaid revenue. The rent received is recorded as a debit to the **bank** column and a credit to the **rent** column. The annual rent is recorded as a debit to the **rent** column and a credit to the **profit and loss** column. The columns are summed and we find a negative figure in the **rent** column of £300; this is prepaid revenue and is a creditor of the business. It is a current liability as it is expected to cover the first three months of the next year.

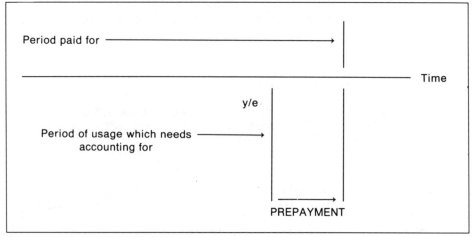

Figure 5.4 Prepaid revenue

The firm often has to estimate the amount of the accrued expense and revenue. It should always bear in mind the concept of prudence. See Figure 5.5 for an explanation of this concept.

Attempt the example in Figure 5.6 to see if you have understood how to account for accruals and prepayments. The accompanying spreadsheet is Spreadsheet 5.3.

Once you have attempted the question compare your spreadsheet with Spreadsheet 5.3 and read the following discussion outlining how the question was tackled.

1. The payment for rent is a credit in the cash account and a debit in the **rent** column. The rent used for the period represents 11/12ths of the £12,000 as the

The prudence concept (sometimes referred to as 'conservatism') is concerned with the situation where, given a choice, the accountant will understate rather than overstate the profit figure. If the choice is between balance sheet items, then the accountant will tend to understate the value placed on assets and overstate the value of liabilities. In this way all losses are charged against profit and no profits are anticipated. The concept is often given overriding status when its application comes into conflict with the application of other concepts.

The concept implies taking the safest course of action and is probably partly responsible for the idea that accountants are boring! The consequence of this is that the owners of the firm can be confident that the figure for profit is not going to be adjusted downwards as a result of some book-keeping indiscretion.

Figure 5.5 The prudence concept

The company's cash transactions for the year to 31 December 1990 include the following transactions:

		£
31 January 1990	Paid year's rent in advance	12,000
28 February 1990	Paid year's insurance premium	360

Received rents of £2,100 from tenents. At the year end £700 was still owing for the year ended 31 December 1990. Commission of £1,000 was received by the business for the period 1 January 1990 to 31 March 1991.

On 31 December 1990 the company sold £115,000 of goods to a customer, who was offered 30-day credit terms. The company buys goods on a 90-day credit basis, and on 31 November it took delivery of £85,000 of stock.

Electricity bills paid during the year amount to £2,000. The company's electricity bill is not due until 28 February 1991, but in the previous quarter last year the bill was £720. Electricity prices have risen by 10 per cent since then.

Other cash transactions during the year can be summarised as follows:

	£
Cash received from customers	100,000
Cash paid for stock sold	60,000

There was £20,000 worth of goods in stock at 31 December 1990.

There were no other transactions during the year.

Figure 5.6   The IOU/UOME Company

£12,000 covers the period from 31 January 1990 to 31 January 1991. The £1,000 is found to be the balancing figure in this column; it represents an amount prepaid by the business at the balance sheet date. This is a prepayment and represents an asset of the business. Alternatively, the amount of prepaid rent can be calculated (i.e. one month's overpayment $-1/12*£12,000$) and inserted as an asset in the closing balance sheet; the rent used is then calculated as the balancing figure in this column and debited to the profit and loss account.

2. The same logic is used to record the insurance payment, rent and commission received.

3. Credit sales and credit purchases are then recorded.

4. The payment for electricity is then recorded by crediting cash and debiting an **electricity** column. The electricity used is then calculated; this represents the electricity paid for (which covers the period from 1 January 1990 to 30 November 1990) plus an estimate of the remaining month's electricity usage. This estimate is obtained by using the last quarter's bill as a guide; this amounted to £720. As electricity prices have risen by 10 per cent, next

Spreadsheet 5.3 The IOU/UOME Company

	Cash	Debtors	Insurance	Rent Payable	Rent Rec'able	Comis.	Creditors	Elec'ty	Stock	Profit & Loss
CASH TRANSACTIONS										
Rent paid	-12000			12000						
Rent used				-11000						11000
Insurance paid	-360		360							
Insurance used			-300							300
Rent received	2100				-2100					
Rent for period					2800					-2800
Commission received	1000					-1000				
Commission for period						800				-800
Sales on credit		115000								-115000
Purchases on credit							-85000		85000	
Electricity Paid	-2000							2000		
Electricity used								-2264		2264
Cash received	100000	-100000								
Cash Paid	-60000						60000			
Cost of Sales									-65000	65000
Closing Balance Sheet	28740	15000	60	1000	700	-200	-25000	-264	20000	-40036	0

quarter's charge is likely to be about £792. This bill will cover the period from 1 December 1990 to 28 February 1992, so only 1/3 relates to the year 1990 (i.e. $1/3*£792 = £264$). Therefore the full usage is £2,264 (i.e. £2,000 + £264), which is credited to the **electricity** column and debited to the **profit and loss** column. The sum of this column is a negative £264 which represents an accrual. Alternatively, the accrual could have been calculated and the usage worked out as a balancing figure.

5. Cash received from debtors and cash paid to creditors are recorded.

Trading and profit and loss account for the year ended 31
December 1990

	£	£
Sales		115,000
Less cost of sales		65,000
GROSS PROFIT		50,000
Add Rent		2,800
Commission		800
		53,600
Less Rent	11,000	
Insurance	300	
Electricity	2,264	
		13,564
NET PROFIT		40,036

Balance sheet as at 31 December 1990

	£	£
Current assets		
Stock		20,000
Trade debtors		15,000
Prepaid expenses – insurance + rent		1,060
Accrued revenue – rent receivable		700
Cash		28,740
		65,500
Current liabilities		
Trade creditors	25,000	
Accrued expenses – electricity	264	
Prepaid revenue – commission	200	
		25,464
		40,036
Financed by:		£
Profit and loss		40,036

Figure 5.7 Trading and profit and loss account and balance sheet

6. The closing stock figure of £20,000 is recorded at the foot of the **stock** column and the cost of goods sold obtained as the balancing figure; its double entry is to the **profit and loss** column.

7. Finally, all columns with the exception of stock are summed.

The balance sheet and profit and loss account are also shown in Figure 5.7.

CHECKLIST

Having completed Chapter 5, you should be able to:

■ explain the differences between cash accounting and accrual accounting;

- define an accrual and a prepayment;
- account for accruals and prepayments;
- identify the limitations of cash accounting and why there is a need to incorporate accruals and prepayments.

Workshop 5.1: The frugal firm

Prepare the business's profit and loss account and balance sheet from the limited information given.

1. The business's cash transactions for the year to 31 March 1990 include the following:

		£
30 April 1989	Paid year's rent in advance	18,000
31 May 1989	Paid insurance for the year	480

2. On 31 March 1990 the business sold £125,000 of goods to a customer on 30-day credit terms.

3. The business buys goods on a 90-day credit basis, and on 31 January it took delivery of £105,000 of stock.

4. Electricity bills paid during the year amount to £3,000. The business's electricity bill is not due until 30 May 1990, but in the previous quarter the bill was £960. Electricity prices have risen by 5 per cent since then.

5. Other cash transactions during the year are summarised as:

	£
Cash received from customers	100,000
Cash paid for stock sold	90,000

6. There were £10,050-worth of goods in stock at 31 March 1991.

Assuming that there were no other transactions during the period and the business started in April 1990, prepare a spreadsheet giving the firm's profit and loss account for the 12 months to 31 March 1990 and the balance sheet as at that date.

Workshop guide

1. The £18,000 for rent is credited to the **cash** column D in row 7, with the corresponding debit in the **rent expense**, column G, achieved using the cell

reference — D7. Row 9 is used to calculate the rent used up (i.e. 11/12ths of the entry in G7 which is then debited to the **profit and loss account** in column K). A similar sequence of transactions are followed with the insurance premium, which is only 10/12ths used up.

2. By selling goods on credit the firm will have debtors. The **debtors** column E therefore carries the debit of £125,000 in row 15, with the opposite entry in the **profit and loss** column, K.

3. The credit purchases are a liability incurred by the firm so the entry — 105000 appears in cell H17. However, the opposite entry is not to the profit and loss account, as this will be charged with the cost of goods sold later. The double entry is in fact reflected in the **stock** account in column J, as the firm has an asset of stock.

4. The cash payment of electricity is simple enough with the entries in the **cash** and **electricity expense** columns. However, instead of just charging this amount to the profit and loss account, i.e. — I19, an additional amount equal to 2/3rds of the estimated bill (£960 + 5 per cent) is added to the entry in cell I21.

Spreadsheet 5.4   Workshop 5.1: The frugal firm – solution

	A	B	C	D	E	F	G	H	I	J	K	L
1												
2												
3											Profit	
4				Cash	Debtors	Insurance	Rent	Creditors	Elec'ty	Stock	& Loss	
5	CASH TRANSACTIONS											
6												
7	Rent paid			−18000			18000					
8												
9	Rent used						−16500				16500	
10												
11	Insurance paid			−480		480						
12												
13	Insurance used					−400					400	
14												
15	Sales on credit				125000						−125000	
16												
17	Purchases on credit							−105000		105000		
18												
19	Electricity Paid			−3000					3000			
20												
21	Electricity used								−3672		3672	
22												
23	Cash received			150000	−150000							
24												
25	Cash Paid			−90000					90000			
26												
27	Cost of Sales									−94950	94950	
28												
29	Closing Balance Sheet			38520	−25000	80	1500	−15000	−672	10050	−9478	0
30												

5. The cash received from the debtors is credited to the **debtors** account, and debited to **cash**. The sum of this column is the debtors outstanding. The converse is true of payments made to the firm's creditors, see row 25, and here the balance outstanding is the firm's remaining liability to its suppliers.

   The remaining accounts are also summed (don't forget to make use of replicate or copy facilities to save time), with the totals in the **rent** and **insurance** columns being prepayments reducing liabilities in future years, and the total in the **electricity** column being an accrual, reducing profit for the period in anticipation of the next bill for electricity used up in this accounting period.

6. The closing stock figure is inserted in cell J29 and used to calculate the **cost of goods sold** figure for the period, i.e. goods purchased less goods not used up (J17 − J29). This is a credit in the **stock** column and a debit in the **profit and loss account**.

Once you are content that your spreadsheet contains the correct cell references attempt the 'what if?' questions for the chapter.

Spreadsheet 5.5   Workshop 5.1: The frugal firm − formulae

	A	B	C	D	E	F	G	H	I	J	K
1											
2											
3											Profit
4				Cash	Debtors	Insurance	Rent	Creditors	Electricity	Stock	& Loss
5	CASH TRANSACTIONS										
6											
7	Rent paid			-18000			-D7				
8											
9	Rent used						-11/12*G7				-G9
10											
11	Insurance paid			-480		-D11					
12											
13	Insurance used					-10/12*F11					-F13
14											
15	Sales on credit				125000						-E15
16											
17	Purchases on credit							-105000		-H17	
18											
19	Electricity Paid			-3000					-D19		
20											
21	Electricity used								-2/3*960*1.05-I19		-I21
22											
23	Cash received			150000	-D23						
24											
25	Cash Paid			-90000				-D25			
26											
27	Cost of Sales									-J17+J29	-J27
28				---							
29	Closing Balance Sheet			SUM(D5:D27)	SUM(E5:E27)	SUM(F5:F27)	SUM(G5:G27)	SUM(H5:H27)	SUM(I5:I27)	10050	SUM(K7:K27)
30				==							

'What if?' problems

1. What if the business pays £10,000 more for its purchases? Does profit rise or fall? By how much?

2. What if the business has already paid £3,400 instead of £3,000? Will this affect the amount charged for electricity in the profit and loss account? Will the accrual be affected? Change the value in D19 to −3400 and watch what happens to cell K21 and I29. (You may need to use the window facility to achieve a vertical screen split, or possibly turn off the automatic recalc.)

3. What if the business paid its rent in advance on 31 December 1989? Amend the cell reference in G9 as appropriate? What is the new profit figure? What is the business's bank balance?

4. What if the electricity bill is expected to rise by 15 per cent? Amend the cell reference in I21 to change the estimate. What has the effect been on profit?

5. What would happen if the business has in fact overpaid its electricity bill due to an oversight and the electricity board *owes the business* £200? Would profit rise? Change the cell contents in cell I23 to reflect the transaction necessary to record correctly this unused expense.

Answers

1. Profit falls by £10,000.

2. The amount charged to the profit and loss account is the amount used. Therefore the accrual is affected.

3. G9 should now contain the formula **−3/12∗F7**. The new profit figure is increased by £12,000, as is the bank balance.

4. I21 should read, **−2/3∗960∗1.15-H19**. Profit will fall.

5. Profit would rise and the cell reference would be **−H19-H29**, with H29 changed to read 200, i.e. a prepayment.

Selected questions and exercises

Question 5.1
R. Smith runs a business whose financial year end is 31 December 1991. You are required to record the following transactions:

1. Rent–paid for the year ended 31 March 1992, £884.
2. Rates–paid on 30 September 1991, £2,400. Prepaid as at 31 December 1991, £560.
3. Petrol expenses–paid in 1991, £567. Owing £239 at 31 December 1991.

4. Electricity–paid £4,400 for the 11 months to 30 November 1991. The usage of electricity was even throughout the year.

Solution on page 511.

Question 5.2

R. Smith continues trading for another year. Record the following transactions:

1. Rent–paid for the year ended 31 March 1993, £946.
2. Rates–paid on 30 September 1992, £2,600. Accrued as at 31 December 1992, £400.
3. Petrol expenses–paid in 1992, £683. Owing £132 at 31 December 1992.
4. Electricity–paid £4,200 for the 15 months to 28 February 1993.
5. Rent–received £1,500 from letting a property recently acquired. The rent is for 15 months to 31 March 1993.
6. Commission–commission received £540. This is commission for the 7 months to 31 July 1990. The outstanding commission for the remaining 5 months of the year amounts to £345.

Solution on page 511.

Question 5.3

Eric Fluffy has extracted the totals shown in Table 5.1 from his records; please prepare a balance sheet and trading and profit and loss account for the year ended 31 December 1991.

Table 5.1   *Details of the accounts for Eric Fluffy*

	£ Debit	£ Credit
Sales		21,456
Purchases	12,418	
Opening stock	2,392	
Capital as at 1 January 1991		8,600
Drawings	2,450	
Bank overdraft		3,291
Rent payable	4,600	
Rent receivable		6,800
Commission receivable		56
Insurance	1,206	
Land	16,390	
Motor van	5,600	
Selling expenses	450	
Office expenses	760	
Wages and salaries	352	
Creditors		3,480
Debtors	4,580	
Cash	45	
Loan		7,560
	51,243	51,243

The following notes are relevant:

1. Closing stock was £2,460.
2. Rent payable accrued was £560.
3. Insurance prepaid, £120.
4. Wages and salaries, accrued £240.
5. Commission due, £68.
6. Rent received overpaid, £124.

Solution on page 512.

6 || *Provisions and debtors*

AIMS OF CHAPTER _____

- to distinguish a provision from an accrual;
- to account for bad debts;
- to account for doubtful debts;

6.1   Introduction: accruals and provisions

In the previous chapter we learnt how to account for accruals and prepayments without giving much consideration to the problem of how these are to be valued. In the case of prepayments there is no problem as the amount is exactly determined in cash terms (i.e. the amount prepaid). In the case of accruals we can imagine two situations. Firstly, if the accrual is paid early in the next accounting period before we prepare the accounts, then we can determine its value exactly. However, if it is not paid until after we prepare the accounts we are forced to estimate its value. In nearly every case we should be able to do this with substantial accuracy. For example, an electricity accrual can be estimated from the last bill (plus allowance for inflation and differing seasonal usages) or from a metre reading.

  We can imagine other situations when the amount cannot be determined with substantial accuracy. These are called provisions, and we will consider them in the next two chapters. For example, we might be doubtful about debtors paying all their debts; we will consider this problem in this chapter. We might want to write down the value of fixed assets as they are used up; we will consider this problem in Chapter 7. We might want to provide for any known liability whose amount we cannot determine with substantial accuracy; we will consider this problem in Chapter 19.

6.2   Accounting for bad and doubtful debts

As we have already discovered, a lot of business is done on a credit basis, either with the company giving its customers time to pay for the sales (or the company being allowed time to pay for goods it purchases). In the course of this sort of trading some debts are likely to go 'bad'. It is useful to distinguish between bad and doubtful debts; we will look at each in turn.

6.2.1   Bad debts

From the point of view of the company's debtors, a bad debt is one where the customer is unlikely to pay all or part of the amount owed. The customer may have gone bankrupt, or cannot be traced, or, in the case of small amounts, it may be more trouble to recover the debt than it is worth. As this is, unfortunately, a common occurrance of modern business life we need to know how to account for such eventualities.

A bad debt is treated as a normal business risk. Therefore the correct accounting treatment is to record it as if it were a normal business expense. This is achieved by debiting the profit and loss account with the amount of the bad debt, *in the expenses section after gross profit has been calculated.* In this way it is net profit that is reduced. The amount owing to the company is reduced by the amount of the bad debt (i.e. credit debtors with the amount of bad debt).

See Spreadsheet 6.1 which shows how we write off a debt of £100 contained in a total debtors figure of £5,500.

It is important to note that we do not reduce sales by the amount owing. This is because accountants view making the sale and collecting the debt as two different operations, so the expense of incurring the bad debt is shown in the profit and loss account and not considered part of trading.

Sometimes debts are written off as bad and then a cheque arrives! This happy course of events is a pleasure to record. See Spreadsheet 6.1(b) for an illustration of this situation. Suppose the debt of £100 is subsequently paid in full. A cash column is debited as money is received and the profit and loss column credited, as this receipt is treated as income in the period in which it is received.

6.2.2   Doubtful debts

As it is a normal occurrence of business life that some debts will eventually go bad, firms often *prudently* make a provision for debts going bad. This is called a provision for *doubtful* debts.

In estimating what figure to provide, the accountant may produce a debtors age listing. This is an analysis of the debtors at the year end, indicating how long each part of the debt has been outstanding. The older the debt, then the more

Spreadsheet 6.1 Accounting for bad debts

```
        :  A   ::  B   ::  C   ::  D   ::  E   ::  F  :
  1
  2
  3   (a)
  4   Description                    Debtors  Profit
  5                                           and
  6                                           Loss
  7
  8   Opening Balances                 5500    -5500
  9
 10   Bad debt written-off             -100      100
 11   -----------------------------------------------
 12   Closing Balances                 5400    -5400
 13   ===============================================
 14
 15
 16   (b)
 17   Description                    Debtors  Profit   Cash
 18                                           and
 19                                           Loss
 20
 21   Opening Balances from above      5400    -5400
 22
 23   Cash Received                            -100     100
 24   ----------------------------------------------------
 25   Closing Balances                 5400    -5500     100
 26   ====================================================
```

likely it is to be a bad one. An example of an age analysis of debtors is shown in Spreadsheet 6.2, together with the accountant's comments on each debt.

This exercise, which can be time-consuming and therefore costly, involves taking a historic perspective and examining how many debtors on average over recent years have failed to pay. Sometimes there is specific knowledge regarding one particular customer that may be taken into consideration, e.g. he may be in the process of being sued for bankruptcy, in which case all debts relating to that customer will be treated as doubtful.

The choice of method will depend upon circumstances and the subjective evaluation of the accountant in the light of considerations such as prudence. A good accountant will try to be as objective as possible, by obtaining as much information as possible from which to evaluate the debtor's ability to pay. However, in the final analysis a degree of subjectivity is inevitable.

It should be realised that recording provisions for doubtful debts is different from recording strightforward bad debts, as they are only estimates and as yet have not happened.

We provide for doubtful debts by creating a provision. Let us consider the age analysis shown in Spreadsheet 6.2. There is clearly no need to provide for the I. Rubenstein and J. Lucas debts as the accountant expects them to be paid in full

Spreadsheet 6.2 Age analysis of debtors

	A	B	C	D	E	F	G	H	I	J	K	L
1												
2												
3												
4	Number	Debtor's Name		Total	Under	1 to 2	2 to 3	Over	Accountant's Comments			
5				Debt	a	Months	Months	3				
6					Month			Months				
7												
8	1	I.Rubinstein		10000	8000	2000			No real problem			
9									-this customer is a good payer			
10												
11	2	A.Mann		5759				5759	Over a year old			
12									-unlikely to pay			
13												
14	3	J.Lucas		9561	4652	3579	1330		Always a slow payer			
15									-but sound			
16												
17	4	J.Burman		5340	4780			560	The old balance is in dispute			
18				---------	------------------------------------			---				
19				30660	17432	5579	1330	6319				
20				=========	====================================			===				

in the near future. The A. Mann debt is unlikely to be paid so should be fully provided for. The J. Burman debt contains a disputed amount of £560; as we are not sure of receiving this amount it is prudent to provide for it. So total provisions amount to £6,319. The double entry to record these provisions is shown in Spreadsheet 6.3a. A new column is opened called **provision for doubtful debts** to house this provision (i.e. a credit entry) and the debit entry taken to the **profit and loss** column as it is an expense of the period. The credit is not put in the **debtors** column as the debt has not as yet gone bad, so it is not written off.

Of course, the accountant may have been overcautious and the provision may prove too high. In this instance, in the next period the converse entries are necessary, i.e. credit the profit and loss account and debit the provision account with the amount of overprovision. See Spreadsheet 6.3b for an example of this situation. Say the disputed item with J. Burman is cleared and he pays. The **cash** column is then debited and the **profit and loss** column credited.

Now consider Figure 6.1, which contains an example of these eventualities, with a spreadsheet interpretation presented in Spreadsheet 6.4.

The £2,000 in the opening balance sheet is matched by £2,000 in a column labelled **other net assets and capital**. In reality this would be made up of a number of assets and liabilities and capital producing this net result, but this one column will be sufficient for our purposes.

Spreadsheet 6.3 Accounting for doubtful debts

	A	B	C	D	E	F
1						
2						
3	(a)					
4	Description			Debtors	Profit	Provision
5					and	for
6					Loss	Doubtful
7						Debts
8						
9	Opening Balances			30660	-30660	
10						
11	Provision				6319	-6319
12	--					
13	Closing Balances			30660	-24341	-6319
14	==					
15						
16						
17	(b)					
18	Description			Debtors	Profit	Provision
19					and	for
20					Loss	Doubtful
21						Debts
22						
23	Opening Balances from above			30660	-24341	-6319
24						
25	Provision				-560	560
26	--					
27	Closing Balances			30660	-24901	-5759
28	==					

The transactions for year 1 are duly recorded. Note that sales are recorded in full, quite independently of any cash received, which is treated as a separate transaction. The bad debt is treated as an expense reducing both profit and the debtor balance.

During the second year of operations the transaction to focus on is the bad debt provision. Notice how profit is reduced as before, but the provision is in the balance sheet and separately identified. This is due to the fact that it is not a bad debt, i.e. a written-off expense, but merely a provision, i.e. a prudent reduction in profit to cover the eventuality should it arise.

In year 3, the debt is reinstated by simply debiting **debtors** and crediting the **profit and loss account**. Note, however, that the credit to the **profit and loss account** is not a sale, but a negative expense. This year the provision needs to be reduced and so the opposite transaction to that of year 2 is needed.

Spreadsheet 6.4   Overcautious plc

		Debtors	Cash	Provision for D.Debt	Profit & Loss	Other Assets	
1							
2							
3							
4							
5							
6	Opening Balance Sheet		2000			-2000	
7							
8	YEAR 1						
9							
10	Sales	10000			-10000		
11							
12	Cost of Sales		-6000		6000		
13							
14	Cash Received	-9000	9000				
15							
16	Bad Debt Expense	-500			500		
17		-------	-------	-------	-------	-------	
18	Closing Balance Sheet	500	5000	0	-3500	-2000	0
19							
20	YEAR 2						
21							
22	Sales	12000			-12000		
23							
24	Cost of Sales		-8000		8000		
25							
26	Cash Received	-10500	10500				
27							
28	Bad Debt Provision			-100	100		
29		-------	-------	-------	-------	-------	
30	Closing Balance Sheet	2000	7500	-100	-7400	-2000	0
31							
32	YEAR 3						
33							
34	Sales	14000			-14000		
35							
36	Cost of Sales		-10000		10000		
37							
38	Cash Received	-14500	14500				
39							
40	Reinstate Debt	500			-500		
41							
42	Bad Debt Provision			50	-50		
43		-------	-------	-------	-------	-------	
44	Closing Balance Sheet	2000	12000	-50	-11950	-2000	0
45		=======	=======	=======	=======	=======	

Overcautious plc is a service company, operating with few assets and negligible expenditure. On 31 December 1988, i.e. year 1, it has cash of £2,000 among other net assets. During the first year of operations it sold services of £10,000 on credit, with the cost of these sales being £6,000 (being all purchases for cash). Receipts are £9,000. Of the balance outstanding, one debt for £500 has remained unpaid for a number of months and the company decides to write off the debt.

During 1989, sales rose to £12,000 (cost of sales £8,000 paid in cash), but once again receipts were less, amounting to only £10,500. While none of these debts are particularly worrying, following from the experience of the previous year, the company decides to provide for 5 per cent of its closing debtors to be classed as doubtful.

In 1990, sales amounted to £14,000 (and cash cost of sales £10,000), but cash receipts came to £14,500. The original debtor in year 1 eventually paid the £500 outstanding and the debt is reinstated.

As a result of this reinstated debt, the company's bad debt provision policy is reviewed and it is agreed that only £50 should be provided for in the accounts for year 3.

Figure 6.1   Overcautious plc

CHECKLIST

Having completed Chapter 6, you should be able to:

- distinguish between an accrual and a provision;
- account for bad and doubtful debts;

Workshop 6.1: Bad and doubtful debts

Prudent's business is a service company, operating with few assets and negligible expenditure. On 31 December 1987, i.e. year 1, it has cash of £5,000 among other net assets. During the first year of operations it sold services of £20,000 on credit, with the cost of these sales being £14,000 (being all purchases for cash). Receipts are £17,000. Of the balance outstanding, one debt for £750 has remained unpaid for a number of months and the company decides to write off the debt.

Spreadsheet 6.5 Workshop 6.1: Prudent plc – solution

	A	B	C	D	E	F	G	H	I
1									
2									
3				Debtors	Cash	Provision	Profit	Other	
4						for D.Debt	& Loss	Assets	
5									
6	Opening Balance Sheet				5000			-5000	
7									
8	YEAR 1								
9									
10	Sales			20000			-20000		
11									
12	Cost of Sales				-14000		14000		
13									
14	Cash Received			-17000	17000				
15									
16	Bad Debt Expense			-750			750		
17									
18	Closing Balance Sheet			2250	8000	0	-5250	-5000	0
19									
20	YEAR 2								
21									
22	Sales			17000			-17000		
23									
24	Cost of Sales				-12000		12000		
25									
26	Cash Received			-16000	16000				
27									
28	Bad Debt Provision					-163	163		
29									
30	Closing Balance Sheet			3250	12000	-163	-10088	-5000	0
31									
32	YEAR 3								
33									
34	Sales			22000			-22000		
35									
36	Cost of Sales				-14000		14000		
37									
38	Cash Received			-18000	18000				
39									
40	Reinstate Debt			750			-750		
41									
42	Bad Debt Provision					-88	88		
43									
44	Closing Balance Sheet			8000	16000	-250	-18750	-5000	0

Spreadsheet 6.6 Workshop 6.1: Prudent plc – formulae

	A	B	C	D	E	F	G	H	I
1									
2									
3				Debtors	Cash	Provision	Profit	Other	
4						for D.Debt	& Loss	Assets	
5									
6	Opening Balance Sheet				5000			-E6	
7									
8	YEAR 1								
9									
10	Sales			20000			-D10		
11									
12	Cost of Sales				-14000		-E12		
13									
14	Cash Received			-E14	17000				
15									
16	Bad Debt Expense			-750			-D16		
17				-------	-------	-------	-------	-------	-------
18	Closing Balance Sheet			SUM(D6:D16)	SUM(E6:E16)	SUM(F6:F16)	SUM(G6:G16)	SUM(H6:H16)	SUM(D18:H18)
19									
20	YEAR 2								
21									
22	Sales			17000			-D22		
23									
24	Cost of Sales				-12000		-E24		
25									
26	Cash Received			-E26	16000				
27									
28	Bad Debt Provision					-SUM(D18:D28)*.05	-F28		
29				-------	-------	-------	-------	-------	-------
30	Closing Balance Sheet			SUM(D17:D28)	SUM(E17:E28)	SUM(F17:F28)	SUM(G17:G28)	SUM(H17:H28)	SUM(D30:H30)
31									
32	YEAR 3								
33									
34	Sales			22000			-D34		
35									
36	Cost of Sales				-14000		-E36		
37									
38	Cash Received			-E38	18000				
39									
40	Reinstate Debt			-D16			-D40		
41									
42	Bad Debt Provision					-F30+F44	-F42		
43				-------	-------	-------	-------	-------	-------
44	Closing Balance Sheet			SUM(D30:D42)	SUM(E30:E42)	-250	SUM(G30:G42)	SUM(H30:H42)	SUM(D44:H44)

During 1988, sales fell to £17,000 (cost of sale £12,000 paid in cash), but once again receipts were less, amounting to only £16,000. While none of these debts are particularly worrying, following from the experience of the previous year, the company decides to provide for 5 per cent of its closing debtors to be classed as doubtful.

In 1989, sales amounted to £22,000 (and cash cost of sales £14,000), but cash receipts came to £18,000. The original debtor in year 1 eventually paid the £750, included in the cash receipts, and the debt is reinstated.

As a result of this reinstated debt, the company's bad debt provision policy is reviewed and it is agreed that only £250 should be provided for the closing balance sheet for year 3.

Workshop guide

1. The £5,000 in the opening balance sheet is matched by £5,000 in a column labelled **other net assets and capital** by using the negative cell reference −E6 in cell H6. In reality this would be made up of a number of assets, liabilities and capital, producing this net result, in which instance a negative sum command would be used; but this one column will be sufficient for our purposes.

2. The transactions for year 1 are duly recorded. Sales of £20,000 are debited to the **debtors** column in cell D10, with the double entry in the **sales** column in cell G10 through the cell reference −D10. The cost of sales has been paid for in cash, i.e. −14000 in row 6 of the **cash** column E, which is debited to the **profit and loss** column G with the reference E12. Note that sales are recorded in full, quite independently of any cash received, which is treated as a separate transaction. The bad debt is treated as an expense reducing both profit and the debtor balance, and is totally independent of any cash transactions. The entry necessary to reduce the debt outstanding is −750 in column D, with the **profit and loss** column bearing the debit through the cell reference −D16.

3. During the second year of operations the transaction to focus on is the bad debt provision. Here 5 per cent of the contents of cell D30 are calculated and placed as a credit entry in cell F28 using the formula −SUM (D18:D28)∗.05. This is then debited to the **profit and loss** column in cell G28 using the reference −F28. Notice how profit is reduced as before, but the provision is in the balance sheet and separately identified. This is due to the fact that it is not a bad debt, i.e. a written-off expense, but merely a provision, i.e. a prudent reduction in profit to cover the eventuality should it arise. This prevents profit being distributed when all the costs accruing to earning it have not been taken into account.

4. In year 3, the debt is reinstated by simply debiting **debtors** and crediting the **profit and loss account**. Note, however, that the credit to the **profit and loss**

account is not a sale, but a negative expense. Treating it as a sale would cause the sort of distortion to profit margins and mark-ups that have been discussed earlier. This year the provision needs to be reduced and so the opposite transaction to that of year 2 is needed. Note how the spreadsheet is calculating the double entry required, i.e. the reinstatement is achieved by the reference **−D16** which reverses the original entry, which is then cancelled out of the **profit and loss** column with the reference **−F42**.

Once you have completed the spreadsheet workings and you are happy that all cell references are correct, attempt the 'what if?' questions.

'What if?' problems

1. What if sales in year 1 fall to £18,000? Will this affect the bad debt expense or the bad debt provision?

2. What happens to profit in year 1 if we increase the bad debt expense to £1,000?

3. What is the long-term effect of being overcautious in writing out bad debts if the debts are reinstated? Adjust cell D40 by inserting the value 800, to reflect a reinstatement of 80 per cent of the original bad debt. What happens to the final year profit figure? Is this an increase or decrease in profit? What policy should the firm adopt, i.e. should it be prudent and write out all of the debt or should it write out only the part it thinks it will lose?

4. What would happen if, instead of the debt being reinstated, another debtor of £200 failed to settle in year 3? Amend row 40, recording:
    row 40 **bad debt expense** **− 200** in cell _____; **double entry** in cell _____?

5. Is the bad debt provision dependent upon:
    a.   sales
    b.   cash received
    c.   both?
    Change the sales of year 3 to 30,000 in cell D34 and then change the cash received in E38, monitoring the amount calculated as bad debt provision in F44.

Answers

1. The provision in year 2 changes to £62.5 and in year 5, £187.5

2. Profit falls by £250.

3. Profit increases by £50; the company should be prudent, but not overcautious. It should therefore only write out the part of the debt it thinks it will lose.

4.   D40; G40.

5.   Sales.

Selected questions and exercises

Question 6.1

D. Morse started business on 1 January 1989. Her accounting year end is 31 December.

You are required to account for the following:

Year ending 31 December 1989–sales amounted to £113,890 and receipts £109,654. £450 debts were considered to be bad and £560 were found to be doubtful.

Year ending 31 December 1989 – sales amounted to £113,890 and receipts £109,654. £450 debts were considered to be bad and £560 were found to be doubtful.

Year ended 31 December 1990 – sales amounted to £134,800 and receipts £129,786. £1,769 debts were considered to be bad and written off. A debt of £65 written off as bad in 1989 was paid in full. The provision for doubtful debts was to be increased to 5 per cent of the year-end debtors figure.

Year ended 31 December 1991–sales amounted to £167,439 and receipts £159,879. £3,673 debts were considered to be bad and written off. The provision is to be maintained at 5 per cent.

You are also required to show the extracts from the balance sheet and profit and loss account.

Solution on page 513.

Question 6.2

Hywel Williams has extracted the totals shown in Table 6.1 from his records, from which he intends to prepare a balance sheet and trading and profit and loss account for the year ended 31 December 1991:

The following notes are relevant:

1.	Closing stock was	17,220
2.	Rent payable accrued was	3,920
3.	Insurance prepaid	840
4.	Wages and salaries acrued	1,680
5.	Commission due	476
6.	Rent received overpaid	868
7.	Provision for doubtful debts to be increased to	2,450

Solution on page 514.

Table 6.1 *Details of accounts of Hywel Williams*

	£ Debit	£ Credit
Sales		150,192
Purchases	86,926	
Opening stock	16,744	
Capital as at 1 January 1991		60,200
Drawings	17,150	
Bank overdraft		23,037
Bad debts	568	
Doubtful debt provision		1,692
Rent payable	32,200	
Rent receivable		47,600
Commission receivable		392
Insurance	8,442	
Land	114,730	
Motor van	39,200	
Selling expenses	3,150	
Office expenses	5,320	
Wages and salaries	2,464	
Creditors		24,360
Debtors	31,492	
Cash	315	
Loan		51,228
	358,701	358,701

Question 6.3

The balance sheet as at 31 May 1987 of Forest Traders Limited included a provision for doubtful debts of £2,300.

The company's accounts for the year ended 31 May 1988 are now being prepared.

The company's policy now is to relate the provision for doubtful debts to the age of debts outstanding. The debts outstanding at 31 May 1988 and the required provisions for doubtful debts are shown in Table 6.2.

Table 6.2 *Details of accounts of John Banks*

Debts outstanding	Amount £	Provision for doubtful debts %
Up to 1 month	24,000	1
More than 1 month and up to 2 months	10,000	2
More than 2 months and up to 3 months	8,000	4
More than 3 months	3,000	5

Customers are allowed a cash discount of $2\frac{1}{2}$ per cent for settlement of debts within one month. It is now proposed to make a provision for discounts to be allowed in the company's accounts for the year ended 31 May 1988.

You are required to prepare the following accounts for the year ended 31 May 1988 in the books of Forest Traders Limited to record the above transactions:

Provision for doubtful debts;
Provision for discounts to be allowed on debtors.

No solution provided.   *Source: AAT, Accounting, June 1988.*

7 | *Depreciation and the disposal of fixed assets*

AIMS OF CHAPTER _____

- to introduce the concept of depreciation;
- to show how to calculate two different methods of depreciation;
- to explain the distinction between an asset and an expense;
- to use the spreadsheet approach to account for different methods of depreciation, with an examination of the effect on profit;
- to outline the concept of objectivity;
- to consider the accounting treatment of the sale of assets;
- to examine the guidelines issued to assist accountants to account for depreciation.

7.1 The concept of depreciation

Assets that are expected to last for more than one accounting period are called 'fixed assets' and include such items as land and buildings, plant and machinery, fixtures, fittings, tools and equipment, and so on. They are bought to be used in the business and so help produce or sell its product.

As the business continues its operations, these assets (with the exception of land) will be used up. For example, consider a machine which costs £15,000 and is expected to last four years, at which time it is expected to be of no further use to the business and is to be sold for £3,000. How are we to reflect this usage in the accounts? The way in which accountants reflect this using up of fixed assets in accounts is through the concept of depreciation.

As you might already have realised, it is unfair to charge the profit and loss account with the full cost of an asset in the year in which it was acquired, since it will be used in the business and hence generate profits for the business throughout its economic life. Depreciation is a way of spreading the cost of the fixed asset over

Years	Accumulated depreciation £	Unused cost £
0	0	15,000
1	3,000	12,000
2	6,000	9,000
3	9,000	6,000
4	12,000	3,000

At the end of the first year its unused cost (more often called 'net book value') is £12,000, a reduction of £3,000 from its full cost of £15,000. At the end of the second year its unused cost is £9,000, a reduction of £3,000 from its first year net book value of £12,000. The net book value continues to be reduced accordingly until the end of year 4.

It is important to realise that we are allocating the cost of the asset over its useful economic life and making no attempt to determine the market value of the asset. A layman who happens to look at a balance sheet seeing the net book value of a fixed asset is likely to think this is what the asset could be sold for; this is incorrect. It is merely a residual amount after charging for asset consumption to date.

Figure 7.1   Calculation of the unused cost of a machine which cost £15,000 and is expected to last four years and be sold for £3,000.

its useful economic life. Therefore, if we assume that the above-mentioned machine will be used up in equal amounts over its four-year useful life, it is reasonable to charge £3,000 per year to the profit and loss account for annual usage. How is this £3,000 arrived at? The cost to be charged over the four-year period is £12,000; the £15,000 purchase cost less the £3,000 to be recovered at the end of the fourth year. Since the machine is to be kept for four years, the annual cost of £3,000 is obtained by dividing the £15,000 by the four years.

We now know how depreciation affects the profit and loss account (i.e. it is an expense). How does it effect the balance sheet? The cost of the fixed asset is reduced to leave the amount of unused cost. Let us consider the machine previously mentioned. See Figure 7.1, which shows how its unused cost is calculated.

7.2   Methods of calculating depreciation

The two main ways of calculating depreciation are the straight-line method and the reducing balance method. There are other methods, but these are the ones in common usage and will serve our purposes adequately.

7.2.1   The straight-line method

This is a way of depreciating an asset so that the profit and loss account bears an equal charge each year. An example of such an asset is the machine we have already considered. To calculate this charge, three pieces of information are required. Firstly, the purchase cost of the asset; this is easily obtained as the purchase has recently been made. The other two pieces of information are not so easily obtained. They are the residual or scrap value and the economic life of the asset.

Some assets are used to destruction and when they are used up there is nothing left of them, so their scrap value is very small or zero. However, this is unusual and most assets are kept by a firm until the cost of maintenance means that the asset has become uneconomic and it is cheaper to replace it. Many companies do not keep cars for longer than three years, for example they sell them at auction. The use of the term 'scrap' can therefore be misleading as some assets can be put to use by another company or by an individual (e.g. an aircraft is seldom scrapped, but is sold to a smaller company that will have a lighter schedule and so does not need to own planes capable of non-stop flying).

The other piece of information required to calculate straight-line depreciation is the estimated useful economic life of the asset to the business, that is, the time period between acquisition and disposal. In trying to determine this information the advice of an expert, such as a production manager in the case of a machine, or a surveyor in the case of a building, can be sought. Once again the overriding concept of prudence will guide the accountants through any disagreements regarding either the life of the asset or the residual value.

To work out the annual charge the following expression is used:

$$\text{Annual charge} = \frac{\text{Historic cost} - \text{Residual value}}{\text{Economic life (in years)}}$$

Using the formula to calculate the annual depreciation charge for our machine we get the same answer as we derived before:

$$£3,000 = \frac{£15,000 - £3,000}{4 \text{ years}}$$

7.2.2 The reducing balance method

The straight-line method is suitable for an asset which is used up in equal amounts each year. Often more of an asset's cost is used up in the earlier years than in the latter years. Accountants have developed many methods of depreciation which take this usage pattern into consideration. We will examine one such method, the reducing balance method.

Instead of charging a fixed amount each year, this method charges a fixed percentage of the previous year's net book value. In this way the depreciation charge is highest in the early years and lowest in the later years. Let us reconsider our machine example. To calculate this fixed percentage this rather complex formula is used:

$$\text{Percentage rate} = 1 - n\sqrt{\frac{s}{c}}$$

where:

n = the economic life of the asset in years
s = the scrap or residual value
c = the historic cost of the asset

Spreadsheet 7.1   Different methods of calculating depreciation charges

	A	B	C	D	E	F	G	
1								
2								
3								
4		Asset Cost		15000		Reducing Balance %		
5								
6		Economic Life		4		s/c =	.2	
7								
8		Residual Value		3000		Rate =	.33	
9								
10				Straight		Reducing		
11				Line		Balance	N.B.V.	
12								
13		Year 1		3000		4969	10031	
14		Year 2		3000		3323	6708	
15		Year 3		3000		2222	4486	
16		Year 4		3000		1486	3000	
17								
18								
19		Total		12000		12000		

	A	B	C	D	E	F	G	H
1								
2								
3								
4		Asset Cost		15000		Reducing Balance %		
5								
6		Economic Life		4		s/c =	D8/D4	
7								
8		Residual Value		3000		Rate =	1-(G6^(1/D6))	
9								
10				Straight		Reducing		
11				Line		Balance	N.B.V.	
12								
13		Year 1		(D4-D8)/D6		D4*G8	D4-F13	
14		Year 2		(D4-D8)/D6		G13*G8	G13-F14	
15		Year 3		(D4-D8)/D6		G14*G8	G14-F15	
16		Year 4		(D4-D8)/D6		G15*G8	G15-F16	
17								
18								
19		Total		SUM(D13:D17)		SUM(F13:F17)		

This formula can be calculated if you have a scientific calculator, or if you can rearrange the expression to enable a spreadsheet package to handle it.

To recap on some basic mathematics may be beneficial at this point. If an expression reads 3^2, or three squared, most readers will be familiar with it. Similarly, the expression $\sqrt{3}$, or the square root of three, is familiar. Perhaps what most readers have forgotton is that $\sqrt{3}$ is the same as 3 to the power of 1/2. So to find the *n*th root you need to place the expression to the power of $1/n$.

In spreadsheet language this expression can be rearranged to give:

Percentage rate $= 1 - ((s/c) \wedge (1/n))$

There are differences between spreadsheet packages, especially over the use of $\wedge$ to mean 'to the power of'. You may need to refer to your manual. Just in case you need to return to your calculator, Spreadsheet 7.1 calculates the depreciation charges for our machine using the reducing balance method (as well as the straight-line method).

It is interesting to see the differences between the two methods. Firstly, both methods will produce the same depreciation charge in total over the four years.

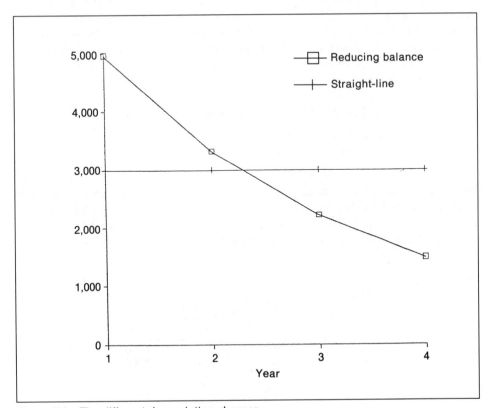

Figure 7.2 The different depreciation charges

This is shown to be £12,000 in row 19 of the spreadsheet. Secondly, as planned the reducing balance method produces a higher depreciation charge in the early years of the asset's life than the straight-line method (i.e. years 1 and 2) and a lower charge in its later years (i.e. years 3 and 4). This is because it is the previous year's net book value (NBV) that is applied to the rate, which produces a smaller charge as the years go by. These charges have been graphed in Figure 7.2 (this is a feature of most spreadsheet packages, so your spreadsheet may be able to produce such a graph).

7.3   Accounting for depreciation

As we have seen, it is necessary to reflect depreciation in both the profit and loss account and the balance sheet. The charge to the profit and loss account is called the depreciation *expense* for the year. This can be confusing, as in practice the term 'expense' is dropped and the item in the profit and loss account is just labelled 'depreciation'. As we know, all expenses are a debit.

The credit is recorded in the balance sheet. This is achieved by opening up a column called **provision for depreciation** and recording the credit entry in this column. This is a **provision** column, as the exact usage of the asset's cost cannot be determined exactly; the depreciation charge is only an estimate of this usage. It is possible to record the credit entry in the **fixed asset** column; however, to do so reduces the amount of information available (i.e. only the net book value is available when the column is summed rather than its original cost and depreciation to date); this is often referred to as the old method of accounting for depreciation. The recommended method is sometimes referred to as the 'new method'.

So, to summarise, the double entry to record depreciation is as follows:

debit the **profit and loss** column and
credit the **provision for depreciation** column

The provision for depreciation column builds up year by year as the depreciation charges accumulate, and tells the reader of the balance sheet how much of the asset's value has been used up. The original cost of the asset is also shown, together with the next book value (i.e. how much of the original cost has not as yet been used up). The fixed assets are shown in Table 7.1.

Table 7.1   *Cost and depreciation of fixed assets*

Fixed assets	Cost £000	Depreciation £000	NBV £000
Land	1,000	0	1,000
Buildings	3,000	1,000	2,000
Machinery	500	400	100
Vehicles	200	150	50
	4,700	1,550	3,150

Spreadsheet 7.2a Accounting for depreciation

	A	B	C	D	E	F	G	H	I
				Asset HC	Provision for Depreciation	Profit and Loss	Net Inc. Cash	Sale of Fixed Asset	Capital
8	Year 1			15000			-15000		
10	Profit or period					-10000	10000		
12	Depreciation Expense				-3000	3000			
14	Profit after Dep'n					7000			-7000
16	Closing Balance Sheet			15000	-3000	0	-5000	0	-7000
18	Year 2								
20	Profit or period					-10000	10000		
22	Depreciation Expense				-3000	3000			
24	Profit after Dep'n					7000			-7000
26	Closing Balance Sheet			15000	-6000	0	5000	0	-14000
28	Year 3								
30	Profit or period					-10000	10000		
32	Depreciation Expense				-3000	3000			
34	Profit after Dep'n					7000			-7000
36	Closing Balance Sheet			15000	-9000	0	15000	0	-21000
38	Year 4								
40	Profit or period					-10000	10000		
42	Depreciation Expense				-3000	3000			
44	Sale of Asset								
46	Write out asset			-15000				15000	
48	Write out dep'n				12000			-12000	
50	Record receipt						3000	-3000	
52	Transfer P/L on Sale					0		0	
54	Profit after Dep'n and Sale					7000			-7000
56	Closing Balance Sheet			0	0	0	28000	0	-28000

Spreadsheet 7.2b   Accounting for depreciation (formulae)

	A	B	C	D	E	F	G	H	I
1									
2									
3									
4				Asset	Provision	Profit	Net Assets	Sale of	Capital
5				HC	for	and	Inc. Cash	Fixed	
6					Depreciation	Loss		Asset	
7									
8	Year 1			15000			-D8		
9									
10	Profit or period					-10000	-F10		
11									
12	Depreciation Expense				-3000	-E12			
13									
14	Profit after Dep'n					-SUM(F8:F13)			-F14
15	-------------								
16	Closing Balance Sheet			SUM(D8:D14)	SUM(E8:E14)	SUM(F8:F14)	SUM(G8:G14)	SUM(H8:H14)	SUM(I8:I14)
17									
18	Year 2								
19									
20	Profit or period					-10000	-F20		
21									
22	Depreciation Expense				-3000	-E22			
23									
24	Profit after Dep'n					-SUM(F18:F23)			-F24
25	-------------								
26	Closing Balance Sheet			SUM(D16:D24)	SUM(E16:E24)	SUM(F16:F24)	SUM(G16:G24)	SUM(H16:H24)	SUM(I16:I24)
27									
28	Year 3								
29									
30	Profit or period					-10000	-F30		
31									
32	Depreciation Expense				-3000	-E32			
33									
34	Profit after Dep'n					-SUM(F28:F33)			-F34
35	-------------								
36	Closing Balance Sheet			SUM(D26:D34)	SUM(E26:E34)	SUM(F26:F34)	SUM(G26:G34)	SUM(H26:H34)	SUM(I26:I34)
37									
38	Year 4								
39									
40	Profit or period					-10000	-F40		
41									
42	Depreciation Expense				-3000	-E42			
43									
44	Sale of Asset								
45	-------------								
46	Write out asset			-D36				-D46	
47									
48	Write out dep'n				-SUM(E36:E45)			-E48	
49									
50	Record receipt						3000	-G50	
51									
52	Transfer P/L on Sale					-H52		-SUM(H46:H50)	
53									
54	Profit after Dep'n and Sale					-SUM(F38:F53)			-F54
55	-------------								
56	Closing Balance Sheet			SUM(D36:D54)	SUM(E36:E54)	SUM(F36:F54)	SUM(G36:G54)	SUM(H36:H54)	SUM(I36:I54)

Spreadsheet 7.3 Accounting for depreciation (using reducing balance figures)

	A ∷ B ∷ C ∷ D	Asset HC	Provision for Depreciation	Profit and Loss	Net Inc. Cash	Sale of Fixed Asset	Capital
1							
2							
3							
4							
5							
6							
7							
8	Year 1	15000			-15000		
9							
10	Profit or period			-10000	10000		
11							
12	Depreciation Expense		-4969	4969			
13							
14	Profit after Dep'n			5031			-5031
15			---------	---------	---------	---------	---------
16	Closing Balance Sheet	15000	-4969	0	-5000	0	-5031
17							
18	Year 2						
19							
20	Profit or period			-10000	10000		
21							
22	Depreciation Expense		-3323	3323			
23							
24	Profit after Dep'n			6677			-6677
25			---------	---------	---------	---------	---------
26	Closing Balance Sheet	15000	-8292	0	5000	0	-11708
27							
28	Year 3						
29							
30	Profit or period			-10000	10000		
31							
32	Depreciation Expense		-2222	2222			
33							
34	Profit after Dep'n			7778			-7778
35			---------	---------	---------	---------	---------
36	Closing Balance Sheet	15000	-10514	0	15000	0	-19486
37							
38	Year 4						
39							
40	Profit or period			-10000	10000		
41							
42	Depreciation Expense		-1486	1486			
43							
44	Sale of Asset						
45	-------------						
46	Write out asset	-15000				15000	
47							
48	Write out dep'n		12000			-12000	
49							
50	Record receipt				3000	-3000	
51							
52	Transfer P/L on Sale			0		0	
53							
54	Profit after Dep'n and Sale			8514			-8514
55			---------	---------	---------	---------	---------
56	Closing Balance Sheet	0	0	0	28000	0	-28000

The depreciation *provision* column is usually just labelled **depreciation** or **depreciation to date**; the fact that it is a provision is accepted, as it is in the balance sheet. Until you are well versed in the differences, it is better to label the columns fully.

Spreadsheet 7.2a shows how we account for the depreciation on our machine using depreciation charges calculated using the straight-line method. The underlying formulae are shown in Spreadsheet 7.2b.

To simplify the explanation and to show the effect on profit more clearly, let's assume that the firm earns £10,000 profit annually which is matched by an increase in net assets. Column G on the spreadsheet has been used to accommodate entries that may take place elsewhere in the accounts; this is called **net assets,** and is done so that we can concentrate on the effects of depreciation.

So in the first year, the asset is purchased using cash, and the firm makes £10,000 profit. The depreciation charge is £3,000, which is charged as a debit to the **profit and loss** column and a credit to the **provision for depreciation** column. The net profit of £7,000 is then transferred to capital. This situation is repeated for the four years, *but* notice how the provision for depreciation in the balance sheet is increasing.

The accounting procedures are exactly the same when the reducing balance method has been used; see Spreadsheet 7.3. The same transactions take place, only the figures are different. The effect on profit of using the two different depreciation methods can be seen by looking at Table 7.2.

Table 7.2   *Net profit comparison using different depreciation methods*

	Net profit	
Year	Straight-line	Reducing balance
1	7,000	5,031
2	7,000	6,677
3	7,000	7,778
4	7,000	8,514
	28,000	28,000

As can be seen, the two methods produce the same total profit of £28,000 over the four-year period, but they do not distribute this profit in the same way between years. The reducing balance method leads to lower profits in the early years and higher profits in the later years, while the straight-line method produces the same profit in each year.

Which method is correct? The answer is that we cannot decide between them on the information given. See Figure 7.3, which looks at this problem in more detail.

The financial accountant fulfils a stewardship function, reporting the performance of a company to its owners. As such, he is in a position of trust to some extent and therefore needs to prove that his accounting treatment of the company has been fair. In order to satisfy this criteria he needs to be objective. Whereas the accountant must exercise his better judgement and apply the interpretation of other concepts and principles as he sees fit, he should always do so without the influence of any personal bias.

Objectivity in an accounting sense means that if the same accounting information were given to a number of accountants and they were asked to prepare a set of accounts from this information, it would be likely that they would produce the same set of accounts with the same profit figure. This situation is to be contrasted with subjectivity, which means that if the same accounting information were given to a number of accountants and they were asked to prepare a set of accounts from this information, it would be unlikely that they would produce the same set of accounts with the same profit figure. This latter situation is more likely if certain items of information need to be subjectively interpreted, such as depreciation or which method/rate to use.

What we can do is reduce our reliance to a minimum on estimates or subjective valuations. It is for this reason that historic cost is the basis for the final accounts of business today, as costs are objective. In times of rising prices, this produces some problems as asset valuations can be significantly understated in the balance sheet. There are more of these problems in Chapter 24.

Figure 7.3 The concept of objectivity

7.4 The disposal of fixed assets

At the end of the useful life of a fixed asset, a business may be able to sell it. The residual value is unlikely to exactly equal the sale proceeds as it was only an estimated figure made when the asset was purchased. A business may decide to sell a fixed asset before the end of its estimated life if it can obtain a good price for the asset or if the asset becomes obsolete. We need to be able to account for these sales.

The recommended accounting treatment is to open a **sale of fixed asset** column. To this column we transfer the cost and accumulated depreciation of the asset being sold by recording the following transactions:

Transfer of the asset's cost:
  debit the **sale of fixed asset** column and
  credit the **fixed asset** column.

Transfer of the asset's accumulated depreciation:
  Debit the **fixed asset accumulated depreciation** column and
  credit the **sale of fixed asset** column.

Spreadsheet 7.4   Sale of a fixed asset

	A	B	C	D	E	F	G	H	I
1									
2									
3	(a) Profit								
4									
5			Cost	Dep'n	Capital	Cash	Profit	Sale	
6							and	of	
7							Loss	Asset	
8									
9	Position before disposal		15000	-12000	-3000	0			
10									
11	Transfer assets cost		-15000						15000
12									
13	Transfer assets depreciation			12000					-12000
14									
15	Sale proceeds					5000			-5000
16									
17	Profit on sale						-2000	2000	
18			--						
19			0	0	-3000	5000	-2000	0	
20									
21	Transfer profit to capital				-2000		2000		
22			--						
23	Balance Sheet		0	0	-5000	5000	0	0	
24			==						
25									
26									
27	(b) Loss								
28									
29			Cost	Dep'n	Capital	Cash	Profit	Sale	
30							and	of	
31							Loss	Asset	
32									
33	Position before disposal		15000	-12000	-3000	0			
34									
35	Transfer assets cost		-15000						15000
36									
37	Transfer assets depreciation			12000					-12000
38									
39	Sale proceeds					2500			-2500
40									
41	Loss on sale						500	-500	
42			--						
43			0	0	-3000	2500	500	0	
44									
45	Transfer profit to capital				500		-500		
46			--						
47	Balance Sheet		0	0	-2500	2500	0	0	
48			==						

The proceeds of sale (if any) are recorded by:
  debiting the **cash/bank/debtors** column and
  crediting the **sale of fixed asset** column.

Finally, the **sale of fixed asset** column is summed to zero and the difference taken to the **profit and loss** column. If the difference is a debit in the **profit and loss** column and a credit in the **sale of fixed asset** column then a loss has been made on the sale (i.e. the original cost of the asset is greater than the accumulated depreciation and the sale proceeds). If the difference is a credit in the **profit and loss** column and a debit in the **sale of fixed asset** column, then a profit has been made on the sale (i.e. the original cost of the asset is less than the accumulated depreciation and the sale proceeds).

Spreadsheet 7.4 shows the accounting entries for the sale of a fixed asset which originally cost £15,000 and had £12,000, provided by way of depreciation at the date of sale. In Spreadsheet 7.4a the sale proceeds were £5,000, which produces a profit on sale of £2,000. In Spreadsheet 7.4b the sale proceeds were £2,500, which produces a loss on sale of £500. Spreadsheets 7.2a and 7.2b continue to dispose of the asset in year 4 as an additional example.

7.5 Statement of standard accounting practice on depreciation

Statements of standard accounting practice (SSAPs) are guidelines issued for accountants to follow. These are examined in more detail in Chapter 20. However, now might be an appropriate point to examine some details of SSAPs apertaining to the subject of depreciation.

As depreciation directly affects the amount of profit a business makes, the professional accountancy bodies have issued a SSAP to regulate and clarify the accounting for depreciation. This is SSAP 12, accounting for depreciation. The following points are made:

1. All fixed assets that have a finite life must be depreciated; therefore all fixed assets with the exception of land are required to be depreciated (these fixed assets include mines, oil and gas fields, as well as all the other fixed assets you have already come across). Before SSAP 12, some companies did not depreciate buildings at all, as they rose in value. However, the guidelines stated that buildings have a limited life and should be depreciated. Some companies invest in property, making this guideline particularly harsh, so SSAP 19 was issued, which allowed investment properties not to be depreciated.

2. No specific method of depreciation was recommended. However, the standard does state that the cost of the asset less its estimated residual value should be allocated as fairly as possible over the periods expected to benefit from its use.

3. The following information requires disclosure:
   a. the method of depreciation used;
   b. the useful life or the depreciation rates used;
   c. the depreciation charge for the period;
   d. the total cost of the depreciable fixed assets, together with their accumulated depreciation.

4. When there is a revision of the estimated useful economic life of the asset, the net book value should be depreciated over the revised remaining life of the asset.

5. If at any time the net book value of the asset becomes irrecoverable it should be written down immediately to its estimated recoverable amount.

6. If there is a change in method of depreciation, the remaining net book value should be written off over the remaining useful economic life on the new basis. The effect of the change needs to be disclosed if material.

7. As some assets are rising in value, it may be decided to revalue the assets. The double entry for revaluation is to debit the fixed asset column and credit a new column called a **revaluation reserve**. See Chapter 16 for a detailed analysis of how to account for revaluation of fixed assets. The depreciation charge should then be based upon the revalued amount and the new estimate of the asset's remaining useful life.

CHECKLIST _____

Having completed Chapter 7, you should be able to:

- define the concept of depreciation;
- calculate depreciation charges under straight-line and reducing balance methods;
- explain the difference between an asset and an expense;
- account for depreciation charges using the spreadsheet method;
- outline the concept of objectivity;
- account for asset disposal;
- show an understanding of SSAP 12 and 19.

Workshop 7.1: Depreciation and sale of fixed assets

The Wornout business has the following net profit record:

Year 1	£20,000
Year 2	£25.000
Year 3	£15,000

Unfortunately, the firm's accountants have omitted a machine from the accounts. It was bought in year 1 for £30,000 and sold in year 3 for £3,000.

Using the straight-line method of depreciation calculate the adjusted profit figure for each of the years in question, together with the appropriate balance sheet extracts.

Workshop guide

1. A word of advice when compiling a spreadsheet model is to think ahead. If you will need a constant cell reference that is a large formula, then why not take the formula out of the accounting spreadsheet and use the area outside to calculate the value for the entry required. Hence H2 uses the cells H1 – the historic cost, F1 – the scrap value and F2 – the life of the asset, to calculate the depreciation charge for the year. Instead of constantly updating this formula year on year with changing cell references and other complications, the depreciation expense can be charged by referencing this cell. If this advice is followed then the rest becomes quite easy.

2. The assets cost is placed in cell D8 with the double entry made up in column G. This column represents all the other accounts not specified by the example. There is no question regarding the validity of any of the other accounts so they are ignored in this manner.

3. The same accounting logic is used for the profit figure in row 10, with the depreciation expense utilising the value calculated in cell H2 in row 12. The net profit is then recalculated by the formula in cell F14 and this returns to the balance sheet.

4. Similar entries follow in years 2 and 3, but in the latter the asset is written out. This is done in the following stages: first, the cost of the asset is removed by reversing the original entry. This is debited to an account labelled **sale of fixed asset** in column H in row 36. Any accumulated depreciation to date is similarly written out as in row 38. Finally, the cash receipt (cash is part of the **other assets** column, G) is recorded and credited to column H in row 40. The balance of column H is the profit or loss on disposal which is credited or debited to the **profit and loss** account as the case may be (see row 42). This amended profit figure is then added to capital.

'What if?' problems

1. What if the original asset cost £50,000? Change the cell contents of H1 to see the effect on profit in year 1. Use the window command simultaneously to view row 44. What are the new profit figures in year 1, year 2 and year 3?

Spreadsheet 7.5 Workshop 7.1: Accounting for depreciation – formulae

	A	B	C	D	E	F	G	H
1					Scrap	3000	Cost	30000
2					Life	3	Charge	(H1-F1)/F2
3								
4				Asset	Provision	Profit	Net Assets	Sale of
5				HC	for	and	Inc. Cash	Fixed
6					Depreciation	Loss	& Capital	Asset
7								
8	Year 1			H1			-D8	
9								
10	Profit or period					-20000	-F10	
11								
12	Depreciation Expense				-H2	-E12		
13								
14	Profit after Dep'n					-SUM(F8:F13)	-F14	
15					---			
16	Closing Balance Sheet			SUM(D8:D14)	SUM(E8:E14)	SUM(F8:F14)	SUM(G8:G14)	
17								
18	Year 2							
19								
20	Profit or period					-25000	-F20	
21								
22	Depreciation Expense				-H2	-E22		
23								
24	Profit after Dep'n					-SUM(F18:F23)	-F24	
25					---			
26	Closing Balance Sheet			SUM(D16:D24)	SUM(E16:E24)	SUM(F16:F24)	SUM(G16:G24)	
27								
28	Year 3							
29								
30	Profit or period					-15000	-F30	
31								
32	Depreciation Expense				-H2	-E32		
33								
34	Sale of Asset							
35	------------							
36	Write out asset			-D26				-D36
37								
38	Write out dep'n				-SUM(E26:E35)			-E38
39								
40	Record receipt						3000	-G40
41								
42	Transfer P/L on Sale					-H42		-SUM(H36:H40)
43								
44	Profit after Dep'n and Sale					-SUM(F30:F33)	-F44	
45					--			
46	Closing Balance Sheet			SUM(D26:D44)	SUM(E26:E44)	SUM(F26:F44)	SUM(G26:G44)	SUM(H26:H44)

Spreadsheet 7.6 Workshop 7.1 Accounting for depreciation – solution

	A	B	C	D	E	F	G	H
1					Scrap	3000	Cost	30000
2					Life		3 Charge	9000
3								
4				Asset	Provision	Profit	Net Assets	Sale of
5				HC	for	and	Inc. Cash	Fixed
6					Depreciation	Loss	& Capital	Asset
7								
8	Year 1			30000			−30000	
9								
10	Profit or period					−20000	20000	
11								
12	Depreciation Expense				−9000	9000		
13								
14	Profit after Dep'n					11000	−11000	
15					---------------------------------------			
16	Closing Balance Sheet			30000	−9000	0	−21000	
17								
18	Year 2							
19								
20	Profit or period					−25000	25000	
21								
22	Depreciation Expense				−9000	9000		
23								
24	Profit after Dep'n					16000	−16000	
25					---------------------------------------			
26	Closing Balance Sheet			30000	−18000	0	−12000	
27								
28	Year 3							
29								
30	Profit or period					−15000	15000	
31								
32	Depreciation Expense				−9000	9000		
33								
34	Sale of Asset							
35	------------							
36	Write out asset			−30000				30000
37								
38	Write out dep'n				27000			−27000
39								
40	Record receipt						3000	−3000
41								
42	Transfer P/L on Sale					0		0
43								
44	Profit after Dep'n and Sale					6000	−6000	
45					--			
46	Closing Balance Sheet			0	0	0	0	0

2. Repeat the requirements of question 1, but this time change the contents of F1 to reflect a scrap value of 10 per cent of the assets historic cost. What are the new profit figures in year 1, year 2 and year 3?

3. What if the asset's life was expected to be five years and it was disposed of early? Change the contents of cell F3 to 5. What are the new profit figures in year 1, year 2 and year 3?

4. If the asset is disposed of sooner than expected its scrap value will rise. Assume that the receipt of £6,000 in row 40. Note that the scrap value in cell F3 does not alter as the business did not know of this early disposal. What is the profit/loss on disposal, i.e. cell H42?

5. Finally, what if the company chose a reducing balance depreciation policy? Again, in a separate area of the spreadsheet, calculate the charges for each year in the way shown in the preceding chapter and use the cell references to give the accounting entries for cells E12, E22 and E32. Use the initial data in the first instance and repeat questions 1 to 4.

Answers

1. Profit figures: year 1, £4,333; year 2, £9,333; year 3, £667.

2. Change F1 to the formula **H1*.1**.
   Profit figures: year 1, £5,000; year 2, £10,000; year 3, nil.

3. Change contents of F2 to 5.
   Profit figures: year 1, £11,000; year 2, £16,000; year 3, £6,000.

4. Change contents of G40 to £6,000.
   Loss on disposal, £17,000.

5.(1) Profit figures: year 1, £10,426; year 2, £13,089; year 3, £10,337.

5.(2) Profit/loss figures: year 1, £(6,792); year 2, £12,564; year 3, £9,228.

5.(3) Profit figures: year 1, £1,548; year 2, £13,357; year 3, £7,654.

5.(4) Profit/loss on disposal, £(6,559).

Selected questions and exercises

Question 7.1
A business starts up on 1 January 1989, with a financial year end of 31 December. You are required to account for fixed assets and depreciation for the following transactions in years ended 31 December 1989, 1990, 1991 and 1992. (See Table 7.3.)

Table 7.3 *Fixed assets and depreciation 1989–91*

1 July 1989	Bought 1 machine costing £1,300 Expected life 10 years
1 April 1990	Bought 2 machines costing £9,000 each Expected life 10 years
1 February 1991	Bought 1 machine costing £5,500 Expected life 10 years Residual value £500
1 August 1991	Bought 2 machines costing £7,000 each Expected life 10 years Residual value £500 each

You are required to use the straight-line method, with machines being depreciated for each proportion of a year.

Solution on page 515.

Question 7.2

You are required to account for the machines bought in question 7.1 using the reducing balance method of depreciation. A full year's depreciation is to be charged in the year of purchase.

No solution provided.

Question 7.3

The business in question 7.1 sold the machines it bought on 1 April 1990 for £8,000 each on 1 July 1993. You are required to account for the machine's depreciation and the sale of the machine in the year ended 31 December 1993.

Solution on page 516.

Question 7.4

Peter Luffrum has extracted the totals shown in Table 7.4 from his records, from which he intends to prepare a balance sheet and trading and profit and loss account for the year ended 31 December 1991.

The following notes are relevant	£
1. Closing stock was	95,940
2. Rent payable accrued was	21,840
3. Insurance prepaid	4,680
4. Wages and salaries accrued	9,360
5. Commission due	2,652
6. Rent received overpaid	4,836
7. Provision for doubtful debts to be increased to	2,450

Table 7.4 *Details of the accounts of Peter Luffrum*

	£ Debit	£ Credit
Sales		836,784
Purchases	484,302	
Opening stock	93,288	
Capital as at 1 January 1991		335,400
Drawings	95,550	
Bank overdraft		128,349
Bad debts	568	
Doubtful debt provision		1,692
Rent payable	179,400	
Rent receivable		265,200
Commission receivable		2,184
Insurance	47,034	
Land	639,210	
Motor vans	218,400	
Machinery	56,320	
Provisions for depreciation as at 1 January 1991		
motor vans		56,980
machinery		24,592
Profit on sale of motor van		680
Selling expenses	17,550	
Office expenses	29,640	
Wages and salaries	13,728	
Creditors		135,720
Debtors	203,984	
Cash	1,755	
Loan		293,148
	2,080,729	2,080,729

8. Motor vans are to be depreciated using the straight-line method at a rate of 25 per cent p.a. on cost.

   A full year's depreciation is to be charged in the year of purchase and none in the year of sale.

9. Machinery is to be depreciated using the reducing balance method at a rate of 10 per cent p.a.

   A full year's depreciation is to be charged in the year of purchase and none in the year of sale.

No solution provided.

Question 7.5

a. On 1 January 19X1 a business purchased a laser printer costing £1,800. The printer has an estimated life of four years, after which it will have no residual

Table 7.5 *Number of sheets printed, by year*

Year	Sheets printed
19x1	35,000
19x2	45,000
19x3	45,000
19x4	55,000
	180,000

value. It is expected that the output from the printer will be as shown in Table 7.5.

You are required to calculate the annual depreciation charges for 19X1, 19X2, 19X3 and 19X4 on the laser printer on the following bases:

(i) the straight-line basis;
(ii) the diminishing balance method at 60 per cent per annum;
(iii) the units of output method.

Note: your workings should be to the nearest £.

b. Suppose that in 19X4 the laser printer were to be sold on 1 July for £200 and that the business had chosen to depreciate it at 60 per cent per annum using the diminishing balance method applied on a month for month basis.

You are required to reconstruct the following accounts for 19X4 only:

(i) the laser printer account;
(ii) the provision for depreciation–laser printer account;
(iii) the assets disposals account.

Solution on pages 517–18. *Source: AAT, Basic Accounting, June 1988.*

Question 7.6

Spire and Tower started trading on 1 January 1984 and decided to depreciate their motor vehicles by 25 per cent per annum using the reducing balance method. Their purchases and disposals of motor vehicles over the next three years were as shown in Table 7.6.

Table 7.6 *Motor vehicle transactions of Spire and Tower*

Vehicle	Purchase date	Cost	Date of sale	Sale proceeds
A321 BOY	1 January 1984	£6,000	1 January 1986	£2,850
B987 GAL	1 January 1985	£7,200	—	—

From the information in Table 7.6, prepare for the years 1984, 1985 and 1986:

1. The motor vehicles accounts.
2. The provision for depreciation accounts.
3. The asset disposal account.

No solution provided.   *Source: RSA, Accounting II, March 1987.*

8 ‖ *Stock valuation*

AIMS OF CHAPTER _____

- to analyse some of the basic concepts of cost accounting;
- to examine the constituent parts of inventory—raw materials, work in progress and finished goods;
- to examine the valuation of stocks of raw materials including the method of FIFO, LIFO and AVCO;
- to outline the consistency concept;
- to introduce students to the accounts of a manufacturing business.

8.1 Manufacturing companies

Until now we have examined the accounts of *trading* concerns (i.e. businesses that buy goods as finished products and resell them in their original state). Not every business restricts its activities to this shopkeeping role; a large number of small businesses *produce* goods for resale (i.e. they buy in raw materials and convert them into finished goods through a process of *manufacture*). We will examine how to account for a manufacturing business in this chapter. However, to account for manufacturing businesses, some concepts of cost accounting must first be outlined.

8.2 Basic cost accounting

This book concentrates on financial accounting, i.e. reporting to the owners and other third parties on the firm's performance. Another important area of accounting is management accounting which involves preparing and reporting financial information for users within the company to enhance company performance or to assist decision-making generally. As the two are specialities of the same subject, there are areas of overlap and the valuation of stocks is one such topic where duplication occurs. As most readers will be studying cost or management accounting as a parallel course, there is no need to examine the concepts of cost accounting in any depth in this text. However, some consideration is necessary to allow for possible differences in approach or in timing of material coverage.

In cost accounting, similar expenses are grouped together. This is necessary as in a manufacturing firm there are many different elements of expenditure which are incurred in the business. The finished product may have hundreds of components in it, and these in turn may be made from an equally wide range of raw materials. There will be workers involved in production, administration, selling and delivery, and some workers who split their time between production and other activities, such as distribution. Most firms identify three main subheadings under which to group the expenditure which accounts for the full cost of the product:

8.2.1   Manufacturing or production cost

This category is composed of three elements.

1. Direct materials are materials (sometimes called 'raw' materials) which form part of the product. For example, in the manufacture of a computer the silicon chips are often bought in as direct materials. These materials are distinguished from indirect materials; these are materials used up in the manufacturing process such as cleaning fluids.

2. Direct wages are the wages of workers who spend their time producing goods for resale. The wages of workers who assemble the various parts of a computer would constitute direct wages.

3. Overhead costs: apart from the direct expenditure there will be other costs of production incurred indirectly, e.g. you could not produce anything in the dark so the factory must be lit; the workers must be kept warm in winter and cool in summer; machinery breaks down and needs repairing. These indirect costs of manufacture are called 'production overheads'.

The direct, aggregated costs are called 'prime cost' and when added to overheads the total cost of manufacture is arrived at.

8.2.2   Administration expenses

Even if the workers and machinery are present, the firm still needs to be managed. The work of office staff may include calculating the wages of the workers and paying the bills. All this expenditure is concerned with the running of the firm and is not directly related to manufacture. This does not mean that it is unnecessary expenditure, it is just a different classification.

8.2.3 Selling and distribution expenditure

There is a misconception in the manufacturing industry that emphasises the efficient manufacture of goods as the road to success. Whereas this is an essential ingredient to the long-term survival of the company, the marketing of the product plays just as important a role. You can produce the best product in the world at the cheapest price, but you must make the customers aware of this fact through advertising the other promotions. The goods also need to be delivered to retail or wholesale outlets, or even direct to the customer. All this expenditure is important and is placed in this cost grouping. Figure 8.1 illustrates the above constituent components of full product cost.

So, just because a cost is placed in a group does not mean it is to be minimised or is unimportant. It is only through this sub-division that effective control can be exercised in the manufacturing firm to isolate areas of inefficiency or to assist year on year comparisons.

Some costs will cut across the groupings chosen, in which instance they are shared between them. The term 'allocation' is used when this division can be done with a degree of accuracy, e.g. Mr Brown spends two days a week delivering goods and the rest of his time is spent helping out on the shop floor. If the term 'apportion' is used then this implies a degree of estimation is incorporated, e.g. Mr Brown works on the shop floor, but sometimes he helps out on deliveries if they are busy. In the former case two-fifths of Mr Brown's weekly wage is *allocated* to selling and distribution, with the rest *allocated* to manufacturing overhead. In the

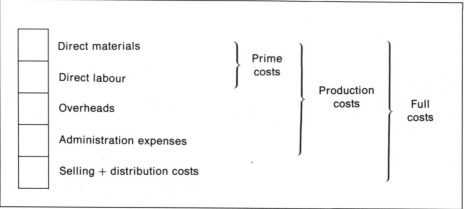

Figure 8.1 Components of full product cost

latter instance an estimate of his time must be taken, e.g. from the supervisor's records or even a 'guesstimate' made if the amount is immaterial.

8.3 Stock valuation

Unlike a trading firm, the manufacturing business will have stocks of raw materials, i.e. items purchased but not yet used in production, work in progress (i.e. products in various stages of completion) and finished goods on which there is no more work to do other than to sell them. All these constituent parts of total stocks need to be valued so that a total stock figure can be used in the accounts.

Before an organisation can value its stocks it must ensure that it knows precisely what stock it owns. This can be done by physically counting its stock at the year end. The results of this count can be used to update its stock records. Errors can occur in these stocktaking procedures, due to human error and faulty measuring equipment (e.g. weighing scales may have to be used to count powder). In an attempt to keep these and other errors down to a minimum, double counting and careful supervision are often used.

We will examine the different valuation methods later; however, before doing so, it is important to understand why accountants spend so much time and effort in valuing stocks.

The main reason accepted methods of valuing stocks have been developed is because of the effect on profit, probably the most popular measure of a business's success. Any change in the value placed on a business's closing stock will change profit by the same amount. If the closing stock valuation is increased by £100, profit increases by £100; if the closing stock is reduced by £50, profit is reduced by £50. This is apparent by viewing a simple profit and loss account as shown in Spreadsheet 8.1. Column D contains the original profit and loss account with a

Spreadsheet 8.1 Stock valuation and profit

	A	B	C	D	E	F
1						
2						
3				Original	(1)	(2)
4						
5	Sales			5000	5000	5000
6						
7	Opening Stock			−500	−500	−500
8	Purchases			−3600	−3600	−3600
9	Closing Stock			600	700	550
10						
11	GROSS PROFIT			1500	1600	1450
12						
13	Expenses			−950	−950	−950
14						
15	NET PROFIT			550	650	500
16						

closing stock value of £600 and a net profit of £550. In column E the closing stock has been increased by £100 to £700 and net profit increases to £650. In column F the closing stock has been reduced by £50 to £550 and the net profit falls to £500. Try changing the stock valuation yourself and see how you can change the profit figure.

Therefore careful attention needs to be paid to the way stocks are valued to prevent the profit figure being manipulated.

Why is there a problem? Up to now we have been assuming that the value of stock is exactly determined by its purchase cost. This is rarely the case due to:

a. the amalgamation of purchases of similar stocks at different prices;

b. cost having many (often quite different) meanings;

c. the possibility of selling some part of the stock at lower than cost.

Let us consider each of these problems in turn as they affect the three component parts of stock:

8.3.1 Raw material valuation

The valuation of raw materials is a matter of assumptions. The physical stock count will produce a number or quantity estimate, but the cost of the raw materials in stock will depend on their date of purchase and which items have been used in production. The stock is made up of items bought at different times and at different prices. In most cases this is indeterminate as the business's stock records often fail to show exactly which item has been used in production, although computerised stock records are improving the information provision. So how do we value what stock there is left at the year end?. We will examine three methods:

1. *First in first out (FIFO)*. This method assumes that the first items to be used in production are those purchased first, so that the items in closing stock will be the items purchased last at more recent prices.

2. *Last in first out (LIFO)*. Here the assumption is the converse to the above, i.e. the items in closing stock are those purchased first.

3. *Average cost (AVCO)*. The stock is valued at the average price paid during the accounting period. This should be a weighted average.

The above three methods are not the only methods available; however, this text will not consider any other alternatives.

An example at this point to illustrate the consequences of the different stock valuations is given in Figure 8.2.

> Morgan Micros plc produce computers which have a key component imported from Taiwan by Davies International Traders. These, micro processors, tend to fluctuate in price, due partly to currency changes and partly to technology advances. There was no opening stock of micro processors and during the year three orders were placed. In January, an order for 400 chips was received at £10 per chip. In June, 500 were received at a price of £12, and the last order for 100 chips was received in September at a price of £14 each. In October 800 chips were sold at £20 each. Therefore at the end of the year there were 200 chips in stock. What should they be valued at and what is the gross profit for the year?

Figure 8.2   Morgan Micros plc

Spreadsheet 8.2 shows the calculations used in the following discussion.

Under the FIFO systems the 200 in stock would be made up of the 100 of the last order (100 × £14 = £1,400) plus 100 of the previous delivery (100 × £12 = £1,200), i.e. total value £2,600. The gross profit is £7,200.

LIFO would assume that the items in stock were those bought in January, i.e. £2,000 in value (200 × £10). Notice that LIFO produces a lower value than FIFO in times of rising prices. The LIFO gross profit is also lower than the FIFO gross profit: £6,600 compared with £7,200. This lower profit figure reflects the fact that it now costs more to replace the stock sold than before. See Chapter 24 for an analysis of how inflation effects financial statements.

Under the AVCO system the average cost is used. In order to calculate average cost the total number purchased is divided into the total price paid (£11,400/1,000), i.e. £11.40 each. This is then applied to the closing stock quantity - 200 × £11.40 = £2,280. As expected the average cost method produces a stock valuation and a gross profit figure somewhere in between the FIFO and LIFO methods.

Which method is correct? The simple answer is all of them are correct in their own way, as they are based on different assumptions. In Great Britain, FIFO is favoured by the tax authorities. The accounting standard on stocks (see page 375) allows FIFO but disallows LIFO. The Companies Act 1985 allows both methods. In the United States LIFO is commonly used.

Consistency is an important concept when valuing stock. Once a valuation method is chosen by a business it should be used from year to year. The business should not change its valuation method unless it has a valid reason for doing so; such a reason does not include the artificial increasing or lowering of the profit figure. See Figure 8.3 for a more detailed discussion of the consistency concept.

8.3.2   Work in progress valuation

Work in progress, or WIP, represents all the partly finished goods in production at the closing balance sheet date. In valuing WIP it is important to include all

Spreadsheet 8.2   Purchases, closing stock and trading accounts

```
     !  A   ::   B   ::   C   ::   D   ::   E   ::   F   :
 1
 2
 3   (a)       Purchases
 4
 5   Month    Qty.       Price      Value
 6
 7   January            400        10      4000
 8
 9   June               500        12      6000
10
11   September          100        14      1400
12                                       -----------
13   Total Purchases                       11400
14                                       ===========
15
16
17   (b)       Closing Stock - FIFO
18
19   Month    Qty.       Price      Value
20
21   September          100        14      1400
22
23   June               100        12      1200
24                                        -----------
25                                          2600
26                                        ===========
27
28   (c)       Closing Stock - LIFO
29
30   Month    Qty.       Price      Value
31
32   January            200        10      2000
33                                       ============
34
35
36   (d)       Closing Stock - AVCO
37
38                     Total Purchases
39   Average Cost
40                     Total Qty.
41
42                        1140
43             =       ---------------
44                        100
45
46             =        11.4
47
48   Closing Stock    =           11.4*200     =     2280
49
50   (e)  .   Trading Accounts
51
52                              FIFO      LIFO      AVCO
53
54   Sales                     16000     16000     16000
55
56   Purchases                -11400    -11400    -11400
57
58   Closing Stock              2600      2000      2280
59
60                            ------------------------------
61   GROSS PROFIT               7200      6600      6880
62                            ==============================
```

The concepts that accountants turn to when deciding how to treat various business transactions are open to interpretation. There are subjective elements in any decision that will lead to differences in reported accounting statements, for example:

which depreciation method to use—straight-line or reducing balance?
which stock valuation method to use—FIFO, LIFO or AVCO?

However, once a specific method has been chosen it becomes the firm's accounting policy and the concept of consistency ensures that this accounting treatment is maintained in future accounting periods.

The company may want to change its policy on certain accounting methods, but this should only apply if they are 'more appropriate to its circumstances and best suit its results and financial position'. This quote has been taken from an accounting standard (SSAP 2); more of this in Chapter 19.

The main reason for this concept is that it adds quality to accounting information, enabling year on year comparisons to be made in the secure knowledge that the basis of the accounts has remained unaltered. It also prevents some of the worst excesses of creative accounting, i.e. the manipulation of the final accounts to present a different picture of the company's performance and position for short-term benefit.

Example
A company has always used a FIFO basis for stock valuation, but prices have recently fallen. This has decreased the closing stock valuation, increasing cost of goods sold and thus reducing gross profit. By changing to a LIFO basis, the profit could be enhanced, but the consistency concept would be breached. A one-off change is acceptable, but frequent changes in valuation policy are not.

Figure 8.3   The concept of objectivity

expenditure incurred in manufacturing the product. We have already identified three types of product cost: prime cost, production cost and full cost. An organisation could chose either of these cost concepts to value its stocks. However, the professional accounting bodies (see Chapter 19 for a description of accounting standards) have agreed a standard definition of cost. This definition is found in Statement of Standard Accounting Practice 9. Cost is defined as 'the expenditure incurred in the normal course of business, in bringing the product to its present location and condition'. This cost concept clearly includes all direct costs together with related overheads incurred at the normal level of activity. Therefore abnormal overhead costs should be excluded from product cost and written off to the profit and loss account in the year in which they occurred. What constitutes normal is left up to the individual accountant to decide.

8.3.3   Finished goods valuation

The guidance in SSAP 9 that cost should include all expenditure incurred in bringing the products to their present location and condition applies to finished stock as well as WIP. Therefore selling and some distribution costs should be excluded from product cost.

There is futher guidance within the standard which states that the value placed on closing stock should be the lower of cost and net realisable value, NRV. The latter is the disposal value of the stock (i.e. price obtained less any selling costs). Using this guideline, overvaluation of stock is prevented and the profit figure reported presents a prudent view of the company's operations.

Sometimes stock will become obsolete and so it is prudent to reduce the carrying value in the balance sheet. This is done by crediting a stock provision account and debiting the profit and loss account with the expense.

8.4 Accounting for stocks

We will now examine how to account for the processing of stock from raw material, through WIP to its finished state. Figure 8.4 shows how the system works.

The solution, in spreadsheet format, is given in Spreadsheet 8.3. Please note that there are now three stock columns: raw materials, work in progress and finished goods, rather than just one column. The accounting procedures are as follows:

1. Opening balances are recorded along row 7 of the spreadsheet, with capital being the balancing figure. For the moment ignore the final column (entitled **manufacturing account**) as it does not form part of the double entry.

2. Record the purchases of raw materials as credits to the **cash** column and debits to the **raw materials stock** column, reflecting the fact that these raw materials are now available to be used in the production process.

3. Note (5) of Figure 8.4 tells us that there are four tons of raw materials in stock at the year end and the company uses the FIFO method of stock valuation. Therefore the closing stock valuation is £1,875 (i.e. three tons at £475 each and one ton at £450). This valuation is placed at the closing balance sheet row of the spreadsheet.

4. We can now work out how much of the raw material was used in the production process during the year. This usage was £9,350, which is transferred out of the **raw materials** column into the **work in progress** column.

5. The next step is to record all the other product costs as credits to the **cash** column and debits to the **work in progress** column, reflecting their use in manufacture. These cost are direct labour and overheads. Note how some of these costs are split between the **work in progress** column and the **profit and loss** column, reflecting the proportions used in the production process and elsewhere in the business.

Keith Jenkins Ltd manufactures footballs and rugby balls from a polycarbonate compound that he produces at his rented factory. The following information is provided:

	£
Stocks at 14 December 19X3	
Raw materials at cost	4,000
Work in progress	3,000
Finished goods at cost	3,000
Other balances as at 14 December 19X3	
Office equipment NBV	40,000
Machinery NBV	90,000
Cash as at 14 December 19X3	10,000
Cash transactions	
Purchases of raw materials:	
June: 10 tons at £400 a ton	
September: 4 tons at £450 a ton	
October: 3 tons at £475 a ton	
Direct wages for productive workers	56,000
Maintenance staff	23,000
Factory power and fuel	4,500
Rent and rates	12,000
Heat and light	8,000
Insurance	2,200
Office salaries	21,000
Advertising	2,000
Sales	301,200
Managers' wages	15,000

Assume that there were no accruals or prepayments at the year end, other than stock valuations.

1. The depreciation expense for the year is calculated as 10 per cent of NBV for office equipment and 20 per cent of NBV for machinery.
2. Heat and light is apportioned at a rate of 20 per cent for the office and 75 per cent for the factory. The rent and rates are similarly dealt with.
3. The insurance premium for the factory is £1,500. The balance relates to the office area.
4. The manager divides his time equally between production, administration and sales.
5. There were 4 tons of raw material compound in stock on 13 December 19X4 and the company uses a FIFO valuation method. The stock of finished goods is valued at £4,500, and work in progress is valued at £3,500.

Figure 8.4   Keith Jenkins Limited

Spreadsheet 8.3   Workshop solution for Keith Jenkins Ltd

	Cash	Raw Materials	Work in Progress	Finished Goods	Office Equipment	Machinery	Trading Account	Profit & Loss A/c	Capital	Manufacturing A/c
		<------	Stock	------>						
Opening Balance Sheet	10000	4000	3000	3000	40000	90000			-150000	7000
Purchases of Raw Materials										
June	-4000	4000								4000
September	-1800	1800								1800
October	-1425	1425								1425
Raw Materials to W.I.P.		-9350	9350							
Sales	301200						-301200			
Direct Wages	-56000		56000							56000
Overhead:-										
Maintenance Staff	-23000		23000							23000
Factory Fuel & Power	-4500		4500							4500
Rent & Rates	-12000		9000					3000		9000
Heat & Light	-8000		6000					2000		6000
Insurance	-2200		1500					700		1500
Manager's Wages	-15000		7500					7500		7500
Depreciation: Machinery			18000			-18000				18000
W.I.P. to Finished Goods			-134350	134350						-134350
Cost of Goods Sold				-132850			132850			
Office Salaries	-21000							21000		
Depreciation Office Equipment					-4000			4000		
Advertising	-2000							2000		
Gross Profit							168350	-168350		
Transfer of Net Profit								128150	-128150	
	160275	1875	3500	4500	36000	72000	0	0	-278150	5375

6. Figure 8.4 tells us that the closing work in progress figure is £3,500, so the amount of completed work in progress is £134,350, which is transferred to the **finished goods** column.

7. Figure 8.4 tells us that the closing finished goods figure is £4,500, so the cost of the goods figure is £132,850, which is transferred to the **trading account** column.

8. We can now record the sales figure as a debit to the **cash** column and a credit to the **trading account**.

9. The gross profit can be calculated as £168,350, which is transferred to the **profit and loss** column.

10. The non-product costs are recorded as expenses in the **profit and loss** column and credits in the **cash** column.

11. Finally, the net profit is transferred to the **capital** column and the remaining columns added up.

In addition to the trading and profit and loss account, manufacturing businesses sometimes prepare a manufacturing account. This statement presents an analysis of the costs incurred in the production process. It is simply constructed by summing the entries in the **raw materials** and **work in progress** columns; this is how the final column in Spreadsheet 8.3 was constructed. The conventional layout of the statement is shown in Figure 8.5. The trading and profit and loss account are shown in Figure 8.6.

8.4.1 Limitations to the uses of manufacturing accounts

Whereas the manufacturing account does present the cost of manufacture, this figure in isolation is of limited use. Management needs to compare the cost of manufacture with the cost of buying-in ready made supplies, i.e. so-called 'make or buy' decisions. To do this, information is needed on the product components, but in this form of account the degree of aggregation means that this information is lost. So the firm uses management accountants to supply it with detailed information of this kind, to ensure greater efficiency and control in manufacture. It is relative performance measures that are important, not absolute measures. Just because a profit of £128,150 was achieved does not mean that this is a good performance; it is just a statement of fact. If the goods could have been bought cheaper than the cost of manufacture then the profit could have been higher. This is a subjective evaluation as this information is not available, but clearly the management accountant has a significant role to fulfil.

Manufacturing account for the twelve months to 31 December 19X4	£	£	£
Stock of raw materials	4,000		
Purchase of raw materials	7,225		
	11,225		
Less: closing stock of raw materials	1,875		
Raw materials used	9,350		
Direct wages	56,000		
PRIME COST	65,350		
Indirect cost			
Opening stock of work in progress		3,000	
Maintenance staff	23,000		
Factory fuel and power	4,500		
Rent and rates	9.000		
Heat and light	6,000		
Insurance	1,500		
Manager's salary	7,500		
Depreciation: machinery	18,000		
		69,500	
		72,500	
Less: closing stock WIP		3,500	69,000
COST OF MANUFACTURE			£134,350

Figure 8.5   Manufacturing account for the twelve months to 31 December 19X4

Trading account for the twelve months to 31 December 19X4	£	£
Sales		301,200
Less: cost of goods sold		
Opening stock: finished goods	3,000	
Cost of manufacture	134,350	
	137,350	
Less closing stock	4,500	132,850
GROSS PROFIT		£168,350

Profit and loss account for the 12 months to 13 December 19X4.	£	£
Gross profit		168,350
Less: expenses		
Rent and rates	3,000	
Heat and light	2,000	
Insurance	700	
Manager's salary	7,500	
Office salaries	21,000	
Depreciation: equipment	4,000	
Advertising	2,000	
	40,200	
NET PROFIT		£128,150

Figure 8.6   Trading and profit and loss account for the twelve months to 31 December 19X4

CHECKLIST _____

Having completed Chapter 8, you should be able to:

- explain some of the basic concepts of cost accounting;
- identify the constituent parts of inventory—raw materials, work in progress and finished goods;
- explain and calculate the FIFO, LIFO and AVCO methods of stock valuation;
- outline the consistency concept;
- prepare a manufacturing account for a business.

Workshop 8.1: Manufacturing account

Debbie Alan manufactures bridal gowns from bought-in materials that she produces at her rented factory. The following information is provided:

	£
Stocks at 31 December 19X2	
Raw materials at cost	7,000
Work in progress	6,000
Finished goods at cost	9,000
Other balances as at 31 December 19X2	
Office equipment NBV	10,000
Machinery NBV	40,000
Cash as at 31 December 19X2	10,000

Cash transactions

	£
Purchases of raw materials:	
June: 500 metres of fabric at £30 a metre	
September: 200 metres of fabric at £25 a metre	
October: 400 metres of fabric at £35 a metre	
Direct wages for productive workers	78,000
Maintenance staff	12,000
Rent and rates	15,000
Heat and light	12,400
Insurance	1,400
Office salaries	25,900
Advertising	4,700
Sales	257,900
Manager's wages	21,000

Assume that there were no accruals or prepayments at the year end, other than stock valuations.

1. The depreciation expense for the year is calculated as 15 per cent of NBV for office equipment and 25 per cent of NBV for machinery.

2. Heat and light is apportioned at a rate of 20 per cent for the office and 80 per cent for the factory. The rent and rates are similarly dealt with.

3. The insurance premium for the factory is £1,100. The balance relates to the office area.

4. The manager divides his time equally between production, administration and sales.

5. There were 500 metres of dress fabric in stock on 13 December 19X4 and the company uses a FIFO valuation method. The stock of finished goods is valued at £7,300, and work in progress is valued at £6,200. All purchases and expenses are paid in cash (except depreciation).

You are required to produce Debbie's manufacturing account for the twelve months to 31 December 19X2 and the balance sheet as at that date.

Workshop guide

1. Opening balances are recorded along row 7 of Spreadsheet 8.4, with capital being the balancing figure. This has been calculated using the formula − SUM(D7:K7). For the moment ignore the final column (entitled *manufacturing account*) as it does not form part of the double entry.

2. Record the purchases of dress fabrics as credits to the **cash** column, column D, and debits to the **raw materials stock** column, column E, reflecting the fact that these raw materials are now available to be used in the production process. The cell contents of D11, D12 and D13 calculate the amount paid in terms of price per metre and metres purchased.

3. Note 5 of the question tells us that there are 500 metres of dress fabric in stock at the year end and the company uses the FIFO method of stock valuation. Therefore the closing stock valuation is £16,500 (i.e. 400 metres at £35 a metre and 100 metres at £25 a metre. The calculation is performed in cell E45. This valuation is placed at the closing balance sheet row of the spreadsheet.

4. We can now work out how much of the dress fabric was used in the production process during the year. This is found by summing the entries in the raw materials column (E) and by deducting the amount left, i.e. cell E45. As the entry is to transfer this usage out of the **raw materials** column into the **work in progress** column, then it carries a credit or minus sign. See cell E16, which is matched by the entry in column F, the **work in progress** column.

Spreadsheet 8.4   Workshop 8.1: Debbie Alan Bridal Gowns – Solution

		<---- Stock ---->							
	Cash	Raw Materials	Work in Progress	Finished Goods	Office Equipment	Machinery	Trading Account	Profit & Loss A/c	Capital	Manufact-uring A/c
Opening Balance Sheet	10000	7000	6000	9000	10000	40000			-82000	13000
Purchases of Raw Materials										
June	-15000	15000								15000
September	-5000	5000								5000
October	-14000	14000								14000
Raw Materials to W.I.P.		-24500	24500							
Sales	257900						-257900			
Direct Wages	-78000		78000							78000
Overhead:-										
Maintenance Staff	-12000		12000							12000
Rent & Rates	-15000		12000					3000		12000
Heat & Light	-12400		9920					2480		9920
Insurance	-1400		1100					300		1100
Manager's Wages	-21000		10500					10500		10500
Depreciation: Machinery			10000			-10000				10000
W.I.P. to Finished Goods			-157820	157820						-157820
Cost of Goods Sold				-159520			159520			
Office Salaries	-25900							25900		
Depreciation Office Equipment					-1500			1500		
Advertising	-4700							4700		
Gross Profit							98380	-98380		
Transfer of Net Profit								50000	-50000	
	63500	16500	6200	7300	8500	30000	0	0	-132000	22700

5. The next step is to record all the other product costs as credits to the **cash** column and debits to the **work in progress** column, reflecting their use in manufacture. The maintenance staff is straightforward enough, with cash being credited and charged to the **work in progress** column. However, the costs of rent and rates, heat and light and insurance need to be split between the **work in progress** column and the **profit and loss** column, reflecting the proportions used in the production process and elsewhere in the business. So for the opposite entry for D25, part is in F25 and part is in K25. To be technically correct there should be one entry to an **expense** column or rent and rates, which would then be cleared by two separate double entries. Here we are using the spreadsheet to shortcut this process. The same principles apply for the heat and light apportionment. The insurance entry is split into two components on the same row (27) with cell K27 acting as a balancing figure. The manager's salary is divided equally in its double entry between production in the manufacturing account and other expenses in the profit and loss account. The depreciation on the machinery is calculated using the cell reference to the NBV, i.e. cell 17, and multiplying by the appropriate percentage rate. See cell F29.

6. Figure 8.4 tells us (note 5) that the closing work in progress figure is £6,200, so the amount of complete work in progress is £157,820 which is transferred to the **finished goods** column. This has been calculated in the same way as the raw materials consumed, i.e. by summing the column to date and deducting the value of uncompleted work. See cell F31.

7. Figure 8.4 tells us (note 5) that the closing finished goods figure is £7,300, so the cost of goods figure is £159,520 which is transferred to the **trading account** column in the same way as previous stock transfers. See row 33, column G and J.

8. We can now record the sales figure as a debit to the **cash** column and a credit to the **trading account**.

9. The gross profit can be calculated as £98,380, being the sum of column J, which is transferred to the **profit and loss** column, column K.

10. The non-product costs are recorded as expenses in the **profit and loss** column and credits in the **cash** column; depreciation on office equipment utilising the cell reference to the NBV.

11. Finally, the net profit is transferred to the **capital** column and the remaining columns summed.

The manufacturing account is prepared by summing the entries in the **raw materials** and **work in progress** columns and placing the result in column N. For completeness, the conventional layout of the statement is shown in Table 8.1 together with the trading and profit and loss account (Table 8.2).

Spreadsheet 8.5 Workshop 8.1: Debbie Alan Bridal Gowns – formulae

	A	B	C	D	E	F	G
1							
2							
3					<------	Stock	------>
4				Cash	Raw	Work in	Finished
5					Materials	Progress	Goods
6							
7	Opening Balance Sheet			10000	7000	6000	9000
8							
9	Purchases of Raw Materials						
10							
11		June		-500*30	-D11		
12		September		-200*25	-D12		
13		October		-400*35	-D13		
14							
15							
16	Raw Materials to W.I.P.				-SUM(E7:E14)+E45	-E16	
17							
18	Sales			257900			
19							
20	Direct Wages			-78000		-D20	
21							
22	Overhead:-						
23							
24	Maintenance Staff			-12000		-D24	
25	Rent & Rates			-15000		-D25*.8	
26	Heat & Light			-12400		-D26*.8	
27	Insurance			-1400		1100	
28	Manager's Wages			-21000		-D28/2	
29	Depreciation: Machinery					-I29	
30							
31	W.I.P. to Finished Goods					-SUM(F7:F29)	-F31
32							
33	Cost of Goods Sold						-SUM(G7:G32)+G45
34							
35							
36							
37	Office Salaries			-25900			
38	Depreciation Office Equipment						
39	Advertising			-4700			
40							
41	Gross Profit						
42							
43	Transfer of Net Profit						
44				---			
45				SUM(D7:D43)	(400*35)+(100*25)	6200	7300
46				===			

	H	I	J	K	L	M	N
	Office Equipment	Machinery	Trading Account	Profit & Loss A/c	Capital		Manufact-uring A/c
	10000	40000			-SUM(D7:K7)		SUM(E7:F7)
							SUM(E11:F11)
							SUM(E12:F12)
							SUM(E13:F13)
			-D18				
							SUM(E20:F20)
							SUM(E24:F24)
				-D25*.2			SUM(E25:F25)
				-D26*.2			SUM(E26:F26)
				-D27-F27			SUM(E27:F27)
				-D28/2			SUM(E28:F28)
		-I7*.25					SUM(E29:F29)
							SUM(E31:F31)
			-633				
				-D37			
	-H7*.15			-H38			
				-D39			
			-SUM(J7:J39)	-J41			
				-SUM(K7:K41)	-K43		
	SUM(H7:H43)	SUM(I7:I43)	SUM(J7:J43)	SUM(K7:K43)	SUM(L7:L43)		SUM(E45:F45)

Table 8.1 *Manufacturing account for the twelve months to 31 December 19X2*

	£
Stock of raw materials	7,000
Purchase of raw materials	34,000
	41,000
Less: closing stock of raw materials	16,500
Raw materials used	24,500
Direct wages	78,000
Prime cost	102,500

Indirect cost	£	£	
Opening stock of work in progress		6,000	
Maintenance staff	12,000		
Rent and rates	12,000		
Heat and light	9,920		
Insurance	1,100		
Manager's salary	10,500		
Depreciation: machinery	10,000		
		55,520	
		61,520	
Less: closing stock WIP		6,200	
			55,320
Cost of manufacture			157,820

'What If?' problems

1. What happens to gross profit (cell K41) if the opening stock of raw materials is £13,000?

2. What happens to net profit if advertising costs fall to £2,700?

3. What happens to net profit and gross profit if the manager's salary is wholly apportioned to the factory. Change the entry in row 28 to effect this change? Net profit = _____? Gross profit = _____?

4. What is the effect on cost of goods sold (H33) if the price paid for material in October was only £30 a metre? Remember to change both cell D13 and to adjust the closing stock, cell D45, to reflect this change in price.

5. Amend the spreadsheet to account for a changing treatment for office salaries, which are now to be apportioned between the factory and other expenses in the ratio 10 per cent and 90 per cent.

Table 8.2 *Trading account for the twelve months to 31 December 19X4*

	£	£
Sales		257,900
Less: cost of goods sold		
Opening stock: finished goods	9,000	
Cost of manufacture	157,820	
	166,820	
Less closing stock	7,300	
		159,520
Gross profit		98,380

Profit and loss account for the 12 months to 13 December 19x4

	£	£
Gross profit		98,380
Less: expenses		
Rent and rates	3,000	
Heat and light	2,480	
Insurance	300	
Manager's salary	10,500	
Office salaries	25,900	
Depreciation: equipment	1,500	
Advertising	4,700	
		48,380
Net profit		50,000

Answers

1. Gross profit change to £92,380.

2. Net profit changes to £46,000.

3. Change cell contents of F28 to read $-$**D28** and blank cell contents of K28. Gross profit changes to £81,880. Net profit changes to £46,000 (i.e. remains the same).

4. Change D13 to read $-$**400*30**. Change E45 to read (400*30) + (100*25). Cost of sold changes to £176,020.

5. Move row 38 to row 30. In cell F30 the formula is $-$**D30*.10**. In cell F33 the formula is $-$**sum (F7:F30) + F46**.Cell K30 becomes $-$**D30*.90**.

Selected questions and exercises

Question 8.1

For the six months ended 31 October, an importer and distributor of one type of washing machine has the transactions shown in Table 8.3 in his records. There was an opening balance of 100 units which had a value of £3,900.

Table 8.3 *Transactions for six months ending 31 October*

Date	Bought quantity in units	Cost per unit £
May	100	41
June	200	50
August	400	51,875

Date	Sold quantity in units	Price each £
July	250	64
September	350	70
October	100	74

The price of £51,875 each for the August receipt was £6,125 per unit less than the normal price because of the large quantity ordered.

From the information given in Table 8.3 and using weighted average, FIFO and LIFO methods for pricing issues, you are required for each method to:

a. show the stores ledger records, including the closing stock balance and stock valuation;

b. prepare, in column format, trading accounts for the period to show the gross profit using each of the three methods of pricing issues;

c. comment on which method, in the situation depicted, is regarded as the best measure of profit, and why.

Solution on page 519. *Source: ICMA, Cost Accounting 1, November 1977.*

Question 8.2

a. Three students, K, L and M, are equal partners in a joint venture which involves them, on a part-time basis, in buying and selling sacks of product F. The transactions for the six months ended 30 September were as stated in Table 8.4. You are to assume that purchases at the unit costs given were made at the beginning of each month and that the sales were made at the end of each month at the fixed price of £1.50 per sack.

Table 8.4 *Details of the accounts of K, L and M.*

Month	Purchases		Sales
	Sacks	Unit cost £	Sacks
April	1,000	1.00	500
May	500	1.20	750
June	1,000	1.00	Nil
July	Nil	—	600
August	500	1.20	650
September	500	1.30	600

In October the student partners held a meeting to review their financial position and to share out the profits but there was disagreement because each partner had priced the issues on a different basis. K had used FIFO, L had used LIFO and M had used a weighted average, basing his weighted average on the whole of the six months' purchases. It was, however, agreed that the stock remaining at the end of September should be stored until next April.

You are required to:
(i) show the records which each student kept of the transactions;
(ii) show the amount each student ought to receive if the whole of the profit arising from each method of pricing the issues were distributed;
(iii) comment briefly on the acceptability of the three different results arising from the transactions.
b. In the context of a manufacturing business, explain briefly what is meant by the last sentence of the following statement.

The Statement of Standard Accounting Practice No. 9 on stocks and work in progress (SSAP 9) states in an explanatory note, paragraph 3, that 'In order to match costs and revenue, 'costs' of stocks and work in progress should comprise that expenditure which has been incurred in the normal course of business in bringing the product or service to its present location and condition. Such costs will include all related production overheads, even though these may accure on a time basis.'

No solution provided.   Source: *ICMA, Cost Accounting 1, November 1979.*

Question 8.3
A business includes in its stock three major categories of goods, A, B and C.

At 31 December 1985, the information given in Table 8.5 is available:

1. What is meant by historic cost and net realisable value?
2. How many ways could you value the above stock?
3. Under what circumstances would each method of valuation be most appropriate?

No solution provided.

Table 8.5   *Stock information at 31 December 1985*

Stock item	Historic cost	Net realisable value
A	2,000	1,750
B	3,220	3,300
C	2,400	2,500

Question 8.4

Thomas Dart, builders' merchant, is now completing his stock valuation at 31 May 1988. He fears that his financial results for the year ended 31 May 1988 will be poor as compared with recent years, but nevertheless wishes his accounts to show a favourable view of his business so that his bank manager will approve a renewal of the business bank overdraft.

The stock at 31 May 1988 includes the items shown in Table 8.6.

Table 8.6   *Details of the accounts of Thomas Dart*

	Unit cost price £	Expected sales price £	Replacement price £
200 'padgetts'	200	340	260
100 'wodgetts'	110	280	140

Thomas Dart has now decided that the items should be valued on the bases explained in Table 8.7.

As far as other items of stock are concerned, Thomas Dart proposes to use the last in first out basis of stock valuation instead of the first in first out basis used in previous years.

Table 8.7   *Figures and reasons for valuation*

	Unit valuation £	Reason
200 'padgetts'	340	An important customer has written saying he hopes to buy all the stock of 'padgetts' on 10 June 1988
100 'wodgetts'	140	Anticipating a growing demand for 'wodgetts', Thomas Dart bought a large quantity before the price rose to £140. Most competitors' stocks were bought at a price of £140

As the accounting technician employed by Thomas Dart, prepare a report addressed to him, commenting on his proposed bases for valuing his stock at 31 May 1988. In your report make reference to appropriate accounting concepts.

No solution provided.   *Source: AAT, Accounting, June 1988.*

Question 8.5

Mrs J. Turner presents you with her trial balance for the year ended 31 December 1987 (see Table 8.8).

Table 8.8 *Details of the accounts of Mrs J Turner*

	£	£
Capital		140,000
Assets at cost:		
land and buildings	110,000	
plant and machinery	50,000	
fixtures and fittings	12,000	
Stocks at 31 December 1986		
raw materials	12,000	
work in progress	4,000	
finished goods	15,000	
Debtors/creditors	22,000	16,000
Bank	3,500	
Purchase of raw materials	97,000	
Sales		240,000
Wages	54,000	
Office expenses	5,000	
Selling and distribution costs	6,500	
Rates	4,000	
Plant maintenance	5,000	
Power: factory	3,500	
office	1,500	
Provision for depreciation		
at 31 December 1986		
plant and machinery		24,000
fittings and fixtures		8,000
Drawings	23,000	
	428,000	428,000

You are advised that:

1. Wages are to be split 2/3 factory (£10,000 of which is indirect), the remainder is allocated evenly between sales and the office.
2. Rates are to be split 60 per cent factory indirect, 40 per cent office.
3. Stocks as at 31 December 1987 are raw materials £9,000, work in progress £4,600, finished goods £13,500.
4. Wages accrued are £6.000.
5. Plant and machinery, fixtures and fittings are to be depreciated by 25 per cent p.a. of book value.

You are asked to present the manufacturing, trading and profit and loss account for the year ended 31 December 1987, and a balance sheet as at that date in a vertical format, highlighting: prime cost, production cost of goods completed, gross profit, net profit, working capital, capital employed.

Solution on pages 521–2.

Source: RSA, Accounting II, March 1988.

Question 8.6

The balances in Table 8.9 as at 31 March 1988 have been extracted from the accounting records of Long Measures Limited.

Table 8.9 *Details of the accounts of Long Measures Limited*

	£
Raw material stock at 1 April 1987	4,100
Raw material purchases	39,200
Raw material carriage inwards	1,800
Direct labour	33,000
Variable overheads	23,000
Fixed overheads	34,000
Work in progress at 1 April 1987	12,600
Finished goods stock at 1 April 1987	35,000
Finished goods purchased	67,500
Establishment expenditure	29,400
Administrative expenditure	17,100
Sales and distribution expenditure	23,500
Sales	320,000
Freehold property:	
at cost	80,000
provision for depreciation at 1 April 1987	20,000
Plant and machinery:	
at cost	44,000
provision for depreciation at 1 April 1987	6,000

Additional information:

1. Stock valuations at 31 March 1988 are raw material, 3,600; finished goods, 28,000.
2. The company's work in progress valuations include prime cost, variable overheads and fixed overheads; the work in progress valuation at 31 March 1988 was £9,500.
3. Depreciation is provided annually on the cost of fixed assets at the relevant year end at the following rates: freehold property, 2.5 per cent; plant and machinery, 10 per cent. Only half the freehold property depreciation is charged to manufacturing.
4. Direct labour charges accrued due at 31 March 1988 amounted to £200 while establishment expenditure prepaid at that date was £600.
5. The company only manufactured 2,000 'codgetts' during the year ended 31 March 1988 which were transferred to the trading account at a total market value of £150,000. In addition to 'codgetts', the company sells certain ancillary goods which it buys already manufactured.

You are required to prepare the manufacturing, trading and profit and loss account for the year ended 31 March 1988 of Long Measures Limited and show the following:

- prime cost;
- profit or loss on goods manufactured;
- unit cost of manufacture.

No solution provided. *Source: AAT, Accounting, June 1988.*

9 | The trading, profit and loss and appropriation account and balance sheet

AIMS OF CHAPTER _____

- to lay out the trading, profit and loss account and balance sheet in good form;
- to identify the profit and loss account as a period statement;
- to define the terms gross and net profit;
- to distinguish between capital and revenue expenditure;
- to outline the concept of materiality;
- to examine the correct accounting treatment of returns, carriage and discounts;
- to identify the balance sheet as a position statement;
- to distinguish between fixed and current assets;
- to define the term liability;

9.1 The trading and profit and loss account

In examining the accounts of any business one of the first questions to be asked is, 'How much profit did the firm make?' Make no mistake, the profit figure is probably *the* most significant figure that the accountant produces. It is used for planning purposes, e.g. where to invest in the future; it is used to raise finance, e.g. to show a bank or potential investor that the business is making money; small businesses use the profit figure as the basis for their income tax computation or to attract business partners. The trading and profit and loss accounts are the statements drawn up by the accountant to determine how profit was arrived at.

It is convenient to consider the trading and profit and loss account as being composed of three parts. Firstly, a section showing how the gross profit was arrived at; this is called the 'trading account'. Secondly, a section showing how the net profit was arrived at; this is the 'profit and loss account'. Thirdly, a section showing how profit was appropriated; this is called the 'profit and loss appropriation account'.

9.1.1   The trading account

Gross profit is the difference between the sales revenue realised from the products sold in the accounting period and the cost of the goods sold. This is calculated in a trading account which should contain all the costs of putting goods into a saleable condition. The usual trading account determines the cost of goods sold by adding opening stock to the purchases for the period and deducting closing stock, as shown in Figure 9.1.

However, it is not just purchases that can make up the cost of goods sold, as we saw in Chapter 8. If the firm is involved in the physical manufacture of a product then all costs associated with bringing the goods into a saleable condition will be included in the cost of goods sold. Such costs include factory depreciation and workers' wages.

9.1.2   Profit and loss account

Net profit is simply gross profit less any expenses incurred in selling the goods or service. This calculation is shown in the profit and loss account. What are expenses? This is also the subject of much debate, but for our purposes we will call them 'used up assets', or that part of the asset that has been used up in the accounting period.

Most items readily fall into this category. We have already examined depreciation and when looking at accruals and prepayments we examined rent, electricity and insurance. Other expenses can include wages and transport costs.

	£	£
Sales		100,000
Less cost of goods sold:		
Opening stock	20,000	
Purchases	70,000	
	90,000	
Less closing stock	15,000	
		75,000
GROSS PROFIT		25,000

Figure 9.1   The trading account

9.2   Capital and revenue expenditure

Accountants make distinction between two types of expenditure: capital expenditure and revenue expenditure. Capital expenditure relates to the purchase of fixed assets, including any costs associated with the purchase. For example, when buying land or buildings there is a legal cost in solicitors' fees which is added to the cost of the property, i.e. it is *capitalised*. When purchasing items of plant and machinery there may be delivery or installation expenditure, which is also capitalised. Items of capital expenditure are included in the balance sheet. Only the part that is used up in the current accounting period (i.e. the depreciation expense) appears in the profit and loss account.

Revenue expenditure relates to the everyday running costs of the business. A good example is the purchase of a car for the use of the business. The record of purchase will be a balance sheet transaction, e.g. debit motor vehicle account and credit cash or loan, if debt financed. The insurance premium, road fund license, maintenance and petrol expenditure are all used up during the accounting period and hence appear as an expense in the profit and loss account.

In order to ensure you are clear as to what expenditures are capital and what are revenue, try to classify the following list of expenditures for a retail electrical store.

1. Purchase of new cash tills to be used in the business.

2. Redecoration of the shop premises.

3. Purchase of a second-hand delivery van.

4. Payment for heating the shop.

5. Transport costs of delivering the new cash tills.

Materiality is a concept that can be referred to in nearly every type of transaction. For example, a definition of a fixed asset is an item of value to the business for more than one accounting period. If a firm buys a stapler and a punch for the office, then technically these items are fixed assets. However, the amount of money involved is so small that it is regarded as immaterial and the expenditure is written off to the profit and loss account as office expenses.

The problem is that what is material to one company may be immaterial to another due to the size of other transactions. Large manufacturing concerns may even have a policy that items costing less than £1,000 are not material. A piece of machinery costing £1,000 may be very material indeed to a small businessman – it may be his only piece of equipment. For example, a paint spraying machine may be a vital component in a small car repair shop, but to a large car manufacturer it will be insignificant.

Figure 9.2   The concept of materiality

Capital items are 1, 3 and 5. In item 5 the delivery cost is capitalised as this is a cost associated with purchase. Item 2 is open to debate. This redecoration could be a refurbishment of the premises which would be an asset, however it would depend on the nature of the work carried out–a lick of paint cannot be capitalised!

When deciding whether or not to capitalise, the concept of materiality should be taken into consideration; see Figure 9.2.

9.3 Some additional transactions

Some transactions merit detailed consideration as their accounting treatment is not necessarily obvious.

9.3.1 Returns

Sometimes a business will purchase goods only to find they are faulty or unwanted and they are returned to the supplier. These are referred to as 'returns outwards' as the goods are sent outwards from the business, back to the supplier.

Similarly, a customer of the business may return goods for similar reasons as the business returned goods to its suppliers; these are referred to as 'returns inwards' as the goods are sent inwards to the business from customers.

The accounting treatment for both returns inwards and returns outwards is shown in Spreadsheet 9.1. The business buys goods for £6,000 on credit and on receipt of the goods finds £1,000-worth are faulty and agrees to return these goods to the supplier. The accounting entry to record this return is to debit the **creditors** column so as to reduce the debt, and credit the **stock** column as the goods are no longer available for sale. If the goods had been purchased for cash, the debit entry would have been to a **debtors** column as the supplier would owe the business. The business goes on to sell the remaining £5,000-worth of goods for £8,000. £500-worth (selling value) of these goods are found to be faulty and returned by the customer. The accounting transaction to record this return is to debit the **profit and loss** column in order to cancel out the sale and credit the **debtors** column to reflect the fact that the customer no longer owes the £500. If the sale was for cash, the credit would have been to a **cash** column.

9.3.2 Carriage

While goods may cost or sell for a set price, the delivery charge relating to them can vary according to the nature of the goods (e.g. are they fragile, are they

Spreadsheet 9.1 Returns outwards and inwards

	A	B	C	D	E	F	G
1							
2							
3	Description			Creditors	Stock	Profit	Debtors
4						and Loss	
5							
6	Purchases			-6000	6000		
7							
8	Returns Outwards			1000	-1000		
9	---						
10	Sub-totals			-5000	5000	0	
11							
12	Sales					-8000	8000
13							
14	Cost of sales				-5000	5000	
15							
16	Returns Inwards					500	-500
17	--						
18	Totals			-5000	0	-2500	7500
19	===						

	A	B	D	E	F	G
1						
2						
3	Description		Creditors	Stock	Profit	Debtors
4					and Loss	
5						
6	Purchases		-6000	-D6		
7						
8	Returns Outwards		1000	-D8		
9	--					
10	Sub-totals		SUM(D6:D8)	SUM(E6:E8)	SUM(F6:F8)	
11						
12	Sales				-8000	-F12
13						
14	Cost of sales			-E10	-E14	
15						
16	Returns Inwards				500	-F16
17	--					
18	Totals		SUM(D10:D16	SUM(E10:E16)	SUM(F10:F16)	SUM(G10:G16)
19	===					

Spreadsheet 9.2 Carriage inwards and outwards

```
  |  A   ||  B  ||  C  ||  D  ||  E  ||  F  ||  G  |
1
2
3   Description           Creditors  Stock    Profit   Debtors
4                                             and Loss
5
6   Purchases                -6000    6000
7
8   Carriage Inwards         -200               200
9   ------------------------------------------------------------
10  Sub-totals               -6200    6000      200
11
12  Sales                                      -8000    8000
13
14  Cost of sales                    -6000     6000
15
16  Carriage Outwards        -300               300
17  ------------------------------------------------------------
18  Totals                   -6500       0    -1500     8000
19  ============================================================
```

```
  |  A   ||  B  ||     D     ||    E    ||    F     ||   G   |
1
2
3   Description        Creditors      Stock       Profit       Debtors
4                                                 and Loss
5
6   Purchases          -6000          -D6
7
8   Carriage Inwards   -200                        -D8
9   --------------------------------------------------------------------------
10  Sub-totals         SUM(D6:D8)     SUM(E6:E8)   SUM(F6:F8)
11
12  Sales                                          -8000        -F12
13
14  Cost of sales                     -E10         -E14
15
16  Carriage Outwards  -300                        -D16
17  --------------------------------------------------------------------------
18  Totals             SUM(D10:D16) SUM(E10:E16) SUM(F10:F16) SUM(G10:G16)
19  ==========================================================================
```

Spreadsheet 9.3 Cash discounts

	A	B	C	D	E	F	G	H
1								
2								
3	Description			Creditors	Stock	Cash	Profit	Debtors
4							and Loss	
5								
6	Purchases			-6000	6000			
7								
8	Payment			5880		-5880		
9								
10	Cash Discounts Received 2%			120			-120	
11	--							
12	Sub-totals			0	6000	-5880	-120	0
13								
14	Sales						-8000	8000
15								
16	Cost of sales				-6000		6000	
17								
18	Receipt					7920		-7920
19								
20	Cash Discount Allowed 1%						80	-80
21	--							
22	Totals			0	0	2040	-2040	0
23	==							

	A	B	C	D	E	F	G	H
1								
2								
3	Description			Creditors	Stock	Cash	Profit	Debtors
4							and Loss	
5								
6	Purchases			-6000	-D6			
7								
8	Payment			6000*.98		-D8		
9								
10	Cash Discounts Received 2%			6000*0.02			-D10	
11	--							
12	Sub-totals			SUM(D6:D10)	SUM(E6:E10)	SUM(F6:F10)	SUM(G6:G10)	SUM(H6:H10)
13								
14	Sales						-8000	-G14
15								
16	Cost of sales				-E12		-E16	
17								
18	Receipt					8000*.99		-F18
19								
20	Cash Discount Allowed 1%						-H20	8000*-.01
21	--							
22	Totals			SUM(D12:D20)	SUM(E12:E20)	SUM(F12:F20)	SUM(G12:G20)	SUM(H12:H20)
23	==							

dangerous?), distance travelled, speed of delivery, and so on. Such carriage cost can be incurred in the transportation of both purchases and sales.

The accounting entries necessary to record these carriage costs are shown in Spreadsheet 9.2. The carriage cost incurred for purchases was £200 and for sales £300. The entries are the same, a credit to creditors (or cash if the costs were paid immediately) and a debit to the **profit and loss** column. When the trading, profit and loss account is prepared the carriage inward expense is included in the trading account with purchases, as it is part of the cost of buying the goods, while the carriage outward expense is recorded in the profit and loss account as it is a selling expense.

9.3.3 Cash discounts

It is common business practice to allow a discount for prompt payment of debt, e.g. to sell an item for £100 at a discount of 2 per cent if paid within twenty-eight days. This means that the debtor will only pay £98, but the sales are worth £100. The £2 cash discount is treated as a revenue expense and recorded in the profit and loss account, as discounts allowed. The logic behind this treatment can be justified as the more immediate receipt of cash can reduce the firm's interest payments if the bank account is overdrawn, and interest is a charge on net profit.

Of course, the business may itself be offered a cash discount from its suppliers if it settles within a stated period of time. Such discounts are called 'discounts received' and are accounted for as revenue and included in the profit and loss account.

Spreadsheet 9.3 shows the accounting entries for cash discounts.

It is convenient at this point to talk about 'trade discounts'. Trade discounts are reductions in the purchase price of goods to encourage sales. There are no additional entries to be made as the purchase and sales are recorded at the net price (i.e. after discount has been deducted).

9.4 The appropriation account

After net profit has been derived it is appropriated (i.e. divided up). These appropriations are as follows:

a. to the owners of the business for personal, as distinct from, business, expenditure (e.g. holidays); these expenditures are called drawings;

b. to pay taxation;

	£
NET PROFIT	5,000
Less taxation	2,000
	3,000
Less drawings	2,500
RETAINED PROFIT	500

Figure 9.3 An appropriation account

c. whatever is left over is, by definition, retained by the business for future expansion. This retention is performed by adding the balance on the appropriation account to capital in the balance sheet.

Figure 9.3 shows an appropriation account.

Figure 9.4 gives an example containing most of the content of this chapter and the spreadsheet preparation is given in Spreadsheet 9.4.

Some of the layout and transactions are worthly of comment.

1. We now have separate columns for the **trading account, profit and loss account** and **appropriation account**. The gross profit is built up in the **trading account** column and then transferred to the **profit and loss** column. The net profit is

---

Frazer Jones started his sports supplies business on 1 January 1990 with cash of £9,000 and £1,000-worth of sports equipment. During the year he bought £12,600-worth of stock from a supplier who offered a discount of 5 per cent for prompt payment; this discount was taken up in full. Sales were £25,150 at selling price to various sports organisations, offering a cash discount of 2 per cent for payment within 28 days.

All the customers paid within 28 days, apart from one order which retailed for £150 and was returned after two months. This was for a very specialised badminton racquet and Frazer was able to return it to his supplier for the £100 he paid for it.

In buying the goods, Frazer paid £200 in delivery charges and £250 in delivering the goods to his customers. These were both cash payments.

To help him in his business, Frazer bought a motor vehicle for £7,500, using an extended overdraft facility. Interest on the overdraft came to £250. Running expenses for the motor vehicle came to £2,500, but £250 was for an insurance premium which expires on 1 June 1991. He intends to depreciate the van at 25 per cent on a written-down basis.

His drawings for the year were £6,000. Frazer is liable to tax at a rate of 25 per cent of net profit. At the end of the year he still had stock costing £2,000. No one owed him any money.

Prepare Frazer's trading, profit and loss, and appropriation account, together with his closing balance sheet.

Figure 9.4 Frazer Jones Sports Supplies

built up in the **profit and loss** column and then transferred to the **appropriation** column. The retained profit is built up in the **appropriation** column and then transferred to the **capital** column.

Notice that the **trading account**, the **profit and loss account** and the **appropriation account** all form part of the double-entry system, i.e. they are columns. The balance sheet is just the balances on those accounts forming the double-entry system.

The three accounts all have balances of zero. They are period statements, i.e. they tell the user what has happened in between the two balance sheets. For this reason they are labelled appropriately, followed by a phrase such as 'for the twelve months to (date)'.

2. The £150 badminton racquet was returned late and forms a returns inward.

3. The return to Frazer's supplier is a returns outward, which comes off purchases.

4. The remaining customers all receive the discount for prompt payment which totals £500. Sales should not be affected by this offer and so the correct treatment of this transaction is to credit debtors and debit the profit and loss account as the cash discount is to be treated as an expense.

5. The carriage inwards is debited to the **trading account** column, while the **carriage outwards** is treated as an expense in the **profit and loss account** column.

6. The purchase of the motor vehicle is a straightforward cash purchase, but notice how the motor vehicle account remains in the closing balance sheet, together with the depreciation provision to date. The depreciation expense is charged to the profit and loss account.

7. The interest paid on the overdraft during the year is debited to the **profit and loss** column.

8. The motor expenses paid is placed in an appropriately named account, column K, with the unused expense–the prepayment–forming part of the closing balance sheet. The difference between the two figures is the motor expenses used which is charged to the profit and loss account.

9. Drawings are a appropriation to net profit so are recorded in the **appropriation** column.

Figure 9.5 gives the *vertical* presentation of these accounts which is the normal format. There is a *horizontal* (or two-sided) format, but this is very rarely used these days, so it is not considered in any detail. See Table 9.1 for an example of a two-sided or horizontal set of financial statements for Frazer Jones.

Spreadsheet 9.4 Frazer Jones

		Cash	Stock	Capital	Creditors	Debtors
6	Opening Balance Sheet	9000	1000	-10000		
8	Purchases		12600		-12600	
10	Payments	-11970			11970	
12	Discount				630	
14	Sales					25150
16	Receipts	24500				-24500
18	Discounts					-500
20	Returns Inwards					-150
22	Returns Outwards	100	-100			
24	Carriage Inwards	-200				
26	Carriage Outwards	-250				
28	Purchase Motor Vehicle					
30	Depreciation Expense					
32	Interest on Overdraft					
34	Motor Expenses Paid	-2500				
36	Motor Expenses Used					
38	Drawings	-6000				
40	Cost of Sales		-11500			
42	Gross Profit					
44	Net Profit					
46	Tax Provision					
48	Retained Profit			-510		
50		----------	----------	----------	----------	----------
51	Closing Balance Sheet	12680	2000	-10510	0	0
52		==========	==========	==========	==========	==========

	I		J		K		L		M		N		O		P	
Bank	Motor Vehicle	Motor Expenses		Dep'n. Prov.	Tax Provision	Trading Account	P & L Account	Appropri- ation a/c
							-630	
						-25150		
							500	
						150		
						200		
							250	
-7500	7500							
				-1875			1875	
-250							250	
		2500						
				-2375			2375	
								6000
						11500		
						13300	-13300	
							8680	-8680
				-2170				2170
								510
-7750	7500	125		-1875	-2170	0	0	0

(continued)

Spreadsheet 9.4   *(Continued)*

	A	B	C	D	E	F	G	H	I
1									
2									
3									
4				Cash	Stock	Capital	Creditors	Debtors	Bank
5									
6	Opening Balance Sheet			9000	1000	-SUM(D6:E6)			
7									
8	Purchases				12600		-E8		
9									
10	Payments			-G10			12600*.95		
11									
12	Discount						12600*.05		
13									
14	Sales							25150	
15									
16	Receipts			-H16				-(25150-150)*.98	
17									
18	Discounts							-(25150-150)*.02	
19									
20	Returns Inwards							-150	
21									
22	Returns Outwards			100	-D22				
23									
24	Carriage Inwards			-200					
25									
26	Carriage Outwards			-250					
27									
28	Purchase Motor Vehicle								-J28
29									
30	Depreciation Expense								
31									
32	Interest on Overdraft								-250
33									
34	Motor Expenses Paid			-2500					
35									
36	Motor Expenses Used								
37									
38	Drawings			-6000					
39									
40	Cost of Sales				-SUM(E5:E39)+E51				
41									
42	Gross Profit								
43									
44	Net Profit								
45									
46	Tax Provision								
47									
48	Retained Profit					-P48			
49									
50				------------	------------	------------	------------	------------	------------
51	Closing Balance Sheet			SUM(D5:D49)	2000	SUM(F5:F49)	SUM(G5:G49)	SUM(H5:H49)	SUM(I5:I49)
52				============	============	============	============	============	============

J	K	L	M	N	O	P
Motor Vehicle	Motor Expenses	Dep'n. Prov.	Tax Provision	Trading Account	P & L Account	Appropri- ation a/c
					-G12	
				-H14		
					-H18	
				-H20		
				-D24		
					-D26	
7500						
		-J28*.25			-L30	
					-I32	
	-D34					
	-K34+K51				-K36	
						-D38
				-E40		
				-SUM(N5:N41)	-N42	
					-SUM(O6:O42)	-O44
			-P46			-P44*.25
						-SUM(P6:P46)
SUM(J5:J49)	250/2	SUM(L5:L49)	SUM(M5:M49)	0	SUM(O5:O49)	SUM(P5:P49)

Frazer Jones's trading account for the twelve months to 31 December 1990

	£	£
Sales less returns (25,150 − 150)		25,000
Less cost of goods solds		
Opening stock	1,000	
Purchases less returns (12,600 − 100)	12,500	
Carriage inwards	200	
	13,700	
Closing stock	2,000	
		11,700
GROSS PROFIT		£13,300

Frazer Jones's profit and loss account for the twelve months to 31 December 1990

	£	£
Gross profit		13,300
Cash discount received		630
Less expenses		
Cash discount allowed	500	
Carriage outwards	250	
Depreciation	1,875	
Interest on overdraft	250	
Motor expenses	2,375	
		5,250
NET PROFIT		£ 8,680

Frazer Jones's appropriation account for the twelve months to 31 December 1990

	£	£
Net profit		8,680
Taxation		2,170
Net profit (after tax)		6,510
Drawings		6,000
Retained profit		£ 510

Figure 9.5   Frazer Jones's accounts

The linkage to the spreadsheet can be seen by noticing that all the figures in the trading account are obtained from column N, with the gross profit figure of £13,300 carried into column O: the **profit and loss account**. Similarly the net profit figure is carried into the appropriation account, see column P row 44. The point to note is that there are no new figures or calculations introduced, it is just a case of layout and presentation.

Table 9.1 *A two-sided or horizontal set of financial statements*

Frazer Jones
Trading and profit and loss account for the twelve months to 31 December 1990

	£		£
Purchases	12,500	Sales	25,000
Opening stock	1,000	Closing stock	2,000
Carriage inwards	200		
Gross profit c/d	13,300		
	27,000		27,000
Cash discount allowed	500	Gross profit b/d	13,300
Carriage outwards	250	Cash discount received	630
Depreciation	1,875		
Motor expenses	2,375		
Interest	250		
Net profit c/d	8,680		
	13,930		13,930
Taxation	2,170	Net profit b/d	8,680
Drawings	6,000		
Retained profit	510		
	8,680		8,680

Frazer Jones
Balance sheet as at 31 December 1990

		£			£
Fixed assets			Capital		
motor vehicles			opening capital		10,000
cost		7,500	add retained profit		510
less depreciation		1,875			10,510
		5,625			
Current assets			Current liabilities		
stock	2,000		bank overdraft	7,750	
prepayments	125		tax creditor	2,170	
cash	12,680				9,920
		14,805			
		20,430			20,430

9.5 The balance sheet

The balance sheet is not a period statement like the profit and loss account (as it does not show how things have changed over time); it is just a list of balances at a *point in time*. The balance sheet is therefore a position statement. This is why it is a row on the spreadsheet and not a column. The balance sheet is not a part of the double-entry system *per se*, just an indication of the state of the system. For this reason it is suffixed by the phrase 'as at (date)'. Frazer Jones's balance sheet is given in Figure 9.6.

Fixed assets	Cost	Depreciation	NBV
	£	£	£
Motor vehicle	7,500	1,875	5,625
Current assets			
Stock		2,000	
Prepayments		125	
Cash		12,680	
		14,805	
Less current liabilities			
Bank overdraft	7,750		
Tax credit	2,170		
		9,920	
			4,885
Net assets			£10,510
Financed by:			£
Capital			£10,510

Figure 9.6   Frazer Jones's balance sheet as at 31 December 1990

9.5.1   Balance sheet layout

The layout of the balance sheet given is also *vertical*. Very occasionally the *horizontal* presentation is used with net assets on the left and the capital account and long-term liabilities on the right (see Table 9.1). Whichever presentation is chosen, the same order of items are present, and no matter which accountant has prepared the accounts, another accountant will still know where to find things. It's similar to walking into a supermarket. Even though the store may be in a different town and belong to a different company, shoppers still know where to find things as the layout is familiar. If the store adopted a different layout, then there would be chaos. The same is true of accounts presentation.

9.5.2   Fixed assets

We can consider the balance sheet to be composed of four sections: a fixed asset section, a current asset section, a liability section and a capital section.

The first group of items are the fixed assets. These are items not bought with the intention of resale and are used by the business. In the case of Frazer Jones, this is the motor vehicle. Most businesses have many different types of fixed assets, in which case they are shown in order – the most permanent first, for example:

freehold land
freehold property

leasehold property
machinery and equipment
moveable plant
motor vehicles

In each instance the *historic cost* of the assets are shown in full, together with the accumulated depreciation provision to date, netted off to give the net book value of the assets. If a firm has a lot of each type of fixed asset, e.g. many buildings, then only the total of all buildings is shown to save space.

9.5.3 Current assets

Basically, these are assets that are going to be used up quickly, i.e. they are for conversion into cash. For this reason they are shown in order of liquidity, as shown in Chapter 5.

9.5.4 Liabilities

Liabilities are amounts owed by the business. They are sometimes described as an asset source external to the business. If the business buys any item it can pay in cash, in which case it is using an asset of the business, or it can take out a loan or other credit terms, in which case the business has not used any of its assets, but someone else's. For example, buying a car using a loan from a bank means that the cash has been supplied by an external source. The business owes the bank the amount of the loan (i.e. it is liable for it). Therefore an overdraft is a liability. A loan, or any external source that lasts for more than one accounting period, is a *long-term liability*.

Trade credit, i.e. paying for goods some time after you have received them, is an example of a *current liability*, i.e. a debt that the business will repay within one year. It is still an asset source as the business has stock, a current asset, which has been provided externally to the business, i.e. the business has not parted with any of its cash to pay for it yet.

9.5.5 Capital

The capital section of the balance sheet is made up of the capital account. It is arrived at by adding/deducting this year's profit/loss and deducting this year's drawings from the opening capital figure.

CHECKLIST _____

Having completed Chapter 9, you should be able to:

- present a trading, profit and loss, appropriation account and balance sheet in good format;
- clearly distinguish between a profit and loss account as a *period* statement and the balance sheet as a *position* statement;
- know the difference between the terms net and gross profit;
- know the difference between capital and revenue expenditure, and fixed and current assets;
- outline and apply the concept of materiality;
- account correctly for returns, carriage and discounts;
- clearly distinguish a liability, provision and contigent liability.

Workshop 9.1: Trading and profit and loss accounts

1. Howard Cramp started his cricket supplies shop on 1 January 19X5 with cash of £11,000 and £4,000-worth of cricket equipment.

2. During the year he bought £15,700 worth of stock from a supplier that offered a discount of 10 per cent for prompt payment; this discount was taken up in full.

3. Sales were £35,750 at selling price to various cricket organisations, offering a cash discount of 5 per cent for payment within 28 days.

4. All the customers paid within 28 days, apart from one order which retailed for £450 and was returned after 2 months. This was for a very specialised cricket bat and Howard was able to return it to his supplier for the £100 he paid for it.

5. In buying the goods, Howard paid £350 in delivery charges to his suppliers and £450 in delivering the goods to his customers. These were both cash payments.

6. To help him to his shop, Howard bought a motor vehicle for £9,500 using an extended overdraft facility. Interest on the overdraft came to £550.

7. Running expenses for the motor vehicle came to £1,500, but £240 was for an insurance premium which expires on 30 June 19X6. He intends to depreciate the van at 25 per cent on a written-down basis.

8. His drawings for the year were £8,000. Howard is liable to tax at a rate of 25 per cent of net profit. At the end of the year he still had stock costing £3,600. No one owed him any money.

Prepare Howard's trading, profit and loss, and appropriation account for the 12 months to 31 December 19X5, together with his closing balance sheet, as at that date.

Workshop guide

1. The opening entries are on row 6 with the debits in the **cash** and **stock** column matched by their credit total in the capital column, F.

2. The full purchase price is recorded for the goods purchased on credit and the indebtedness credited as a liability to a **creditors** column. The discount is only available if payment is prompt, therefore it is not prudent to record the purchase net of discount. This would be misrepresenting the transaction anyway. The payment, net of discount, is shown in row 10 and the discount recorded as a credit to the **profit and loss account** in column O, row 12. The corresponding debit is used to illuminate the final indebtedness.

3. Once again, the sales are shown at their gross price in row 14 with the discounted value of cash receipts shown in row 16. Note in cells H16 and H18 how the returned goods are removed from the discount calculation. They have been returned, and so are not paid for.

4. Row 22 reverses the original purchase. Note that Howard only paid £100 net of any discount so no adjustment is necessary for any discount taken on these items. He may have had to return any discount received from his supplier for prompt settlement of that portion of the order that related to this purchase.

5. The carriage inwards is debited to the trading account, while the carriage outwards is a business expense and charged to the profit and loss account.

6. The motor vehicle purchase is financed by the bank in row 28.

7. The running expenses are duly recorded in row 34 as **expenses paid**. Expenses used are calculated in cell K36 utilising the prepayment calculation in cell K51. It is this value that is debited to the **profit and loss account**. The original cell references that recorded the vehicle purchase are used to calculate the depreciation provision in cell L30; the depreciation expense is shown in O30, i.e. in the **profit and loss account**.

8. The drawings are an appropriation of profit. They could have been charged to the capital account which would have had the same net effect. The stock figure is entered into cell E51 and is used to calculate the **cost of sales** in cell E40.

The **gross profit** is derived in cell N42 being the balance on the trading account; this is transferred to the profit and loss account. The net profit is the sum of column O which is transferred to the **appropriation account**, column P, on row

Spreadsheet 9.5a Workshop 9.1: Howard Cramp—solution

	A	B	C	D	E	F	G	H
1								
2								
3								
4				Cash	Stock	Capital	Creditors	Debtors
5								
6	Opening Balance Sheet			11000	4000	-15000		
7								
8	Purchases				15700		-15700	
9								
10	Payments			-14130			14130	
11								
12	Discount						1570	
13								
14	Sales							35750
15								
16	Receipts			33535				-33535
17								
18	Discounts							-1765
19								
20	Returns Inwards							-450
21								
22	Returns Outwards			100	-100			
23								
24	Carriage Inwards			-350				
25								
26	Carriage Outwards			-450				
27								
28	Purchase Motor Vehicle							
29								
30	Depreciation Expense							
31								
32	Interest on Overdraft							
33								
34	Motor Expenses Paid			-1500				
35								
36	Motor Expenses Used							
37								
38	Drawings			-8000				
39								
40	Cost of Sales				-16000			
41								
42	Gross Profit							
43								
44	Net Profit							
45								
46	Tax Provision							
47								
48	Retained Profit					-2500		
49								
50				---				
51	Closing Balance Sheet			20205	3600	-17500	0	0
52				===				

¦ I ¦¦	J ¦¦	K ¦¦	L ¦¦	M ¦¦	N ¦¦	O ¦¦	P ¦
Bank	Motor Vehicle	Motor Expenses	Dep'n. Prov.	Tax Provision	Trading Account	P & L Account	Appropri- ation a/c
						-1570	
					-35750		
						1765	
					450		
					350		
						450	
-9500	9500						
			-2375			2375	
-550						550	
		1500					
		-1380				1380	
							8000
					16000		
					18950	-18950	
						14000	-14000
				-3500			3500
							2500
-10050	9500	120	-2375	-3500	0	0	0

(*continued*)

Spreadsheet 9.5b   Workshop 9.1: Howard Cramp—formulae

	A	B	C	D	E	F	G	H
1								
2								
3								
4				Cash	Stock	Capital	Creditors	Debtors
5								
6	Opening Balance Sheet			11000	4000	-SUM(D6:E6)		
7								
8	Purchases				15700		-E8	
9								
10	Payments			-610			-68*.9	
11								
12	Discount						-68*.1	
13								
14	Sales							35750
15								
16	Receipts			-H16				(-H14-H20)*.95
17								
18	Discounts							(-H14-H20)*.05
19								
20	Returns Inwards							-450
21								
22	Returns Outwards			100	-D22			
23								
24	Carriage Inwards			-350				
25								
26	Carriage Outwards			-450				
27								
28	Purchase Motor Vehicle							
29								
30	Depreciation Expense							
31								
32	Interest on Overdraft							
33								
34	Motor Expenses Paid			-1500				
35								
36	Motor Expenses Used							
37								
38	Drawings			-8000				
39								
40	Cost of Sales				-SUM(E5:E39)+E51			
41								
42	Gross Profit							
43								
44	Net Profit							
45								
46	Tax Provision							
47								
48	Retained Profit					-P48		
49								
50				--				
51	Closing Balance Sheet			SUM(D5:D49)	3600	SUM(F5:F49)	SUM(G5:G49)	SUM(H5:H49)
52				==				

	I	J	K	L	M	N	O	P
	Bank	Motor Vehicle	Motor Expenses	Dep'n. Prov.	Tax Provision	Trading Account	P & L Account	Appropri- ation a/c
							-G12	
						-H14		
							-H18	
						-H20		
						-D24		
							-D26	
	-J28	9500						
				-J28*.25			-L30	
	-550						-I32	
			-D34					
			-K34+K51				-K36	
								-D38
					-E40			
					-SUM(N5:N41)	-N42		
							-SUM(O6:O42)	-O44
				-P46				-P44*.25
								-SUM(P6:P46)
	SUM(I5:I49)	SUM(J5:J49)	240/2	SUM(L5:L49)	SUM(M5:M49)	0	SUM(O5:O49)	SUM(P5:P49)

Howard Cramp's trading account for the twelve months to 31 December 19X5

	£	£
Sales less returns (35,750 − 450)		35,300
Less cost of goods sold		
Opening stock	4,000	
Purchases less returns (15,700 − 100)	15,600	
Carriage inwards	350	
	19,950	
Closing stock	3,600	
		16,350
Gross profit		£18,950

Howard Cramp's profit and loss account for the twelve months to 31 December 19X5

	£	£
Gross profit		18,950
Cash discount received		1,570
Less expenses		
Cash discount allowed	1,765	
Carriage outwards	450	
Depreciation	2,375	
Interest on overdraft	550	
Motor expenses	1,380	
		6,520
Net profit		£14,000

Howard Cramp's appropriation account for the twelve months to 31 December 19X5

	£	£
Net profit		14,000
Taxation		3,500
Net profit (after tax)		10,500
Drawings		6,000
Retained profit		£4,500

Howard Cramp's balance sheet as at 31 December 19X5

Fixed assets	Cost	Depreciation	NBV
	£	£	£
Motor vehicle	9,500	2,375	7,125
Current assets			
Stock		3,600	
Prepayments		120	
Cash		20,205	
		23,925	
Less current liabilities			
Bank overdraft	10,050		
Tax creditor	3,500		
		13,550	
			10,375
Net assets			£17,500
Financed by:			£
Capital			£17,500

Figure 9.7 Howard Cramp's accounts

44. Tax provided for is an appropriation of profit, see row 46, which is shown as a current liability in the balance sheet in column M. The balance on the appropriation account is retained profit which is added to any capital balance. Balances are taken in those columns that do not have any entries in them in row 51 to the closing balance sheet.

The accounts in good format are presented in Spreadsheet 9.5 and Figure 9.7.

'What if?' problems

1. What if Howard only introduced £10,000 in cash at the start of the year? What is the effect on profit? What is the effect on the balance sheet?

2. What effect does increasing the tax provision to 30 per cent have on Howard's retained profit?

3. What if the insurance premium had been paid up to 1 September 19X6? What is the effect on net profit?

4. What if Howard's suppliers lowered their discount rate to 7 per cent? What is the effect on profit? What is the effect on the closing cash balance?

Answers

1. No effect on profit but initial capital decreases to £14,000.
2. Change contents of P46 to read **−P44∗.3**. The retained profit figure changes to £1,800.
3. Change contents of K51 to read **240∗.75**. The profit figure changes to £14,060.
4. Change contents of G10 to read **−G8∗.93**. Change contents of G12 to read **−G8∗.07**. The profit figure changes to £13,589. The closing cash balance is £18,734.

Selected questions and exercises

Question 9.1

1. Explain briefly the terms capital expenditure and revenue expenditure.
2. State the effect the following transactions would have on the capital, working capital and profit of a sole trader.
   a. The account of a creditor £2,000 is paid by cheque, he allows us 2 per cent cash discount.
   b. A fixed asset book value £1,000 is sold for cash £850.
   c. Goods for resale costing £100 are purchased on credit.
   d. Purchased shelves for stock room at a cost of £500. Payment is made by cheque.

Table 9.2 *Answer grid for question 9.1*

Capital	Working capital	Profit
a.		
b.		
c.		
d.		

Your answer should be tabulated as shown in Table 9.2. Under each heading you should put either increase by £?, decrease by £? or no effect.

No solution provided.   *Source: RSA, Accounting II, March 1987.*

Question 9.2

Edward Peter has extracted the totals shown in Table 9.3 from his records. Prepare a balance sheet and trading and profit and loss account for the year ended 31 December 1991.

The following notes are relevant:	£
1. Closing stock was	66,420
2. Rent payable accrued was	15,120
3. Insurance prepaid	3,240
4. Wages and salaries accrued	6,480
5. Commission due	1,836
6. Rent received overpaid	3,348
7. Provision for doubtful debts to be increased to	2,450

8. Motor vans are to be depreciated using the straight-line method at a rate of 25 per cent p.a. on cost. A full year's depreciation is to be charged in the year of purchase and none in the year of sale.
9. Machinery is to be depreciated using the reducing balance method at a rate of 10 per cent p.a. A full year's depreciation is to be charged in the year of purchase and none in the year of sale.
10. Taxation of the year's profits is 35 per cent of net profit.

Solution on page 523–4.

Question 9.3

Hickson Blunt is the proprietor of 'Astra Grocers'. He has presented you with the financial statements shown in Table 9.4. They contain a number of faults.
1. In so far as the available information permits, identify as many of the faults in the above financial statements as you can.
2. Compute the corrected figure for net profit for the year.

Solution on page 524–5.   *Source: AAT, Basic Accounting, June 1988.*

Table 9.3 *Details of the accounts of Edward Peter*

	£s Debit	£s Credit
Sales		579,312
Sales returns	2,450	
Carriage outwards	12,359	
Discounts allowed	4,500	
Purchases	335,286	
Purchase returns		10,765
Carriage inwards	25	
Discounts received		13,420
Opening stock	64,584	
Capital as at 1 January 1991		232,200
Drawings	66,150	
Bank overdraft		88,857
Bad debts	568	
Doubtful debt provision		1,692
Rent payable	124,200	
Rent receivable		183,600
Commission receivable		1,512
Insurance	32,562	
Land	442,530	
Motor vans	151,200	
Machinery	56,320	
Provisions for depreciation as at 1 January 1991		
motor vans		56,980
machinery		24,592
Profit on sale of motor van		680
Selling expenses	12,150	
Office expenses	20,520	
Wages and salaries	9,504	
Creditors		93,960
Debtors	203,984	
Cash	1,215	
Loan		252,537
	1,540,107	1,540,107

Question 9.4

Table 9.5 shows the cumulative effects of a succession of separate transactions on the assets and liabilities of a business.

Identify clearly and as fully as you can what transaction has taken place in each case. Do not copy out the table but use the reference letter for each transaction.

Solution on page 526.   *Source: AAT, Basic Accounting, June 1988.*

Table 9.4　*Details of the accounts of Hickson Blunt as at 31 May 1988*

Hickson Blunt
Final accounts as at 31 May 1988

Sales		127,000
Add: return outwards		3,600
		130,600
rents received		2,500
		133,100
Less: cost of goods sold:		
stock at 31 May 1988	7,450	
purchases	111,090	
returns inwards	2,140	
discounts received	11,800	
	132,480	
Less: stock at 31 May 1987	6,780	
		125,700
Gross profit		7,400
Less: operating expenses:		
selling and distribution	11,800	
drawings	10,060	
administration	4,670	
		26,530
Net profit		33,930

Balance sheet for 31 May 1988

Fixed assets		
equipment at cost		28,500
stock at cost		6,780
		35,280
accumulated depreciation		(14,250)
		21,030
Current assets		
cash on hand	130	
trade debtors	11,090	
accrued expenses	230	
bank overdraft	1,050	
	12,500	
Current liabilities		
trade creditors	7,530	
prepaid expenses	140	
	7,670	
Working capital		20,170
Net assets		41,200
Financed by capital		
as at 1 June 1987		18,400
Add: net profit		33,930
		52,370
Difference		11,170
		41,200

Table 9.5 *Effects of transactions on a business's assets and liabilities*

Transaction	£000	A £000	B £000	C £000	D £000	E £000	F £000	G £000	H £000	I £000	J £000
Assets:											
buildings	80	80	80	80	80	80	80	80	80	72	72
equipment	78	78	88	88	88	88	88	88	70	63	63
stocks	33	38	38	36	36	36	36	35	35	35	35
trade debtors	37	37	37	37	37	26	26	26	26	26	22
prepayments	5	5	5	5	5	5	6	6	6	6	6
bank	11	11	8	11	7	18	14	14	29	29	29
cash	3	3	3	3	3	3	3	3	3	3	3
	247	252	259	260	256	256	253	252	249	234	230
Liabilities:											
capital	126	126	126	127	127	127	124	123	120	105	105
loan	75	75	82	82	82	82	82	82	82	82	82
trade creditors	38	43	43	43	43	43	43	43	43	43	39
accrued expenses	8	8	8	8	4	4	4	4	4	4	4
	247	252	259	260	256	256	253	252	249	234	230

Question 9.5

On 1 May 1987 Century Ltd had trade debtors of £35,780 and owed its suppliers £44,210. Receipts from credit customers during the year ended 30 April 1988 were £268,420 and payments to suppliers were £397,600. There were also cash sales of £433.740 during the year. Discounts allowed to customers and discounts received from suppliers were £3,100 and £1,980 respectively. Credit notes issued to customer totalled £5,560 while credit notes received from suppliers were £4,670.

Bad debts of £2,080 were written off during the year. This amount includes £440 which was specifically provided for in the provision for bad debts as at 30 April 1987.

In January 1988 a balance of £3,000 owing to a supplier was offset against an invoice issued to the supplier.

At 30 April 1988 Century Ltd had unpaid invoices from suppliers totalling £43,110 while customers owed a total of £36,550. The amount owing from customers included an invoice issued for £640 which may be uncollectable and specific provision for this is to be made in the provision for bad debts as at 30 April 1988.

Stocks of unsold goods at the beginning and end of the year were valued at £29,730 and £30,100 respectively.

1. Calculate Century Ltd's total sales for the year ended 30 April 1988.
2. Calculate Century Ltd's total purchases for year ended 30 April 1988.
3. Prepare Century Ltd's trading account for the year ended 30 April 1988.

Solution on page 526.

Source: AAT, Basic Accounting, June 1988.

Question 9.6

Ms Price set up a business on 1 January 1986 with a loan of £10,000 from a friend and £10,000 of her own. With this cash she purchased a machine for manufacturing a new board game called 'Chairmanship'. She submits the account shown in Table 9.6 for her first year's trading.

Table 9.6   *Details of the accounts of Ms Price*

	£
Cash received from sale of games (2,000 @ £20 each)	40,000
Less: cash paid: wages	14,000
rent	4,000
raw materials	6,800
general expenses	2,400
part repayment of loan	3,000
Net income	£9,800

Ms Price is somewhat doubtful whether the above statement is very reliable and asks you to prepare a trading and profit and loss account and balance sheet. In addition to the above information you discover:

1. Ms Price has sold a further 300 units at £20 each for which she has not yet been paid.
2. She owes £1,800 for materials already received.
3. The machine has a ten year life and no anticipated scrap value.
4. Ms Price owes her secretary £400 for working overtime.
5. There are raw materials at cost £800 left in stock but no work in progress or finished goods.
6. The rent payment covers the period from 1 January 1986 to 31 March 1987.
7. The wages include £8,000 withdrawn by Ms Price for her own use.
8. She has incurred further general expenses of £200 which she has not yet paid.

You are required to:

1. Prepare a revised trading and profit and loss account for the year ending 31 December 1986 and a balance sheet as at that date.
2. Explain to Ms Price the accounting conventions you have adopted which are primarily responsible for the difference between the original account and your revised trading and profit and loss account and why such conventions are considered necessary.

No solution provided.   Source: *JMB GCE A Level, 1987.*

Question 9.7

The balance sheet as at 29 February 1988 of Mark Bean, retailer, is as shown in Table 9.7.

Table 9.7 *Details of the accounts of Mark Bean*

	£	£	£
Fixed assets:			
fixtures and fittings:			
at cost		76,000	
Less: provision for depreciation		18,000	
			58,000
Current assets:			
stock	16,000		
trade debtors	13,000		
balance at bank	10,000		
		39,000	
Less: current liabilities:			
trade creditors		11,000	
			28,000
			£86,000
Mark Bean: Capital account			£86,000

The unexpected opportunity to acquire new business premises has necessitated 'final accounts' being required for the three months ended 31 May 1988. Accordingly, the information in Table 9.8 has been prepared from the business's bank account.

Additional information:

1. All receipts and payments are passed through the business bank account.
2. A half of credit sales are paid for in the month sales take place and the balance of the cash due is received in the following month.
3. Purchases are paid for in the month following the receipt of the goods; all general expenses are paid on a cash basis. Purchase creditors at 31 May 1988 amounted to £9,600.
4. A gross profit of 30 per cent is obtained on all sales.

Table 9.8 *Receipts and payments accounts for the three months ended 31 May 1988*

		1988	
	March £	April £	May £
Receipts:			
sales: cash	6,000	9,000	8,000
credit	15,500	11,500	13,000
sale of surplus display cabinet		500	
Payments:			
purchases	11,000	11,900	10,900
general expenses	4,600	3,700	2,700
drawings	1,200	1,400	1,500

5. During March, April and May 1988. Mark Bean withdrew from the business, goods for his own use of £600 at cost price.
6. The display cabinet sold in April 1988 cost £2,000 when bought in 1985 and had a written-down book value in fixtures and fittings at 29 February 1988 at £1,400.
7. The depreciation charge for fixtures and fittings for the three months to 31 May 1988 is £1,850.

1. Prepare a computation of the business bank account balance at 31 May 1988 of Mark Bean.
2. Prepare Mark Bean's trading and profit and loss account for the three months ended 31 May 1988.
3. Prepare Mark Bean's balance sheet as at 31 May 1988.

No solution provided.   *Source: AAT, Accounting, June 1988.*

10 Errors in the spreadsheet: the use of a trial balance, suspense accounts and journals

AIMS OF CHAPTER _____

- to identify the types of errors that can occur in preparing accounts;
- to examine the creation of suspense accounts;
- to correct errors, once identified, with the use of journals.

10.1 Introduction

All human beings make errors and accountants are no exception. The aim of this chapter is to enable you to identify the different types of errors it is possible to make and to correct these errors.

10.2 Using the spreadsheet for error detection

In the manual preparation of the accounts of a business, a check on the double entry is performed by constructing a trial balance immediately prior to preparing the trading, profit and loss account and balance sheet. The trial balance is a listing of all the debit balances and all the credit balances, whose totals should be equal. See Table 10.2 later in this chapter for an example of a trial balance. If this is not the case the trial balance will not balance (i.e. the sum of the debits will not equal the sum of the credits). What the trial balance does not tell us is where the mistake or mistakes have occurred. We have to go back through the originating double entry, which is a time-consuming process.

The reason a trial balance is prepared is to check that for every debit there has been a credit entry of equal amount. It does not mean that the accounts are correct, as we shall soon see.

The equivalent of this trial balance check in the spreadsheet approach is to ensure the final row of the spreadsheets sums to zero. This is done by summing all

Spreadsheet 10.1 Spreadsheet containing errors and corrected spreadsheet

```
    :  A  ::  B  ::  C  ::  D  ::  E  ::  F  ::  G  ::  H  :
 1
 2
 3  (a) Spreadsheet Containing Revealed Errors
 4             (ii) and (iii).
 5
 6  Description    Cash   Capital Stock   Profit          Control
 7                                        and Loss        Coluan
 8  Cash introduced  1000  -1000                               0
 9
10  Buy goods        -600            600                        0
11
12  Pay for transport -200                      -200        -400
13
14  Pay rent         -100                       100            0
15
16  Sales            1300                                    1300
17
18  Cost of Goods Sold              -600        600            0
19  ----------------------------------------------------------
20  Balance Sheet    1400  -1000     0          500          900
21  ==========================================================
22
23
24  (b) Spreadsheet Containing Revealed Errors
25                  (iii).
26
27  Description    Cash   Capital Stock   Profit          Control
28                                        and Loss        Coluan
29  Cash introduced  1000  -1000                               0
30
31  Buy goods        -600            600                        0
32
33  Pay for transport -200                                  -200
34
35  Pay rent         -100                       100            0
36
37  Sales            1300                      -1100         200
38
39  Cost of Goods Sold              -600        600            0
40  ----------------------------------------------------------
41  Balance Sheet    1400  -1000     0         -400            0
42  ==========================================================
43
44
45  (c) Corrected Spreadsheet
46
47  Description    Cash   Capital Stock   Profit          Control
48                                        and Loss        Coluan
49  Cash introduced  1000  -1000                               0
50
51  Buy goods        -600            600                        0
52
53  Buy Van          -200                       200            0
54
55  Pay rent         -100                       100            0
56
57  Sales            1300                      -1300           0
58
59  Cost of Goods Sold              -600        600            0
60  ----------------------------------------------------------
61  Balance Sheet    1400  -1000     0         -400            0
62  ==========================================================
```

the cells in that row and placing the sum into a newly opened cell, called the **control cell**. If this cell is zero this tells us certain kinds of errors (see later on in this chapter for descriptions of these errors) have not been made. If we want to locate the error(s) in the spreadsheet, this represents no problem as we simply sum all the rows in the spreadsheet and place the sums in a newly created column, called the **control column**. The rows which do not contain zeros are in error.

See Spreadsheet 10.1 for an example of a spreadsheet which contains errors; these errors are identified by a non-zero control cell and their location by non-zero entries in the control column.

We will now examine the kind of errors which can occur in the accounting process, distinguishing between errors revealed and not revealed by the spreadsheet.

10.3 Errors revealed by the spreadsheet

1. A common error in a manual accounting system is an addition error, producing an incorrect account total. Using the spreadsheet system this should never arise, as the spreadsheet program automatically adds columns correctly. However, we must ensure the range of cells in the sum formula in the balance sheet row takes in all entries in a particular column. A conventional trial balance (see page 159) will show that the error has occurred as it will fail to balance, but a laborious checking of transactions is necessary to locate the error.

2. A one-sided entry is made because we fail to record the corresponding negative cell reference. This type of error is shown in Spreadsheet 10.1(a), where the negative cell reference of the sales transaction has been omitted. The control cell indicates that a mistake has been made and the non-zero figure in row 16 locates the mistake. A conventional trial balance will show that the error has occurred as it will fail to balance, but once again a laborious checking of transactions is necessary to locate the error.

3. If there have been two credits or two debits rather than one of each then an error has occurred. This can happen if a minus is omitted from the relative cell reference. Again the control cell will not be zero and the location of the error will be highlighted in the **control** column. An example of such an error is shown in Spreadsheet 10.1(a), row 11. A conventional trial balance will show that the error has occurred as it will fail to balance; however a laborious checking of transactions is necessary to locate the error.

4. In a manual system you can have transcription errors, where one figure is put into one account as a credit, but a different figure is put into another account as a debit; e.g. confusion over the number of noughts is a common mistake with large transactions. Sometimes a numeric dyslexia overcomes the book-keeper and transposition errors occur, e.g. £2,345 becomes £3,245. It's very

easy to do. Using relative cell references this error is avoided. In a manual system a transposition error could also occur when transferring the account balance to the trial balance; such an error cannot occur in the spreadsheet system as no transcription is required. If a manual trial balance does not balance due to a transposition error then the amount of the difference is often difficult to find.

Until now the errors we have discussed have been picked up by the spreadsheet and the trial balance (even though the location of the error was not highlighted). The next error is only picked up by the spreadsheet.

5. Sometimes there may be two errors which cancel each other out. They are said to be compensating errors. A conventional trial balance will not reveal such errors as total debits will equal total credits. In the spreadsheet the control cell will be zero, but there will be two equal and opposite amounts in the **control** column. An example of compensating error is shown in Spreadsheet 10.1(b) in rows 34 and 38.

10.4   Errors not revealed by the spreadsheet

Not all errors are revealed in the spreadsheet control cell and column. These errors are as follows:

1. It is quite common to reverse the entries totally; e.g. take the case of the payment of rent where the **cash** column has been debited and the **profit and loss** column credited. In this case the spreadsheet **control** column will be zero, so this error can go undetected. Such an example is shown in Spreadsheet 10.2(a), row 14. In a manual system the trial balance will still balance, but the sales and cash figures are wrong.

2. Transactions can be totally omitted and there is no record in the accounts that they ever took place, for example, the omission of a sale. Such an example is shown in Spreadsheet 10.2(a).

3. The transaction may record the incorrect figure totally, i.e. the entries may be in the right columns, but the figure is wrong. Such an example is shown in Spreadsheet 10.2(b) in row 32. This is one error that the spreadsheet approach is prone to, as the fact that the computer is doing all the arithmetic work can lead to a false sense of security on the part of the student. Therefore care must be taken when entering data.

4. There are errors called 'errors of commission' which mean that while all the entries have been made correctly, in the right *class* of account, the wrong *account* has been debited or credited. For example, debiting property when land is purchased; both are fixed assets. Such an example is shown in Spreadsheet 10.2(b) in row 32, where rent is misclassified as transport.

Spreadsheet 10.2 Spreadsheet containing errors and corrected spreadsheet

```
           :  A  ::  B  ::  C  ::  D  ::  E  ::  F  ::  G  ::  H  :
   1
   2
   3   (a) Spreadsheet Containing Unrevealed Errors
   4                    (i)
   5
   6   Description      Cash    Capital Stock   Profit          Control
   7                                            and Loss        Column
   8   Cash introduced  1000    -1000                                   0
   9
  10   Buy goods        -600            600                              0
  11
  12   Pay for transport -200                           200             0
  13
  14   Pay rent         100                             -100            0
  15
  16   Cost of Goods Sold                     -600      600             0
  17   ----------------------------------------------------------
  18   Balance Sheet    300     -1000   0     700                       0
  19   =========================================================
  20
  21
  22
  23   (b) Spreadsheet Containing Revealed Errors
  24                    (iii),
  25
  26   Description      Cash    Capital Stock   Profit   CreditorsControl
  27                                            and Loss         Column
  28   Cash introduced  1000    -1000                                   0
  29
  30   Buy goods        -600            600                              0
  31
  32   Pay for transport -300                           300             0
  33
  34   Pay for transport -100                           100             0
  35
  36   Sales            1300                                     -1300  0
  37
  38   Cost of Goods Sold                     -600      600             0
  39   --------------------------------------------------- ---------
  40   Balance Sheet    1300    -1000   0     1000      -1300          0
  41   ===============================================================
  42
  43
  44
  45
  46
  47
  48   (c) Corrected Spreadsheet
  49
  50   Description      Cash    Capital Stock   Profit          Control
  51                                            and Loss        Column
  52   Cash introduced  1000    -1000                                   0
  53
  54   Buy goods        -600            600                              0
  55
  56   Buy Van          -200                            200             0
  57
  58   Pay rent         -100                            100             0
  59
  60   Sales            1300                            -1300           0
  61
  62   Cost of Goods Sold                     -600      600             0
  63   ----------------------------------------------------------
  64   Balance Sheet    1400    -1000   0     -400                      0
```

5.   Finally, there are 'errors of principle' where the wrong class of account has been debited or credited, e.g. crediting sales to creditors instead of to the profit and loss account. The former is a liability in the balance sheet while the latter is an item of revenue in profit and loss account. Such an example is shown in Spreadsheet 10.2(b) in row 36.

As the spreadsheet does not highlight the above errors, there is no foolproof way to ensure they are identified. However, to reduce the chances of these errors going undetected a business can ensure its records are examined by an experienced accountant or have its accounts audited (see Chapter 25).

10.5   Suspense columns

In a business which has thousands of transactions there is likely to be not one, but several errors. Trying to find them all before completing the accounts may not be possible, or too time-consuming, and the net amount involved may be small. So to make the spreadsheet balance, a figure is inserted in a **suspense** column. As the errors are detected so they are corrected by putting the correcting entry in the appropriate column and placing the double entry in the **suspense** column. Once all corrections have been made there should be no amount left in the **suspense** column. The equivalent of the **suspense** column in a manual system is a **suspense account**.

The correction of errors is usually carried out by the use of journal entries.

10.6   Journal entries

The journal entries should identify:

1.   The date of the entry.

2.   The columns to be described and credited.

3.   The amount.

4.   A description of the entry.

10.7   A worked example

Let's have a look at the creation and clearing of a suspense account using the illusration in Figure 10.1. The spreadsheet solution to this problem is given in Spreadsheet 10.3.

John Lucas has a small office cleaning company whose book-keeping is performed by one of the managers. He has prepared the following trial balance for the twelve months to 31 March 1989.

	Debit £	Credit £
Purchases of cleaning materials	4,220	
Sales		82,350
Cleaners' wages	64,345	
Repair of cleaning equipment	820	
General expenses	2,410	
Share capital		10,000
Retained profit as at 31 March 1988		2,710
Creditors		60
Cleaning equipment	14,850	
Provision for depreciation		4,880
Debtors	4,360	
Bank account	2,207	
Managers' salaries	6,980	
	100,192	100,000

Figure 10.1   John Lucas

In an attempt to prepare the final accounts correctly, a suspense account needs to be drawn up and cleared. The following information comes to light during your investigations:

1. A floor polisher purchased during the year for £400 has been charged to the repairs account.

2. One of the cleaner's payslips for the last month of the year was for £210, but the manually prepared cheque was for £120. The cleaner involved has complained to the manager and it appears that the cheque is incorrect.

3. One customer has paid the company £326 for its monthly cleaning contract. While the cheque has been entered in the bank account, the customer is still recorded as a debtor.

4. The depreciation provision for this year has yet to be provided. The company's policy is to charge 10 per cent of NBV.

5. A cheque for £112 was classed as a receipt instead of a payment in the company's cash book.

We will now see how these errors are corrected.

The first task is to reconstruct the traditional trial balance into spreadsheet format, with the columns becoming the account titles. The trial balance is given in

Spreadsheet 10.3 John Lucas

	A	B	C	D	E	F	G	H	I
1									
2									
3			Purchases	Sales	Wages	Repairs	Expenses	Shares	Profit
4									
5	Trial Balance		4220	-82350	64345	820	2410	-10000	-2710
6									
7	Journals:-								
8	----------								
9	Purchase classed								
10	as repair					-400			
11									
12	Creation of Creditor								
13	for cleaners' wage								
14									
15	Removal of debtor								
16	who has paid								
17									
18	Depreciation Expense								
19	for the year								997
20									
21	Cheque Incorrectly								
22	recorded								
23									
24			--						
25	Trial Balance		4220	-82350	64345	420	2410	-10000	-1713
26									
27	Conversion of Trial								
28	Balance to Balance Sheet:								
29									
30	Purchases		-4220						
31									
32	Sales			82350					
33									
34	Wages				-64345				
35									
36	Repairs					-420			
37									
38	Expenses						-2410		
39									
40	Salaries								
41			--						
42	Balance Sheet		0	0	0	0	0	-10000	-1713
43									
44	Transfer of Profit								-3975
45			--						
46	Balance Sheet		0	0	0	0	0	-10000	-5688
47			==						

	J		K		L		M		N		O		P		Q		R	
	Creditors		Equip,t		Dep'n		Debtors		Bank		Salaries		Suspense				P & L A/c	
	-60		14850		-4880		4360		2207		6980		-192				0	
					400													
	-90												90					
							-326						326					
					-997													
									224				-224					
	-150		15250		-5877		4034		2431		6980		0		0		0	
																	4220	
																	-82350	
																	64345	
																	420	
																	2410	
											-6980						6980	
	-150		15250		-5877		4034		2431		0		0		0		-3975	
																	3975	
	-150		15250		-5877		4034		2431		0		0		0		0	

row 5 of Spreadsheet 10.3, with the suspense account in column P. The amount in the suspense account is given in cell P5 as the figure needed to balance the trial balance.

To clear this balance, journal entries are needed and the narrative section gives an indication of the descriptions that the journals may carry.

1. The first entry is to account for the purchase of the floor polisher correctly, i.e. cleaning equipment. When it was purchased the incorrect entries were:

	£	£
Dr. Repairs	400	
Cr. Bank		400

One half of this double entry is correct, i.e. the reduction of the bank balance, but the other half is wrong and the equipment account has been debited. So we need to correct the debit entry by reversing it, and then correctly record the purchase of equipment.

	£	£
Dr. Equipment	400	
Cr. Repairs		400
Purchase classed as repair		

This entry does not affect the suspense account, but nevertheless it is an error – an error of principle – that is not picked up by the trial balance.

2. The cleaner's wage is a transcription error, i.e. an error that is detectable:

	£	£
Dr. Cleaner's wage	210	
Cr. Bank account		120

Note that the difference is divisible by 9. To rectify the error it would be nice to write a cheque for the missing £90, but this remedy would be after 31 March. At that date the company owed the cleaner £90, i.e. a liability or creditor, and so the entry necessary is:

	£	£
Dr. Suspense a/c	90	
Cr. Creditors		90
Creation of creditor for cleaner's wage		

When the cheque is written then the bank account will be credited and the creditors' account debited, clearing the debt.

3. The customer who has paid but is still a debtor is an example of a one-sided entry, i.e. the bank account has been debited, but the debtors' account has not been credited. To correct this error the omission is rectified:

	£	£
Dr. Suspense a/c	326	
Cr. Debtors		326
Removal of debtor that has paid		

4. The depreciation charge for the year is just the normal provision. Note that this does not affect the suspense account, but it will affect the profit for the year.

5. The cheque that was incorrectly recorded is not a reversal of double entries as the one side has been correctly recorded as an expense or whatever. It is the entry in the bank account that is wrong, i.e. it is a debit when it should have been a credit. To resolve this situation correctly the original error should be corrected, i.e. Dr. Bank £112. This only brings half the solution as the next stage is to record the initial transaction correctly, i.e. Dr. Bank £112 again!

	£	£
Dr. Bank	224	
Cr. Suspense a/c		224
Cheque incorrectly recorded		

From the new corrected trial balance the final accounts can be drawn up. Note that the trial balance contains profit and loss account items as well as balance sheet items. This is because the balances on the sales and expenses accounts have not been transferred to the trading, profit and loss account. This is why it is a trial balance and not a balance sheet.

CHECKLIST

Having completed Chapter 10, you should be able to:

■ identify the types of errors that can occur in preparation of accounts;

■ create a suspense account;

■ correct errors (via a suspense account) with the use of journals.

Workshop 10.1:   The trial balance and the correction of errors

Neil James operates a bakery supplying local caterers with a wide range of bread and pastry products. Despite employing a small workforce, Neil still helps out on the baking, especially during the early hours, and is often seen delivering special orders late in the day.

He keeps a manual set of records, which you use to prepare his final accounts. A list of balances produces a situation where debits exceed credits by £679.

Your investigations into Neil's record-keeping bring to light the following errors:

1. One of the debtors' accounts balances for £46 has been left out of the figure in your trial balance.

2. When you added up Neil's cash records, you find that he had overcast his receipts by £340.

3. You find that *you* made a transposition error when recording the sales figure. The sales figure should be £9,765, but you misread it as £7,956.

4. One of Neil's suppliers sent a credit note for £87 which was posted to the wrong side of his account.

5. An invoice for a new mixer for £400 was classed as repairs because the company failed to fix the old one and it had to be replaced.

6. While in Neil's office you find a gas bill for £670 that should have been paid, but hasn't.

7. One customer paid £1,250 for an order which was correctly accounted for in his account, but has not been entered in the cash column.

You are required to show the double entries necessary to clear the suspense account, along with the effects on other accounts of the errors you have found.

Workshop guide

The first task is to open a suspense account, column B in this instance, and place the balance necessary to make all debits equal all credits in the opening cell. As debits exceed credits then a credit balance of £679 is needed to make the accounting identity hold. Then we approach the errors one at a time:

1. This is a straightforward omission, and so the entry needed is to debit debtors by £46 and place the corresponding credit in the **suspense** column, as in row 7 of the answer.

Spreadsheet 10.4   Workshop 10.1: Neil James – solution and formulae

	A	B	C	D	E	F	G	H	I
1									
2		Suspense							
3		Account	Debtors	Machinery	Repairs	Cash	Sales	Creditors	Gas
4									
5	Balance Difference	-679							
6									
7	Debtor Omision	-46	46						
8									
9	Cash Book Overcast	340				-340			
10									
11	Transposition Error	1809					-1809		
12									
13	Credit Note	-174						174	
14									
15	Repairs as Machinery			400	-400				
16									
17	Gas Bill							-670	670
18									
19	Cheque not recorded	-1250				1250			
20		-------	-------	-------	-------	-------	-------	-------	-------
21		0	46	400	-400	910	-1809	-496	670

	A	B	C	D	E	F	G	H	I
1									
2		Suspense							
3		Account	Debtors	Machinery	Repairs	Cash	Sales	Creditors	Gas
4									
5	Balance Difference	-679							
6									
7	Debtor Omision	-C7	46						
8									
9	Cash Book Overcast	-F9				-340			
10									
11	Transposition Error	-G11					-9765+7956		
12									
13	Credit Note	-H13						87*2	
14									
15	Repairs as Machinery			400	-D15				
16									
17	Gas Bill							-I17	670
18									
19	Cheque not recorded	-F19				1250			
20		-------	-------	-------	-------	-------	-------	-------	-------
21		SUM(B5:B19)	SUM(C5:C19)	SUM(D5:D19)	SUM(E5:E19)	SUM(F5:F19)	SUM(G5:G19)	SUM(H5:H19)	SUM(I5:I19)

2. This is an error that can be readily corrected. Cash is credited by the amount of the error, with the opposite entry in the suspense account. Note that all double entries are still achieved through relative cell referencing; in this instance the formula **– F9** in cell B9 creates the debit necessary.

3. Even accountants make mistakes! This is a large transposition error which is corrected by first establishing the difference between what the entry should have been (– 9765) and what actually occurred (– 7956). Cell G11 produces the correcting entry which is completed by cell B11.

4. If a supplier sends a credit note then it means that the business's indebtedness is reduced. In fact the opposite has occurred, and it has been treated as an invoice. Therefore to correct this entry, *twice* the amount needs to be entered, one to clear the error and one to record the credit correctly. This is achieved in row 13.

5. This invoice has been incorrectly treated. This will not be picked up by the trial balance and so the suspense account is unaffected. However, a correction still needs to be made as repairs are charged to the profit and loss account, while a piece of new machinery is an asset. If more information were available, then the original machine would have to be written out and any disposal losses/gains recorded.

6. The gas bill is another omission, with the liability recorded. Payment will now occur in the new accounting period. The suspense account is unaffected.

7. The final entry is to complete the recording of the receipt of the cash as a debit in the **cash** column. As a single entry has only been entered so far then this will affect the suspense account.

Finally, a list of the effects on the account balances are calculated in row 21, with the suspense account successfully cleared and the effect of the other entries established.

Selected questions and exercises

Question 10.1
A trader's trial balance at 31 March 1988 did not agree. He transferred the difference to a suspense account, prepared his trading and profit and loss account and drew up the balance sheet shown in Table 10.1.

The following errors were subsequently discovered:

1. A debit balance of £100 on rent and rates account had been omitted.
2. The purchase of a new fitment for the stockroom at a cost if £150 had been debited to purchases.

Table 10.1 *A trader: balance sheet as at 31 March 1988*

	£	£
Fixed assets		
furniture and fittings	2,800	
motor vehicles	4,500	7,300
Current assets		
stock	4,250	
debtors	1,400	
bank and cash	752	
	6,402	
Current liabilities		
sundry creditors	1,600	4,802
		12,102
Financed by		
capital	11,085	
add net profit	7,180	
	18,265	
less drawings	6,400	11,865
suspense account		237
		12,102

3. A cash payment of £170 by K. Stevens, a debtor, had been correctly entered, in cash but no entry had been made in the debtors' account.
4. A purchase of goods from A. Chubb, £95, was entered in purchases and Chubb's account as £59.
5. A purchase of goods, £90 from T. Smith, has been correctly entered in purchases but debited to Smith's account.
6. A sum of £13 petty cash had not been included in the bank and cash figures.
7. A sale of £10 has been omitted.

You are required:
a. to prepare the suspense account, making the appropriate entries therein to eliminate the balance.
b. to prepare a statement showing the correct net profit for the year.
c. to draw up a corrected balance sheet as at 31 March 1988.

Solution on page 527. *Source: RSA, March 1985.*

Question 10.2
The draft trial balance of Palimo Ltd as at 31 May 1988 agreed. The business proceeded with the preparation of the draft final accounts and these showed a profit of £305,660. However, a subsequent audit revealed the following errors:

1. Bank charges of £56 had been omitted from the cash book.
2. The purchases journal had been overcast by £400.

3. The sales journal had been undercast by £100.
4. An invoice for £127 received from Beta plc had been entered into the purchases journal as £217. (This is quite independent of the error made in the purchase journal referred to above.)
5. It is now considered prudent to write off the balance of £88 on Peter Shadey's account as bad.
6. An invoice from Caring Garages Ltd for £550 in respect of servicing Palimo Ltd's motor vehicles had been posted to the debit of motor vehicles account.
7. Depreciation at 10 per cent per annum has been provided for on motor vehicles inclusive of the £550 invoice referred to in 6 above.

Palimo Ltd maintains control accounts for debtors and creditors in its general ledger. Individual accounts of debtors and creditors are maintained on a memorandum basis only.

1. Prepare journal entries to show how the above errors would be corrected. (Note: dates and narratives are not required.)
2. What is the profit for the year after correcting the above errors?

Solution on page 528.   *Source: AAT, Basic Accounting, June 1988.*

Question 10.3

a. Thomas Smith, a retail trader, has very limited accounting knowledge. In the absence of his accounting technician, he extracted a trial balance as at 31 March 1988 from his business's accounting records (see Table 10.2).

Prepare a corrected trial balance as at 31 March 1988.

Table 10.2 *Details of the accounts of Thomas Smith*

	£	£
Stock in trade at 1 April 1987		10,700
Stock in trade at 31 March 1988	7,800	
Discounts allowed		310
Discounts received	450	
Provision for doubtful debts	960	
Purchases	94,000	
Purchases returns	1,400	
Sales		132,100
Sales returns	1,100	
Freehold property: at cost	70,000	
provision for depreciation	3,500	
Motor vehicles: at cost	15,000	
provision for depreciation	4,500	
Capital – Thomas Smith		84,600
Balance at bank	7,100	
Trade debtors		11,300
Trade creditors	7,600	
Establishment and administrative expenditure	16,600	
Drawings	9,000	
	£239,010	£239,010

b. After the preparation of the above trial balance, but before the completion of the final accounts for the year ended 31 March 1988, the following discoveries were made:

1. The correct valuation of the stock in trade at 1 April 1987 is £12,000; apparently some of stock lists had been mislaid.
2. A credit note for £210 has now been received from J. Hardwell Limited; this relates to goods returned in December 1987 by Thomas Smith. However, up to now J. Hardwell Limited had not accepted that the goods were not of merchantable quality and Thomas Smith's accounting records did not record the return of the goods.
3. Trade sample goods were sent to John Grey in February 1988. These were free samples, but were charged wrongly at £1,000 to John Grey. A credit note is now being prepared to rectify the error.
4. In March 1988, Thomas Smith painted the inside walls of his stockroom using materials costing £150 which were included in the purchase figure in the above trial balance. Thomas Smith estimates that he saved £800 by doing all the painting himself.

Prepare the journal entries necessary to amend the accounts for the above discoveries. (Note: narratives are required.)

Solution on page 529.   *Source: AAT, Accounting, June 1988.*

Question 10.4

Carys has prepared a summary (see Table 10.3) of her assets and liabilities as at 30 June 1984.

Her friend Ann has looked at the books and found out the following:

1. Loan interest due to Jane was outstanding for six months at 6 per cent annum.

Table 10.3 *Balance sheet of Carys as at 30 June*

	£	£
Plant and machinery		6,210
Debtors		12,200
Stock		8,500
Balance at bank		1,000
		£27,910
Capital – 1 July 1983	8,140	
Add profit for the year	3,470	
		11,610
Loan – Jane		6,000
Creditors (goods only)		10,300
		£27,910

2. Ten loads of material had been valued for stock purposes at cost (£30 per load), but Carys explained that they were damaged and only worth £6 per load as scrap.
3. Plant and machinery cost £11,000 and should have a net book value of £6,010.
4. Rent of £300 was due for the quarter ended 30 June.
5. Debtors were shown before deducting a doubtful debt of £150. It was agreed that this debt was bad and that it should be written off, and that provision would be made for further debts, amounting to £70, which were considered doubtful.
6. Goods sold for £60 (20 per cent above their cost) had been included in sales. These goods awaited collection by the customer and had been included in stock at cost.
7. The balance at bank as shown in the cash book was not in accordance with the bank statements on which the following debits had been made but not entered in cash:

	£
Bank charges	60
Carys – drawings	520

You are required to prepare a statement showing the adjustments to the profit for the year, and a balance sheet for Carys as at 30 June 1984.

Solution on page 530.

11 | *Accounting ledger systems*

AIMS OF CHAPTER _____

■ to explain the limitations of the spreadsheet in preparing the accounts of a business and hence the need for other (ledger) systems, manual or computerised;

■ to examine the need for books of prime entry;

■ to prepare books of prime entry;

■ to examine the division of the ledger into its constituent parts;

■ to explain the differences between personal and impersonal accounts, real accounts and nominal accounts;

■ to examine the need for, and the detailed workings of, sales and purchase ledgers;

■ to examine the need for control accounts;

■ to prepare control accounts;

■ to outline the principles relating to micro computer accounting software briefly, specifically modular integrated ledger systems.

11.1   Introduction

The accounts that we have prepared so far have been made up of relatively few transactions; so we could account for them in one spreadsheet. We used a spreadsheet to learn how to account for transactions; now we are going to see how businesses account for transactions in the real world (as distinct from the classroom).

Even small firms can have a large amount of transactions (e.g. thousands of sales and purchases during a year) so they need a system to record all of their transactions, to enable them to prepare accounts. So rather than rely on one

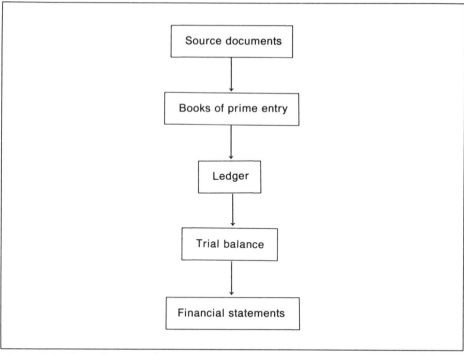

Figure 11.1   Some features of an accounting system

spreadsheet model, they often use an accounting ledger system; this chapter will explain some of the typical features of such a system. It should be realised that each individual business will select those features most suited to its own needs; so each business has its own unique accounting system. We can only look at some of these features. See Figure 11.1

11.2   Books of prime entry

We have already encountered the problem of having to account for a large number of similar transactions. For example, a business may make thousands of sales in a year. Rather than account for each sale separately it would make economic sense to prepare a listing of these sales, say each month, and record the total monthly sales figure in the accounting records. This is indeed what happens in the sales day book, as we will see.

Think of the other types of similiar transactions incurred by most businesses. These transactions include:

purchases
cash receipts

cash payments
sales returns
purchase returns.

All these transactions are listed in what are called 'lists (or books) of prime entry'. They are so called as they represent the first record of the transaction in the firm's accounting system. The sales for the day are contained in the sales day book, the purchases for the day in the purchases day book, the cash receipts and payments in the cash book, the sales returns in the sales day book and the purchase returns in the purchase returns day book. These are not part of the double-entry system (which we will call the ledger system, see page 188), just a list of the day's transactions.

Let's have a look at each of these books of prime entry.

11.2.1 The sales day book

The sales day book prevents unnecessary detail entering the ledger. In retail trade the majority of sales are in cash terms, but for wholesalers and manufacturers the norm is for sales to be made on a credit basis, with payment following some time after the goods have been supplied. The customer is notified of the debt by the business in a document called an 'invoice', prepared by the business and sent to the customer. All invoices are different in design and layout, but they all contain the same minimum details such as:

an invoice number
the name and address of the company supplying the goods
the customer's name and address
the date of delivery
the customer's reference or order number
the firm's VAT number (if registered)
details of cash discounts available for prompt payment.

The invoice is usually a multi-copy document with a copy despatched to the customer and one copy retained by the firm. It is from these copy invoices that the sales day book is written up. The sales day book is no more than a listing of all the sales made in period (it does not have to be a day). Only the main details are recorded such as the date, the customer, invoice number and total amount for each transaction. An example of a sales day book is given in Figure 11.2.

We will explain how the sales day book is used to record sales later in the chapter.

A point to note is the use of trade discounts by businesses to encourage customers to buy their products. These are not the same as cash discounts, which are given to customers for prompt payment. A trade discount is a reduction in the price charged to a customer, usually offered for bulk purchases. If the customer

Sales day book			
	Invoice No.	Folio	Page 12
1 January M. Rowlands	101	SL 34	1,345.75
1 January K. Griffin	102	SL 12	674.00
2 January S. Salmon	103	SL 90	321.50
3 January G. Robbins	104	SL 89	5,689.00
4 January P. Scullion	105	SL 99	67.99
6 January C. MacKenzie	106	SL 14	5,700.00
Transferred to sales account		GL 10	13,798.24

Figure 11.2　An example of a sales day book

attracts a trade discount then the amount on the invoice (the gross amount) is reduced by the amount of the trade discount to show the net amount. It is this net amount that is entered in the sales day book.

11.2.2　The purchase day book

This is a similar to the sales day book. Just as the firm has customers so the firm is a customer to other businesses. It will receive invoices from suppliers of goods and services, and to avoid confusion with sales invoices these are referred to as 'purchase invoices'. The amount outstanding (net of trade but not cash discount), the invoice number, the name of the supplier, the date and any reference numbers are listed in the purchase day book. An example of a purchase day book is given in Figure 11.3.

11.2.3　The returns day books

There are two returns day books, one for returns inwards and one for returns outwards. Returns inwards are good that the firm has sold, but the customer has

Purchases day book			
	Invoice No.	Folio	Page 15
1 January S. Smith	234	PL 22	4,589.00
1 January M. Treharn	345	PL 56	12,760.99
2 January B. Price	690	PL 34	56.00
Transferred to purchases account		PL 20	17,405.99

Figure 11.3　An example of a purchase day book

returned because he had over overordered or bought the wrong item; these sales returns are listed in a sales returns day book. Returns outwards are goods that the business has purchased, but returned to suppliers because they were faulty in some way; these purchase returns are listed in a purchase returns day book.

11.2.4 The cash book

A business is likely to incur a large number of payments (especially to suppliers) and receipts (especially from customers). Rather than clutter up the ledgers with these transactions, they are listed in a book of prime entry called the 'cash book'. The cash book consits of two types of lists: a receipts lists and a payments lists. Let's consider each in turn.

The receipts lists

Receipts usually come in two ways: in cash and in cheques. Both cash and cheques are recorded in the cash book, discounts allowed to customers are also listed. The source document is usually a remittance advice note.

The payments lists

Like receipts, payments usually come in two ways: in cash and in cheques. Both cash and cheques are recorded in the cash book. In addition discounts received from customers are also listed. The source document is usually a cheque stub.

See Figure 11.4 and Spreadsheet 11.1 for an example of a cash book.

You are required to prepare a cash book for the following:

Date	Transaction	Amount £
1 March 19X9	Opening cash balance	240
1 March 19X9	Opening bank balance	−520
3 March 19X9	Paid wages by cheque	2,890
4 March 19X9	Received cheque from J. Jones	9,500
5 March 19X9	Withdrew cash from bank	3,600
6 March 19X9	Paid T. Brown in cash	3,600
7 March 19X9	Cash sales	4,670
7 March 19X9	Deposited takings into bank	4,500
8 March 19X9	Received cheque from A. Ligg − discount allowed £300	5,700
8 March 19X9	Paid F. Benn by cheque − discount received £100	9,900

Figure 11.4 The cash book

Spreadsheet 11.1   The cash book

	A	B	C	D	E	F	G	H	I	J	K	L	M
1													
2													
3				CASH BOOK									
4													
5		--------RECEIPTS ---------						-----------PAYMENTS -----					
6													
7	Date			Discount	Cash	Bank		Date			Discount	Cash	Bank
8													
9	1/3/-9	Opening balance			240			1/3/-9	Opening balance				520
10													
11	4/3/-9	J.Jones				9500		3/3/-9	Wages				2890
12													
13	5/3/-9	Bank			3600			5/3/-9	Cash				3600
14													
15	7/3/-9	Sales			5670			6/3/-9	T.Brown			4670	
16													
17	7/3/-9	Cash				4500		7/3/-9	Bank			4500	
18													
19	9/3/-9	Receipt		300		5700		9/3/-9	Payment		100		9900
20													
21										Balance c/d		340	2790
22				------------------------									
23				300	9510	19700					100	9510	19700
24				=======================							=======================		
25													
26	1/4/90	Balance b/d			340	2790							

11.3   The ledger system

The ledger is in effect the spreadsheet as we know it, written in a slightly different format. Instead of columns, accounts are used. See Figure 11.5 for a comparison of a speadsheet column and an account.

As can be seen, the information is the same. The differences are in layout. The spreadsheet column classifies debit entries as positive figures and credit entries as negative entries, with the closing balance as the sum of the column. The account classifies debits as being located on the left side of the account and credits as being located on the right side (as you can see, the account is divided down the middle to facilitate this classification), with the closing balance being the entry which ensures the two sides of the account equate. The closing balance is transferred down so that it can be used to start recording February's transactions.

We have treated the cash book as a book of prime entry, with separate accounts in the ledger for cash and bank. However, many businesses use the cash book as its cash and bank accounts, in which case they are part of the ledger as well as books of prime entry.

In a business there are often a large number of accounts. For example, businesses may have hundreds of customers, suppliers, fixed assets and stock

We will look at a typical Motor Car column and see how it can be written up in 'account' form:

A spreadsheet column

Date	Description	Motor cars
1 January 1990	Opening balance	1000
4 July 1990	Purchases	8000
7 January 1990	Sales	(6000)
31 January 1990	Closing balance	3000

An account

		Motor cars		
1 January 1990 Opening balance	1000	I	4 January 1990 Sales	6000
7 January 1990 Purchases	8000	I	31 January 1990 Closing balance	3000
	9000	I		9000
1 February 1990 Opening balance	3000			

Figure 11.5 Comparison of a spreadsheet column and an account

items. Therefore it is impractical to have all accounts kept together. So businesses tend to split up the accounts into separate ledgers to break the accounts up into manageable sections; these sections are described below. Other reasons for splitting up the ledger are as follows:

1. To enable different accounts to be written up at the same time by different people.

2. To prevent one person having access to all accounts, and so help reduce the opportunity for fraud (see Chapter 25 for a discussion of this problem).

11.3.1 The division of accounts

Accounts are often classified as either personal or impersonal.

Personal accounts

These accounts relate to individuals, companies or other firms that the business entity deals with. They can be either debtors accounts or creditors accounts, depending upon whether the individual is a customer or supplier. In some instances a business can buy from and sell to the same business, in which case both a debtor and creditor account are kept. Debtors' accounts are kept in a debtors ledger and creditors' accounts in a creditors ledger.

These are often the most widely used ledger systems deployed by businesses due to the number of transactions that they attract. One customer, for example, may have a number of orders each month; he may return some goods relating to various orders; he will pay for some of the goods and he will have an outstanding balance at the end of the accounting period. The company may have hundreds if not thousands of such customers, all with different transaction details.

The same situation is true of the firm's suppliers. The firm's own indebtedness needs to be controlled and monitored in much the same way, and so all these accounts are held in the purchase ledger.

Impersonal accounts

These are the opposite to personal accounts (i.e. they do not relate to customers or suppliers) and are divided into real and nominal accounts.

Real accounts

These accounts are usually characterised by the fact that they deal in property or fixed assets. They tend to attract relatively few transactions as a consequence and

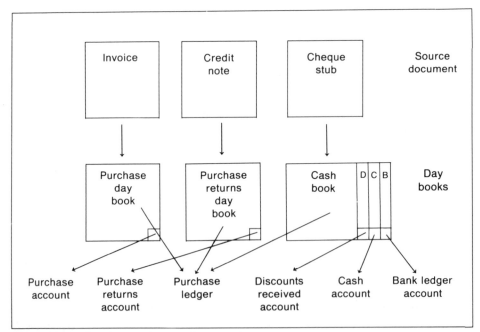

Figure 11.6a   Posting creditors and payments

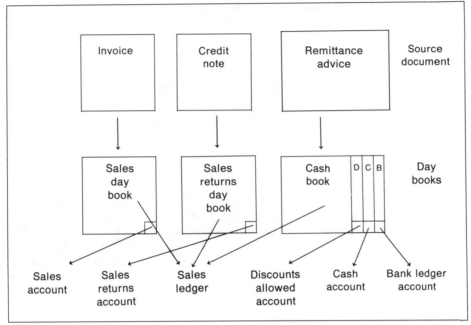

Figure 11.6b Posting debtors and receipts

for this reason they are separated from those accounts that are heavily used. These accounts are kept in a fixed asset ledger (or register).

Nominal accounts

These are all the remaining accounts that have not been dealt with so far and they include the remaining revenue and expenditure accounts that make up the profift and loss account. They are kept in a nominal ledger.

11.3.2 Posting the ledgers

The totals from the books of prime entry are used to post (i.e. write up) the ledgers. Figure 11.6 shows how this posting is carried out.

11.4 Control accounts

As we have seen, the main transactions incurred by a business will often be the sale and purchase of goods and the receipts and payments associated with these sales and purchases. Of course, other transactions are occurring all the time, but for the most part these will account for the majority of transactions.

Imagine a firm dealing with 100 customers on a regular basis. Orders will be sent in and goods delivered more or less daily, with payments following maybe 28 days later.

In the meantime, customers may still be receiving goods, but may not have paid for their last order. Errors take place within the firm's accounts department, with one customer's cheque being credited to another's account and *vice versa*. So how is the company to keep track of all this?

One way is to take all the *personal accounts* out of the double-entry system and use a control account ledger system. To explain the meaning of these terms, let's have a look at the sales ledger. During any particular day the firm may sell tens of thousands of pounds-worth of items to a hundred different customers. To the senior management of the company, their concern is not with the indebtedness of one small customer, but with the overall sales picture (e.g. how much have we sold today?).

The same is true of the cash receipts. Dozens of cheques will arrive, and senior management will want to know the daily total for cash flow monitoring or liquidity planning. They will not be too concerned if Mr Brown's cheque for £40 has arrived.

Accountants have found it convenient to record total amounts (of sales, receipts, purchases, payments, sales returns and purchase returns) in the double-entry system, with the individual entries kept outside the system. This is done via control accounts. A hundred cheques coming to £50,000 will be just one entry in the control account, but a hundred separate entries in the personal accounts of each customer. The same is true of all the sales despatched on given day. Each sale will be entered into the individual customer's personal account, but only the daily total will be entered in the control account. For this reason the control accounts are sometimes referred to as 'total accounts'. The sales ledger control account is sometimes called the 'total debtors account' as its balance will give the total debtors figure. The purchase ledger control account is sometimes called the 'total creditors account' as its balance will give the total creditors figure. Figure 11.7 shows how the control accounts fit into the accounting system.

11.4.1   The advantages of control accounts

1.   Control accounts can then be used to 'separate the duties' of staff to prevent fraud and detect errors. If a member of staff does make a mistake then this will be detected as the total of funds received has been recorded by another member of staff. See Chapter 25 for further discussion of fraud and error.

2.   Control accounts also give quick summary information to management. Any

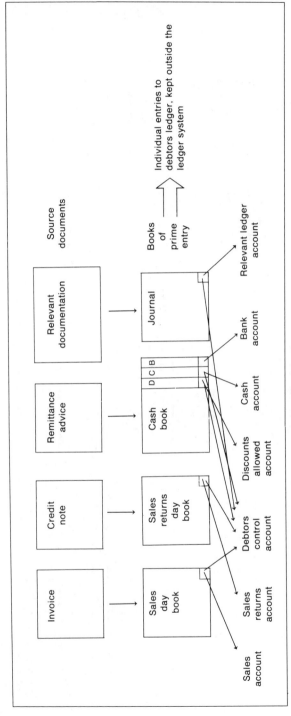

Figure 11.7a The debtors control account and the accounting system

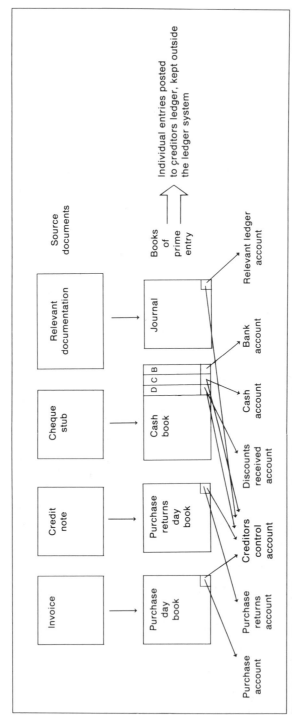

Figure 11.7b The creditors control account and the accounting system

NEG Ltd sells computer games to specialist shops throughout the country. In January the personal accounts of its four customers are as follows:

1. *Stoate Software*
   With an opening balance of £400, the month's sales have been slow at £300. The customer has paid £250 for goods received before Christmas, but has returned some stock of 'Rambo's Machine Gun'—a game that did not sell well—worth £200.
2. *Prudent Electronics*
   The opening balance of £4,000 has grown steadily over a number of months. Sales for this month have been stopped as the firm has not received payment for its November deliveries. Rumour has it that the firm is likely to go bankrupt, so the debt is to be written off.
3. *Madman Electronics*
   This customer has a credit balance of £600 due to some returned goods. The sales for January amounted to £8,900, but no cash has been received.
4. *Richard Summers Ltd*
   An established computer specialist retailer, this customer has a balance of £450, with sales for the month amounting to £360. Payment has been received for the outstanding balance, which attracts a discount of £10.

You are required to write up the individual personal accounts, the sales ledger control account and to complete the double entries in the nominal ledger.

Figure 11.8   NEG Limited

errors are likely to be within the personal accounts of the ledger, which will not effect large-scale decisions that need to be made.

Figure 11.8 gives an example of a sales ledger control account, but only a few personal accounts are mentioned for ease of demonstration. A realistic sales ledger would have hundreds of accounts.

For example, a health authority does not have a sales ledger, but it has up to fifty control accounts to cope with the huge payroll, say 10,000 employees, and the massive spending on drugs, equipment, vehicles, etc. The NHS is the largest organisation in Europe, employing over one million people and spending around £20,000 million pounds a year. It is only through using control accounts that this sort of organisation can keep track of its cash flow.

The solution is given in Spreadsheet 11.2. Note how the control account is part of the double-entry system.

The balance on the control account is the total debtors of the company and this total should match the sum of the personal accounts.

11.4.2   Computerised accounting ledger systems

The growing market for computer ledger systems

The majority of firms that have a computer will often use it to do their accounts. As we discovered in the first chapter, computers are nothing more than

Spreadsheet 11.2   NEG Ltd

	Stoate	Prudent	Madman	Summers	Control Account	Sales	Goods Returned	Bad Debt	Cash Discounts	Cash
	Personal Accounts									
Opening Balance	400	4000	-600	450	4250					
Sales	300		8900	360	9560	-9560				
Goods Returned	-200				-200		200			
Bad Debt		-4000			-4000			4000		
Cash Discounts				-10	-10				10	
Cash Received				-800	-800					800
	500	0	8300	0	8800	-9560	200	4000	10	800

glorified adding machines designed for the automation of clerical and book-keeping tasks. In 1981–2, *Personal Computer World's* survey indicated that 31 per cent of microcomputer applications packages in the UK related to some form of accounting ledger system. IBM produces a new personal computer every seven seconds. These figures can seem quite alarming, with the natural statistical inference that the world will soon be saturated with computers running accounting packages! It does indicate that the current trend in business is increased computerisation, made possible by the availability of cheap hardware, and accounting software packages.

The modular approach of computerised ledger systems

The systems designers and programmers of accounting ledger systems have not strayed far from the manual origins of ledgers and they usually offer a suite of programs designed to replace the ledgers that are commonly used in business. The most basic program is based around the nominal ledger (or general ledger) and the facility to produce financial statements.

The nominal ledger is supplemented by sales ledger, purchase ledger, fixed assets and stock modules (other modules include payroll and job costing). The software manufacturers try to increase their market potential by writing programs of general applicability rather than specific programs for specific firms, and allow the firm to select which modules it will make most use of. For example, a firm with large numbers of employees may purchase the payroll module, whereas a small business may only buy the general ledger and sales ledger.

The important element is that each module can be *integrated* with the others. Details from the purchase ledger can be automatically posted to the nominal ledger at the end of the day, as can details from the sales ledger.

Controls in computer accounting systems

Unlike a manual system the computerised versions offer a number of advantages, especially in the area of controls. Before access to the computer files is achieved a password must be entered. This prevents unauthorised use of the data or the deliberate inputting of false transactions or other aspects of fraud. The password is usually altered periodically by a member of senior management and in some packages the password is used to limit access according to the operators' responsibility level (e.g. sales ledger clerks would find that their access to the cash book is restricted, while the cashier would be unable to access the sales ledger). This is seen as enhancing the separation of duties (see Chapter 25 for more discussion of accounting controls).

During the input process, control totals, enforced balancing and account prompts are used to minimise the errors made by operators. Bogus values may be triggered and questioned before input (e.g. large transactions will require additional operator verification before acceptance, thus eliminating the errors made by missing the decimal point or debiting an account that should be credited). The systems are capable of the production of an audit trial and while errors can be corrected, their original incidence is recorded on the disk for later scrutiny if necessary. These control are in-built into the software and cannot be duplicated by a manual system.

CHECKLIST _____

Having completed Chapter 11, you should be able to:

- identify the limitations of the spreadsheet approach in preparing accounts for a large business;
- understand what is meant by books of prime entry and how they are prepared;
- demonstrate an understanding of the division of the ledger and the classification of accounts;
- explain the term control accounts in relation to the sales and purchase ledger;
- comprehend the growth in the microcomputer market in relation to accounting ledger packages, indicating the advantages that these systems have.

Selected questions and exercises

Question 11.1

Table 11.1   *Details of transactions required to be posted*

Post the following transactions:

1. Purchases

1 January	AB	£108
9 January	CD	£250
16 January	EF	£500
24 January	GH	£650

2. Sales

2 January	XT	£420
9 January	VW	£205
15 January	RS	£108
25 January	CD	£55
30 January	TV	£40

3. Purchase returns

8 January	AB	£58
25 January	GH	£30

4. Sales returns

15 January	VW	£5

5. Bank

(i) Receipts

27 January	XY	£150
31 January	VW	£190 (discount £10)

(ii) Payments

2 January	CD	for goods £170 (discount £25)
7 January	AB	for rent £48 (discount £2)
16 January	EF	for transport £100

6. Journals

(i) Transfer £55 on CD Ltd's a/c from its sales ledger a/c to its purchase ledger a/c

(ii) Write-off TV's debt since the company has gone bankrupt

Solution on pages 531–4.

Question 11.2

The A2Z Company presents you with the balances shown in Table 11.2 for December 1987.

You are required to draw up the debtors control account for December 1987, showing all the closing balances.

Table 11.2   *Details of transactions required to be posted*

			£
1 December 1987	Sales ledger	DR	202,100
		CR	2,800
	Purchase ledger	DR	330
		CR	115,900

31 December 1987   *Transactions*

	£
Credit sales	534,000
Cash sales	213,600
Credit purchases	282,700
Payments to creditors	238,600 (continued)

Table 11.2 (*Continued*)

Payments received from debtors			449,500
Bad debts written off			1,900
Provision for bad debts			9,700
Purchase returns			4,500
Sales returns			5,800
Discounts received			5,900
Discounts allowed			9,500
Balances in debtors ledger set off against			
balances in creditors ledger			3,400
Customer's cheque dishonoured			500
31 December 1987 Sales ledger		DR	?
		CR	2,100
	Purchase ledger	DR	420
		CR	?

Note: not all this data is needed

No solution provided.

Question 11.3

Gala Traders Ltd had £57 cash on hand and a favourable balance of £216 in its business bank account as at the start of business on 2 May 1988. The following is a list of cash and bank transactions for the week ending 7 May 1988:

May 2   Paid an insurance premium of £130 by cheque.

May 3   Made cash sales of £276 inclusive of VAT.

May 3   Paid travelling expenses in cash £17.

May 3   Paid an invoice for £110 from Supplies Ltd in full after deducting 10 per cent for prompt settlement.

May 4   Received a cheque for £114 from Fred Croxter, a credit customer. Mr Croxter was settling an invoice for £120 and had been entitled to £6 discount.

May 5   Made cash sales of £414 inclusive of VAT.

May 6   Made cash purchases of £161 including VAT.

May 6   Paid the week's wages to employees, partly by cheque for £107, and partly in cash £75.

May 6   Paid £620 from the safe into the business bank account.

The rate of VAT is 15 per cent.

1. Write up Gala Traders Ltd's cash book for the week commencing 2 May 1988 with separate columns for discount, VAT, bank and cash. Balance the cash books at 7 May 1988.
2. Describe how the totals for the discount and VAT columns will be entered into the ledger.

No solution provided.   *Source: AAT, Basic Accounting, June 1988.*

12 | *Reconciliation statements*

AIMS OF CHAPTER _____

- to identify the uses of reconciliation statements;
- to examine the need for a statement which reconciles the control account total with the ledger total for both debtors and creditors;
- to prepare a statement which reconciles the control account total with the ledger total for both debtors and creditors;
- to examine the main reconciling items in a control account/list of ledger balances reconciliation statement;
- to look at the need for bank reconciliation statements;
- to prepare a bank reconciliation statement;
- to examine the main reconciling items in a bank reconciliation statement.

12.1 Introduction

In the previous chapter we focused our attention on accounting systems, with all the controls built in to aid the smooth running of the system and to prevent fraud and error occurring in the system. In this chapter we will examine another important technique available to the accountant to find and correct frauds and errors; this technique involves the regular preparation and review of reconciliation statements.

A reconciliation involves the comparison of two figures taken from different sources, which should equate. If they do not equate then the reasons for the differences are identified (called 'reconciling items') and investigated, as they may well have occurred as a result of fraud and/or error.)

We will look at some well-known reconciliation statements:

1. The reconciliation between the sales ledger control and the total of the sales ledger accounts.

2. The reconciliation between the purchase ledger control and the total of the purchase ledger accounts.

3. The reconciliation between the bank account and the bank statement.

Other reconciliations could have been examined, such as the one between suppliers statements and individual purchase ledger accounts. As the same general principles apply, we will not examine such reconciliations.

12.2 Debtors control account reconciliation statements

In order to ensure the debtors control account total is correct (this is important as it is this figure we are going to use in the balance sheet), many businesses reconcile it with the summed total of the individual debtor accounts held in the debtors ledger. In order to see how this is done we will examine the example in Figure 12.1

As you can see, the sales ledger control account total does not agree with the total of the individual balances in the debtors ledger, due to a whole series of errors. These errors could have been made in:

a. the control account, or

b. the sales ledger, or

c. both the control account and the sales ledger.

We need to identify which situation is the case and then make the appropriate correction. The anwer is shown in Spreadsheet 12.1.

The first task is to set up two sections of the spreadsheet: section 12.1a where we are going to correct the control account and section 12.1b where we are going to correct the sales ledger.

Then we work our way down the errors, correcting as necessary.

1. It is clearly stated that these amounts have been omitted from the list of balances; so the missing debits are added to the debtors total (which is of course a debit balance) and the missing credits deducted.

2. The sales return book is used to post the control account so it is this that is in error rather than the ledger, which is posted from the individual sales returns. As sales returns are a credit to the control account the undercast would lead to a lower credit entry than required, so a credit adjustment is needed.

3. It is clearly stated that the list of balances has been overcast; so the total is too large by the amount of the overcast. The amount is therefore deducted from the total.

During the course of the audit of Chappell Ltd, it was found that the net total balances of £28,200 extracted from the sales ledger on 31 December 19X4 did not agree with the net balance on the sales ledger control account, £31,030. On checking, the following errors were discovered, after the adjustment of which the books balanced and the correct net total of the sales ledger balances agreed with the amended balance on the control account.

1. A debit balance of £860 and credit balances amounting to £140 had been omitted from the list of balances.
2. The sales returns book had been undercast by £1,000.
3. The list of balances had been overcast by £100.
4. A balance owing by O'Donnell of £180 had been written off as irrecoverable on 31 December 1984 and debited to bad debts, but no entry had been made in the control account.
5. A debit balance of £140 in the sales ledger had been listed as a credit balance.
6. No entries had been made in the control accounts in respect of a transfer of £410 standing to the credit of Peaman's account in the purchase ledger to his account in the sales ledger.
7. Bosley's account had been credited with £340 for goods returned by him but no other entry had been made in the books.
8. A discount of £50 allowed to Cartwright had been correctly recorded and posted in the books. This item was subsequently disallowed and a corresponding amount entered in the discounts received in the cash book and posted to Cartwright's account in the purchase ledger and included in the total of discounts received.

You are required to prepare:
a. a statement reconciling the original net balances extracted from the sales ledger with the adjusted final balance on the sales ledger control account;
b. the sales ledger control account showing the necessary adjustments and the balance on the account before and after these adjustments.

Figure 12.1   Chappell Limited

4. It is only the control account that has not been adjusted. Bad debts are written off the control account by crediting it.

5. It is clearly stated that the list of balances is in error. A debit balance has been listed as a credit; it is necessary to record a debit balance of double the size to eliminate the credit entry and include the debit entry.

6. In this situation Peaman both owes and is owed £410. To cancel out this interdebtedness, the control account is credited.

7. No entry has been made in the control account. Therefore it is credited as it relates to omitted sales returns.

8. The correction has been incorrectly made in the purchase ledger and purchase control rather than in the debtors ledger and debtors control account; therefore both need correcting. As discount is a credit, disallowed discount is a debit.

Spreadsheet 12.1 Debtors control account reconciliations

```
          !  A  !!  B  !!  C  !!  D  !!  E  !!  F  !!  G  !
    1
    2
    3
    4  (a)       Correction of the Debtors Control Account
    5
    6
    7
    8  Incorrect total                                   31030
    9
   10  (2) Returns book under-cast                       -1000
   11
   12  (4) Bad debt                                       -180
   13
   14  (6) Contra with Creditors Control Account          -410
   15
   16  (7) Returns                                        -340
   17
   18  (8) Contra with Purcahase Ledger                     50
   19                                                  ---------
   20                                                    29150
   21                                                  =========
   22
   23
   24  (b) Correction of Sales Ledger
   25
   26  Incorrect total                                   28200
   27
   28  (1) Debit balances                                  860
   29  (1) Credit Balances                                -140
   30
   31  (3) Overcast in error                              -100
   32
   33  (5) Debit balances listed as credit balances        280
   34
   35  (8) Dissallowed discount                             50
   36                                                  ---------
   37                                                    29150
   38                                                  =========
```

12.3 Creditors control account reconciliation statements

Exactly the same principles apply to the creditors control account. See Figure 12.2 for an example and Spreadsheet 12.2 for the answer. There follows a discussion of the answer:

1. Goods were omitted from the purchase ledger, so the relevant account should be credited. An amount of £1,500 is added to the list of balances total.

2. Discount received had been omitted from the personal accounts which make up the list of balances, so it needs to be entered into the purchase ledger; an amount of £500 is taken off the total of the list of balances.

The total on the creditors control account is £22,000 and the total of the list of balances is £23,800. There were no debit balances. The credit balances were checked and the following errors were discovered:

1. Goods costing £1,500 had been omitted from Collin's account.
2. Discounts received for the month, amounting to £500, had not been entered into the personal accounts.
3. The credit side of Brown's account had been undercast by £1,000.
4. A cash payment of £2,250 to Almond had been credited to his account.
5. A bank payment to Martin of £2,600 had been omitted from his account.
6. Ashton's balance of £2,000 had not been included in the list of balances.
7. The purchase returns book had been undercast by £500.
8. Discounts allowed totalling £350 had been debited to Crosby's account.
9. No entries had been made in the control account in respect of a transfer of £150 standing to the debit of H. Coombe's account in the sales ledger in his account in the purchase ledger.
10. Franklin's account had been debited with £300 for goods returned to him, but no other entries had been made in the books.

You are required to prepare:
   a.   a reconciliation correcting the purchase ledger control account;
   b.   a reconciliation correcting the total of the list of balances.

Figure 12.2 An example to illustrate the purchase ledger reconciliation process

3.   The credit side of Brown's account has been undercast, so his account undercast needs crediting by £1,000. £1,000 is therefore added to the total of the list of balances.

4.   A cash payment of £2,250 to Almond had been credited to his account instead of being debited, therefore an amount of £4,500 (twice £2,250) needs to be debited to his account, so leaving a net debit of the correct amount. An amount of £4,500 is deducted from the total of the list of balances.

5.   A bank payment to Martin of £2,600 had been omitted from his account, so we need to debit his account. An amount of £2,600 is therefore deducted from the total of the list of balances.

6.   Ashton's balance of £2,000 had not been included in the list of balances, so it needs to be added to the total.

7.   The purchase returns book had been undercast by £500. As the purchase returns book is used to prepare the control account (i.e. a debit entry), we need to correct the control account balance by deducting £500.

8.   Discounts allowed totalling £350 had been debited to Crosby's account. Discounts allowed are given by our business to its customers so should not affect creditors. The entry in the personal account of Crosby needs correcting by crediting, therefore £350 is added to the total of the list of balances.

Spreadsheet 12.2   Creditors control account reconciliation

```
         !  A  !!  B  !!  C  !!  D  !!  E  !!  F  !!  G  !
      1
      2
      3
      4
      5
      6
      7
      8   Incorrect total                             22000
      9
     10   (7) Returns book under cast                  -500
     11
     12   (9) Contra with Creditors Control Account    -150
     13
     14   (10) Returns                                 -300
     15                                              ---------
     16                                                21050
     17                                              =========
     18
     19
     20
     21
     22   Incorrect total                             23800
     23
     24   (1)Omitted goods                             1500
     25
     26   (2)Omitted discount                          -500
     27
     28   (3)Credit side of account undercast          1000
     29
     30   (4)Payment recorded as a credit             -4500
     31
     32   (5)Omitted cash payment                     -2600
     33
     34   (6)Omitted balance                           2000
     35
     36   (8)Discounts allowed debited                  350
     37                                              ---------
     38                                                21050
     39                                              =========
```

9. No entries had been made in the control account in respect of a transfer of £150 standing to the debit of H. Coombe's account in the sales ledger to his account in the purchase ledger. We need to put through this entry in the control account by debiting the control account and so deducting if from the total.

10. Franklin's account had been debited with £300 for goods returned to him, but no other entries had been made in the books. We need to reflect this return in the control account by debiting and so the control account total is reduced by £300.

12.4   Bank reconciliation statements

Even individuals not running a business can be quite surprised when the monthly bank statement drops through the letter box. The bank balance is seldom in agreement with the amount the individual thought they had in their bank account (i.e. the total on the cheque stubs). Differences can arise for many reasons. For example, the cheque paid for the electricity bill may still be in the post, it may not have been cashed by the electricity company or not yet cleared by the bank; in any event the amount has not as yet been taken off the account by the bank so will not appear on the bank statement. The individual may have forgotten about a standing order so it has been omitted from the cheque book tally when it does appear on the bank statement.

Individuals often have a much smaller number of bank account entries each month compared to even a small business so there can be more opportunity for mistakes in a business.

Before we examine these reconciling differences in detail, we need to be clear as to which two figures we are reconciling. The business keeps its record of bank movements in its bank column or cash book. The bank keeps its records on its computer system which produces a bank statement for each account and sends its account holders a copy of this statement. Therefore the reconciliation is between the bank column total and the bank statement total.

Now we can examine the differences that are likely to arise in more detail.

1.   Unpresented cheques: these are cheques that have been written and posted to the creditor, thereby writing out the debt in the company's accounts, but as yet have not been paid out of the bank account.

2.   Unrecorded lodgements: these are cheques received from customers which have been entered in the company's records but not as yet paid into the bank account. The phrase 'lodgements' is used, which is legal jargon for a deposit of money not normally used in everyday language.

3.   Standing orders and direct debits: money going in or out of the bank account does not have to be in the form of cash or cheques; some receipts and payments are made automatically to the bank account without any entry in the company's books.

4.   Dishonoured cheques: these are cheques that have 'bounced', i.e. they have been recorded as a receipt by the bank, but on presenting the cheque to the drawer's bank there have been insufficient funds to honour the amount payable. The receipt is then reversed in the bank account of the drawee and the cheque returned. If this happens then the company should restore the debt written off when the cheque was received and try to gain payment in a more direct manner.

5. Errors: banks make mistakes and so do companies. Manual and computerised accounting systems are fallable and the two balances can disagree due to an erroneous entry in one or other of the accounts. A large organisation will have a number of bank accounts and while the overall balance is reconciled, the error lies between the individual accounts held. All the other reconciling items are due to timing differences, these differences are the exception.

So on a routine basis, weekly or monthly, a bank reconciliation statement is drawn up. As we have explained, the reason for preparing the statement is to find errors and frauds. A secondary purpose is to update the business's records for items deducted from and added to their bank account (standing orders and direct debits); these items will appear on the bank statement.

A bank reconciliation statement is shown in Figure 12.3. The bank reconciliation statement starts with the business's bank account total and ends with the bank statement total. This order of course could be reversed. Similar reconciling items are grouped together in the statement for ease of presentation.

One confusing feature for students is the nature of the debits and credits in the bank statement which will be opposite to those of the bank account. If the firm's cash book shows a debit balance of £5,000 then this will be a debit in the firm's accounts. However, this will be a credit balance on the bank statement. Why should this be the case? The bank statement is a document produced by the bank for its purposes as much as the company's. If the company owns £5,000 of the cash held by the bank, then the bank owes the company this amount (i.e. the company is a creditor to the bank). After all, it's not the bank's money, the company is in a way just 'lending' it to the bank.

As the reconciliation is performed at a specific date (like a balance sheet) it carries the phrase '...as at...' in its heading.

	£	£
Balance as per cash book		9,000
Add: credit transfers	500	
counter credit	1,500	2,000
		11,000
Less: payments not in cash book		4,000
Written up cash book balance		7,000
Less: bank charges and commission	700	
dishonoured cheques	500	1,200
		5,800
Add: unpresented cheque		200
Less: unrecorded lodgements		300
Balance as per bank statement (credit)		5,700

Figure 12.3 Bank reconciliation statement as at 31 March 1990

Now we must see how to prepare such a bank reconciliation statement. We will use the example shown in Figure 12.4. As you can see we are given the bank statement for the month ended 30 April 19X8 and the bank account as at that date. We are trying to reconcile the bank account total of £1,310.40 with the bank statement total of £1,166.45. The reconciling process can be performed as follows:

1. The way in which reconciling items are detected is usually by a 'tick and check' manual procedure, whereby items in the bank account are ticked with the corresponding entry in the bank statement (these are also ticked). Any unmarked items in both the company's bank account and in the bank statements will be the reconciling items. This completed ticking procedure is shown in Figure 12.5.

2. The next step is to arrive at the corrected bank account total, as it is the company's correctly written up bank account total that is used in the final balance sheet. This is shown in Figure 12.6 to be £1,296.45. The bank account total of £1,310.40 is taken as the start figure and the bank statement examined for items not found in the bank account.
    a. Bank giro credit – this is an amount paid directly into Lakes's bank.
    b. Difference in cheque 236130, which is an error made by the business in writing up its bank account.
    c. Standing order – an amount withdrawn directly out of Lakes's bank account on a regular basis.
    d. Bank charges – the fee paid by Lakes to the bank for managing his bank account.

    It may be necessary to examine the bank account for items not included in the bank statement to find errors made by the business in writing it up.

3. The corrected bank account total is then reconciled to the bank statement total of £1,166.45. The bank account is examined for items not included in the bank statement.
    a. Unpresented cheques.
    b. Unrecorded lodgements.

    It may be necessary to examine the bank statement for items not included in the bank account, to find errors made by the bank, such as a rogue cheque – the bank has made a mistake by charging Lakes's account with someone else's cheque.

4. Finally, for completeness we have reconciled the opening bank position as at 1 April 19X8.

As you can see the preparation of the bank reconciliation identifies those items which require further investigations. These are:

1. Bank giro credits – who paid the money in?
    – is any more due?

On 15 May 19X8, Mr Lakes received his monthly bank statement for the month ended 30 April 19X8. The bank statement contained the following details.

Mr Lakes's statement of account with
Baroyds Ltd. (*Balance indicates account is overdrawn)

Date	Particulars	Payments	Receipts	Balance
		£	£	£
1 April	Balance			1,053.29
2 April	236127	210.70		842.59
3 April	Bank Giro Credit		192.35	1,034.94
6 April	236126	15.21		1,019.73
6 April	Charges	12.80		1,006.93
9 April	236129	43.82		963.11
10 April	427519	19.47		943.64
12 April	236128	111.70		831.94
17 April	Standing Order	32.52		799.42
20 April	Sundry Credit		249.50	1,048.92
23 April	236130	77.87		971.05
23 April	236132	59.09		911.96
25 April	Bank Giro Credit		21.47	933.43
27 April	Sundry Credit		304.30	1,237.63
30 April	236133	71.18		1,166.45

For the corresponding period, Mr Lakes's own records contained the following bank account:

Date	Detail	£	Date	Detail	Cheque No.	£
1 April	Balance	827.38	5 April	Purchases	128	111.70
2 April	Sales	192.35	10 April	Electricity	129	43.82
18 April	Sales	249.50	16 April	Purchases	130	87.77
24 April	Sales	304.20	18 April	Rent	131	30.00
30 April	Sales	192.80	20 April	Purchases	132	59.09
			25 April	Purchases	133	71.18
			20 April	Wages	134	52.27
			30 April	Balance		1,310.40
		£1,766.23				£1,766.23

You are required to:
a. prepare a statement reconciling the balance at 30 April as given by the bank statement to the balance at 30 April as stated in the bank account;
b. explain briefly which items in your bank reconciliation statement would require further investigation.
(Association of Certified Accountants)

Figure 12.4 Mr Lakes – statement of account

On 15 May 19X8, Mr Lakes received his monthly bank statement for the month ended 30 April 19X8. The bank statement contained the following details.

Date	Particulars	Payments	Receipts	Balance
		£	£	£
1 April	Balance			1,053.29
2 April	236127	210.70		842.59
3 April	Bank Giro Credit		192.35✓	1,034.94
6 April	236126	15.21		1,019.73
6 April	Charges	12.80		1,006.93
9 April	236129	43.82✓		963.11
10 April	427519	19.47		943.64
12 April	236128	111.70✓		831.94
17 April	Standing Order	32.52		799.42
20 April	Sundry Credit		249.50✓	1,048.92
23 April	236130	77.87		971.05
23 April	236132	59.09✓		911.96
25 April	Bank Giro Credit		21.47	933.43
27 April	Sundry Credit		304.20✓	1,237.63
30 April	236133	71.18✓		1,166.45

For the corresponding period, Mr. Lakes's own records contained the following bank account:

Date	Detail	£	Date	Detail	Cheque No.	£
1 April	Balance	827.38	5 April	Purchases	128	111.70✓
2 April	Sales	192.35✓	10 April	Electricity	129	43.82✓
18 April	Sales	249.50✓	16 April	Purchases	130	87.77
24 April	Sales	304.20✓	18 April	Rent	131	30.00
30 April	Sales	192.80	20 April	Purchases	132	59.09✓
			25 April	Purchases	133	71.18✓
			20 April	Wages	134	52.27
			30 April	Balance		1,310.40
		£1,766.23				£1,766.23

You are required to:
a. prepare a statement reconciling the balance at 30 April as given by the bank statement to the balance at 30 April as stated in the bank account;
b. explain briefly which items in your bank reconciliation statement would require further investigation.
(Association of Certified Accountants)

Figure 12.5   Mr Lakes – statement of account following 'tick and check' process

	£	£
Balance as per bank account		1,310.40
Items in bank statement but not in bank account:		
Add bank giro credits	21.47	
Difference in cheque 236130	9.90	
		31.37
Less standing order	32.52	
bank charges	12.80	
		(45.32)
Corrected bank account total		1,296.45
Items in bank account but not in bank statement:		
Add unpresented cheques:		
131	30.00	
134	52.27	
		82.27
Less unrecorded lodgement		(192.80)
Items in bank account but not in bank statement:		
Less rouge cheque		(19.47)
Total per bank statement		£1,166.45
Reconciliation of opening balance		
Balance per bank account		827.38
Add unpresented cheques:		
236127	210.70	
236128	15.21	
		225.91
Balance per bank statement		1,053.29

Figure 12.6 Mr Lakes – bank reconciliation statement as at 30 April 19X8

2. Difference in cheque 236130 – why was the mistake made?
 – could it happen again?
 – how could it have been prevented?

3. Standing order – who is being paid?
 – has it been properly authorised?
 – is it a legitimate business expense?

4. Bank charges – how are they calculated?
 – are they reasonable?
 – can they be reduced?

5. Rogue cheque – bank to be informed to correct account?
 – has it happened before?

CHECKLIST _____

By the end of Chapter 12, you should be able to:

■ explain the need for a statement which reconciles the control account total with the ledger total for both debtors and creditors;

■ prepare a statement which reconciles the control account total with the ledger total for both debtors and creditors;

■ explain how the main reconciling items in a control account/list of ledger balances reconciliation statement occurred;

■ outline the reasons for preparing reconciliation statements;

■ prepare a bank reconciliation statement;

■ explain how the main reconciliating items in a bank reconciliation statement occurred.

Selected questions and exercises

Question 12.1
George is the book-keeper for a small trading concern. He has again unfortunately failed to balance his control accounts for the sales and purchase ledgers at the year end, 31 May 1987. The position is as follows:

Net debit balance on sales ledger control	£45,124
Net credit balance on purchase ledger control	£29,461
Net total of balances in sales ledger (debit)	£45,560
Net total of balances in purchase ledger (credit)	£28,912

He called in his close friend Ian (who is good at accounts) to help him sort out the situation. Ian has discovered the following:
1. A sales invoice of £1,316 has been posted to the debit of G. Daye in the sales ledger and then posted again to the debit of Daye Ltd in the sales ledger.
2. The total of the credit balances in the purchase ledger has been under-added by £100.
3. A bad debt of £100 has been written off an account in the sales ledger but no entry has been made in the control account.
4. Contra items totalling £460 have been put through the personal accounts but not entered in the control accounts.
5. The sales day book has been under-added by £200.
6. The purchase returns book has been over-added by £20.
7. A debit balance of £520 has been omitted from the sales ledger list of balances.

8. A purchase invoice of £21 has been posted as £12 to L. Dineen's account in the purchase ledger.

You are required to show the corrections needed to sort out the above errors in:
a. the sales ledger control account;
b. the purchase ledger control account;
c. the list of sales balances;
d. the list of purchase ledger balances.

Solution on page 535.

Question 12.2

The figures shown in Table 12.1 appeared in the purchases ledger control account of Hudson and Co. Ltd on 31 March 1987.

Table 12.1 *Details of the accounts of Hudson and Company Limited*

	£
Creditor balances 1 April 1986	36,846
Debtor balances 1 April 1986	328
Discount received	1,957
Purchases	276,220
Payments to creditors	258,972
Purchase returns	3,116
Cash refunded from creditors	262
Bills payable	1,118
Debtor balances 31 March 1987	419
Contras: sales ledger	784

The control account creditor balance at 31 March 1987 failed to agree with the total of the list of balances of creditors extracted from the purchase ledger. Subsequent examination revealed the following errors.

1. A credit balance of £176 on the account of a creditor had been omitted from the list of creditors balances.
2. Discount received of £28 had been entered in the cash book and discount received account but not in the creditors account in the ledger.
3. The purchase day book had been undercast by £200.
4. An item of £186 in the purchase day book had been posted to the creditors account as £168.
5. Discount received for one month of £137 had been posted to the debit instead of the credit side of the cash book.
6. Goods returned to a supplier valued at £82 had been correctly entered in the creditors account but entered in the purchases returns day book as £182.

1. Show how the control account would appear in the ledger before making any corrections.
2. Prepare a statement showing the adjustment of the balance in the control account in 1 above to the correct balance, giving details of the errors.
3. Prepare a statement reconciling the corrected balance with the totals as shown by the list of balances before the errors were found, giving details of the relevant errors.

Solution on page 536.

Question 12.3

You are required to prepare a statement reconciling the balance at 28 January as given in the bank statement (Table 12.2) to the balance at 28 January as given in the cash book (Table 12.3).

Table 12.2   *Bank statement of R. T. Ewing*

Bank statement

Cannon Bank
123 Tree Street Cardiff S. Glamorgan

R. T. Ewing Esq
34 Jock Road
Muddlewich
Cardiff

Details	Payments	Receipts	Date	Balance
Balance forward			1 Jan	16,575.87
15367	567.01		3 Jan	16,008.86
15365	6,741.94		4 Jan	9,266.92
Bank credit		100.05	5 Jan	9,366.97
Standing order	357.82		5 Jan	9,009.15
Remittance		1,367.96	9 Jan	10,377.11
15366	56.87		11 Jan	10,320.24
15368	1,200.09		12 Jan	9,120.15
Bank credit		1,300.75	14 Jan	10,420.9
15370	2,378.94		17 Jan	8,041.96
Standing order	156.95		19 Jan	7,885.01
Remittance		1,453.98	21 Jan	9,338.99
15371	2,316.89		24 Jan	7022.1
Charges	101.78		25 Jan	6,920.32
Remittance		5,600.01	26 Jan	12,520.33
15372	2,300.65		28 Jan	10,219.68
Bank credit		106.89	28 Jan	10,326.57

Table 12.3 *Cash book entries of R. T. Ewing*

Date	Details		Date	Details	Cheque No.	
1 Jan	Balance	9,777.06	1 Jan	Rent	15367	567.01
2 Jan	Sales	100.05	6 Jan	Stock	15368	1,200.09
5 Jan	Sales	1,367.96	8 Jan	Stock	15369	4,500.89
10 Jan	Sales	1,300.75	11 Jan	Repairs	15370	2,378.94
18 Jan	Sales	1,453.98	20 Jan	Fittings	15371	2,316.89
24 Jan	Sales	5,600.01	22 Jan	Stock	15372	2,300.65
29 Jan	Sales	4,560.75	24 Jan	Stock	15373	56.75
			28 Jan	Machine	15374	1,360.09
		24,160.56				14,681.31
			31 Jan	Balance		9,479.25
		24,160.56				24,160.56

Solution on page 537.

Question 12.4

The A2Z Company presents you with the balances shown in Table 12.4 for December 1987.

Table 12.4 *A2Z Company balances as at December 1987*

			£
1 December 1987	Sales ledger	DR	202,100
		CR	2,800
	Purchase ledger	DR	330
		CR	115,900
31 December 1987	*Transactions*		
			£
Credit sales			534,000
Cash sales			213,600
Credit purchases			282,700
Payments to creditors			238,600
Payments received from debtors			449,500
Bad debts written off			1,900
Provision for bad debts			9,700
Purchase returns			4,500
Sales returns			5,800
Discounts received			5,900
Discounts allowed			9,500
Balances in debtors ledger set off against balances in creditors ledger			3,400
Customer's cheque dishonoured			500
31 December 1987	Sales ledger	DR	?
		CR	2,100
	Purchase ledger	DR	420
		CR	?

Note: not all this data is needed.

You are required to draw up the debtors control account for December 1987, showing all the closing balances.

No solution provided.

Question 12.5

Dai A. Bolical's cash book on 30 June showed a balance due to his bank of £4,840, and a balance of £2,824 overdrawn appeared on his bank statement. On investigation you find:

1. Cheques drawn amounting to £1,680 had not been presented to the bank for payment.
2. The receipts side of the cash book had been undercast by £400.
3. Cheques of £1,440 entered in the cash book as paid into the bank had not been credited by the bank.
4. A cheque of £2,080 drawn on Dai's account had been charged by the bank in error to another customer's account.
5. Bank charges of £304 entered on the bank statement had not been entered in the cash book.
6. A dividend of £120 paid direct to the bank had not been entered in the cash book.
7. A cheque drawn for £192 had been entered in the cash book for £120.
8. A cheque for £280 paid into the bank had been dishonoured, but no entry relating to this dishonoured cheque had been made in the cash book.
9. A cheque for £168 drawn by another customer of the same name had been charged in error to Dai's bank account.

1. Show the appropriate adjustments to be made in the cash book and prepare a bank reconciliation.
2. Since bank reconciliations are merely a matter of arithmetic, just add the right figures and a balance is assured. If this is the case then what use is a bank reconciliation?

No solution provided.

Part C

Application of basic financial accounting practice to different types of organisation

13 | *The accounts of the sole trader: incomplete records*

AIMS OF CHAPTER _____

- to introduce the sole trader as a form of business enterprise, with an indication of the advantages and disadvantages of this form of organisation;
- to produce a set of final accounts from a limited amount of financial information, using the spreadsheet approach.

13.1 Introduction

Many businesses operate as one-man enterprises, i.e. they are 'sole traders'. Do not let the terminology confuse you: a sole trader refers to the ownership and legal status of the enterprise and can involve a number of employees. However, for the most part such organisations are small in terms of turnover, as there are advantages to be gained from partnership agreements or even company status as the firm grows.

13.2 The advantages and disadvantages of being a sole trader

Many people have the ambition to 'work for myself', and this can be a rewarding experience, both financially and in terms of job satisfaction. Most would point to the independence of being your own boss and the feeling of being personally responsible for one's actions. In recent times there have been government initiatives to help people start their own businesses, with allowances and loans granted to people with sound business ideas, but with insufficient financial backing.

In some cases the sole trader is the best form of organisation for a particular enterprise, offering a great degree of flexibility, personal supervision of staff and direct customer contact. Good examples exist in service industries such as hairdressing, small scale retailing (especially for specialist products), and tradesmen such as plumbers or painters and decorators.

It is not the idyllic life, as most sole traders will soon inform you. Legally, the business has unlimited liability, which means that financial ruin results in personal belongings being possessed to pay creditors. Bankruptcy, or even the possibility of it, is very stressful as is the burden of shouldering the responsibility of possibly providing the livelihood of other people, i.e. the employees. Sometimes the sole trader can be frustrated by lack of capital for expansion or by lack of expertise to adopt new technology. Government assistance is not always forthcoming and banks usually lend money to people who do not need it! Locally sponsored enterprise agencies exist to serve the need of the sole trader, or potential small business.

13.3   The accounts of the sole trader

Large companies are legally obligated to maintain a proper accounting system; indeed their accounts are audited by professional accountants to ensure that their final accounts present a true and fair view of the business (see Chapter 25). The sole trader has no shareholders to satisfy and is not encumbered by the regulations of Acts of Parliament that govern partnerships or companies. This may have been a motivating factor in starting the business. The sole trader is usually only obligated to satisfy the tax inspector, or possibly the bank manager, and as a consequence often does not keep a full double-entry accounting system.

The financial records of a small business can be subject to neglect on the part of the owner and not all transactions may be recorded. We say the records are 'incomplete'. Some owners lack the ability to keep proper books, but maintain a cash book or the like in which details of transactions are recorded only once. This gives rise to the expression 'single-entry book-keeping'. Incidentally, there is nothing wrong with this accounting system, which was widely used in Great Britain before the adoption of the Venetian 'double-entry system' (see Chapter 1).

In any case, most small firms do not need a complex accounting system, with the owner keeping a 'little black book'. A substantial number keep all invoices and records in a small box or tin, giving rise to the term 'shoebox accounting'.

It can be ironic, as the poor accounting system deployed can result in the financial downfall of the entire business. Most small firms fail not because they are not making a profit, but because they have cash flow problems. A lack of information for management and control purposes can affect general business performance and lead to financial strife. Many do not provide for any tax liability payable in the year following the accounts preparation, and find themselves floundering because they thought they were 'doing fine' simply because they had some cash in the bank.

13.3.1 Preparing accounts from incomplete records

This is normally a year-end task, but sometimes accounts are drawn up to estimate stock losses incurred through accidents such as fire, or through burglary and theft. Preparing a set of accounts from incomplete records is often an examinable area, as it reinforces the student's understanding of the underlying concepts through solving problems containing fragmented and disorganised data.

In the examples you will encounter there is enough information to complete the question without any estimation on your part, e.g. the cash account may be complete apart from a figure for drawings. Typically you will have sufficient opening balance sheet figures to work out the opening capital, and closing balance sheet figures for current assets and liabilities are normally given. Figure 13.1 is a good illustration of the incomplete records of a sole trader.

In order to prepare the full set of accounts we need to calculate the following:

1. Ray Milward's capital on 1 June 1988.

2. Purchases for the year ended 31 May 1989.

3. Sales for the year ended 31 May 1989.

4. The amount for expenses for the year ended 31 May 1989.

Ray Milward is an ice cream salesman who does not keep a full set of books. He buys his stock on credit terms, but all sales are strictly cash. All takings are paid into his bank account apart from his own drawings and all business payments are made by cheque.

A summary of his bank account for the year ended 31 May 1989 is as follows:

	£		£
Balance 1 June 88	900	Paid for creditors	12,400
Received for cash sales	20,700	Motor expenses	2,450
		Laundry	150
		Drawings	?
		Balance 31 May 89	400

The following information is available:

	1 June 1988 £	31 May 1989 £
Creditors	200	300
Accrued motor expenses	50	30
Stock in trade	150	100
Ice cream van	3,000	2,250

Using the information above, prepare a trading account and a profit and loss account for the year ended 31 May 1989 and a balance sheet on that date. Ignore taxation.

Figure 13.1 Ray Milward

13.3.2   The method of solution

The following stages are generalised rules for the completion of such accounts:

1. Place the opening balance sheet figures along the first row of the spreadsheet after you have labelled the columns appropriately. The balancing figure, i.e. to make the balance sheet equal zero, is capital and is calculated as minus the sum of the other entries.

2. The bank account entries are then inserted in the **bank** column, with the corresponding double entry achieved by a negative relative cell reference. It is important to take a new line for each transaction to avoid confusion.

3. Leave room for the final transactions needed to complete the accounts and insert the known figures in the closing balance sheet. The amount of rows to leave is a matter of experience and personal judgement. You can insert new rows or delete unused rows as necessary anyway.

4. Deduce the missing entries, using your accounting knowledge. This may seem very haphazard, but it is difficult to state general rules for what in reality amount to specialist problems. However, here are a few examples:

    a. Dr. Debtors   Cr. P & L a/c
        with the period's sales
    b. Dr. Stock   Cr. Creditors
        with the period's purchases
    c. Dr. P & L a/c   Cr. Stock
        with the cost of goods sold
    d. Dr. P & L a/c   Cr. Accrual/prepayment a/c
        with the expenses for the period
    e. Dr. P & L a/c   Cr. Provision for depreciation
        with the period's depreciation charge

5. Total the columns without final balance sheet figures inserted and ensure that the final balance sheet sums to zero. Note that this is best done using a control cell, outside the double-entry part of the spreadsheet. Using the closing capital cell as the sum of the closing balance sheet is inadequate, as it will not contain the profit for the period.

Spreadsheet 13.1 gives the solution for the Ray Milward illustration. (Spreadsheet 13.1a gives the formulae.) In practice, the accounts would then be written out in good format, as in Figure 13.2.

Note that the cost of goods sold is calculated using a stock change figure. In most cases it is usual to see cost of goods sold calculated as opening stock + purchases − closing stock, but using this presentation we are rearranging the equation to read: purchases + (opening stock − closing stock). The only reason for this is to match the spreadsheet workings.

Spreadsheet 13.1   Ray Milward

	A	B	C	D	E	F	G	H	I	J	K
1											
2											
3	Account Type --->			ASSET	LIAB.	LIAB.	ASSET	ASSET	EQUITY	EQUITY =	0
4											
5	Account Title -->			Bank	Creditor	Creditor	Stock	Ice Crea	Capital	Profit	
6					(Stock)	(Motor		Van		& Loss	
7	Narrative					Expenses)					
8											
9	Opening Balance Sheet			900	-200	-50	150	3000	-3800		0
10											
11	Bank Account Entries										
12											
13	Received from Cash Sales			20700						-20700	
14	Paid to Creditors			-12400	12400						
15	Paid for Motor Expenses			-2450		2450					
16	Laundry			-150						150	
17	Drawings			-6200					6200		
18											
19				--							
20	Trial Balance			400	12200	2400	150	3000	2400	-20550	0
21											
22											
23	End of Year Adjustments										
24											
25	Purchases for year				-12500					12500	
26	Motor Expenses for year					-2430				2430	
27	Stock Change						-50			50	
28	Depreciation							-750		750	
29											
30	Profit for year								-4820	4820	
31											
32				--							
33	Closing Balance Sheet			400	-300	-30	100	2250	-2420	0	0

Note also how drawings is a charge on capital, not profit. Similarly, the tax liability is based on the profit figure. This may seem strange at first, but remember you are taxed on your income, not on your wealth (i.e. for income tax), and if drawings exceed profit made then the businessman is using some of his wealth to supplement his income. As this wealth was at some time income then it has already been subject to income tax.

From the formula back-up it is evident how much work the spreadsheet is doing, given the correct use of relative cell referencing and other formulae. This is a good feature in practice, as changes to figures are frequently made as more information comes to light.

To take you through a few of the calculations may prove beneficial. The bank account entries are straightforward, but the term trial balance for row 20 is a misnomer as it is really just a balance calculation.

Spreadsheet 13.1a   Ray Milward (formulae)

	A	B	C	D	E	F	G	H	I	J
1										
2										
3	Account Type --->			ASSET	LIAB.	LIAB.	ASSET	ASSET	EQUITY	EQUITY
4										
5	Account Title -->			Bank	Creditor	Creditor	Stock	Ice Cream	Capital	Profit
6					(Stock)	(Motor		Van		& Loss
7	Narrative					Expenses)				
8										
9	Opening Balance Sheet			900	-200	-50	150	3000	-SUM(D9:H9)	
10										
11	Bank Account Entries									
12										
13	Received from Cash Sales			20700						-D13
14	Paid to Creditors			-12400	-D14					
15	Paid for Motor Expenses			-2450		-D15				
16	Laundry			-150						-D16
17	Drawings			-SUM(D9:D16)+D20					-D17	
18										
19				---						
20	Trial Balance			400	SUM(E9:E17)	SUM(F9:F17)	SUM(G9:G17)	SUM(H9:H17)	SUM(I9:I17)	SUM(J9:J17)
21										
22										
23	End of Year Adjustments									
24										
25	Purchases for year				-E20+E33					-E25
26	Motor Expenses for year					-F20+F33				-F26
27	Stock Change						-G20+G33			-G27
28	Depreciation							-H20+H33		-H28
29										
30	Profit for year								-J30	-SUM(J20:J28)
31										
32				---						
33	Closing Balance Sheet			SUM(D20:D31)	-300	-30	100	2250	SUM(I20:I31)	SUM(J20:J31)

The purchases figure is the sum of what we paid for during the year plus what we owed at the end, less what we owed at the beginning. The same logic underlies the motor expenses. The stock change is dealt with above, while the fall in NBV of the van is depreciation. The profit for the year is the sum of the entries in that column which is taken to the capital account.

CHECKLIST

Having completed Chapter 13, you should be able to:

- indicate some advantages and disadvantages of operating as a sole trader;
- produce a set of final accounts for a sole trader from a limited amount of financial information, using the spreadsheet approach.

Trading, Profit and Loss Account for the year ended 31 May 1989

	£	£
Sales		20,700
Less cost of goods sold:		
Purchases	12,500	
Stock change	50	12,550
Gross profit		8,150
Less expenses:		
Motor expenses	2,430	
Laundry	150	
Depreciation	750	3,330
Net profit		4,820

Balance sheet as at 31 May 1989

	£	£	£
Fixed assets	Cost	Depreciation	NBV
Ice cream van	3,000	750	2,250
Current assets			
Stock			100
Bank			400
			2,750
Less *current liabilities*			
creditors and accruals			330
			2,420
Financed by:			£
Capital 1 June 1988			3,800
Add profit for period			4,820
			8,620
Less drawings			6,200
			2,420

Figure 13.2 Account for the twelve months to 31 May 1989 for Ray Milward

Workshop 13.1: Incomplete records

This workshop is in the form of a case study based on the letter from David Pentost and Figures 13.3 and 13.4. Prepare the accounts on the spreadsheet and answer the letter as a separate exercise.

You are working in an accountant's office as a trainee and one of the partners has asked you to reply to the letter from Mr David Pentost which is attached. The partner would like to see the completed financial statements with your workings, together with a draft reply ready for signing.

David Pentost
Carpenter
12 Plane Street
Notty Ash

28 February 1989

Wood & Window
Accountants
High Street
Forseton

Dear Dickie

Thank you for reminding me that my books were due. My wife has been busy sorting out my bank account for you which you said would help you. I don't know if she's done it right, but the summary she prepared is enclosed.

I also enclose last year's balance sheet prepared by my previous accountants, Brace & Bit, who were not very helpful when it came to explaining what they did to some of the business transactions. For example, they 'depreciated' my van and my tools at 25 per cent of something called 'net book value'. I find this hard to follow, especially when my van is not worth the same as their valuation. There was no mention of where the money was coming from to replace it. I thought that was what depreciation meant, after all it comes off my profit, doesn't it? As to depreciating my tools, I really object to that. I look after them well and I should have them for donkey's years yet – I only buy the best you know.

I bought a new van as a Christmas present to myself as the old one was on its way out. I had a good deal from DeLorean Evans who sold one of these snazzy Japanese pick-up trucks to me at discount for £8,300, allowing me £4,000 for the old one. He even said I could have the balance on loan, payments starting in the month after purchase. You won't have any record of this in the bank or cash account.

I've also jotted down some notes from my little black book. This is where I record my cash dealings. Don't worry, I've got receipts for all purchases and invoices to cover any jobs I've done.

Other information you'll probably need from past experience with accountants is my stock of materials, which was £250 on 31 December 1988, but at that time I was working on a job costing £1,500 which was three quarters complete. This cost includes wages and material, but no mark-up. My account at the builders' merchant Q & B, where I buy all my materials, showed that I owed £1,450 at the end of December.

Of my sundry expenses, which I tend to pay in cash, I owed £230 going by the unpaid invoices. Having said that, some of the stuff I've bought I've used on my own house, about £500-worth.

Jack Lumber still hasn't paid for the job I did for him before Christmas. He owes me £690, but I don't know if I'll see all of it since he went bankrupt in January! My customers owed me £2,130 – most of whom have now paid me.

Good luck with preparing my accounts. If you have any problems you'll have to sort them out yourself as I'm usually busy working all over the place during the day. I'll have to get one of those flashy car phones, only my wife says that yuppies drive Porsches not pick-ups! I look forward to hearing from you before the end of March.

All the best.

Dai

Fixed assets	Cost £	Depreciation £	NBV £
Van	7,000	1,750	5,250
Tools	450	150	300
			5,550
Current assets			
Stock—work in progress	980		
materials	230		
Debtors	1,245		
Bank	345		
Cash	325		
			3,125
Current liabilities			
Creditors—materials	1,890		
—sundries	325		
			(2,215)
			£6,460
Financed by:			
Capital			£6,460

Figure 13.3 Balance sheet as at 31 December 1987

Deposits	£
Cheques from customers paid in	27,980
Cash paid in	3,765

Withdrawals	£
Suppliers of materials	9,765
Sundry expenses	2,486
Transfers to joint account	7,984
New tools	240
Cash withdrawn	8,450
Closing bank balance	£3,165

Little Black Book details

	£
Invoices paid	9,875
Materials bought	329
Wages to labourer	4,671

Wife's earnings, £45 per week
Drawings £600 a month approx.

Other odds and sods, i.e. sundry items, I wouldn't have a clue about. I suppose they must be the balance as I only had £200 in cash according to my little book on 31 December 1988.

Figure 13.4 Analysis of bank statements for 1988

Workshop guide

This case study represents a scenario found all too often in the real world. You are presented with a situation where you have to construct the accounts of a business from only limited information. So before we go any further reread the details given so that they are clear in your mind and you will know where to find things.

The first stage is to open columns for each of the accounts contained in last year's balance sheet, putting in the opening balances, either debit or credit, in row 5 of the spreadsheet. You may wish to open a **control** column, column U, to sum the entries of the balance sheet to ensure that it balances. Don't worry about the number of columns yet, as you can insert or delete column accounts as and when necessary.

Having completed this stage, let's complete the bank account transactions. There are no tricky transactions so the explanations in the chapter will be adequate to sort any problems you might have. When you have completed all the entries, open up a closing balance sheet in row 52 and place a sum command to find the balance on the bank account. Any row would do really as you can insert additional rows as you need them, with the relative cell reference in cell K52 changing accordingly. You can replicate this reference for the remaining columns to take the totals automatically.

The next stage is to tackle the **cash account**, column L in the answer given. All entries are quite straightforward except the sundry expenses calculation. We know the balance is £200, therefore the entry for sundries is the balancing figure. To find this we take the sum of the column to date and deduct the closing balance. However, as we wish to transfer this balance to the **sundry creditors** column, the formula $-\text{SUM(L5:L23)} + \text{L52}$ is used in cell L24 with the double entry carried in cell N24.

The next stage is to examine the contents of the letter for other information. We know that tools are depreciated at 25 per cent of net book value; therefore the first calculation is to find NBV which is the previous balance on the tools account less any provision to date, plus any purchases of tools during the year. This figure is then multiplied by 25 per cent to find this year's depreciation charge as in cell G28.

Some of the sundry items are to be treated as drawings; therefore in row 29 column N is credited, thus reducing the sundries charge, and debited to drawings.

One debtor is unlikely to pay. As this is still uncertain, two courses of action could be taken; either write off the debt by reducing total debtors and charging the amount to the profit and loss account or create a provision for a doubtful debt. Either course of action is equally prudent as the profit figure is reduced by this increased provision. As very little is known about the bankruptcy, and sometimes creditors do receive part of the amount owing, provision seems to be an acceptable treatment. See row 30.

Sundry expenses to be charged to the profit and loss account are the expenses paid to date plus any amounts owing. We insert the balance owing in cell N52 and the formula in row 31 represents the figure needed to allow that column to balance. This is then charged to the **profit and loss account**, column T.

Mr Pentost also changes his van, i.e. he disposes of a fixed asset. To record these transactions a **disposal account** is opened, column S. The first stages are to write out the old asset, both in terms of cost and depreciation provision, and charge the entries to the disposal account. This is done in rows 35 and 36. The loan is shown in full in the first instance, i.e. by debiting the asset account and crediting the loan account. No cash has changed hands in this instance, but a liability has been established. The allowance for the old van has been treated as a debit to offset the loan and credited to the disposal account. The balance on the disposal column is then taken to the profit and loss account, in this case a loss of £1,250, as in row 39.

The new vehicle is depreciated in the year of acquisition. This may seem inappropriate as the van is only a few days' old, but it can be argued that this is an objective treatment and vehicles do lose a significant amount of value when they leave the showroom. The depreciation charge is debited to the profit and loss account and credited to the provision account as in row 41.

Only a few final adjustments remain. The materials purchased, if not paid for, are calculated in row 45 by extracting the balance needed in column M after inserting the closing balance in cell M52. In this instance the figure is taken to the stock of materials account. The materials used are established in much the same manner, i.e. by inserting the closing stock and deriving the balancing figure. This is then taken to the **work in progress** column, H. It is this column that is used to find the cost of goods sold. One job was partly complete and this represents a closing balance. The balancing figure is the work performed at cost which is charged to the profit and loss account.

The sales figure is found after taking account of debtors likely to pay. The bad debt is still included in sales through the cheque received in row 9.

The net profit is the sum of column T which is taken to the **capital** column, O. The total of any drawings are also charged against capital as in row 50.

The final transaction is to sum any columns without balances inserted, as in row 52, which becomes the closing balance sheet. Column U is used as a **control** column to ensure that the balance sheet balances and all transactions have two sides. Figure 13.5 illustrates the accounts in good format.

'What if?' problems

1. What would be the effect on sundry expenses and profit if the closing cash balance was £250?

2. What would be the effect on profit if the work in progress was only half complete? Amend cell H52 to change the closing valuation.

Spreadsheet 13.2a   Workshop 13.1: David Pentost—solution

	A	D Van	E Provision for Dep'n	F Tools	G Provision for Dep'n	H Stock W.I.P.	I Stock Materials	J Debtors
5	Balance Sheet 31/12/87	7000	-1750	450	-150	980	230	1245
7	Bank Account							
9	Cheques paid in							-27980
10	Cash paid in							
11	Suppliers paid							
12	Sundries paid							
13	Drawings							
14	New Tools			240				
15	Cash Withdrawn							
17	Cash Account							
19	Invoices paid by customers							-9875
20	Materials bought							
21	Labourers wages							
22	Wife's earnings							
23	Drawings							
24	Sundry Expenses							
26	Other Details							
28	Tools Depreciation				-135			
29	Drawings							
30	Provision for Bad Debt							
31	Sundry Expenses							
33	Disposal of Fixed Asset							
35	Write out asset	-7000						
36	Write out depreciation		1750					
37	Loan for new vehicle	8300						
38	Allowance for old vehicle							
39	Loss on disposal							
41	Depreciation on Van		-2075					
43	Final Adjustments							
45	Purchases of Materials						9654	
46	Usage of Materials					9634	-9634	
47	Cost of Goods Sold					-9489		
48	Sales							38740
49	Net Profit							
50	Drawings							
52	Balance Sheet 31/12/88	8300	-2075	690	-285	1125	250	2130

: K :	: L :	: M :	: N :	O :	: P :	: Q :	: R :	: S :	: T :	: U :
Bank	Cash	Creditors Materials	Creditors Sundries	Capital	Drawings	Bad Debt Provision	Loan	Disposal	Profit & Loss	
345	325	-1890	-325	-6460						0
										0
27980										0
3765	-3765									0
-9765		9765								0
-2486			2486							0
-7984					7984					0
-240										0
-8450	8450									0
	9875									0
	-329	329								0
	-4671							4671		0
	-2340							2340		0
	-7200				7200					0
	-145		145							0
								135		0
			-500		500					0
						-690		690		0
			-2036					2036		0
								7000		0
								-1750		0
							-8300			0
							4000	-4000		0
								-1250	1250	0
									2075	0
		-9654								0
										0
									9489	0
									-38740	0
				-16054					16054	0
				15684	-15684					
3165	200	-1450	-230	-6830	0	-690	-4300	0	0	0

(*continued*)

Spreadsheet 13.2b   Workshop 13.1: David Pentost – formulae

	A	B	C	D	E	F	G	H	I	J	K
1	David Pentost										
2					Provision		Provision	Stock	Stock		
3				Van	for Dep'n	Tools	for Dep'n	W.I.P.	Materials	Debtors	Bank
4											
5	Balance Sheet 31/12/87			7000	-1750	450	-150	980	230	1245	345
6											
7	Bank Account										
8											
9	Cheques paid in									-K9	27980
10	Cash paid in										3765
11	Suppliers paid										-9765
12	Sundries paid										-2486
13	Drawings										-7984
14	New Tools				-K14						-240
15	Cash Withdrawn										-8450
16											
17	Cash Account										
18											
19	Invoices paid by customers									-L19	
20	Materials bought										
21	Labourers wages										
22	Wife's earnings										
23	Drawings										
24	Sundry Expenses										
25											
26	Other Details										
27											
28	Tools Depreciation					-(F5+F14+G5)*.25					
29	Drawings										
30	Provision for Bad Debt										
31	Sundry Expenses										
32											
33	Disposal of Fixed Asset										
34											
35	Write out asset			-D5							
36	Write out depreciation				-E5						
37	Loan for new vehicle			8300							
38	Allowance for old vehicle										
39	Loss on disposal										
40											
41	Depreciation on Van				-D37*.25						
42											
43	Final Adjustments										
44											
45	Purchases of Materials								-M45		
46	Usage of Materials							-I46	-SUM(I5:I45)+I52		
47	Cost of Goods Sold							-SUM(H5:H46)+H52			
48	Sales									-SUM(J5:J47)+J52	
49	Net Profit										
50	Drawings										
51				--							
52	Balance Sheet 31/12/88			SUM(D5:D50)	SUM(E5:E50)	SUM(F5:F50)	SUM(G5:G50)	1500*.75	250	2130	SUM(K5:K50)

	L	M	N	O	P	Q	R	S	T	U
	Cash	Creditors Materials	Creditors Sundries	Capital	Drawings	Bad Debt Provision	Loan	Disposal	Profit & Loss	
	325	-1890	-325	-6460						SUM(D5:T5)
										SUM(D7:T7)
										SUM(D9:T9)
	-K10									SUM(D10:T10)
		-K11								SUM(D11:T11)
			-K12							SUM(D12:T12)
					-K13					SUM(D13:T13)
										SUM(D14:T14)
	-K15									SUM(D15:T15)
	9875									SUM(D19:T19)
	-329	-L20								SUM(D20:T20)
	-4671								-L21	SUM(D21:T21)
	-45*52								-L22	SUM(D22:T22)
	-600*12				-L23					SUM(D23:T23)
	-SUM(L5:L23)+L52	-L24								SUM(D24:T24)
									-G28	SUM(D28:T28)
			-500		-N29					SUM(D29:T29)
						-690			-Q30	SUM(D30:T30)
			-SUM(N5:N30)+N52						-N31	SUM(D31:T31)
								-D35		SUM(D35:T35)
								-E36		SUM(D36:T36)
							-D37			SUM(D37:T37)
							4000	-R38		SUM(D38:T38)
								-SUM(S35:S39)	-S39	SUM(D39:T39)
									-E41	SUM(D41:T41)
		-SUM(M5:M44)+M52								SUM(D45:T45)
										SUM(D46:T46)
									-H47	SUM(D47:T47)
									-J48	SUM(D48:T48)
				-T49					-SUM(T7:T48)	SUM(D49:T49)
				-P50	-SUM(P5:P49)					
	200	-1450	-230	SUM(O5:O50)	SUM(P5:P50)	SUM(Q5:Q50)	SUM(R5:R50)	SUM(S5:S50)	SUM(T5:T50)	SUM(D52:T52)

Income statement for the twelve months to 31 December 1981

	£	£
Sales		38,740
Cost of goods sold		(9,489)
Gross profit		29,251
Loss on disposal of fixed asset		(1,250)
Less expenses:		
Wages	4,671	
Wife's earnings	2,340	
Tools depreciation	135	
Provision for bad debt	690	
Sundry expenses	2,036	
Van depreciation	2,075	
		(11,947)
Net profit		16,054

Balance sheet as at 31 December 1988

Fixed assets	Cost £	Depreciation £	NBV £
Van	8,300	2,075	6,225
Tools	690	285	405
			6,630
Current assets			
Stock – work in progress		1,125	
– materials		250	
Debtors		2,130	
Less provision		(690)	
Bank		3,165	
Cash		200	
			6,180
Current liabilities			
Creditors – materials		1,450	
– sundries		230	
			(1,680)
			£11,130
Financed by:			£
Capital			6,830
Loan			4,300
			£11,130

Figure 13.5 Dai Pentost's final accounts

3. What if Jack Lumber's receivers announced that creditors would receive two-thirds of their debts upon sale of his assets? Amend the provision in row 29. What is the effect on profit?

4. What if the partner disagrees with your treatment of depreciation on the new vehicle and states that the old vehicle should be depreciated in full prior to sale? What is the effect on the disposal account? What is the effect on net profit?

5. What if one of the cheques paid in bounced in January? What effect would this have on the accounts, if any?

Answers

1. Profit increases by £50, Sundry expenses decrease by £50.

2. H52 changes to **1,500∗.5**. Profit decreases by £375.

3. Profit increases by £235.

4. Profit on disposal of £500. Net profit increases by £500 plus the decrease in the depreciation charge.

5. No effect on the accounts for the year unless this is a post balance sheet event (see Chapter 19).

Selected questions and exercises

Question 13.1

Ms Mary Martin, a retailer, was due to present her accounts on 6 January 1987, but a fire on 5 January 1987 destroyed her stock and accounts.

Her assets and liabilities as at 1 January 1986 were as shown in Table 13.1.

Table 13.1 *Details of assets and liabilities of Mary Martin*

	£	
Capital	31,000	
Loan	3,300	
Trade creditors	8,000	
Accrued wages	1,500	
Fixtures and fittings	11,000	(book value) original cost £27,500
Vehicle (one only)	5,000	(book value) original cost £9,000
Stock	22,500	
Debtors	2,600	
Bank	2,700	

Ms Martin held her bank statements, cheque books and paying in slips at home. From this and from other data you have determined that for the year ended 31 December 1986:

1. Cash received was £255,000, which included £8,000 from rent received from Mr L. Hageman, and £5,500 from the sale of vehicle.

2. Payments made were as shown in Table 13.2

Table 13.2 *Details of Mary Martin's payments*

Purchase new vehicle	£14,000
Purchase new fixtures/fittings	£3,400
Wages	£48,000
Purchases for resale	£158,000
Rent/rates	£12,000
Light/heat	£7,000
Drawings	£14,500
Loan interest	£561

3. Other facts (as at 31 December 1986) are:
   a. Cost of goods sold in 60 per cent of sales.
   b. All sales in 1986 were on a cash basis, all debtors are fully paid up.
   c. Wages owing – £3,500.
   d. Light and heat owing – £2,000.
   e. Rent/rates prepaid £3,000.
   f. Creditors had increased by 10 per cent over the year.
   g. Depreciation on fixtures/fittings and vehicles is 20 per cent of the book value at the end of the year.
   h. The bank balance was £239.

You are asked to prepare a trading, profit and loss account for the year ended 31 December 1986 and a balance sheet at that date.

Solution on pages 538–9. *Source: RSA, Accounting II, June 1987.*

Question 13.2
Happy Holidays Ltd is in the business of providing package camping holidays in Europe. The information of its activities during the year to 31 March is provided in Table 13.3.

Other facts are:

1. No camping equipment was lost or disposed of during the year.
2. Camping equipment is to be depreciated at $33\frac{1}{3}$ per cent of cost.
3. Sales are regarded, for the purpose of calculating annual profit/loss, as the total value of holidays provided during the year.

You are required to:
a. prepare a profit and loss account for the year ended 31 March 1987;
b. prepare a balance sheet as at 31 March 1987.

Table 13.3 *Details of the accounts of Happy Holidays Limited*

Transactions during the year ended 31 March 1987	
	£000
Cash receipts from customers	2,000
Cash payments to ferry operators and camp-site proprietors	710
Administration and advertising expense payments	245

Balances:	At 31 March 1986	At 31 March 1987
	£000	£000
deposits received from customers	200	230
deposits paid to ferry operators and camp-site proprietors	110	160
creditors (for camping equipment)	300	40
camping equipment (at cost)	3,000	3,400
advertising expenditure paid, but deferred to following period	60	60

Solution on page 540.

Question 13.3

Table 13.4 is a summary of the entries on the payments side of the bank statement of Eric, the owner of a shop specialising in banana products, for the year 1986.

Table 13.4 *Entries on the payments side of bank statement*

	£
Balance, 31 December, 1985 (overdrawn)	568
Trade creditors	33,442
Rent of business premises for 15 months to 31 March 1987	1,000
General expenses	2,872
Drawing	696
Balance 31 December 1986	234

Cheques drawn in favour of trade creditors which had not been presented amounted, at 31 December 1985, to £350 and at 31 December 1986 to £138. These cheques were presented and were paid by the bank in January 1986 and January 1987 respectively. No amounts other than business takings were paid into the bank in 1986.

The figures in Table 13.5 were taken from Eric's books.

Table 13.5 *Details of the accounts of Eric*

	31 December 1985	31 December 1986
	£	£
Stock in trade, at cost	2,540	2,832
Trade creditors	1,824	1,616
Creditors for general expenses	78	126
Furniture and fittings	1,000	1,000

All sales were for cash and, with the exception of the sale, for £660, of goods which cost £720, the gross profit margin on all sales in 1985 was 25 per cent of selling price.

Wages, £1,788, were paid out of cash takings during 1986. The balance of cash not accounted for by wages and payments into bank is to be treated as Eric's drawings.

Provide for depreciation of furniture and fittings, £100.

You are required to prepare a trading and profit and loss account for the year ended 31 December 1986 and a balance sheet as at that date and submit all workings.

Solution on page 540.

Question 13.4

a. P. Dwarf owns a retail shop, and the balances shown in Table 13.6 were taken from her balance sheet at 1 September 1984.

Table 13.6 *Balance sheet details of Ms P Dwarf*

	£
Shop fittings (cost £1,000)	800
Stock in hand	1,900
Debtors	200
Cash at bank	440
Cash in till (float)	40
Creditors	980

Table 13.7 is a summary of the bank statements for the year ended 31 August 1985.

Table 13.7 *Bank statement summary for Ms P Dwarf*

	£
Takings banked	27,932
Payments to suppliers	25,160
Rent of premises	1,600
Light and heat	340
Advertising	200
Sundry expenses	152

You were given the following additional information:

1. Takings are banked daily and all suppliers are paid by cheque, but Ms P. Dwarf keeps £60 per week for herself and pays her assistant wages of £44 per week out of cash takings prior to banking the balance.

2. The cash float was increased to £60.
3. The sundry expenses include the cost of new shelving at £100.
4. Ms P. Dwarf took £300-worth of goods for her own use.
5. Your charge for preparing the accounts has been agreed at £100.
6. The outstanding invoices show £920 due to suppliers, £40 accrued for light and heat and the customers credit accounts £340 for debts due to Ms P. Dwarf.
7. Depreciation of shop fittings is to be provided at 10 per cent on cost, a full year's charge being made in the year of purchase.
8. Stock in hand on 31 August 1985 is summarised in Table 13.8. Prepare Ms P. Dwarf's trading and profit and loss account for the year ended 31 August 1985 and her balance sheet at that date.

Table 13.8 *Stock in hand, by group*

	Cost £	Net realisable value £
Group A	720	560
Group B	1,080	1,720
Group C	920	1,160
Group D	440	280

b. Explain to Ms Dwarf what double-entry book-keeping is and advise her of the advantages accruing from adopting the system in her business.

No solution provided.

Question 13.5
Brian is considering the amount of drawings his business will be in a position to pay in respect of the year ending 31 December, year 7. The information in Table 13.9 is available.

He budgets that in year 7:

1. Though selling prices will remain the same, the volume of sales will increase by 10 per cent with sales commission increasing proportionately. By the end of year 7, it is expected that the credit period allowed to debtors will be half that allowed at 31 December, year 6.
2. Due to improved purchasing arrangements, the proportion of gross profit to sales will increase by 5 per cent.
3. Both administration expenses and wages will increase by 5 per cent.
4. Bank overdraft interest will fall by 50 per cent.
5. Loan interest will be at the same rate as in year 6.
6. Stock and creditors at 31 December will be the same amounts as they were at the end of year 6.

Table 13.9   *Details of the account of Brian's business*

Trading and profit and loss account for the year ended 31 December, year 6

	£000	£000
Sales		30,000
Less cost of goods sold		20,000
Gross profit		10,000
Less sales commissions (1 % of sales)	300	
loan interest for one year	150	
administration expenses	3,500	
wages	300	
bank overdraft interest	300	
depreciation – calculated on the reducing balance basis	2,000	
uninsured fire loss (April, year 6)	950	7,500
Net profit		2,500

Balance sheet as at 31 December, year 6

	£000	£000		£000	£000
Capital		25,000	*Fixed assets*		18,000
Retained profit		1,000			
		26,000			
Loan (repayable 30 June, year 7)		1,500	*Current assets*		
Current liabilities			Stock	5,000	
Creditors	500		Debtors	7,500	12,500
Bank	2,500	3,000			
		30,500			30,500

Prepare, for Brian, a budgeted:
1. Trading and profit and loss account for the year to 31 December, year 7.
2. Summarised bank account for the year to 31 December, year 7.
3. Balance sheet as at 31 December, year 7.

No solution provided.

14 | *Club and society accounts*

_____

- to introduce you to the accounting statements of non-profit-making organisations;
- to examine alternative methods of accounting for these organisations;
- to use the spreadsheet to prepare receipts and payments accounts, and income and expenditure accounts.

14.1   Introduction

Commercial and industrial organisations are usually run to make a profit, with profit-making their single most important goal. However, many other organisations such as clubs and societies do not share this aim. These organisations exist to provide services to their members. As a consequence, the way in which they report financial information needs to reflect this change in emphasis and this chapter will consider how we account for such organisations.

There are two main ways we can account for clubs and societies. Firstly, a receipts and payments account can be prepared and secondly an income and expenditure account and balance sheet can be prepared. We will examine each in turn.

14.2   Receipts and payments account

A receipts and payments account is no more than a summary of bank and cash transactions for the period. It is equivalent to a cash flow statement for a business, as explained in Chapter 21.

Let us consider an example. The VI Club incurs the receipts and payments as shown in Figure 14.1

Receipts:	£	£
Members' subscriptions		2,260
Donations		50
Bar takings		4,565
Raffle ticket sales		125
		7,000
Payments:		
Payments for bar supplies	157	
Bar staff wages	679	
Repairs	134	
Transfer to current account	5,460	
Transfer to deposit account	500	
		6,930
Closing recorded balance		£ 70

Figure 14.1a The VI Club – cash receipts and payments for the twelve months to 31 December 1988

	+ £	− £	Balance £
Bankings	5,460		5,460
Purchase of equipment		1,680	3,780
Raffle prizes		56	3,780
Payments for bar supplies		2,568	1,156
Rental payments		1,750	(594)
Transfer to deposit account		400	(994)

Figure 14.1b The VI Club – current bank account receipts and payments for the twelve months to 31 December 1988

	+ £	− £	Balance £
Bankings	500		500
Transfer from current account	400		900
Interest	30		930

Figure 14.1c The VI Club – deposit bank account receipts and payments for the twelve months to 31 December 1988

Cash receipts and payments are shown in Figure 14.1a, current bank account receipts and payments in 14.1b and deposit bank account receipts and payments in 14.1c.

These receipts and payments are transferred to Spreadsheet 14.1 where they are accumulated into a **total receipts and payments** column.

As can be seen, the transfers between cash and bank accounts are cancelled out, as we are not interested in such internal transfers, only the transactions with

Spreadsheet 14.1 The VI Club: receipts and payments account.

```
      |  A   ||   B   ||   C   ||   D   ||   E   ||   F   ||   G   ||   H   |
  1
  2
  3
  4   Description                    Cash    Current  Deposit          Receipts
  5                                           Bank     Bank             and
  6                                          Account  Account          Payments
  7
  8   Members Subscriptions          2260                               2260
  9   Donations                        50                                 50
 10   Bar takings                    4565                               4565
 11   Raffle Ticket Sales             125                                125
 12   Payment for Bar Supplies       -157                               -157
 13   Bar Staff Wages                -679                               -679
 14   Repairs                        -134                               -134
 15   Transfers to Current A/c      -5460     5460
 16   Transfers to Deposit A/c       -500             500
 17
 18   Purchase of Equipment                  -1680                     -1680
 19   Raffle Prizes                            -56                       -56
 20   Payment for Bar Supplies               -2568                     -2568
 21   Rental Payments                        -1750                     -1750
 22
 23   Transfers to Deposit Account            -400    400
 24
 25   Interest on Deposit Account                      30                 30
 26
 27   --------------------------------------------------------------------------
 28   Totals                           70     -994    930                  6
 29   ==========================================================================
```

```
      |  A   ||   B   ||  C  ||    D    ||    E    ||    F    ||    H    |
  1
  2
  3
  4   Description                    Cash     Current   Deposit    Receipts
  5                                            Bank      Bank       and
  6                                           Account   Account    Payments
  7
  8   Members Subscriptions          2260                          SUM(D8:F8)
  9   Donations                        50                          SUM(D9:F9)
 10   Bar takings                    4565                          SUM(D10:F10)
 11   Raffle Ticket Sales             125                          SUM(D11:F11)
 12   Payment for Bar Supplies       -157                          SUM(D12:F12)
 13   Bar Staff Wages                -679                          SUM(D13:F13)
 14   Repairs                        -134                          SUM(D14:F14)
 15   Transfers to Current A/c      -5460      -D15
 16   Transfers to Deposit A/c       -500               -D16
 17
 18   Purchase of Equipment                   -1680                SUM(D18:F18)
 19   Raffle Prizes                            -56                 SUM(D19:F19)
 20   Payment for Bar Supplies                -2568                SUM(D20:F20)
 21   Rental Payments                         -1750                SUM(D21:F21)
 22
 23   Transfers to Deposit Account            -400      -E23
 24
 25   Interest on Deposit Account                        30        SUM(D25:F25)
 26
 27   -----------------------------------------------------------------------
 28   Totals                  SUM(D1:D26) SUM(E1:E26) SUM(F1:F26) SUM(D28:F28)
 29   =======================================================================
```

		£
Receipts:		
Members' subscriptions		2,260
Donations		50
Bar takings		4,565
Raffle ticket sales		125
Interest on deposit account		30
		7,030
Payments:		
Payments for bar supplies	2,725	
Bar staff wages	679	
Repairs	134	
Purchase of equipment	1,680	
Raffle prizes	56	
Rental payments	1,750	
		7,024
Closing cash and bank		£6

Figure 14.2   The VI Club–receipts and payments account for the twelve months to 31 December 1988

outsiders. This gives us the receipts and payments account as shown in Figure 14.2.

The only difference between this account and the receipts and payments column in Spreadsheet 14.1 is that like items are grouped together; for example, bar payments (i.e. cash payments of £157 and cheque payments of £2,568 are added together to give total bar payments of £2,725).

14.3   Income and expenditure accounts

A receipts and payments account may be sufficient for a small club or society, but for a larger organisation it is often considered inadequate as it fails to disclose much important information which the members may want to know. This additional information is shown in Figure 14.3.

It consists of details of assets and liabilities at the end of the year, such as how much stock the bar contains and the amount of subscriptions owing. Such additional information can be presented to the members by way of notes to the receipts and payments account; however, it is usual to find it integrated with the receipts and payments information in the form of an income and expenditure account and balance sheet.

The balance sheet is a familiar statement to you, but the income and expenditure account is new. It is similar to a profit and loss account in that it contains income less expenditure for the period. This net figure is not called profit or loss as the organisation does not think in profit or loss terms. It is called

1. At 31 December 1988 a stocktake of bar stocks was undertaken and the value of stocks was found to be £137.
2. Unpaid bar invoices at 31 December 1988 amounted to £245.
3. Rent prepaid at 31 December 1988 amounted to £250.
4. Subscriptions paid in advance on 31 December 1988 amounted to £1,530, while £1,305 of subscriptions relating to the year ended on that date still remained due for payment.
5. The equipment purchased should last 4 years, by which time it is expected to have a negligible value. It is to be depreciated using the straight-line method.
6. The cash balance was counted on 31 December 1988 and found to be £67.

Figure 14.3 Additional information

'surplus of income over expenditure' or 'surplus of expenditure over income' depending upon whether the figure is positive or negative.

Let us see how an income and expenditure account and balance sheet can be prepared for the VI Club. The workings are shown in Spreadsheet 14.2. It takes as its base Spreadsheet 14.1, excluding the summary **receipts** and **payments** columns, and extends this single-entry system to our familiar double-entry system of recording transactions (i.e. all transactions have two entries, a positive entry termed a 'debit' and a negative entry termed a 'credit').

The income and expenditure account and balance sheet are shown in Figure 14.4.

It is worth taking a brief look at the income and expenditure account before seeing how the spreadsheet is constructed. As can be seen items of income are listed followed by items of expenditure.

If we look for details of the raffle we find a single entry (raffle profit £69) rather than two separate entries (raffle ticket sales of £125 and cost of raffle prizes £56). This netting-off is considered desirable as it shows the members the net result to club finances of this money-raising venture. It is in fact a profit-making venture for the club and enables subscriptions to be lower than would otherwise be the case. The bar is a similar example of such a profit-making activity within a non-profit-making organisation. A separate column of the spreadsheet is used to accumulate these costs and revenues before the column totals are transferred to the **income and expenditure** column.

Spreadsheet 14.2 is constructed in a similar way to that used to prepare final accounts from incomplete records in Chapter 13.

Firstly, opening balances are listed along the top row of the spreadsheet; in the case of the VI Club there are none as it only started this year.

Secondly, bank and cash entries are listed as in Spreadsheet 14.1.

Thirdly, the double entry for the bank and cash entries is recorded using conventional accounting logic, remembering to post any entries relating to a profit-making activity within the club to a separate column.

Fourthly, the columns are sub-totalled.

Fifthly, the closing balances given by way of note are recorded along the bottom row of the spreadsheet.

Sixthly, the missing accounting transactions are deduced (which makes the columns sum correctly) using your accounting knowledge; and the profit or loss on profit-making activities (i.e. the raffle and the bar) are transferred to the **income and expenditure** column.

Finally, the **income and expenditure** column is summed and the income and expenditure account and balance sheet written out in good form.

There are often other, associated problems when accounting for clubs and societies.

Firstly, many clubs offer life membership for a one-off payment. If strict matching rules are to apply, the club should capitalise these payments (i.e. credit a deferred revenue account and debit cash), and release it to the income and expenditure account over the active club life of the member. In practice, it is difficult to estimate this active club life and, since the sums of money involved are often small, any monies for granting life membership are taken to the income and expenditure account in the year it is receivable.

Secondly, many clubs require a joining or entrance fee to be paid separately from the yearly subscription. If such fees are to cover the administrative costs associated with admitting a new member, it is sensible to take the monies received as income in the period in which they are due. However, if they represent an advanced payment to cover many years (i.e. as a sort of commitment payment), then they should be released to income over the active club life of the member. Normally, they are treated as income in the year of receipt for similiar reasons to the life member situation.

Thirdly, at the year end all subscriptions owing to the club should be re-viewed to see that they are still collectable. As members often move from the area, leaving no forwarding address, some of these debts may have to be written off or provided against. See Chapter 6 for the procedure to account for bad and doubtful debts.

CHECKLIST

Having completed Chapter 14, you should be able to:

- discuss alternative methods of accounting for non-profit-making organisations;
- use the spreadsheet to prepare receipts and payments accounts, and income and expenditure accounts.

Spreadsheet 14.2 The VI Club: income and expenditure account

	A		C	D	E	F	G	H	I	J	K	L	M	N
1														
2														
3														
4	Description		Cash	Current Bank Account	Deposit Bank Account	Subs	Income And Expend're	Bar Profit and Loss	Bar Stocks	Bar Creditors	Raffle	Equipment	Rent	
8	Members Subscriptions		2260			-2260								
9	Donations		50				-50							
10	Bar takings		4565					-4565						
11	Raffle Ticket Sales		125								-125			
12	Payment for Bar Supplies		-157							157				
13	Bar Staff Wages		-679					679						
14	Repairs		-134				134							
15	Transfers to Current A/c		-5460	5460										
16	Transfers to Deposit A/c		-500		500									
18	Purchase of Equipment			-1680								1680		
19	Raffle Prizes			-56							56			
20	Payment for Bar Supplies			-2568						2568				
21	Rental Payments			-1750									1750	
23	Transfers to Deposit Account			-400	400									
25	Interest on Deposit Account				30		-30							
27	-----													
28	Subtotals		70	-994	930	-2260	54	-3886	0	2725	-69	1680	1750	
30	Cash Loss		-3				3							
31	-----													
32	Subtotals		67	-994	930	-2260	57	-3886	0	2725	-69	1680	1750	
34	Subscriptions					2485	-2485							
35	Bar Purchases								2970	-2970				
37	Bar Cost of goods sold							2833	-2833					
38	Bar Profit						-1053	1053						
39	Raffle Profit						-69				69			
40	Rent						1500						-1500	
41	Depreciation Equipment						420					-420		
45	-----													
46	Closing Balance Sheet		67	-994	930	225	-1630	0	137	-245	0	1260	250	
47	=====													

(*continued*)

Spreadsheet 14.2 *(Continued)*

	A	B	C	D	E	F	G
1							
2							
3							
4	Description		Cash		Current Bank	Deposit Bank	Subs
5					Bank	Bank	
6					Account	Account	
7							
8	Members Subscriptions		2260				-D8
9	Donations		50				
10	Bar takings		4565				
11	Raffle Ticket Sales		125				
12	Payment for Bar Supplies		-157				
13	Bar Staff Wages		-679				
14	Repairs		-134				
15	Transfers to Current A/c		-5460	-D15			
16	Transfers to Deposit A/c		-500			-D16	
17							
18	Purchase of Equipment			-1680			
19	Raffle Prizes			-56			
20	Payment for Bar Supplies			-2568			
21	Rental Payments			-1750			
22							
23	Transfers to Deposit Account			-400	-E23		
24							
25	Interest on Deposit Account					30	
26							
27	--						
28	Subtotals			SUM(D1:D26)	SUM(E1:E26)	SUM(F1:F26)	SUM(G1:G26)
29							
30	Cash Loss		-3				
31	--						
32	Subtotals			SUM(D28:D30)	SUM(E28:E30)	SUM(F28:F30)	SUM(G28:G30)
33							
34	Subscriptions						-G32+G46
35	Bar Purchases						
36							
37	Bar Cost of goods sold						
38	Bar Profit						
39	Raffle Profit						
40	Rent						
41	Depreciation	Equipment					
42							
43							
44							
45	--						
46	Closing Balance Sheet			SUM(D32:D44)	SUM(E32:E44)	SUM(F32:F44)	225
47	==						

	H	I	J	K	L	M	N
	Income And Expend're	Bar Profit and Loss	Bar Stocks	Bar Creditors	Raffle	Equipment	Rent
	-D9						
		-D10					
					-D11		
				-D12			
		-D13					
	-D14						
						-E18	
					-E19		
				-E20			
							-E21
	-F25						
	SUM(H1:H26)	SUM(I1:I26)	SUM(J1:J26)	SUM(K1:K26)	SUM(L1:L26)	SUM(M1:M26)	SUM(N1:N26)
	-D30						
	SUM(H28:H30)	SUM(I28:I30)	SUM(J28:J30)	SUM(K28:K30)	SUM(L28:L30)	SUM(M28:M30)	SUM(N28:N30)
	-G34						
			-K35	-K32+K46			
		-J37	-J35-J36+J46				
	-I38	-I32-I37					
	-L39				-L32-L46		
	-N40						-N32+N46
	-M41					-(M18/4)	
	SUM(H32:H44)	SUM(I32:I44)	137	-245	0	SUM(N32:N44)	250

Balance sheet as at 31 December 1988

	Cost £	Depreciation £	£
FIXED ASSETS			
Equipment	1680	420	1260
CURRENT ASSETS			
Bar stocks		137	
Debtors for subs		1530	
Rent prepaid		250	
Deposit account		930	
Cash		67	
		2914	
LESS CURRENT LIABILITIES			
Bar creditors	245		
Sub. creditors	1305		
Current account	994		
		2544	
			370
			1630
FINANCED BY			
Surplus of income over expenditure			1630

INCOME AND EXPENDITURE ACCOUNT
for the year ended 31 December 1988

INCOME			
Subscriptions			2485
Bar profit			1053
Raffle profit			69
Donations			50
Interest on deposit account			30
			3687
EXPENDITURE			
Repairs		134	
Cash Loss		3	
Rent		1500	
Depreciation on equipment		420	
			2057
			1630

Figure 14.4 The VI's Club's Final Accounts

Workshop 14.1: Club and society accounts

The Sharks Swimming Club incurs the cash receipts and payments, current bank account receipts and payments and deposit bank account receipts and payments shown in Figure 14.5 during its first year of operating.

Additional information

1. At 31 December 19X8, a stocktake of bar stocks was undertaken and the value of stocks was found to be £464.

2. Unpaid bar invoices at 31 December 19X8 amounted to £592.

3. Hire charges prepaid at 31 December 19X8 amounted to £157.

4. Subscriptions paid in advance on 31 December 19X8 amounted to £920, while £605 of subscriptions related to the year ended on that date still remained due for payment.

5. The equipment purchased should last four years, by which time it is expected to have a negligible value. It is to be depreciated using the straight-line method.

Cash receipts and payments for the year ended 31 December 19X8.

Receipts:	£	£
Members' subscriptions		4,620
Donations		140
Bar takings		9,620
Sponsored events		490
		14,870
Payments:		
Payments for bar supplies	420	
Bar staff wages	2,170	
Repairs	244	
Transfer to current account	10,350	
Transfer to deposit account	1,600	
		14,784
Closing recorded balance		£ 86

Current bank account receipts and payments for the year ended 31 December 19X8.

	+ £	− £
Bankings	10,350	
Purchase of equipment		672
Swimming prizes		642
Payments for bar supplies		5,948
Hire of pool		2,918
Transfer to deposit account		200

Deposit bank account receipts and payments, for the year ended 31 December 19X8.

	+ £	− £
Bankings	1,600	
Transfer from current account	200	
Interest	120	

Figure 14.5 The Sharks Swimming Club

6. The cash balance was counted on 31 December 19X8 and found to be £81.

7. Some of the galas are sponsored by local organisations who supply the money for prizes. However, the club sometimes has to contribute to such activities.

Workshop guide

1. The first stage is to construct the double entries for the cash and bank accounts on the spreadsheet. Most of these are straightforward, but care should be taken not to double count the entries between cash and bank accounts. Accounts need to be opened for any working capital balances that exist at the year end.

2. The adjustments for accruals and prepayments, including stock adjustments, need to be completed before the income and expenditure account can be drawn up. However, this is a similar process to the incomplete records workshop.

3. The cash loss is charged to the income and expenditure account, and the depreciation charge is netting-off the cost of the asset in column M.

4. The completed accounts are given in Spreadsheet 14.3 and Figure 14.6.

'What if?' problems

1. What would happen to the surplus if the cash balance, when counted, came to £96?

2. What would be the effect on the surplus if £200 was transferred from the deposit account to cash account? Record this entry in place of row 22.

3. Change the formula for calculating the depreciation charge in cell M40 to take account of the newly assessed scrap value of £200. What effect does this have on the accumulated fund and the balance sheet?

4. Subscriptions prepaid and owing were recorded incorrectly. It should have been £920 owing and £605 prepaid. Change cell G45 to correct this error. What is the effect on the income and expenditure account?

5. One member of the committee does not understand an income and expenditure account and would prefer a receipts and payments account instead. Provide one for him in column Q.

Spreadsheet 14.3a   Workshop 14.1: The Sharks Swimming Club–solution

	Cash	Current Bank Account	Deposit Bank Account	Subs	Income And Expend're	Bar Profit and Loss	Bar Stocks	Bar Creditors	Sponsored Events	Equipment	Rent
Member's Subscriptions	4620			-4620							
Donations	140				-140						
Bar takings	9620					-9620					
Sponsored Events	490								-490		
Payment for Bar Supplies	-420							420			
Bar Staff Wages	-2170					2170					
Repairs	-244				244						
Transfers to Current A/c	-10350	10350									
Transfers to Deposit A/c	-1600		1600								
Purchase of Equipment		-672								672	
Swimming Prizes		-642							642		
Payment for Bar Supplies		-5948						5948			
Hire of Pool		-2918									2918
Transfers to Deposit Account		-200	200								
Interest on Deposit Account			120		-120						
Subtotals	86	-30	1920	-4620	-16	-7450	0	6368	152	672	2918
Cash Loss	-5				5						
Subtotals	81	-30	1920	-4620	-11	-7450	0	6368	152	672	2918
Subscriptions				4935	-4935						
Bar Purchases							6960	-6960			
Bar Cost of goods sold						6496	-6496				
Bar Profit					-954	954					
Sponsored Events					152				-152		
Rent					2761						-2761
Depreciation Equipment					168					-168	
Closing Balance Sheet	81	-30	1920	315	-2819	0	464	-592	0	504	157

(continued)

Spreadsheet 14.3b   Workshop 14.1: The Sharks Swimming Club—formulae

	A	B	C	D	E	F	G
1							
2							
3	Description			Cash	Current	Deposit	Subs
4					Bank	Bank	
5					Account	Account	
6							
7	Member's Subscriptions			4620			-D7
8	Donations			140			
9	Bar takings			9620			
10	Sponsored Events			490			
11	Payment for Bar Supplies			-420			
12	Bar Staff Wages			-2170			
13	Repairs			-244			
14	Transfers to Current A/c			-10350	-D14		
15	Transfers to Deposit A/c			-1600		-D15	
16							
17	Purchase of Equipment				-672		
18	Swimming Prizes				-642		
19	Payment for Bar Supplies				-5948		
20	Hire of Pool				-2918		
21							
22	Transfers to Deposit Account				-200	-E22	
23							
24	Interest on Deposit Account					120	
25							
26	---						
27	Subtotals			SUM(D1:D25)	SUM(E1:E25)	SUM(F1:F25)	SUM(G1:G25)
28							
29	Cash Loss			-5			
30	---						
31	Subtotals			SUM(D27:D29)	SUM(E27:E29)	SUM(F27:F29)	SUM(G27:G29)
32							
33	Subscriptions						-G31+G45
34	Bar Purchases						
35							
36	Bar Cost of goods sold						
37	Bar Profit						
38	Sponsored Events						
39	Rent						
40	Depreciation	Equipment					
41							
42							
43							
44	---						
45	Closing Balance Sheet			SUM(D31:D43)	SUM(E31:E43)	SUM(F31:F43)	920-605
46	===						

H	I	J	K	L	M	N
Income And Expend're	Bar Profit and Loss	Bar Stocks	Bar Creditors	Sponsored Events	Equipment	Rent

-D8

    -D9

                                  -D10

                        -D11

    -D12

-D13

                                                -E17

                                  -E18

                        -E19

                                                    -E20

-F24

```
----------------------------------------------------------------------------
SUM(H1:H25)  SUM(I1:I25)  SUM(J1:J25)  SUM(K1:K25)  SUM(L1:L25)  SUM(M1:M25)  SUM(N1:N25)

-D29
----------------------------------------------------------------------------
SUM(H27:H29) SUM(I27:I29) SUM(J27:J29) SUM(K27:K29) SUM(L27:L29) SUM(M27:M29) SUM(N27:N29)

-G33
                          -K34         -K31+K45
              -J36         -J34+J45
-I37          -I31-I36
-L38                                    -L31-L45
-N39                                                              -N31+N45
-M40                                                 -(M17/4)

----------------------------------------------------------------------------
SUM(H31:H43) SUM(I31:I43) 464          -592         0           SUM(M31:M43) 157
============================================================================
```

Income and expenditure account for the year ended 31 December 19X8

INCOME	£	£	£
Subscriptions			4935
Bar profit			954
Sponsored events			− 152
Donations			140
Interest on deposit account			120
			5997
EXPENDITURE			
Repairs		244	
Cash loss		5	
Rent		2761	
Depreciation on equipment		168	
			3178
			2819

Balance sheet as at 31 December 19X8

FIXED ASSETS

	Cost	Depreciation	
Equipment	672	168	504

CURRENT ASSETS			
Bar stocks		464	
Debtors for subs		920	
Rent prepaid		157	
Deposit account		1920	
Cash		81	
		3542	
LESS CURRENT LIABILITIES			
Bar creditors	592		
Sub. creditors	605		
Current account	30		
		1227	
			2315
			2819

Figure 14.6   The Sharks' Swimming Club Final Accounts

Answers

1.   It would increase by £15.

2.   No effect on surplus, just bank balances.

3.   Formula becomes   **−(M17 − 200)/4**. Depreciation then falls to £118. The fund balance is now £2,884.

4.   Cell becomes 605–920. Surplus becomes £2,254.

5.   All columns E and F. Balance = £1,890 Dr.

Selected questions and exercises

Question 14.1
Table 14.1 is a summary of the bank account of the Northminster Arts Centre for the year ended 31 December 1986.

Table 14.1 *Northminster Arts Centre Bank Account for year ended 31 December 1986*

Bank summary			
	£		£
Balance at bank @		Payments for bar supplies	56,100
1 January 1986	7,200	Rates	3,600
Bar takings	84,200	Equipment	30,400
Rents received	6,400	Light and heat	3,800
Members' subscriptions	7,800	Telephone	1,800
Overdrawn balance @		General expenses	2,900
31 December 1986	2,700	Administrator's salary	9,700
	108,300		108,300

You are able to ascertain the following:

1. Weekly wages for part-time bar staff amounting to £60 per week are paid in cash before takings are banked.
2. Suppliers' invoices for crisps, tobacco, etc., which have been resold in the bar amount to £4900. These have been paid in cash.
3. Ten members have prepaid their 1987 subscriptions of £5 each.
4. Equipment is to be depreciated by £7,500.
5. Bar stocks on 31 December increased by £200 since 1 January while creditors for the bar purchases fell by £100 in the same period.

Assets and liabilities on 1 January 1986 were as shown in Table 14.2

Table 14.2 *Assets and liabilities as at 1 January 1986*

	£
Premises (at cost)	60,000
Equipment (book value)	50,000
Bar stocks	8,100
Creditors for bar supplies	6,200

You are required to prepare a bar trading and an income and expenditure account for the year ended 31 December 1986 and a balance sheet as at that date.

Solution on pages 541–3. *Source: RSA, Accounting II, March 1987*

Question 14.2

The Allied Bowls Club presents you with the data in Table 14.3 for the year ended 31 December 1987.

Table 14.3 *Details of accounts of Allied Bowls Club*

Receipts	£	Payments	£
Subscriptions received	34,000	Rates	1,200
Dance takings	15,000	General expenses	28,000
		Dance expenses	8,000

You are also advised that:

	31 December 1986 £	31 December 1987 £
Subscriptions owing	1,400	1,200
Subscriptions pre-paid	200	300
Premises (at cost of £90,000)	40,000	36,000
Fixtures and fittings		
(at cost of £20,000)	6,000	4,000
Bank	2,000	13,800

You are asked to:

1. Present the income and expenditure account for the year ended 31 December 1987, highlighting the surplus/deficit of the dance.
2. Calculate the accumulated fund as at 31 December 1986 and at 31 December 1987.

Solution on pages 543–4.

15 | *Partnership accounts*

AIMS OF CHAPTER _____

- to introduce the student to the concept of a business trading as a partnership;
- to specify the rules of accounting for partnerships;
- to examine the accounts initiating the partnership, and the allocation of profits among partners, using a spreadsheet approach;
- to record interest on capital, drawings and the payment of salaries, using the spreadsheet to examine 'what if?' scenarios and the impact on the final accounts;
- to examine the accounting procedures for changes in partnership structure, including the introduction and exit of partners;
- to introduce students to the concept of goodwill, its measurement and accounting treatment;
- to record the accounting transactions necessary to dissolve a partnership using a realisation account.

NB Some of the workshops in this chapter rely on the model used in the text. It is therefore recommended that the student works through the material inputting the example as he/she goes along.

15.1 Introduction

Up to now we have only considered businesses owned by one person, that is, sole traders. Now it is time to consider how we can account for businesses owned by more than one person. This chapter will examine how we can account for partnerships and the next chapter will examine how we can account for companies.

A partnership can be defined as a business owned by between two and twenty people. The upper limit is placed upon the organisation by the 1890 Partnership Act. The Act does allow professional businesses such as accountants and solicitors to exceed this upper limit of twenty members, as the rules of the professional bodies prevent these businesses trading as companies.

A partnership can come into being when a sole trading business grows to such a size that the original owner can no longer supply all the resources necessary to enable the business to develop as they wish. Alternatively, a business can start off as a partnership with the individuals involved pooling their resources; one individual may not have sufficient resources or be willing to risk all their capital in the business.

15.1.1   What are these resources?

They can be capital in the form of money or other assets invested in the business, or expertise possessed by one of the partners, such as marketing or accounting skills.

Each partner is liable for the full debts of the partnership. This means if the business cannot pay its debts, then the partners' personal wealth, such as their houses and motor cars, will be sold to pay the partnership's creditors. If one partner does not possess sufficient wealth to pay his/her share of the debts the other partners have to make good any deficiency. Therefore it is essential to be very careful about who one goes into partnership with!

The exception to this unlimited liability rule are limited partners, allowed by the 1907 Partnership Act, whose liability is limited to the money they invest in the business. (This idea of limited liability will be fully explained in Chapter 16.) However, the price paid for this limited liability is that the partners concerned cannot take part in the running of the business; this means that in effect there must be at least one non-limited partner.

15.2   Accounting for partners

Now we are in the situation of having more than one owner of the business, it becomes necessary to establish rules as to how much capital is to be introduced by each partner and how the business profits (and losses should they arise) are to be allocated. These rules are usually laid down in a partnership agreement drawn up by a solicitor, so that it can be referred to by the accountant (i.e. you) when preparing the organisation's financial statements, and to enable the individual partners to see that they are being fairly treated. If a partnership agreement does not exist or does not cover a certain point, Section 24 of the Partnership Act 1890 comes into force. These requirements are shown in Figure 15.1.

1. All partners are entitled to share equally in the capital and profits of the business, and must contribute equally to losses.
2. The firm must indemnify every partner in respect of payments made or liabilities incurred by him in the ordinary and proper conduct of the business.
3. A partner making any payment or advance *beyond* the amount of capital which he has agreed to subscribe is entitled to interest at 5 per cent per annum from the date of the payment or advance.
4. A partner is not entitled, before the ascertainment of profits, to interest on the capital subscribed by him.
5. No partner shall be entitled to remuneration (salaries, wages, etc.) from the partnership.
6. The partnership books are to be kept at the place of business of the partnership, and every partner may have access to inspect and copy them.

Figure 15.1   Partnership Act 1890: Section 24 rules

Let us now look in some detail at how we can record the effects of the partnership agreement on our spreadsheet (Spreadsheet 15.1).

15.2.1   Introduction of capital into the business

It is necessary to have a separate column in the spreadsheet for each partner's capital, so that we maintain a record of how much each partner has introduced into the business. For example, if partner A contributes £1,500 in cash and partner B contributes £2,500 (£1,000 in cash and £1,500 in the form of a motor car), these transactions can be recorded as shown in Spreadsheet 16.1. Partner A has a total of £1,500 in his capital column and partner B a total of £2,500 in his capital column. The assets they contributed total £2,500 of cash and £1,500 in the form of a motor car to be used in the business.

Spreadsheet 15.1   Partners starting a business

	A	B	C	D	E	F	G
1							
2							
3		Description		Capital	Capital	Cash	Motor
4				A	B		Car
5							
6		A Contributes Cash		−1500		1500	
7							
8		B Contributes Cash			−1000	1000	
9							
10		B Contributes a			−1500		1500
11		Motor Car					
12							
13							
14		Balance Sheet		−1500	−2500	2500	1500

15.2.2   Allocation of profits and losses

We need to consider the following points.

Ratio used to divide up the profits and losses

There are many ways in which the profits and losses of the business can be allocated between the partners. Some of these ways are listed below:

a. equally between the partners, so if there are two partners each gets 50 per cent;

b. in proportion to the amount of capital each has invested in the business. For example, if partner A contributes £2,000 and partner B £3,000, then profits and losses are split 2:3.

These profit (and loss) splits represent allocations of profit to the partners' capitals.

For convenience it is common practice to provide each partner with two capital columns; these are rather confusingly referred to as a 'capital column' and a 'current column'. The reason for this division is to enable capital introduced to be recorded in the **capital** column and the partner's share of profit (or loss) to be recorded in the **current** column.

Let us see how this works by considering the following illustrative example. There are two partners A and B, who agree to split profits and losses in the ratio 2:3. The business has been trading for a year and its balance is shown in Table 15.1.

This balance sheet, together with the profit allocation, is shown in Spreadsheet 15.2. As can be seen, each partner has both a **capital** and a **current** column. The profit is split in the agreed ratio of 2:3, so A is credited with £1,600 and B with £2,400. These amounts are recorded as increases in the partners' **current** columns and reductions in the **profit and loss** column.

Notice the use made of relative cell referencing utilising cells F2 and G2. By

Table 15.1   *Partnership balance sheet of A and B*

	£s
Assets	10,000
Liabilities	2,000
	8,000
Capitals: A	1,500
B	2,500
Profit for year	4,000
	8,000

Spreadsheet 15.2a and b Dividing the profits in the partners' allocation ratio

	A	B	C	D	E	F	G	H	I	J
1										
2		Allocation Ratio:			2	3				
3										
4		Description		Assets	Liabilities	Capital	Capital	Profit	Current	Current
5						A	B		A	B
6		Balance Sheet		10000	-2000	-1500	-2500	-4000		
7		before allocation								
8										
9		A's profit alloacation						1600	-1600	
10										
11		B's profit allocation						2400		-2400
12										
13		---------								---------
14		Balance sheet		10000	-2000	-1500	-2500	0	-1600	-2400
15		after allocation								
16		=======								=======

	A	B	C	D	E	F	G	H	I	J
1										
2		Allocation Ratio:				2	3			
3										
4		Description		Assets	Liabilities	Capital	Capital	Profit	Current	Current
5						A	B		A	B
6		Balance Sheet		10000	-2000	-1500	-2500	-4000		
7		before allocation								
8										
9		A's profit alloacation						-H6*F2/(F2+G	-H9	
10										
11		B's profit allocation						-H6*G2/(F2+G2)		-H11
12										
13		---------								---------
14		Balance sheet		SUM(D6:D11)	SUM(E6:E11)	SUM(F6:F11)	SUM(G6:G11)	SUM(H6:H11)	SUM(I6:I11)	SUM(J6:J11)
15		after allocation								
16		=======								=======

changing the ratio, the effect on profit allocation can be readily seen. Why not try some of your own 'what if?' problems to see the effect of changing the ratio, or try changing the profit figure. It is important to isolate the ratios in separate cells, as we will see later.

Interest on capital

It is frequently the case that partners contribute different amounts of capital into the business. Rather than split the profits in this proportion (which might not be fair, as the partners may put in roughly the same amount of work effort and skills

Spreadsheet 15.3   Allocating interest on capital before dividing profits

	A	B	C	F	G	H	I	J
1		Interest Rate		10%				
2		Allocation Ratio:		2	3			
3								
4		Description		Capital	Capital	Profit	Current	Current
5				A	B		A	B
6		Balance Sheet		-1500	-2500	-4000		
7		before allocation						
8								
9		A's Interest on Capita				150	-150	
10								
11		B's Interest on Capita				250		-250
12		--------					--------	
13		Balance Sheet		-1500	-2500	-3600	-150	-250
14								
15		A's profit allocation				1440	-1440	
16								
17		B's profit allocation				2160		-2160
18								
19		--------					--------	
20		Balance sheet		-1500	-2500	0	-1590	-2410

```
 J11        Form=G6*F1/100
Width:  9  Memory: 254  Last Col/Row:K34     ? for HELP
   1>
F1=Help F2=Cancel F9=Plot F10=View
```

into the business), the partners may decide to pay each other interest on the capital they invest before splitting up the profits. The interest rate used should be specified in the partnership agreement. It may be fixed at 10 per cent, say, or be a variable rate such as the rate paid by a commercial bank on deposit account.

Interest on capital represents an allocation of profits before it is split in the profit-sharing ratio. Let us extend our example to see how this works. Suppose each partner is entitled to 10 per cent p.a. interest on their capital. A is therefore entitled to £150 and B to £250. Spreadsheet 15.3 shows these allocations of profit. Now there is only £3,600 of profit remaining to be split between the partners in the agreed profit-sharing ratio of 2:3; partner A receives £1,440 and partner B £2,160.

Notice how 'title' facilities have been used to present 'screen prints' of the spreadsheet. These are useful features contained in most good packages which are well worth mastering. They enable you to see exactly which column the entry is being recorded in. Notice also that rows have been inserted and column widths varied. This displays the versatility of the spreadsheet. You do not have to start from the beginning, as such amendments are easy to do and undo. These are all good presentational features. The important element is the use of the relative cell referencing. What if the interest rate changes to 20 per cent? Try it and see what happens. Does your balance sheet still balance? If not, check your spreadsheet formulae with the model at the end of the chapter.

If we compare the bottom line of Spreadsheet 15.3 with that of 15.2, we see that the current column totals are different. With no interest on capital, A is entitled to £1,600 and B to £2,400, while with interest on capital A is entitled to £1,590 and B £2,410. This increase in B's entitlement is due to B investing £1,000 more in the business than A.

Interest on drawings

Partners may decide to draw cash (or other assets) out of the business during the year, for their own personal expenditures (such as living expenses and holidays). To ensure equality between partners (as one partner may be continually drawing out assets, while the others do not), and to discourage the drawing of excessive amounts of cash out of the business, partners can be charged interest on their drawings. The rate of interest is usually established in the partnership agreement and is usually charged from the date the withdrawal is made. These charges represent reductions in the individual partner's **current** column and increases in the total profit available for allocation.

Let us extend our example once more to include interest on drawings at 20 per cent p.a. We need to know how much each partner has drawn out during the year and when the drawing took place. If we assume A drew out £1,000 on 31 March 1988 and B £600 on 1 June 1988 and £2,400 on 30 November 1988, the interest on drawings is shown in Table 15.2.

Note how we only charge interest on the number of months between the date of withdrawal and the year end, since this is the time period the partners had use of the cash.

Spreadsheet 15.4 shows how this interest on drawings is recorded. The **profit and loss** column is increased and the partners' **current** columns are reduced. The now increased profit available for splitting is £3,935, which is split in the agreed ratio of 2:3.

Salaries

A partner may be entitled (as specified in the partnership agreement) to receive a salary as well as any profit split and interest on capital. This may be to

Table 15.2 *Interest on drawings for A and B*

$$A \quad £1,500 * \frac{20}{100} * \frac{9}{12} = £225$$

$$B \quad £\ 600 * \frac{20}{100} * \frac{7}{12} = 70$$

$$£2,400 * \frac{20}{100} * \frac{1}{12} = 40$$

$$£110$$

Spreadsheet 15.4a and b   Recording the interest on drawings

	B	C	D	E	F	G	H	I	J
1	Interest Rate				10%				
2	Allocation Ratio:			2	3				
3									
4	Description		Assets	Liabilities	Capital	Capital	Profit	Current	Current
5					A	B		A	B
6	Balance Sheet		10000	-2000	-1500	-2500	-4000		
7	before allocation								
8									
9	A's Interest on Capital						150	-150	
10									
11	B's Interest on Capital						250		-250
12									
13	A's Interest on Drawings						-225	225	
14									
15	B's Interest on Drawings						-110		110
16	--
17	Balance Sheet		10000	-2000	-1500	-2500	-3935	75	-140
18									
19	A's profit allocation						1574	-1574	
20									
21	B's profit allocation						2361		-2361
22									
23	--
24	Balance sheet		10000	-2000	-1500	-2500	0	-1499	-2501
25	after allocation								
26	==

	B	C	F	G	H	I	J
1	Interest Rate	10	%				
2	Allocation Ratio:	2	3				
3							
4	Description		Capital	Capital	Profit	Current	Current
5			A	B		A	B
6	Balance Sheet		-1500	-2500	-4000		
7	before allocation						
8							
9	A's Interest on Capital				-I9	F6*F1/100	
10							
11	B's Interest on Capital				-J11		66*F1/100
12							
13	A's Interest on Drawings				-I13	1500*(20/100)*(9/12)	
14							
15	B's Interest on Drawings				-J15		((600*20/100*7/12)+(2400*20/100*1/12))
16	---
17	Balance Sheet		SUM(F6:F15)	SUM(G6:G15)	SUM(H6:H15)	SUM(I6:I15)	SUM(J6:J15)
18							
19	A's profit allocation				-H17*F2/(F2+G2)	-H19	
20							
21	B's profit allocation				-H17*G2/(F2+G2)	-H21	
22							
23	---
24	Balance sheet		SUM(F17:F22)	SUM(G17:G22)	SUM(H17:H22)	SUM(I17:I22)	SUM(J17:J22)
25	after allocation						
26	===

Spreadsheet 15.5 The payment of salaries to partners

	A	B	C	D	E	F	G	H	I	J
1		Interest Rate					10%			
2		Allocation Ratio:				2	3			
3										
4		Description		Assets	Liabilities	Capital	Capital	Profit	Current	Current
5						A	B		A	B
6		Balance Sheet		10000	-2000	-1500	-2500	-4000		
7		before allocation								
8										
9		A's Interest on Capital						150	-150	
10										
11		B's Interest on Capital						250		-250
12										
13		A's Interest on Drawings						-225	225	
14										
15		B's Interest on Drawings						-110		110
16										
17		A's Salary						2500	-2500	
18										
19		-------								---
20		Balance Sheet		10000	-2000	-1500	-2500	-1435	-2425	-140
21										
22		A's profit allocation						574	-574	
23										
24		B's profit allocation						861		-861
25										
26		-------								---
27		Balance sheet		10000	-2000	-1500	-2500	0	-2999	-1001
28		after allocation								
29		=======								===

compensate for additional duties, special expertise (e.g. marketing) or a poor or even no allocation of profits (this is often the case with a junior partner). These salaries are allocations of profit (just like interest on capital) to the respective partner's **current** column. We can extend our example to show how partners' salaries are recorded. If A receives a salary of £2,500 p.a. the allocation out of profit into A's **current** column is shown in Spreadsheet 15.5. The reduced profit of £1,435 is then split in the agreed ratio of 3:3, giving A £574 and B £861.

The allocation of the business profit as shown in the profit and loss column is often written up as a separate statement (or as a continuation of the profit and loss account) and called a profit and loss appropriation account. This is shown in Figure 15.2.

Workshop 15.1

A partnership consisting of three partners has made a profit of £10,000 for the year ended 31 December 1988. The profit sharing ratio is A = 25 per cent, B = 45

Profit and loss appropriation account for the year ended 31 December, 1988

	£	£
Net profit		4,000
Less interest on capital:		
A	150	
B	250	
		400
		2,600
Add interest on drawings:		
A	225	
B	110	
		335
		3,955
Less A's salary		2,500
		1,455
Less profit split:		
A	574	
B	861	
		1,455

Figure 15.2 Profit and loss appropriation account for the year ended 31 December 1988

per cent and C = 30 per cent. During the year A drew £2,000 out of the business on 1 July, B £500 on 31 March and C £5,000 on 1 February. The balance sheet for the year ended 31 December 1988, before the allocation of profit, is shown in Table 15.3.

You are required to use your spreadsheet to:

1. Record the allocation of profit by accounting for interest on capital of 7 per cent p.a. and salaries of £2,000 to A and £4,000 to C, interest on drawings of 15 per cent p.a. and the profit split.

2. Prepare a profit and loss appropriation account.

Table 15.3 *A, B and C's partnership balance sheet before allocation of profit*

	£s
Assets	54,000
Liabilities	7,000
	47,000
	£s
Capital accounts: A	5,000
B	12,000
C	20,000
Profit for the year	10,000
	47,000

Spreadsheet 15.6   Workshop 15.1 – solution

	Description	Assets	Liabilities	Capital A	Capital B	Capital C	Profit	Current A	Current B	Current C
1										
2	Interest on Capital		7%							
3	Interest on Drawings		15%							
4	Allocation Ratio:			25	45	30				
5										
6	Description	Assets	Liabilities	Capital	Capital	Capital	Profit	Current	Current	Current
7				A	B	C		A	B	C
8	Balance Sheet	54000	-7000	-5000	-12000	-20000	-10000			
9	before allocation									
10										
11	A's interest on						350	-350		
12	capital									
13									0	
14	B's interest on						840			
15	capital									
16										
17	C's interest on						1400			
18	capital									
19										
20	A's interest on						-150	150		
21	drawings									
22										
23	B's interest on						-56		56	
24	drawings									
25										
26	C's interest on						-688			688
27	drawings									
28										
29	A's salary						2000	-2000		
30										
31	C's salary						4000			-4000
32	----------									
33	Balance sheet	54000	-7000	-5000	-12000	-20000	-2304	-2200	56	
34	before profit split									
35										
36	A's profit alloacation						576	-576		
37										
38	B's profit allocation						1037		-1037	
39										
40	C's profit allocation						691			-691
41	----------									
42	Balance sheet	54000	-7000	-5000	-12000	-20000	0	-2776	-980	-691
43	after allocation									
44	==========									

Workshop guide

As the workshop is based on the model in the text, no guide is necessary. For explanations refer to the preceeding pages.

'What if?' problems

1. The interest on capital changes from 7 per cent to 10 per cent. What is the new profit allocation?

2. What is the new profit allocation if the interest on drawings changes from 15 per cent to 10 per cent?

Answers

1. Profit allocation: A = £298; B = £537; C = £358.

2. Profit allocation: A = £224; B = £403; C = £269.

15.3   Accounting for changes in partners

Partnerships are often subject to changes. For example, a partner may leave the partnership (or die), a new partner may be admitted or the existing partners may simply decide to change their agreed profit-sharing ratio. We need to account for these changes and it is these tasks that we will now consider.

The first step is to determine how much the partnership is worth, so that we have a current valuation for the business, which is used to see how much each partner is entitled to. We cannot use the partnership balance sheet because it is not designed to measure the current value of the business; this is a result of two conventions used in its construction.

15.3.1   The historic cost convention

Assets are recorded at their historic cost and no value change is made in the carrying value of assets, until they are sold. Therefore unsold assets are recorded at their historic cost, which may bear no relationship to the asset's current value (i.e. what it would cost to replace or the proceeds it would realise if sold). Let us consider a piece of land owned by the business, which was purchased for £1,000 five years ago. It will still be recorded at £1,000 in the partnership balance sheet, while its current value may be £5,000. We need to record this extra £4,000 in the balance sheet, to show its up-to-date value. This is achieved by uplifting the

Table 15.4 *Partnership balance sheet as at 31 December 1988*

	£
Land	1,000
Machine	2,000
Stock	900
Debtors	800
Bank and cash	200
Creditors	(400)
	4,500
Capitals: A	1,000
B	1,500
C	2,000
	4,500

recorded value of the asset in the **asset** column (i.e. debit the **asset** column) and record the other side of the entry (i.e. a credit entry) in a newly opened column entitled **revaluation**.

Of course, we may need to record a fall in the value of an asset; for example a computer bought last year may now have been superseded by a new, much improved version which sells at half the price of the original version. We record this fall in value of an asset by reducing the asset value (net of any depreciation or other provision already recorded) to its current cost (i.e. a credit entry) and reducing the **revaluation** column (i.e. a debit entry).

Let us consider the following example, to see how to use the revaluation column. The partnership balance sheet as at 31 December 1988 is as shown in Table 15.4. The partners have agreed to share profits in the ratio A = 10 per cent B = 35 per cent and C = 55 per cent.

The current value of the land is £5,000, the machine £1,500 and the stock £850. Included in the debtors is a debt of £150 which is irrecoverable; no adjustment has yet been made in the above balance sheet to reflect this.

You are required to prepare, using a spreadsheet, a balance sheet to reflect the current value of assets.

Spreadsheet 15.7 shows how the balance sheet is adjusted to reflect the current value of the assets.

Notice this time how we abide by the rule of making the computer work for us by 'forcing' the double entry necessary out of the machine, e.g. the revalued land figure is inserted in cell D19 and hence cell D10; the entry needed is calculated by the spreadsheet and then shown in cell M10 in the **revaluation** column.

Once all revaluations have been made the **revaluation** column is summed and the total allocated to the partners' **capital** columns in their agreed profit-sharing ratio.

Spreadsheet 15.7   Revaluing the partnership

	A	B	C	D	E	F	G	H	I	J	K	L	M
1													
2	Allocation Ratio:									10	35	55	
3													
4	Description			Land	Machine	Stock	Debtors	Bank	Creditors	Capital	Capital	Capital	Revalua-
5								Cash		A	B	C	tion A/c
6													
7	Balance Sheet												
8	before Revaluation			1000	2000	900	800	200	-400	-1000	-1500	-2000	
9													
10	Revaluation of Land			4000									-4000
11													
12	Revaluation of Machine				-500								500
13													
14	Revaluation of Stock					-50							50
15													
16	Bad Debt						-150						150
17													
18	-------												---
19				5000	1500	850	650	200	-400	-1000	-1500	-2000	-3300
20													
21	Transfer of Revaluation: A									-330			330
22	Surplus to Capitals												
23		B									-1155		1155
24													
25		C										-1815	1815
26	-------												---
27	Balance Sheet												
28	after Revaluation			5000	1500	850	650	200	-400	-1330	-2655	-3815	0

	A	B	C	D	E	F	G	H
1								
2	Allocation Ratio:							
3								
4	Description			Land	Machine	Stock	Debtors	Bank
5								Cash
6								
7	Balance Sheet							
8	before Revaluation			1000	2000	900	800	200
9								
10	Revaluation of Land			D19-D8				
11								
12	Revaluation of Machine				E19-E8			
13								
14	Revaluation of Stock					F19-F8		
15								
16	Bad Debt						-150	
17								
18	-------							---
19				5000	1500	850	SUM(G8:G16)	SUM(H8:H16)

Is the business now worth the current net assets total of £7,800 (i.e. the physical assets of the business less any liabilities accruing)? No, because we have not yet included goodwill; we will now see what is meant by goodwill.

15.3.2 The money measurement concept

Only those transactions that can be objectively measured in money terms are recorded (see Figure 15.3). Therefore the following assets of the business are not recorded:

1. Skilled and well-motivated employees. A business may have built up an efficient workforce and management team who would be difficult to replace and costly to retrain.

Accounting is sometimes constrained by its exact rules. One such instance is when the rule of money measurement is deployed. The concept refers to the fact that only items that can be measured in money terms are recorded in the accounts of a business. The underlying logic is that in this way objectivity is preserved, i.e. there can be no dispute as to the cost of the asset or how much the business owes, etc. However, this does mean that a lot of useful information is not contained in the firm's accounts. One omission relates to the human element of the firm. A company may have good employees, steady customers, first-class management, innovative designers, a good reputation, good product brand names and other things that cannot be put in terms of money, but which may well affect the performance of the company both now and in the future.

There are accountants interested in changing this concept; for example:

'human asset accounting' is a subject under reseach which aims to place a monetary value upon a firm's employees;
the valuation of the future benefits to be derived from a well-known product.

However, the subjective nature (see Figure 7.3) of these measurements are a serious drawback.

The following senario is not unusual. A firm has spent a lot of time researching a new product and has invested heavily in new production facilities. It has firm orders for the product from established customers and the design team is enthusiastically preparing the final details. The factory staff have all undergone an expensive training programme to work the new equipment. All this has been achieved at the cost of lost production this year and sales of the old product have fallen away in anticipation of the new replacement. Stocks of the old product are therefore high and the firm has reduced the price to try and shift them. As a consequence of this activity, the accounts present a picture of a fall in sales, reduced gross profit margins, increased expenses, and an even lower net profit margin. The company's balance sheet reflects the increase in fixed assets in the new factory, but the old factory has had to be written off. The new factory has been debt financed so the company's gearing has worsened. The accounts therefore present a bleak picture which is unrepresentative of the real position. This is because the preparations made for the future are not capable of being measured in money terms, and it is not prudent to include cash flows not yet realised.

Figure 15.3 The money measurement concept

2. Loyal customers who regularly trade with the business because of the service it provides.

3. The location of the business may be advantageous, over and above what it could be sold for.

4. A good business name, such as Marks and Spencer plc.

5. Research and development projects which might result in high profits in future years, whose costs have been written off.

It is apparent that these assets are very difficult to measure with any degree of accuracy as they are intangible in nature and they have been built up over the life of the business. Therefore they are placed together and collectively known as 'goodwill'. However, when valuing a business we do need to attach a value of good will as its value might be considerable.

In theory, goodwill represents the difference between the value of the business (to a prospective purchaser) and the sum of the current (i.e. revalued) values of the business's net assets. As we do not know the former value since we are not selling the business it is not possible to find an exact value for goodwill. What have been developed are several methods which provide rough approximations to its value. Some of these methods are described in Figure 15.4.

These methods can then be used to generate figures for use as the basis of negotiation between the established and/or new partners.

Once an agreed valuation has been placed upon goodwill, we need to record it in our spreadsheet. This is done by opening up a new asset column called **goodwill** to record the goodwill valuation (i.e. a debit entry) and split the credit entry

---

There are various methods of calculating goodwill. Firstly, there is purchased good will, which arises when a business is bought. In this instance goodwill will be the difference between the purchase price and the fair value of the firm's net assets.

Difficulties arise with non-purchased goodwill, which can only be subjectively estimated. How do you place a value on a firm's good custom or the loyalty of the workforce?

There are a number of methods:

1. Revalue all assets and liabilities and take away what is considered to be a fair value for the firm, usually obtained by a professional valuer.

2. Analyse a number of years' profits, possibly placing more stress on recent years e.g. If we are trying to measure goodwill in 1989, we might use:

$$\frac{4}{10} \times 1988 \text{ profits} + \frac{3}{10} \times 1987 \text{ profits} + \frac{2}{10} \times 1986 \text{ profits} + \frac{1}{10} \times 1985 \text{ profits}$$

Don't look for any scientific rationale in these procedures, as they are only guesstimates.

Figure 15.4   How to calculate goodwill

between the partners in accordance with their agreed profit-sharing ratio. That is to credit the partners with their share of this asset which they have built up. In our example, let us assume the goodwill has been valued at £5,000. Spreadsheet 15.8 shows how this goodwill has been recorded. Note that cell B30 contains the *value* of goodwill that the partners have agreed and does not form part of the double entry.

So the first step in accounting for a change in partners is to revalue the assets of the business and, if necessary, to open a good will account. The second step in accounting for the change is to record the actual change in the partnership. This change can include one or more of the following.

A change in the profit sharing ratio of the partners

The partnership agreement is changed to reflect the new ratio and future profits and losses are split accordingly.

Admittance of a new partner

The new partner is likely to introduce some new assets into the partnership in exchange for a share in future profits (and losses). The introduction of new assets (usually cash) is to increase (i.e. debit) the relevant **asset** column and the **new partner's** capital column (i.e. a credit entry). The partnership agreement is changed to reflect the new profit-sharing ratio as per 1 above.

Exit of a partner

The retiring partner will usually, in exchange for his profit share, be compensated by receiving partnership assets. These assets can be:

a. a cash payment, in which case the **cash** column is reduced as is the **retiring partner's capital** column;

b. a loan, in which case a **loan** column is created to house the loan made by the partnership to the retired partner and the **retiring partner's capital** column is so reduced;

c. any other asset (e.g. a motor car), in which case the relevant **asset** column is reduced as is the **retiring partner's capital** column.

The example is extended to illustrate how these changes are accounted for. Let us assume partner A retires and in exchange for his profit share he agrees to accept cash of £100, part of the land (current value £1,000) and a loan (bearing interest of 10 per cent p.a.) of £730. A new partner is to be admitted, D, who has agreed to contribute cash of £1,200 and a machine whose current value is £2,000.

Spreadsheet 15.8 Recording goodwill

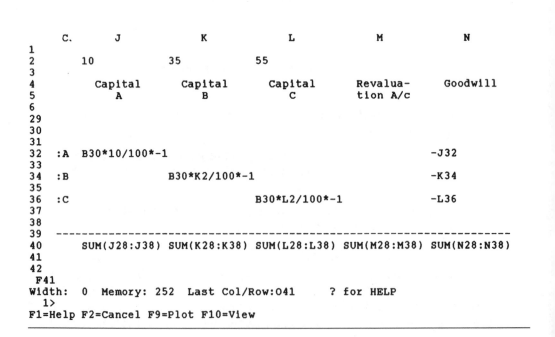

	A	B	C	J	K	L	M	N	O
1									
2	Allocation Ratio:			10	35	55			
3									
4	Description			Capital	Capital	Capital	Revalua-	Goodwill	
5				A	B	C	tion A/c		
6									
29									
30	Goodwill	5000							
31									
32	Goodwill :A			−500				500	
33									
34	:B				−1750			1750	
35									
36	:C					−2750		2750	
37									
38									
39	--								
40	Balance Sheet			−1830	−4405	−6565	0	5000	
41	including Goodwill								
42									

```
N40          Form=SUM(N28:N38)
Width:  9  Memory: 252  Last Col/Row:041      ? for HELP
   1>
F1=Help F2=Cancel F9=Plot F10=View
```

	C.	J	K	L	M	N
1						
2		10	35	55		
3						
4		Capital	Capital	Capital	Revalua-	Goodwill
5		A	B	C	tion A/c	
6						
29						
30						
31						
32	:A	B30*10/100*-1				-J32
33						
34	:B		B30*K2/100*-1			-K34
35						
36	:C			B30*L2/100*-1		-L36
37						
38						
39		---				
40		SUM(J28:J38)	SUM(K28:K38)	SUM(L28:L38)	SUM(M28:M38)	SUM(N28:N38)
41						
42						

```
 F41
Width:  0  Memory: 252  Last Col/Row:041      ? for HELP
   1>
F1=Help F2=Cancel F9=Plot F10=View
```

Spreadsheet 15.9 Exit and introduction of partners

	A	B	C	D	E	H	J	M	R
1									
2	Allocation Ratio:						10		
3									
4	Description			Land	Machine	Bank	Capital	Capital	Loan
5						Cash	A	D	
6									
40	Balance Sheet			5000	1500	200	-1830		
41	including Goodwill								
42									
43	Retirement of A:								
44		Cash				-100	100		
45		Land		-1000			1000		
46		Loan					730		-730
47	Admittance of D:								
48		Cash				1200		-1200	
49		Machine			2000			-2000	
50	------								----
51	Balance Sheet			4000	3500	1300	0	-3200	-730
52	after restructuring								
53									

```
P40
Width:   0   Memory: 251   Last Col/Row:R52      ? for HELP
   1>
```

F1=Help F2=Cancel F9=Plot F10=View

Spreadsheet 15.10 Writing out good will

	A	B	C	J	K	L	M	O	U
1									
2	Allocation Ratio:			10	35	55			
3				0	30	45	25		
4	Description			Capital	Capital	Capital	Capital	Goodwill	Loan
5				A	B	C	D		
6									
51	Balance Sheet			0	-4405	-6565	-3200	5000	
52	after restructuring								
53									
54	Writing Off Goodwill								
55		B			1500			-1500	
56		C				2250		-2250	
57		D					1250	-1250	
58	------								
59	Balance Sheet			0	-2905	-4315	-1950	0	
60	after W/O Goodwill								
61									
62									
63									
64									

```
O59              Form=SUM(O51:O57)
Width:   9   Memory: 250   Last Col/Row:S60      ? for HELP
   1>
```

F1=Help F2=Cancel F9=Plot F10=View

The new profit-sharing ratio is to be B = 30 per cent, C = 45 per cent and D = 25 per cent.

Spreadsheet 15.9 shows the transactions necessary to record these changes. Notice that this is an extension of the existing model.

The final step in the process is to decide whether to keep goodwill in the accounts. The partners might decide that it is a business asset, just as the land and the other assets are business assets, so it should remain in the balance sheet. If this is the case we need do no more; the accounting process is complete. Alternatively, they might decide that goodwill is unlike any other asset as it is not objectively determined, so it is best left out of the balance sheet. If this is the case we need to eliminate the goodwill asset account and take out of the partner's capital account their share of the goodwill. Remember the new partner has now bought his share of this goodwill so we reduce the partners' capital accounts in their new profit-sharing ratio. This treatment is shown in Spreadsheet 15.10.

Notice that the capital account of the existing partners has changed, e.g. B is now £2,905, whereas it was £2,655 in Spreadsheet 15.6. It has increased because when the goodwill account was created, B's share was £1,750 whereas when goodwill was written off B's share was only £1,500. This is due to the change in the allocation ratio.

A further treatment is to consider the goodwill as an asset whose value will fall over its useful life, in which case we amortise (i.e. depreciate) the asset. This approach has a practical problem associated in that we need to determine an economic life for goodwill; since it is composed of a hybrid of elements this is no easy task. Further analysis of this method, eliminating goodwill from the accounts, is, however, outside the scope of this book. The methods mentioned are the ones favoured by SSAP 22, which is only applicable to companies, although there are other ways.

Spreadsheet 15.11 gives a summary of the transactions completed so far.

15.4 Dissolution of a partnership

We will now consider how to account for the winding up of a partnership. The end of a partnership can occur due to a wide range of reasons, such as the conversion of the partnership to a company or a dispute between the partners leading to its break-up. The way we account for this dissolution will be explained by means of an example. However, before we do this a number of factors require explanation.

1. A partner may purchase some of the partnership assets (e.g. a motor car). In this case, the agreed valuation of these assets is set off against any monies the partner in question would have received.

2. A **realisation** column is used to calculate the profit and loss upon realisation. Assets are transferred to this column at their balance sheet value and any proceeds arising upon sale are credited to this column (the debit going to the

Spreadsheet 15.11   A summary of completed transactions

`: A :: B ::C:: D :: E :: F :: G :: H:: I :: J :: K :: L :: M :: N :: O ::P :`

	A Description	B Land	C Machine	D Stock	E Debtors	F Bank Cash	G Creditors	H Capital A	I Capital B	J Capital C	K Capital D	L Revaluat-ion A/c	M Goodwill	N Loan
1														
2	Allocation Ratio:							10	35	55				
3								0	30	45	25			
4	Description	Land	Machine	Stock	Debtors	Bank	Creditors	Capital	Capital	Capital	Capital	Revaluat-	Goodwill	Loan
5						Cash		A	B	C	D	ion A/c		
6														
7	Balance Sheet													
8	before Revaluation	1000	2000	900	800	200	-400	-1000	-1500	-2000				
9														
10	Revaluation of Land	4000										-4000		
11														
12	Revaluation of Machine		-500									500		
13														
14	Revaluation of Stock			-50								50		
15														
16	Bad Debt				-150							150		
17														
18	-------													
19		5000	1500	850	650	200	-400	-1000	-1500	-2000		-3300		
20														
21	Transfer of Revaluation: A							-330				330		
22	Surplus to Capitals													
23	B								-1155			1155		
24														
25	C									-1815		1815		
26	-------													
27	Balance Sheet													
28	after Revaluation	5000	1500	850	650	200	-400	-1330	-2655	-3815		0		
29														
30	Goodwill 5000													
31														
32	Goodwill :A							-500					500	
33														
34	:B								-1750				1750	
35														
36	:C									-2750			2750	
37														
38														
39	-------													
40	Balance Sheet	5000	1500	850	650	200	-400	-1830	-4405	-6565		0	5000	
41	including Goodwill													
42														
43	Retirement of A:													
44	Cash					-100		100						
45	Land	-1000						1000						
46	Loan							730						-730
47	Admittance of D:													
48	Cash					1200					-1200			
49	Machine		2000								-2000			
50	-------													
51	Balance Sheet	4000	3500	850	650	1300	-400	0	-4405	-6565	-3200	0	5000	-730
52	after restructuring													
53														
54	Writing Off Goodwill													
55	B								1500				-1500	
56	C									2250			-2250	
57	D										1250		-1250	
58	-------													
59	Balance Sheet	4000	3500	850	650	1300	-400	0	-2905	-4315	-1950	0	0	-730
60	after W/O Goodwill													

(continued)

Spreadsheet 15.11   *(Continued)*

	A	B	C	D	E	F	G	H	I
1									
2	Allocation Ratio:								
3									
4	Description			Land	Machine	Stock	Debtors	Bank	Creditors
5								Cash	
6									
7	Balance Sheet								
8	before Revaluation			1000	2000	900	800	200	-400
9									
10	Revaluation of Land			D19-D8					
11									
12	Revaluation of Machine				E19-E8				
13									
14	Revaluation of Stock					F19-F8			
15									
16	Bad Debt						-150		
17									
18	--								
19				5000	1500	850	SUM(G8:G16)	SUM(H8:H16)	SUM(I8:I16)
20									
21	Transfer of Revaluation: A								
22	Surplus to Capitals								
23			B						
24									
25			C						
26	--								
27	Balance Sheet								
28	after Revaluation			SUM(D19:D25)	SUM(E19:E25)	SUM(F19:F25)	SUM(G19:G25)	SUM(H19:H25)	SUM(I19:I25)
29									
30	Goodwill	5000							
31									
32	Goodwill :A								
33									
34			:B						
35									
36			:C						
37									
38									
39	--								
40	Balance Sheet			SUM(D28:D38)	SUM(E28:E38)	SUM(F28:F38)	SUM(G28:G38)	SUM(H28:H38)	SUM(I28:I38)
41	including Goodwill								
42									
43	Retirement of A:								
44	Cash							-100	
45	Land			-1000					
46	Loan								
47	Admittance of D:								
48	Cash							1200	
49	Machine				2000				
50	--								
51	Balance Sheet			SUM(D40:D49)	SUM(E40:E49)	SUM(F40:F49)	SUM(G40:G49)	SUM(H40:H49)	SUM(I40:I49)
52	after restructuring								
53									
54	Writing Off Goodwill								
55			B						
56			C						
57			D						
58	--								
59	Balance Sheet			SUM(D51:D57)	SUM(E51:E57)	SUM(F51:F57)	SUM(G51:G57)	SUM(H51:H57)	SUM(I51:I57)
60	after W/O Goodwill								

J	K	L	M	N	O	P
10	35	55				
0	30	45	25			
Capital A	Capital B	Capital C	Capital D	Revaluation A/c	Goodwill	Loan
-1000	-1500	-2000				
				-D10		
				-E12		
				-F14		
				-G16		
SUM(J8:J16)	SUM(K8:K16)	SUM(L8:L16)		SUM(N8:N16)		
-N21				-N19*J2/100		
	-N23			-N19*K2/100		
		-N25		-N19*L2/100		
SUM(J19:J25)	SUM(K19:K25)	SUM(L19:L25)		(SUM(N19:N25))		
B30*10/100*-1					-J32	
	B30*K2/100*-				-K34	
		B30*L2/100*-1			-L36	
SUM(J28:J38)	SUM(K28:K38)	SUM(L28:L38)		SUM(N28:N38)	SUM(O28:O38)	
-H44						
-D45						
-P46					-730	
			-H48			
			-E49			
SUM(J40:J49)	SUM(K40:K49)	SUM(L40:L49)	SUM(M40:M49)	SUM(N40:N49)	SUM(O40:O49)	SUM(P40:P49)
	-O55				-O51*K3/100	
		-O56			-O51*L3/100	
			-O57		-O51*M3/100	
SUM(J51:J57)	SUM(K51:K57)	SUM(L51:L57)	SUM(M51:M57)	SUM(N51:N57)	SUM(O51:O57)	SUM(P51:P57)

bank column). The total of the **realisation** column is transferred to the partners' **capital** columns in accordance with their agreed profit-sharing ratio (unless there is any other agreed ratio in the partnership agreement to be used in the event of realisation). Any costs of dissolution, such as accountants' and solicitors' costs, are to be charged to the **realisation** column.

3.   Liabilities are paid off from the partnership bank account.

4.   The total of the **current** columns are transferred to the respective partners' **capital** columns as this distinction is no longer useful as the partnership is to close down.

5.   If the resultant **capital** column of any partner results in a debit (i.e. positive balance), they will be asked to pay this amount into the partnership bank account. However, if they are unable to do this, the other partners must bear the loss, not in their profit-sharing ratios, but in the ratio of 'their last agreed capitals', usually measured by the capital in the previous period's balance sheet. This rather odd requirement results from the legal case of *Garner* vs *Murray* (1904), which does not apply in Scotland. The partnership agreement can contain provisions to override this case, if the partners so decide.

The following question will be used to illustrate the winding-up procedure:

The partnership of X, Y and Z is to be dissolved on 31 December 1988. The profit sharing ratio is X = 30 per cent, Y = 30 per cent and Z = 40 per cent. The land is sold for £7,500, the machine for £2,300 and the stock for £4,560. The motor car was taken over by Y at an agreed valuation of £2,750. £5,430 was collected from debtors and the creditors agreed to a payment of £3,160 as full and final settlement of their claim. The costs of dissolution were £2,100.

The balance sheet as at 31 December 1988 was as shown in Figure 15.5.

You are required to record on a spreadsheet the closing down of the partnership.

The solution to this question is present in Spreadsheet 15.12. Firstly, the sale proceeds from the land, machinery and stock are recorded as additions to **bank** and **cash** (i.e. debit entries) and credit entries in the **realisation** column. The motor car is taken by Y as part settlement of their interest in the partnership, so no monies are received. The current value of the motor car, £2,750, is recorded as a debit entry in the **capital** column and the credit entry taken to the **realisation** column. The monies collected from debtors are debited to the **bank** and **cash** columns and the credit entry taken to the **realisation** column. Creditors are then paid out of **bank** and **cash**. The costs of dissolution are charged to the **realisation** column and paid out of **bank** and **cash**. Then the book value of all assets except **bank** and **cash** are transferred to the **realisation** column. The discount received from creditors is credited to the **realisation** column. Then the current totals are transferred to the **capital** columns for each partner.

The next stage is to divide the profit on realisation of £2,680 among

	£	£
Fixed assets		
Land		3,000
Machinery		2,200
Motor car		2,600
		7,800
Currents assets		
Stock	4,600	
Debtors	5,500	
Bank and cash	560	
	10,660	
Current liabilities		
Creditors	3,300	
		7,360
		15,160
	£s	£s
Capitals:		
X	4,000	
Y	3,000	
Z	5,000	
		12,000
Current accounts:		
X	246	
Y	1,478	
Z	1,436	
		3,160
		15,160

Figure 15.5 Balance sheet as at 31 December 1988

the partners in their profit-sharing ratio. Finally the bank and cash balance of £15,160 is used to pay off the partners' outstanding capital.

CHECKLIST _____

Having completed Chapter 15, you should be able to:

- explain why a business would wish to trade as a partnership;
- apply the rules of accounting for partnerships;
- prepare the accounts of a partnership and allocate profits among partners;
- record interest on capital, drawings and the payment of salaries, using the spreadsheet to examine 'what if?' scenarios and the impact on the final accounts;

Spreadsheet 15.12 Dissolution of a partnership

	A	B	C	D	E	F	G	H
1								
2								
3								
4	Description			Land	Machinery	Motor Car	Stock	Debtors
5								
6								
7	Balance Sheet			3000	2200	2600	4600	5500
8								
9	Sale of assets:	Land						
10								
11		Machinery						
12								
13		Stock						
14								
15		Motor Car						
16								
17	Collection of debtors							
18								
19	Payment of Creditors							
20								
21	Costs of Disolution							
22								
23	Transfer to							
24	Realisation :	Land		-3000				
25								
26		Machinery			-2200			
27								
28		Motor Car				-2600		
29								
30		Stock					-4600	
31								
32		Debtors						-5500
33								
34	Discounts on creditors							
35								
36	Transfer of Current							
37	Balances : X							
38								
39		Y						
40								
41		Z						
42	---							
43	Sub Totals			0	0	0	0	0
44								
45	Profit on Realisation : X							
46								
47		Y						
48								
49		Z						
50	---							
51	Sub Total			0	0	0	0	0
52								
53	Cash Settlement : X							
54								
55		Y						
56								
57		Z						
58	===							

	I	J	K	L	M	N	O	P	Q
	Bank and Cash	Creditors	Capital X	Capital Y	Capital Z	Current X	Current Y	Current Z	Realisation Column
	560	-3300	-4000	-3000	-5000	-246	-1478	-1436	
	7500								-7500
	2300								-2300
	4560								-4560
				2750					-2750
	5430								-5430
	-3160	3160							
	-2100								2100
									3000
									2200
									2600
									4600
									5500
		140							-140
			-246			246			
				-1478			1478		
					-1436			1436	
	15090	0	-4246	-1728	-6436	0	0	0	-2680
			-804						804
				-804					804
					-1072				1072
	15090	0	-5050	-2532	-7508	0	0	0	0
	-5050		5050						
	-2532			2532					
	-7508				7508				

(continued)

Spreadsheet 15.12 *(Continued)*

	A	B	C	D	E	F	G	H	I
1									
2									
3									
4	Description			Land	Machinery	Motor	Stock	Debtors	Bank
5						Car			and Cash
6									
7	Balance Sheet			3000	2200	2600	4600	5500	560
8									
9	Sale of assets:	Land							7500
10									
11		Machinery							2300
12									
13		Stock							4560
14									
15		Motor Car							
16									
17	Collection of debtors								5430
18									
19	Payment of Creditors								-3160
20									
21	Costs of Disolution								-2100
22									
23	Transfer to								
24	Realisation :	Land		-D7					
25									
26		Machinery			-E7				
27									
28		Motor Car				-F7			
29									
30		Stock					-G7		
31									
32		Debtors						-H7	
33									
34	Discounts on creditors								
35									
36	Transfer of Current								
37	Balances :	X							
38									
39		Y							
40									
41		Z							
42	--								
43	Sub Totals			SUM(D7:D41)	SUM(E7:E41)	SUM(F7:F41)	SUM(G7:G41)	SUM(H7:H41)	SUM(I7:I41)
44									
45	Profit on Realisation : X								
46									
47		Y							
48									
49		Z							
50	--								
51	Sub Total			SUM(D43:D49)	SUM(E43:E49)	SUM(F43:F49)	SUM(G43:G49)	SUM(H43:H49)	SUM(I43:I49)
52									
53	Cash Settlement : X								-K53
54									
55		Y							-L55
56									
57		Z							-M57
58	==								

J	K	L	M	N	O	P	Q
Creditors	Capital X	Capital Y	Capital Z	Current X	Current Y	Current Z	Realisation Column
-3300	-4000	-3000	-5000	-246	-1478	-(SUM(D7:O7))	
							-I9
							-I11
							-I13
		2750					-L15
							-I17
-I19							
							-I21
							-D24
							-E26
							-F28
							-G30
							-H32
-(J7+J19)							-J34
	-N37			-N7			
		-O39			-O7		
			-P41			-P7	
SUM(J7:J41)	SUM(K7:K41)	SUM(L7:L41)	SUM(M7:M41)	SUM(N7:N41)	SUM(O7:O41)	SUM(P7:P41)	SUM(Q7:Q41)
	-Q45						-Q43*.3
		-Q47					-Q43*.3
			-Q49				-Q43*.4
SUM(J43:J49)	SUM(K43:K49)	SUM(L43:L49)	SUM(M43:M49)	SUM(N43:N49)	SUM(O43:O49)	SUM(P43:P49)	SUM(Q43:Q49)
	-K51						
		-L51					
			-M51				

- examine the accounting procedures for changes in partnership structure, including the introduction and exit of partners;
- understand the concept of goodwill, its measurement and accounting treatment;
- record the accounting transactions necessary to dissolve a partnership using a realisation account.

Workshop 15.2: Partnership accounts

Jeremy, Leigh and Nigel have been operating as a partnership making heating equipment for greenhouses. However, Nigel has a new invention which the rest of the partners do not wish to develop. As a result, Nigel decides to retire from the business and set up his own company. This will leave the partnership with a problem, as Jeremy and Leigh will have to finance Nigel's share of the business.

Fortunately, Nigel's cousin Barry is keen to take his place, but only if all partners are on equal terms. Currently the partnership shares profits and losses in the ratio of Jeremy 3, Leigh 2 and Nigel 1. The balance sheet at the current date, 31 March 19X5, is given below.

The assets of the partnership were revalued, with premises now worth £167,000, plant and machinery £42,000 and stock £32,700. All other assets remained unchanged, apart from one debtor (for £3,000) who might not pay.

The partners agree on a value for goodwill of £63,000, but this is written off in the new profit-sharing ratio.

Nigel chose to take one of the motor vehicles (valued at £8,100) with him on his departure, and agreed to leave £15,000 in the firm as a loan; the balance due to him would be paid from the partnership's bank account.

As Barry's condition of joining the partnership, he contributed an amount equal to the lowest partner's capital balance, the higher partner's balance being reduced through a cheque payment. The same principles apply to the current account balances (Figure 15.6).

Using the information in Figure 15.6, account for the transactions necessary to replace Nigel with Barry in the partnership. Draw up a new balance sheet when all transactions are completed (a solution is provided in Figure 15.7).

Workshop guide

1. The first stage is to open a series of columns containing the balance sheet's opening balance. This is row 6 of Spreadsheet 15.13 with rows 1 and 2 used to record useful reference cells for the profit-sharing ratios (old and new), and the goodwill valuation. We will refer to these later.

	£	£
Fixed assets (at NBV)		
Premises		124,000
Machinery		56,000
Motor vehicles		23,500
Fixtures and fittings		14,000
		217,500
Current assets		
Stock	36,800	
Debtors	24,670	
Bank	—	
Cash	2,460	
	63,930	
Less: current liabilities		
Creditors	27,330	
Bank overdraft	1,500	
Loan (Nigel)	32,000	
	60,830	
Net current assets		3,100
		220,600
Financed by:		
Capital accounts:		
Jeremy		90,000
Leigh		76,000
Nigel		43,000
		209,000
Current accounts:		
Jeremy	6,782	
Leigh	(1,780)	
Nigel	6,598	
		11,600
		220,600

Figure 15.6   Balance sheet as at 31 March 19X5

2.   The next stage is to record the new asset valuations in the balance sheet in row 38. The balance for premises, plant and stock are entered, with entries placed in the columns to ensure that this balance is met; e.g. for premises, this will be the difference between the opening and closing balance D38 − D6. The opposite entry is placed in the revalution account in column W. It is irrelevant whether the asset's value has risen or fallen. The treatment of the debtors provision has been to write this off to the revaluation account, with the credit entered in the **debtors** column. A separate **provision** column could have been opened, but this is not really necessary.

3. The balance on the **revaluation** column needs to be apportioned over the partners' capital accounts in the profit-sharing ratio. Once you have entered the formula for one partner you can replicate it for the other two partners, *without altering the cell references.* Your spreadsheet should have a feature to allow absolute cell references to be maintained. Of course, the cell formula is not correct, but using an edit facility you should be able to change the reference cell giving the required profit-sharing ratio.

4. Goodwill is created by a similar process, but this time a cell reference is used to refer to the cell giving the goodwill valuation, in this case cell X2. This has been done to assist in the 'what if?' questions that follow. To write off goodwill, reverse the creation entries, only this time in the new profit-sharing ratio.

5. As one partner is to retire from the business, then a retirement account is opened. This is column T on the spreadsheet. This takes the opposite entries necessary to write out the car, Nigel's capital account, current account and the loan. A new loan is issued and the balance on the account calculated in cell T35, which is paid from the partnership's bank account. The entries for the loan could be simplified by just taking £17,000 from the existing loan account. The net effect is the same.

6. To place the partners on an equal footing requires some 'human' observations. You will need to refer to the cell containing the lowest balance, so first of all a balance must be taken. Possibly the neatest way is to create an interim balance sheet at this point, i.e. row 38. Scrutiny of the columns K to M and O to P will direct the relative cell references needed to achieve the equality desired. It is possible to program some spreadsheets using the **if** command, but for the few entries needed it is not worth the effort. All entries in the capital and current accounts are matched by either debits or credits to the **bank** account, column V.

7. A closing balance sheet is taken by summing the columns between rows 38 and 45.

'What if?' problems

1. What is the effect on the amount of cash the partnership has to pay Nigel (cell T35), if the premises are revalued at £200,000?

2. What is the effect on the amount of money Barry has to contribute (cells V41 and V42) if good will (cell X2) is changed to £40,000?

3. What would be the effect on the capital accounts of Jeremy and Leigh if the old ratios were maintained, i.e. Barry taking Nigel's place (assume that the other conditions of equality of final balance is still maintained)?

Spreadsheet 15.13a Workshop 15.2: Partnership–formulae

	A	B	C	D	E	F	G	H	I	J
1									New	Ratios:
2									Old	Ratios:
3										
4				Premises	Plant	Vehicles	Fixtures	Stock	Debtors	Cash
5										
6	Opening Balance Sheet			124000	56000	23500	14000	36800	24670	2460
7										
8	Revaluation of Assets									
9	Premises			D38-D6						
10	Plant				E38-E6					
11	Stock							H38-H6		
12	Provision for Doubtful Debts								-3000	
13										
14	Profit On Revaluation:									
15	Jeremy									
16	Leigh									
17	Nigel									
18										
19	Goodwill Created									
20	Jeremy									
21	Leigh									
22	Nigel									
23										
24	Goodwill Written Off									
25	Jeremy									
26	Leigh									
27	Barry									
28										
29	Nigel's Retirement									
30	Car					-8100				
31	Capital Account									
32	Current Account									
33	Loan Repaid									
34	Loan Issued									
35	Cash Balance									
36										
37	---------									
38	Interim Balance Sheet			167000	42000	SUM(F6:F36)	SUM(G6:G36)	32700	SUM(I6:I36)	SUM(J6:J36)
39										
40	Placing Partners Equal									
41	Barry: Capital									
42	Barry: Current									
43	Alan: Capital									
44	Alan: Current									
45										
46	---------									
47	Closing Balance Sheet			SUM(D38:D45)	SUM(E38:E45)	SUM(F38:F45)	SUM(G38:G45)	SUM(H38:H45)	SUM(I38:I45)	SUM(J38:J45)

(continued)

Spreadsheet 15.13a   *(Continued)*

	K		L		M		N		O		P		Q	
1	2		2				2		2		2			
2	3		2		1				3		2		1	
3	<---------	Capital	--------->						<---------	Current	--------->			
4	Jereay		Leigh		Nigel		Barry		Jereay		Leigh		Nigel	
5														
6	-90000		-76000		-43000				-6782		1780		-6598	
7														
8														
9														
10														
11														
12														
13														
14														
15									-W15					
16											-W16			
17													-W17	
18														
19														
20	-X20													
21			-X21											
22					-X22									
23														
24														
25	-X25													
26			-X26											
27							-X27							
28														
29														
30														
31					-SUM(M6:M22)									
32													-SUM(Q6:Q17)	
33														
34														
35														
36														
37	--													
38	SUM(K6:K36)		SUM(L6:L36)		SUM(M6:M36)		SUM(N6:N36)		SUM(O6:O36)		SUM(P6:P36)		SUM(Q6:Q36)	
39														
40														
41							-N38+L38							
42														
43	L38-K38													
44									P38-O38					
45														
46	--													
47	SUM(K38:K45)		SUM(L38:L45)		SUM(M38:M45)		SUM(N38:N45)		SUM(O38:O45)		SUM(P38:P45)		SUM(Q38:Q45)	

:	R	::	S	::	T	::	U	::	V	::	W	::	X	::	Y	:

R	S	T (Nigel Retirement)	U (Creditors)	V (Bank)	W (Revaluation)	X (Goodwill)	Y
2							
						63000	
Barry	Loan	Nigel Retirement	Creditors	Bank	Revaluation	Goodwill	
	-32000		-27330	-1500			SUM(C6:X6)
					-D9		
					-E10		
					-H11		
					-I12		
					-SUM(W9:W12)*D2/SUM(D2:Q2)		
					-SUM(W9:W12)*P2/SUM(D2:Q2)		
					-SUM(W9:W12)*Q2/SUM(D2:Q2)		
						X2*K2/SUM(K2:M2)	
						X2*L2/SUM(K2:M2)	
						X2*M2/SUM(K2:M2)	
						-X2*K1/SUM(K1:N1)	
						-X2*L1/SUM(K1:N1)	
						-X2*N1/SUM(K1:N1)	
		-F30					
		-M31					
		-Q32					
	-S6	-S33					
	-T34	15000					
		-SUM(T30:T34)		-T35			
SUM(R6:R36)	SUM(S6:S36)	SUM(T6:T36)	SUM(U6:U36)	SUM(V6:V36)	SUM(W6:W36)	SUM(X6:X36)	SUM(C38:X38)
				-N41			
P38				-R42			
				-K43			
				-O44			
SUM(R38:R45)	SUM(S38:S45)	SUM(T38:T45)	SUM(U38:U45)	SUM(V38:V45)	SUM(W38:W45)	SUM(X38:X45)	SUM(C47:X47)

(continued)

Spreadsheet 15.13b   Workshop 15.2: Partnership – solution

	A	B	C	D Premises	E Plant	F Vehicles	G Fixtures	H Stock	I Debtors	J Cash	K Jeremy	L Leigh	M Nigel	N Barry
1									New	Ratios: 2	2			2
2									Old	Ratios: 3	2	1		
3											<-------- Capital -------->			
4				Premises	Plant	Vehicles	Fixtures	Stock	Debtors	Cash	Jeremy	Leigh	Nigel	Barry
5														
6	Opening Balance Sheet			124000	56000	23500	14000	36800	24670	2460	-90000	-76000	-43000	
7														
8	Revaluation of Assets													
9	Premises			43000										
10	Plant				-14000									
11	Stock							-4100						
12	Provision for Doubtful Debts								-3000					
13														
14	Profit On Revaluation:													
15	Jeremy													
16	Leigh													
17	Nigel													
18														
19	Goodwill Created													
20	Jeremy										-31500			
21	Leigh											-21000		
22	Nigel												-10500	
23														
24	Goodwill Written Off													
25	Jeremy										21000			
26	Leigh											21000		
27	Barry													21000
28														
29	Nigel's Retirement													
30	Car					-8100								
31	Capital Account												53500	
32	Current Account													
33	Loan Repaid													
34	Loan Issued													
35	Cash Balance													
36														
37	-------													
38	Interim Balance Sheet			167000	42000	15400	14000	32700	21670	2460	-100500	-76000	0	21000
39														
40	Placing Partners Equal													
41	Barry: Capital													-97000
42	Barry: Current													
43	Alan: Capital										24500			
44	Alan: Current													
45														
46	-------													
47	Closing Balance Sheet			167000	42000	15400	14000	32700	21670	2460	-76000	-76000	0	-76000

	O	P	Q	R	S	T	U	V	W	X	Y
		2	2		2						
		3	2	1							63000
		Jeremy	Leigh	Nigel	Barry	Loan	Nigel Retirement	Creditors	Bank	Revaluation	Goodwill
		-6782	1780	-6598		-32000		-27330	-1500			0
									-43000		
									14000		
									4100		
									3000		
		-10950							10950		
			-7300						7300		
				-3650					3650		
											31500
											21000
											10500
											-21000
											-21000
											-21000
							8100				
							-53500				
				10248			-10248				
						32000	-32000				
						-15000	15000				
							72648		-72648		
		-17732	-5520	0	0	-15000	0	-27330	-74148	0	0	0
									97000		
					-5520				5520		
									-24500		
		12212							-12212		
		-5520	-5520	0	-5520	-15000	0	-27330	-8340	0	0	0

	£	£
Fixed Assets (at NBV)		
Premises		167,000
Machinery		42,000
Motor vehicles		15,400
Fixtures and fittings		14,000
		238,400
Current assets		
Stock	32,700	
Debtors	21,670	
Bank	—	
Cash	2,460	
	56,830	
Less: current liabilities		
Creditors	27,330	
Bank overdraft	8,340	
Loan (Nigel)	15,000	
	50,670	
Net current assets		6,160
		244,560
Financed by:		
Capital accounts:		
Jeremy		76,000
Leigh		76,000
Barry		76,000
		228,000
Current accounts:		
Jeremy	5,520	
Leigh	5,520	
Barry	5,520	
		16,560
		244,560

Figure 15.7   New balance sheet as at 31 March 19X5

4. In the workshop guide, it was mentioned that an **if** formula could be used to make the computer decide which balance was the lowest and proceed accordingly. Write such a statement for cell K43.

Answers

1. The cell changes from £72,648 to £78,148.

2. Barry's capital contribution changes from £97,000 to £89,333. The current account remains the same.

3. The capital accounts of Jeremy and Leigh do not alter.

4. **If ((L38 − K38 > L43), (L38 − K38), 0).** This must be repeated for L43 with the appropriate cell references.

Selected questions and exercises

Question 15.1
Angie and Ben set up in partnership on 1 May 1987 with capitals of £50,000 and £40,000 respectively. Their partnership agreement provides for the following:

1. Profits and losses are to be shared between Angie and Ben in the ratio 3:2 respectively.
2. Ben is to be given a salary of £1,500 per annum.
3. The partners are entitled to withdraw from the partnership the following amounts in arrears: Angie, £2,000 quarterly; Ben, £1,500 quarterly. During the year ended 30 April 1988, the partners withdrew these amounts on 31 July 1987, 31 October 1987, 31 January 1988 and 30 April 1988.
4. Interest is to be charged on drawings at 12 per cent per annum.
5. Interest is to be allowed on capital invested at 12 per cent per annum.

According to the profit and loss account for the year ended 30 April 1988, the partnership earned a profit of £42,000.

1. Show clearly your calculation of the amount of interest chargeable on drawings for each partner for the year ended 30 April 1988.
2. Draw up the partnership appropriation account for the year ended 30 April 1988.
3. Show clearly your calculation of the balance on each partner's current account as at 30 April 1988.

Solution on page 545.   *Source: AAT, Basic Accounting, June 1988.*

Question 15.2
Peter Pale, who has been in business for several years as a sole trader, was joined in partnership on 1 April 1987 by Roger Rains.
   Roger Rains brought into the partnership, as his initial capital, his existing business whose summarised balance sheet as at 31 March 1987 was as shown in Table 15.5.

Table 15.5 *Details of Roger Rain's existing business balance sheet*

	£
Tangible fixed assets	40,000
Net current assets	11,000
	£51,000
Capital – R. Rains	£51,000

For purposes of the partnership, the business of Roger Rains was valued at £60,000 at 1 April 1987.

It has been agreed that the accounting records of Peter Pale will become those of the partnership from 1 April 1987; however, it has now been discovered that Roger Rains' initial capital at 1 April 1987 has not been brought into the partnership accounts, nor has effect been given to the goodwill of Roger Rains at 1 April 1987.

A summarised trial balance at 31 March 1988 has been extracted from the partnership accounts (see Table 15.6).

Table 15.6 *Trial balance as at 31 March 1988*

	£	£
Tangible fixed assets	100,000	
Net current assets	123,000	
Capital account: Peter Pale		170,000
Current accounts: Peter Pale		18,000
Roger Rains	3,000	
Net profit for the year ended 31 March 1988		38,000
	£226,000	£226,000

The net profit for the year ended 31 March 1988 as stated above arose uniformly throughout the year.

The partnership agreement includes the following:

1. A goodwill account is not to be maintained.
2. Roger Rains is to be credited with a partner's salary of £8,000 per annum.
3. Partners are to be credited with interest on their capital account balances at the rate of 5 per cent per annum.
4. As from 1 October 1987, £40,000 is to be transferred from Peter Pale's capital account to the credit of a loan account in that partner's name; interest is to be credited at the rate of 10 per cent per annum.
5. The balance of profits and losses are to be shared between Peter Pale and Roger Rains as follows: up to 30 September 1987, Peter Pale three-fifths, Roger Rains two-fifths; from 1 October 1987, equally.

1. Prepare the partnership's profit and loss appropriation account for the year ended 31 March 1988.
2. Prepare the partners' capital accounts for the year ended 31 March 1988.
3. Prepare the partners' current accounts for the year ended 31 March 1988.

Solution on pages 546–7.   *Source: AAT, Accounting, June 1988.*

Question 15.3

Chair and Table were in partnership as surveyors sharing profits (and losses) in the ratio of 2:1 respectively. Their business was conducted from offices in Leeds and Manchester. It was agreed that the partnership should be dissolved as from 31 March Year 8 with Chair taking over the Leeds office and Table taking over the Manchester office. Their balance sheet at that date is shown in Table 15.7.

Table 15.7   *Partnership balance sheet of Chair and Table.*

Balance sheet

	£000		£000
Capital accounts: Chair	50	Good will	10
Table	13	Furniture	9
	63	Debtors: Leeds	10
Creditors	11	Manchester	5
		Bank	40
	74		74

Good will was revalued at: Leeds £7,000; Manchester £5,000
Furniture was revalued at: Leeds £5,000; Manchester £3,000

Besides this, each partner agreed to take over the debtors associated with his office at their book value less 8 per cent provision for bad debts. Chair agreed to pay off all the partnership creditors on which cash discounts received amounted to £300.

It was also agreed (1) that amounts of £2,500 and £700 should be allowed to Chair and Table, respectively, towards redecorating the premises previously occupied by the partnership and (2) that the dissolution costs of £1,100 should be paid by the partnership.

Assuming that all the transactions relating to the partnership dissolution were carried out as agreed, show:

1. The realisation account.
2. The bank account.
3. The capital accounts (in columnar form).

Solution on page 548.   *Source: LCCI, Third Level Accounting, 1988.*

Question 15.4

Glynn and Fearn are partners in a retail business, sharing profits and losses in the ratio of 3:2 after charging interest on capital of 5 per cent. A trial balance was extracted from their books as at 31 May 1986 (see Table 15.8).

Table 15.8 *Partnership trial balance of Glynn and Fearn*

	DR	CR
Purchases and sales	595,400	810,500
Capital accounts at 1 June 1985		
Glynn		40,000
Fearn		50,000
Glynn	46,000	
Fearn	28,000	
Drawings		
Fixtures		
at cost	40,000	
provision for depreciation		
at 1 June 1985		30,000
Stock in trade at 1 June 1985	51,100	
Debtors and creditors	15,000	25,000
Premises at cost	110,500	
Discounts allowed and received	3,400	3,052
Wages and salaries	89,400	
Rent, rates and insurance	41,500	
Bank account		43,450
General expenses	10,580	
Cash	4,742	
Repairs to premises	3,450	
Current account at 1 June 1985		
Glynn	1,450	
Fearn		1,800
Loan account – Dobson		40,000
Sales commissions	3,250	
Bad debt – written off	580	
Bad debt provision at 1 June 1985		550
	1,044,352	1,044,352

1. Stock at 30 May 1986 was valued at £59,250 at cost according to a check by Glynn. Sales on 31 May amounted to £1,248, and Glynn and Fearn normally expect a gross profit of 33.33 per cent on sales.
2. Provision for bad debts should be adjusted to 5 per cent of balance sheet debtors at 31 May 1986; Glynn has heard that the bad debt written off is likely to be recovered, as the customer concerned has been persuaded by Dobson that it might be in its best interests to pay up.
3. Depreciation of fixtures is 5 per cent per annum on cost.

4. Wages and salaries due at 31 May 1986 amounted to £2,750, while rates and insurance were prepaid by £14,500.
5. Interest of 10 per cent per annum should be provided for the loan from Dobson.

1. Prepare a trading profit and loss account for the year ended 31 May 1986 and a balance sheet as at that date. The profit and loss appropriation account and partners' current accounts are required.
2. Dobson lent £40,000 to the business in its formative years and now feels he would like to participate in the management. Glynn and Fearn would welcome his financial expertise, and see the conversion of the loan into capital as a welcome alternative to repayment. The two existing partners are somewhat perplexed as to how the good will might be valued on the entry of Dobson as a partner and have asked you to offer advice as to how and why a valuation should take place. (Note the book-keeping entries are not required.)

No solution provided.

Question 15.5

Amis, Lodge and Pym were in partnership, sharing profits and losses in the ratio 5:3:2. The trial balance in Table 15.9 has been extracted from their books of account as at 31 March 1988.

Additional information:

1. Stock at 31 March 1988 was valued at £35,000.
2. Depreciation on the fixed assets is to be charged as follows:
     motor vehicles 25 per cent on the reduced balance;
     plant and machinery, 20 per cent on the original cost.
   There were no purchases or sales of fixed assets during the year to 31 March 1988.
3. The provision for bad and doubtful debts is to be maintained at a level equivalent to 5 per cent of the total trade debtors as at 31 March 1988.
4. An office expense of £405 was owing at 31 March 1988, and some rent amounting to £1,500 had been paid in advance as at that date. These items had not been included in the list of balances shown in the trial balance.
5. Interest on drawings and on the debit balance on each partner's current account is to be charged as follows: Amis, £1,000; Lodge, £900; Pym, £720.
6. According to the partnership agreement, Pym is allowed a salary of £13,000 per annum. This amount was owing to Pym for the year to 31 March 1988, and needs to be accounted for.
7. The partnership agreement also allows each partner interest on his capital account at a rate of 10 per cent per annum. There were no movements on the respective partners' capital accounts during the year to 31 March 1988, and the interest had not been credited to them as at that date. (Note: the

Table 15.9 *Partnership trial balance of Amis, Lodge and Pym*

	£	£
Bank interest received		750
Capital accounts (as at 1 April 1987):		
Amis		80,000
Lodge		15,000
Pym		5,000
Carriage inwards	4,000	
Carriage outwards	12,000	
Cash at bank	4,900	
Current accounts:		
Amis	1,000	
Lodge	500	
Pym	400	
Discounts allowed	10,000	
Discounts received		4,530
Drawings:		
Amis	25,000	
Lodge	22,000	
Pym	15,000	
Motor vehicles:		
at cost	80,000	
accumulated depreciation (at 1 April 1987)		20,000
Office expenses	30,400	
Plant and machinery:		
at cost	100,000	
accumulated depreciation (at 1 April 1987)		36,600
Provision for bad and doubtful debts		
(at 1 April 1987)		420
Purchases	225,000	
Rent, rates, heat and light	8,800	
Sales		404,500
Stock (at 1 April 1987)	30,000	
Trade creditors		16,500
Trade debtors	14,300	
	£583,300	£583,300

information given above is sufficient to answer part 1 of the question and notes 8 and 9 below are pertinent to part 2 of the question.)

8. On 1 April 1988, Fowles Limited agreed to purchase the business on the following terms:

   a. Amis to purchase one of the partnership's motor vehicles at an agreed value of £5,000, the remaining vehicles being taken over by the company at an agreed value of £30,000;

   b. the company agreed to purchase the plant and machinery at a value of £35,000 and the stock at a value of £38,500;

c. the partners to settle the trade creditors; the total amount agreed with the creditors being £16,000;

d. the trade debtors were not to be taken over by the company, the partners receiving cheques on 1 April 1988 amounting to £12,985 in total from the trade debtors in settlement of the outstanding debts;

e. the partners paid the outstanding office expense on 1 April 1988, and the landlord returned the rent paid in advance by cheque on the same day;

f. as consideration for the sale of the partnership, the partners were to be paid £63,500 in cash by Fowles Limited, and to receive £75,000 in £1 ordinary shares in the company, the shares to be appointed equally among the partners.

9. Assume that all the matters relating to the dissolution of the partnership and its sale to the company took place on 1 April 1988.

1. Prepare:
   a. Amis's, Lodge's and Pym's trading, profit and loss and profit and loss appropriation account for the year to 31 March 1988;
   b. Amis's, Lodge's and Pym's current accounts (in columnar format) for the year to 31 March 1988 (the final balance on each account is then to be transferred to each partner's respective capital account).

2. Compile the following accounts:
   a. the partnership realisation account for the period up to and including 1 April 1988;
   b. the partners' bank account for the period up to and including 1 April 1988;
   c. the partners' capital accounts (in columnar format) for the period up to and including 1 April 1988.

Note: detailed workings should be submitted with your answer.

Solution on page 549–50.   *Source: AAT, Financial Accounting, June 1988.*

16 | *Introduction to company accounts*

AIMS OF CHAPTER _____

- to introduce students to the idea of limited liability and other legal requirements relating to businesses operating as companies;
- to understand the different ways profits can be appropriated;
- to prepare a profit and loss appropriation account for a company.

16.1 Limited liability and other legal requirements

As a sole trader or partnership expands it usually requires additional capital to take advantage of market opportunities. It often finds these funds difficult to raise in its present form, as any person investing money into the business as a partner is not just risking their investment, but also all their personal wealth. This is due to partnership having no limited liability.

In order to attract such funds, partnerships often convert into limited liability companies, so that any investment is limited to the amount of funds invested in the business. Therefore the liability of an investor in a company is limited to the amount invested in that company; if the company should go into liquidation with more liabilities than assets available to pay these liabilities, the creditors of the company would have no claim on the investors' personal wealth (i.e. houses, cars, savings, etc.) to cover the shortfall.

Another important advantage of a business trading as a company instead of as a partnership is the relaxation in the need to limit members to twenty; companies can have more than twenty members.

The availability of limited liability status for companies could lead to abuse, with investors starting companies which incur large debts and then go out of business, leaving liabilities unsettled. Therefore the way companies are run is governed by an Act of Parliament, the Companies Act 1985. The Companies Act 1985 contains a considerable amount of detailed clauses; the main provisions, as they affect the accountant, are outlined in this chapter and those following. For a full explanation of the provisions of the Act the reader is referred to a company law textbook.

The Companies Act 1985 is a consolidating act, bringing together the provisions previously contained in many separate companies acts. It does not apply to banks, insurance and shipping companies, who have their own separate governing legislation (this specialised legislation is outside the scope of this text). The Act also covers unlimited companies (i.e. companies without limited liability) and companies limited by guarantee. In the latter case the owners agree to contribute a fixed sum of money in the event of the company winding-up. As unlimited companies and companies limited by guarantee are rarely found, we will restrict our future discussion to limited liability companies.

A company can be either a private company or a public company. A private company is usually a small- to medium-sized business, run by its owners, while a public company is usually a large business which looks to the stock exchange to raise most of its finance. Therefore the owners of public companies are usually not the persons who run the company. The owners entrust the running of the company to specialised managers called 'directors'.

The Companies Act 1985 outlines the differences between a private company and public company, of which the following are important.

1. A public company must have an authorised share capital of not less than £50,000, while no limit is placed upon private companies. The Secretary of State for Trade and Industry can change the limit for public companies from time to time as needs arise (e.g., inflation).

2. A private company cannot (unlike public companies) invite the general public to invest in its business.

3. The name of a public company must end with 'plc' ('ccc' in Wales).

A company must have two documents drawn up:

1. A memorandum of association which indicates the relationship between the company and the outside world. It must contain the following clauses:
   a. the name of the company, so it can be identified;
   b. the location of its registered office, so it can be contacted;
   c. whether it is a private or public company;
   d. whether it has limited liability status;
   e. the authorised share capital (see Chapter 17);
   f. the objectives of the company.

The objectives clause spells out the type of business the company is allowed to engage in. Investors and persons transacting business with the company (e.g. suppliers and customers) want to know that the company is acting within its powers, as any transactions engaged in outside the stated objectives are termed *ultra-vires* and are void. In order to provide sufficient freedom for the company to function, these objectives are usually widely drawn-up.

Changes in the memorandum of association require a special resolution to be passed by the members (i.e. a three-quarters majority).

2. Articles of association which detail the rights of members and contain other information. The matters usually covered include:

    a. changes in capital and the way capital is split up into shares (see Chapter 17 for a detailed explanation of share capital);
    b. voting rights of members;
    c. duties of directors, who are accountable to members for the running of their business;
    d. how the company is to be wound-up, should it become necessary.

The Companies Act 1985 has a model set of articles of association referred to as Table A, which most companies adopt, in whole or in part.

Changes in the articles of association require an ordinary resolution to be passed by the members (i.e. a 50 per cent majority).

16.2   Appropriations of profit

The way a company allocates (i.e. what it decides to do with) its profits must be clearly shown in the profit and loss account. The relevant portion of the profit and loss account is called the 'profit and loss appropriation account' and is shown in Figure 16.1.

	£s
Profit before taxation	100,000
Taxation	35,000
Profit after taxation	65,000
Transfer to reserves	10,000
Profit available for distribution	55,000
Dividends	20,000
Undistributed profit carried forward to next year	£35,000

Figure 16.1 shows three allocations of profit: taxation, transfer to reserves and dividends. We will discuss each in turn.

The profits of companies are subject to Corporation Tax, which is payable to the Inland Revenue. The double entry to record taxation in our spreadsheet is to debit the **profit and loss** column (to show that the company has incurred a taxation expense) and credit a **taxation** column (to show that the tax has to be paid over to the Inland Revenue some time in the future). The double entry for taxation in Figure 16.1 is shown in Spreadsheet 16.1.

Figure 16.1   Profit and loss appropriation account

Spreadsheet 16.1 An example of a transfer to reserves

	A	B	C	D	E	F	G	H	I
1									
2									
3	Description			Profit	Assets –	Taxation	Fixed	General	Dividends
4				and Loss	Liabilities	Owing	Asset	Reserve	Owing
5					(inc. Bank)		Replacement		
6							Reserve		
7									
8	Profit for the year			-100000	100000				
9									
10	Taxation			35000		-35000			
11									
12	Transfer to Fixed Asset								
13	Replacement Reserve			7000			-7000		
14									
15	Transfer to General Reserve			3000				-3000	
16									
17	Final Dividend			10000					-10000
18									
19	Interim dividend			10000	-10000				
20	---								
21	Closing Balances			-35000	90000	-35000	-7000	-3000	-10000
22	===								

The topic of taxation is a complex one and is dealt with in Chapter 18.

The directors of the company may decide to put away part of the profit to be used in the future. This is done by transferring part of the profit to reserves. The transfer can be for a specific future expenditure such as the replacement of a fixed asset (in which case a fixed asset replacement reserve is created) or for general future expenditure (in which case a general reserve is created). The double entry to record this transaction is to debit the **profit and loss** column (so reducing the remaining profit) and credit the appropriate **reserve** column (to show where the appropriated profit has gone).

An example of transfer to reserves is shown in Spreadsheet 16.1.

The final appropriation of profit we are considering is dividends.

Investors buy shares in companies for two reasons: firstly, to receive income and secondly for capital gain. Income is received in the form of dividends, which are sums of money paid over to the investors by the company out of its profits. Capital gains accrue from the undistributed profits (and transfers to reserves) kept within the company and used for expanding the business. For example, suppose you own 100 shares in a company whose share price at the beginning of the year is £1 and £2 at the end of the year; and during the year it pays a dividend of 50 pence per share. Your total income from this investment is shown in Table 16.1.

The amount of profits paid as dividends is decided upon at the annual general meeting of the company by passing an ordinary resolution. The amount of dividend is recommended by the directors and cannot exceed this amount.

Table 16.1   *Total income for year from 100 shares*

	£
Dividend 50 pence per share * 100 shares	50
Capital gain £1 * 100 shares	100
Total income	£150

Companies are required to have an annual general meeting at which the dividend is fixed, the accounts approved and other business decided upon. All members are invited to attend and vote at these meetings.

The dividend is often paid in two parts: an interim dividend paid out during the year and a final dividend still owing at the year end. Spreadsheet 16.1 shows the double entry necessary to record dividends.

The dividend can only be paid out of profits available for distribution, which include undistributed profits from previous years.

The percentage of profits paid as dividends is an important decision for the company's directors. The result of this decision is known as the company's dividend policy. The pros and cons of paying different proportions of profits as dividends is discussed in business finance literature. Such a discussion is therefore outside the scope of this textbook.

Dividends are paid net of the basic rate of income tax. The income tax is collected by the company on behalf of its shareholders and paid over to the Inland Revenue. If the shareholder pays income tax at more than the basic rate, he is responsible for paying over the balance to the Inland Revenue. See Chapter 18 for a fuller discussion on tax payable on dividends.

CHECKLIST

Having completed Chapter 16, you should be able to:

■ discuss the idea of limited liability and other legal requirements relating to businesses operating as companies;

■ understand the different ways profits can be appropriated;

■ prepare a profit and loss appropriation account for a company.

Selected questions and exercises

Question 16.1

Julie Morse plc has the totals shown in Table 16.2 in its records from which you are required to prepare a balance sheet and trading and profit and loss account for the year ended 31 December 1991.

Table 16.2 *Details of accounts of Julie Morse plc*

	£ Debit	£ Credit
Sales		2,918,016
Sales returns	2,450	
Carriage outwards	12,359	
Discounts allowed	4,500	
Purchases	1,688,848	
Purchase returns		10,765
Carriage inwards	25	
Discounts received		13,420
Opening stock	325,312	
Share capital £1 shares		1,169,600
Reserves		329,342
Profit and loss account		15,658
Interim dividend	53,000	
Bank overdraft		447,576
Bad debts	568	
Doubtful debt provision		1,692
Rent payable	625,600	
Rent receivable		924,800
Commission receivable		7,616
Insurance	164,016	
Land	2,229,040	
Motor vans	761,600	
Machinery	56,320	
Provisions for depreciation as at 1 January 1991		
motor vans		56,980
machinery		24,592
Profit on sale of motor van		680
Selling expenses	61,200	
Office expenses	103,360	
Wages and salaries	47,872	
Creditors		193,080
Debtors	203,984	
Cash	6,120	
Loan		232,357
	6,346,174	6,346,174

The following notes are relevant:	£
1. Closing stock was	334,560
2. Rent payable accrued was	76,160
3. Insurance prepaid	16,320
4. Wages and salaries accrued	32,640
5. Commission due	9,248
6. Rent received overpaid	16,864
7. Provision for doubtful debts to be increased to	2,450

8. Motor vans are to be depreciated using the straight-line method at a rate of 25 per cent p.a. on cost.

    A full year's depreciation is to be charged in the year of purchase and none in the year of sale.

9. Machinery is to be depreciated using the reducing balance method at a rate of 10 per cent p.a.

A full year's depreciation is to be charged in the year of purchase and none in the year of sale.

10. Corporation tax on profits is 35 per cent

11. The final dividend is to be 15 pence per share.

12. Transfer to reserves £100,000

Solution on pages 551–2.

17 Sources of finance

AIMS OF CHAPTER _____

- to introduce students to the various sources of finance available to companies;
- to examine the suitability of each source in different circumstances in view of cost-reduction objectives;
- to record the transactions necessary to account for these sources of finance using the familiar spreadsheet approach.

17.1 Introduction

A company requires finance in order to purchase items it requires, such as a new machine, or more working capital. It is the function of the financial manager or accountant to ensure sufficient funds are available at the right time, for the right length of time and at lowest cost.

It is sensible that the company obtains the amount of finance it requires, as to obtain too little would prevent the company purchasing the items it needs, and to obtain too much finance would be wasteful. All finance has a cost, i.e. a return payable to the supplier, so the company should consider all the different types of finance available, ensuring that it obtains funds at lowest cost.

It is necessary to ensure that the finance does not have to be paid back until the assets purchased produce a return. It makes little sense to finance a long-term project with a short-term source of finance. This would leave the company seeking additional finance, often at a higher cost, to cover this period of financial shortfall. Alternatively, the project could be sold at a loss or the company may even be forced into liquidation. Many companies in the early 1970s financed purchases of property (a long-term investment) with short-term finance; when property prices fell they found themselves in serious trouble.

This chapter will outline the different sources of finance available to a company, and how to account for them.

17.2   Types of finance

It is convenient to divide the different types of finance into two categories: short-term and long-term.

Short-term finance is used to finance the purchase of assets with a short life (i.e. less than three years, say), while assets with longer lives require long-term finance.

Figure 17.1 shows some of the different types of finance available to a company, together with examples of the assets acquired. We will now consider each type of finance in turn.

17.2.1   Bank borrowing

Funds can be obtained from the high street banks in two main ways. Firstly, overdrafts, which are arrangements made between the company and its bank so that sums of money can be drawn up to a previously agreed amount. Secondly, short-term loans where the bank lends the company an agreed amount of money for a fixed period.

Life of asset	Examples of assets requiring financing	Types of suitable finance
Short term – up to three years	Fluctuations in working capital, e.g. increase in stocks and seasonal demand Equipment with a short life Developing a new product or service which is payable in less than three years	Bank borrowing Trade credit Factoring Bills of exchange Hire purchase Leasing
Long term – three years and over	Permanent increases in working capital Purchase of fixed assets with a long life Taking over an existing business	Hire purchase Leasing Long-term loans Equity capital Preference shares

Figure 17.1   Types of finance

The main differences between these two sources of bank borrowing are as follows:

1. Interest is paid only on the outstanding daily balance in the case of an overdraft, so it can be flexible and cheap. Interest is payable on the full amount of the short term loan, however, so it is not so flexible.

2. The interest rate charged on an overdraft is usually based upon market rates, which vary; this can cause problems when interest rates increase. The interest interest rate charged on a term loan can be fixed so the company is certain of the amount of interest it has to pay over the life of the loan.

3. Overdrafts are repayable on demand. However, if they are properly handled, with the bank kept fully informed of the company's performance, they can usually be renewed.

4. Term loans are usually secured against fixed assets or guarenteed by the owners of the company, while an overdraft is treated as just another creditor if the company goes into liquidation. Term loans are over a fixed period of time.

5. Loans are available to small businesses backed by the government loan guarantee scheme. This enables banks to lend small businesses money at low interest rates, knowing that if the business defaults the government will repay the bank 80 per cent of the loan.

17.2.2 Trade credit

It is possible to raise short-term funds by delaying paying creditors, i.e. making them wait for their money while the company uses it. However, this can lead to complications, such as:

a. being put on 'stop lists' by your suppliers who will only sell to your company if payment is made when the supplies are received;

b. discounts for early settlement being lost;

c. a loss of reputation;

d. your customers doing the same to you;

e. being sued and even being put into liquidation if this is taken to extremes.

17.2.3 Factoring

A factoring company buys your trade debtors, providing up to 80 per cent of their face value in advance. It can also carry out a debtors accounting and administration service for you, sending out invoices and statements. Such a service is most helpful for small growing companies who do not have, and do not want to be concerned with, the administrative burden of collecting debts. This allows the company's management to concentrate upon what it does best, which may be producing and marketing its products. Larger companies will usually find it is more effective to manage their own debtors ledger. Also available is an insurance scheme whereby the company receives 100 per cent protection against bad debts.

The cost of factoring involves an interest charge on the money received before customers pay, plus commission. These charges vary depending upon numbers and value of customer sales.

17.2.4   Bills of exchange

This type of finance enables a company to obtain settlement of a sale immediately rather than waiting for the customer to pay up. The company does this by drawing up a bill of exchange on its customer (i.e. a commitment by the customer to settle the debt at a future specified date) and selling it to a discount house (a specialist financial institution), which pays the company the face value of the bill, less a commission. When the bill is due for payment the discount house presents it to the customer for payment.

The major problem with this source of finance is the cost of commission, which varies with the length of time between the money being advanced, the customer settling the bill and the credit-worthiness of the customer.

The bill of exchange is often used for financing export sales as the credit period is often much longer than that associated with home trade.

17.2.5   Hire purchase

Plant and equipment can be purchased by hire purchase. The company has use of the asset while it pays for it over a number of years. Interest is charged, often at an expensive rate, on the outstanding balance and an initial down-payment is often required. However, the company can utilise certain tax advantages such as capital allowances and tax relief on the interest payments (see Chapter 18).

17.2.6   Leasing

The company acquires the use of an asset in exchange for rental payments. Leases can be of two main types, firstly, operating leases where equipment is used for less than its full economic life; examples of assets acquired on operating leases are motor cars and photocopiers. In this case the company does not bear the full risks of the asset becoming obsolete or inoperational. Secondly, finance leases where equipment is used for its full economic life so the company bears the risks of obsolesence. Operating leases tend to be more expensive than finance leases. There are certain tax advantages associated with leasing.

Companies can raise funds by selling freehold property owned by the business to a financial institution which agrees to lease the property back to the company. This is called a 'sale and lease back arrangement'.

17.2.7 Long-term loans

Long-term loans can be in the form of one large loan from a financial institution or in a series of small loans from individual investors. These loans are usually secured on the assets of the company in which case they are called 'debentures'. If the company defaults on interest or capital repayments, the lenders have first call on the sale proceeds of the assets on which the loans are secured. These securities are called 'charges' and can be 'fixed' on a specific asset, such as a freehold building, or 'floating' on the assets of the business generally. The date the capital has to be repaid is usually fixed within a number of years (e.g. 1993–6 debentures) during which period the company has to repay the capital.

A company can at any time repurchase its debentures at their current market price, if it has sufficient funds. It may want to do this if interest rates have fallen since the issue date of the debenture, and cheaper forms of finance are now available.

Convertable debentures can be 'converted' into ordinary shares at some future date at the option of the holder. The terms of the conversion are laid out in the debenture deed. These debentures give the holder the option of entering into the company's equity capital at favourable terms sometime in the future. The company can gain from this since it can issue them at lower rates of interest than non-convertible debentures.

Debentures can be issued with 'warrants', which give the holder the option to buy a certain number of shares at a favourable price sometime in the future. Warrants differ from convertibles in that the debenture continues to exist after the option has been taken up or not as the case may be. The advantages to the company are lower rates of interest payable than non-warrant debentures and a potential future inflow of finance if the warrants are taken up.

17.2.8 Equity capital

Equity capital comes directly or indirectly from the owners of the business. It can come directly in the form or ordinary share capital or indirectly in the form of retained profits. Ordinary share capital represents funds invested in the company by investors in exchange for a share in future profits. By law, shares must have a nominal value (e.g. £1 shares) which is usually the price at which the shares were first issued, but now bears no relationship to their current price.

Investors purchase shares for two reasons: firstly for dividends and secondly for capital gains. Dividends are cash payments made to shareholders out of company profits. Dividends are paid twice a year, once during the year, an interim payment, and once at the end of the year, a final dividend. The amount of dividends often varies according to whether the profits are good or bad, so the shareholder cannot rely upon this source of income. Capital gains arise when shares are sold at an amount greater than the original purchase price. Public company shares can be sold and purchased on the Stock Exchange, while private company shares have to be sold privately.

Shares can be issued in four main ways:

1. The public can be invited to subscribe for shares. Only fairly large companies use this procedure as it is expensive. A prospectus detailing the terms of the offer and other information about the company is prepared and made available to the public, often by publishing it in the press. The public then applies for the shares by filling in the application form and sending a cheque for an initial payment upon application. The company then allots the shares. Should the issue be over-subscribed some applicants may not receive any shares or all applicants may receive less than the number applied for. Unsuccessful applicants will have their application monies returned by the company. Applicants who receive less shares than they applied for may have their surplus monies retained by the company to be offset against later installments. These later installments are referred to as 'allotments and calls.'

   For example, an applicant may apply for 100 shares at a price of £1, payable 20p on application, 30p on allotment, 25p on first call and 25p on second call. A cheque will be sent for £20 (100 × 20p application) together with the application form. If only 90 shares are alloted there is an over-payment of £2. The company may keep this money to reduce the sum due on allotment to £25 (i.e. 90 shares × 30p less £2 over-payment on application). The two future payments are £22.50 for both the first and second call.

   The price of the issue may be at a fixed price or by tender. In the latter case the applicant must state the maximum price he is willing to pay and send that amount together with his application form. The company will collate these prices from all application forms and a price will be fixed, called the 'striking price'. This price is the minimum price which is sufficient to sell all the issue. Applications below the striking price are rejected and applications at more than the striking price have a refund or their allotment debts reduced.

2. A 'rights issue' is an issue to existing shareholders giving them the opportunity to buy an amount of new shares at a price less than the market price of the current shares or to sell the rights (clearly the rights themselves are valuable as they confer upon the holder the privilege of purchasing shares at less than

market value). Established companies often use this method since issue costs are much less than with a public issue. The apparent cheapness of the new issue is illusionary, as the market price of the shares after the issue will adjust to the weighted average of the old price and the rights price.

3. A 'placing' is an issue of shares to a single or small group of investors who are usually clients of a merchant bank or other financial institution (e.g. pension funds) or company (e.g. insurance companies). These investors probably intend to keep the majority of shares as a long-term investment, but may want to sell some of them as investment opportunities arise or cash needs occur. This method of issue is usually the least expensive, as so few investors are involved.

4. Bonus issues are sometimes made by companies. These issues are different from the others we have considered as no cash is received by the company for the shares. Bonus shares are issued only to existing shareholders in proportion to their existing holding (say two bonus shares for each one already held). Why should the company want to issue bonus shares? They are usually issued as reserves have built up over the years of trading to large amounts and the shares market price has become large or heavy. In order to reduce both reserves and market price, free shares are issued to existing shareholders in proportion to their existing holding. The important point to note is that a bonus issue is not a method of raising finance but a book-keeping exercise.

Ordinary shares held by the owners of the company usually carry voting rights. This means that shareholders can influence company policies and appoint or dismiss directors. There are non-voting shares issued by companies who want to keep control in the hands of a few original investors.

Companies can purchase their own shares or can sell them, but they have to replace this capital by a new issue of shares or take the amount out of profits available for distribution and place it into a specially created, non-distributable reserve, the capital redemption reserve fund (CRRF). When a company is wound up, the ordinary shareholders are only entitled to the remaining assets once all creditors and loans have been repaid. This may be more or less than their original investment.

The second form of equity capital is 'retained profits'. These are the amount of profit left over once the dividend has been paid. The decision as to how much profit to pay by way of dividend is left to the directors to decide. The main advantage of retaining profits is that it avoids all the costs involved in issuing shares.

17.2.9 Preference shares

Preference shares are legally part of equity capital. However, they have preference over ordinary shares as far as their dividend is concerned, and in repayment of

· their capital in the case of a winding-up. So they are usually far less risky than ordinary shares.

They receive a final dividend each year, unless they are 'participating', in which case they receive a variable dividend if profits exceed some certain predetermined level. They carry no voting rights, unless their dividend is in arrears.

Preference shares can be 'cumulative'. This comes into effect when their dividend is not paid in any year (due to insufficient profits), and it becomes due in the next year if there are sufficient profits to meet this claim. Like ordinary shares, preference shares can be redeemed, but capital must be made good by a new share issue or a transfer of distributable profits to the non-distributable reserve, the CRRF.

17.3 How to account for the sources of finance

We will now consider how to account for each type of finance already considered. You may need to remind yourself of the types described in Section 17.2.

17.3.1 Bank borrowing

Overdrafts are accounted for in the same way as bank transactions are recorded. It is good practice to reconcile the balance on the bank account to bank statements received from the bank; see Chapter 12 which explains how to perform this reconciliation and the central reasons for doing it.

Bank loans are recorded by debiting the **bank** column when the loan is received and crediting a **liability** column to reflect the fact that the loan will eventually have to be repaid. If it has to be repaid within a year, a **current liability** column is credited; if it has to be repaid in over a year's time a **long-term liability** column is credited. Spreadsheet 17.1 shows transactions for a company raising a short-term loan of £10,000 and a long-term loan of £20,000.

17.3.2 Trade credit

We have already seen how to account for trade credit in Chapter 3. All that is involved is delaying settling the creditor, i.e. crediting the **bank** column with the payment and debiting the **creditor** column to extinguish the liability.

17.3.3 Factoring

When cash is received from the factoring company the **bank** column is debited and the **debtors** column credited. Any commission reduces the debtor balance and is entered in the profit and loss account as an expense.

Spreadsheet 17.1 Recording bank borrowing

A	B	C	D	E	F	G
Bank Borrowing						
				Short	Long	
		`ank	Term	Term		
				Loan	Loan	
Short Term Loan			10000	−10000		
Long Term Loan			20000		−20000	

Closing Balance			30000	−10000	−20000	0

A	B	C	D	E	F	G
Bank Borrowing						
				Short	Long	
			Bank	Term	Term	
				Loan	Loan	
Short Term Loan			10000	−D9		
Long Term Loan			20000		−D11	

Closing Balance			SUM(D9:D11)	SUM(E9:E11)	SUM(F9:F11)	SUM(D13:F13)

Let us consider an example. Suppose a company sells £100,000-worth of goods to a customer and then sells this debt to a factoring company for 80 per cent of the debt up-front with the balance to be paid less commission when the debtors pay. Commission charged is 2 per cent of sales. See Spreadsheet 17.2 for the accounting transactions needed to record this situation.

The credit sale is recorded in the usual way by debiting **debtors** and crediting **profit and loss account**. The 80 per cent received from the factoring company is credited to **debtors** and debited to **bank**. The commission is debited to the **profit and loss** column since it is a business expense and credited to **debtors** to extinguish the £2,000 which is no longer owed. Finally, when the final balance of £18,000 is received, the **bank** column is debited and the **debtors** column credited.

If the company's year end falls before the debtor pays the factoring company the spreadsheet would look like Spreadsheet 17.3.

Spreadsheet 17.2   The accounting treatment of factored debts

	A	B	C	D	E	F
1						
2						
3			Factor	P and L	Bank	Customer
4			Debtor	A/c		Debtor
5						
6	Sale of Goods			-100000		100000
7						
8	Sale of Debt		100000			-100000
9						
10	Money from Factor					
11		80 %	-80000		80000	
12						
13	Commission					
14		2 %	-2000	2000		
15						
16	Balance paid		-18000		18000	
17			---
18	Closing Balance		0	-98000	98000	0

	A	B	C	D	E	F
1						
2						
3			Factor	P and L	Bank	Customer
4			Debtor	A/c		Debtor
5						
6	Sale of Goods			-F6		100000
7						
8	Sale of Debt		-F8			-F6
9						
10	Money from Factor					
11	80	%	-C8*A11/100		-C11	
12						
13	Commission					
14	2	%	-C8*A14/100	-C14		
15						
16	Balance paid		-SUM(C8:C14)		-C16	
17			--
18	Closing Balance		SUM(C6:C16)	SUM(D6:D16)	SUM(E6:E16)	SUM(F6:F16)

If there is any doubt about the debtor not paying then the £18,000 needs to be provided for. Of course if the factoring company provides insurance against this problem then no such provision is necessary.

17.3.4   Bills of exchange

Let us consider how to account for a bill of exchange by considering the example in Figure 17.2.

Spreadsheet 17.3 Accounting for unpaid factored debts

	A		B		C		D		E		F	
1												
2												
3					Factor		P and L		Bank		Customer	
4					Debtor		A/c				Debtor	
5												
6	Sale of Goods						-100000				100000	
7												
8	Sale of Debt				100000						-100000	
9												
10	Money from Factor											
11		80 %			-80000				80000			
12												
13	Commission											
14		2 %			-2000		2000					
15												
16												
17					------		------		------		------	
18	Closing Balance				18000		-98000		80000		0	

XYZ Company owes ABC Company £100,000 for goods or services received, so ABC has drawn up the bill of exchange and presented it to XYZ Company who have written 'accepted' on the bill. ABC Company wants its money immediately so takes the bill to a discount house, which gives ABC Company £98,000 retaining £2,000 as its commission. The discount house subsequently presents the bill to XYZ Company when the ninety days are up and XYZ pays over to the discount house the £100,000. If XYZ did not pay up, the discount house would have recourse to ABC for its money.

Spreadsheet 17.4 shows the accounting entries necessary to record the bill in ABC's records. Once the bill is accepted by XYZ the debt is a negotiable bill of exchange which can be discounted, so the debt is transferred from the XYZ column to a **bills receivable** column. Once the bill has been discounted, a £98,000

Cardiff 15 April 1988

90 days after the above date please pay to my order the sum of One Hundred Thousand Pounds sterling for value received.

TO: XYZ Company   SIGNED: ABC Company

Figure 17.2 A sample bill of exchange

Spreadsheet 17.4   Accounting for bills of exchange

	A	B	C	D	E	F
1						
2						
3						
4				P and L	Bills	Bank
5			Debt	A/c	Receivable	
6						
7	Sales		100000	-100000		
8						
9	Bill Accepted		-100000		100000	
10						
11	Bill Discounted				-98000	98000
12						
13	Commission					
14		2 % rate		2000	-2000	
15			----	-------------	----------	------
16	Closing Balance		0	-98000	0	98000

	A	B	C	D	E	F
1						
2						
3						
4				P and L	Bills	Bank
5			Debt	A/c	Receivable	
6						
7	Sales		100000	-C7		
8						
9	Bill Accepted		-C7		-C9	
10						
11	Bill Discounted				C9*(100-A14)/100	-E11
12						
13	Commission					
14	2	% rate		-C9*A14/100	-D14	
15			-------	-------------	----------------	-------
16	Closing Balance		SUM(C7:C14)	SUM(D7:D14)	SUM(E7:E14)	SUM(F7:F14)

cheque is received so the **bank** column is debited and the **bills receivable** column is credited. The £2,000 commission is debited to the **profit and loss** column as an expense and credited to extinguish the remaining debt.

17.3.5   Hire purchase

The accounting entries necessary to record the purchase of assets on hire purchase are similar to those of a short-term loan. However, the ownership of the asset does not pass to the company until all the payments have been made, prior to this time the outstanding balance must be shown as a liability.

17.3.6 Leasing

The accounting entries necessary to record the acquisition of assets on a lease are the subject of SSAP 21. The traditional way of dealing with leases is merely a charge to the profit and loss account for the payments due during the accounting period. However, SSAP 21 places leases on the balance sheet. A finance lease is 'capitalised', with the asset depreciated over its economic life. This is offset by a liability for the outstanding lease payments.

17.3.7 Long-term loans

The accounting entries to record the issue of a simple long-term loan has been dealt with in 17.3.1 above.

The accounting entries to record the issue of debentures are similar to those for shares dealt with in 17.3.8 below.

The redemption of debentures, however, does require more consideration. The company can redeem its debentures in the open market when it considers their price to be favourable or at the end of their life, often with the use of a sinking fund. We will look at each in turn.

Redemption of debentures during their life

Let us consider an example. Suppose the company's balance sheet is as shown in Table 17.1. It wants to redeem £1,000 of the debentures at a premium of 40 per cent.

Table 17.1 *Redemption of debentures: sample balance sheet*

Balance sheet as at 31/12/89	
	£
Net assets other than bank	20,000
Bank	6,000
	26,000
Finance by:	
share capital	15,000
share premium	3,000
debentures	6,000
profit and loss account	2,000
	26,000

The accounting entries necessary to redeem these debentures are shown in Spreadsheet 17.5.

The £1,000 debentures are taken out of the **debentures** column (i.e. debit) and credited to the **bank** column. The £400 premium also is a cash payment so the **bank** is credited; the debit is taken to the **share premium** column rather than the **profit and loss** column, as this is one of the few uses allowed to be made of the **share**

Spreadsheet 17.5   Redemption of debentures

	A	B	C	D	E	F	G	H	I	J	K
1											
2											
3											
4				Other	Bank	Share	Share	Debentures	P and L	Debenture	
5				Assets		Capital	Premium			Redemption	
6										Reserve	
7											
8	Opening Balance Sheet			20000	6000	-15000	-3000	-6000	-2000		0
9											
10	Redemption of Debt				-1000			1000			
11											
12	Redemption Premium										
13	40 % rate				-400		400				
14											
15	Transfer to Debenture										
16	Redemption Reserve								1400	-1400	
17											
18				--							
19				20000	4600	-15000	-2600	-5000	-600	-1400	0

	A	B	C	D	E	F	G	H	I	J	K
1											
2											
3											
4				Other	Bank	Share	Share	Debentures	P and L	Debenture	
5				Assets		Capital	Premium			Redemption	
6										Reserve	
7											
8	Opening Balance Sheet			20000	6000	-15000	-3000	-6000	-2000		SUM(D8:J8)
9											
10	Redemption of Debt				-H10			1000			
11											
12	Redemption Premium										
13	40	% rate			E10*A13/100		-E13				
14											
15	Transfer to Debenture										
16	Redemption Reserve								-SUM(E10:E1	-I16	
17											
18				--							
19				SUM(D8:D17)	SUM(E8:E17)	SUM(F8:F17)	SUM(G8:G17)	SUM(H8:H17)	SUM(I8:I17)	SUM(J8:J17)	SUM(D19:J19)

Table 17.2 *The effect on the balance sheet of redeeming debentures*

	Before	After
Share capital	15,000	15,000
Share premium	3,000	2,600
Debentures	6,000	5,000
Debenture redemption reserve	—	1,400
	£24,000	£24,000

premium column by company law. The final entry is to debit the **profit and loss** column and credit a new column, the **debenture redemption reserve**, with the nominal value of the debentures redeemed. The reason for such an entry is not company law, but prudential accounting practice: to maintain non-distributable capital of which debentures were a part at their previous level (see Table 17.2).

Redemption of debentures at the end of their life with the use of a sinking fund

The company knows when it issues the debentures that it will have to redeem them sometime in the future. It may decide to put aside an amount of cash each year into an investment account which will be sufficient to pay for the redemption on the due date. This is called a 'sinking fund'.

Let us consider an example. Suppose the company had to redeem £100,000-worth of debentures in 5 years' time, and it could earn 10 per cent interest per annum. It would need to put aside £16,380 each year into a debenture sinking fund investment account, so that after 5 years it would amount to the £100,000 needed. See Spreadsheet 17.6, which shows how this sum builds up to the required £100,000. The £16,380 is calculated using annuity tables, i.e.:

$$\frac{£100,000}{6.105} = £16,380$$

17.3.8 Equity capital

Many individuals now own shares, but not many apply for a new share issue. The privatisation issues with which most are familiar are not typical of the normal raising of finance on the stock market by large companies when they issue new shares. Accounting for share issues can be complicated by the fact that in the real world there will not be exactly the required number of potential shareholders as there are new shares to be issued. Nor is the finance raised on a simple basis. Most new issues only require subscribers to put down a deposit on application, with a further installment due on 'allotment'. The final balance may be due in a number of installments, or 'calls'.

Spreadsheet 17.6   Build-up of a sinking fund

	A	B	C	D	E	F	G
1							
2							
3	Year	Annual	Capital	Capital	Interest	Capital	Annuity
4		Investment	b/f	c/f	Rate %	After	Construction
5					10	Interest	
6							
7	1	16380		16380	1638	18018	1
8							
9	2	16380	18018	34397	3440	37837	1.1
10							
11	3	16380	37837	54217	5422	59639	1.21
12							
13	4	16380	59639	76018	7602	83620	1.331
14							
15	5	16380	83620	100000			1.4641
16							
17							6.1051

	A	B	C	D	E	F	G
1							
2							
3	Year	Annual	Capital	Capital	Interest	Capital	Annuity
4		Investment	b/f	c/f	Rate %	After	Construction
5					10	Interest	
6							
7	1	D15/G17		B7+C7	D7*E5/100	D7+E7	1
8							
9	2	D15/G17	F7	B9+C9	D9*E5/100	D9+E9	G7*(1+E5/100)
10							
11	3	D15/G17	F9	B11+C11	D11*E5/10	D11+E11	G9*(1+E5/100)
12							
13	4	D15/G17	F11	B13+C13	D13*E5/10	D13+E13	G11*(1+E5/100)
14							
15	5	D15/G17	F13	100000			G13*(1+E5/100)
16							
17							SUM(G7:G15)

Some investors put down their deposit and then, for reasons sometimes better known to themselves, decide they do not want their shares. They may feel that the company is not such a good buy, and cut their losses before any further installments are due.

Let's have a look at an example which contains a few of the complications mentioned and the accounting treatment necessary to record the transactions. Figure 17.3 gives the example of Gas Fuels plc.

The transactions necessary are given in Spreadsheet 17.7.

In tackling a problem of this sort, it is wise to enumerate the transactions taking place before trying to 'put the figure in'. Only when you have a clear

Gas Fuels plc has authorised and issued share capital of £100,000, consisting of 100,000 fully paid up ordinary shares of £1 each. On 2 June 1989, the authorised share capital was increased to £200,000 and 80,000 £1 shares were offered to the public at £1.50 each, i.e. a premium of 50p a share. The terms of the offer were that 75p was payable on application, with a further 45p payable when the shares were allotted. The 75p due on application included the share premium. The final 30p a share was due on 2 November 1989.

The offer finished on 16 June 1989, and 105,000 applications were received. Of these, 5,000 were returned, leaving the balance to be allocated amongst the shares available on a *pro rata* basis.

Of the successful applicants, one for 500 shares was declared forfeited. These shares were reissued at £1.35 on 3 December 1989. The call due on 2 November 1989 was paid by the other shareholders.

Figure 17.3 Gas Fuels plc

picture of the sequence of events and the build-up of the issue can you possibly correctly record the accounting transactions necessary.

In the opening balance sheet, merely for the sake of convenience, it is assumed that the share capital fully paid and issued is matched by cash. Of course, in the real world this would be made up of a number of assets and liabilities, but the number of columns are kept to a minimum through this assumption.

If there are applications for 105,000 shares at 75p a share then the company must have received $105,000 \times 75p = £78,750$ in the first instance. The company decides to return 5,000 applications – this may be decided by ballot, or some other decision criteria – hence the unsuccessful deposits are returned, i.e. $5000 \times 75p = £3,750$. The entries in the **cash** column are matched by entries in the **application and allotment** column. This is a form of suspense account, as no shares have been issued as yet.

There is a total of £1.20 payable on each share once it has been allotted, but of this amount 50p relates to share premium, i.e. that amount above the par value of the share. Therefore only 70p of the £1.20 due relates to share capital. So from the application and allotment account come two amounts relating to share capital, $80,000 \times 70p = £56,000$ and share premium, $80,000 \times 50p = £40,000$.

By performing these entries it is evident that there will be a debit balance on the application and allotment account. This balance is £21,000, representing the total amount owed by the purchasers of the shares at this stage. This is made up as shown in Table 17.3. This is to be gained from the sale of just 80,000 shares as the issue has been over-subscribed. Therefore for each ten shares applied for, the applicant will only receive eight. This means that for each share now allotted the applicant has to pay just $21,000/80,000 = 26.25p$.

The fact that one applicant has forfeited his shares means that 500 shares will not be issued. Note that at this time only 70p relates to share capital and so

Spreadsheet 17.7 Share issue including forfeiture

	A	B	C	D	E	F	G	H	I	J
					Application					
				Cash	&	Share	Share	Forfeited	Call	
					Allotment	Capital	Premium	Shares		
8	Opening Balance Sheet			100000		-100000				
10	Application for Allotment									
11		105000	.75	78750	-78750					
13	Share Applications Returned									
14		5000	.75	-3750	3750					
16	Due on Application & Allot.									
17		80000	.7		56000	-56000				
19	Share Premium									
20		80000	.5		40000		-40000			
22	Forfeited Shares									
23		500	.7			350		-350		
25	Cash Received									
26		21000	.2625	20869	-20869					
28	Balance Transferred				-131			131		
30	Call Received									
31		79500	.3	23850					-23850	
33	Transferred to Share Capital					-23850			23850	
35	Cash Paid for Shares									
36		500	1.35	675				-675		
38	Transferred to Share Capital					-500		500		
40	Balance to Share Premium						-394	394		
42	Closing Balance Sheet			220394	0	-180000	-40394	0	0	0

$500 \times 50p = £350$ is debited from the share capital account and placed into **forfeited shares**. As this applicant has forfeited, he will not be contributing to the £21,000 outstanding, i.e. the company will not receive $500 \times 26.25p = £131.25$, only £21,000 less £131.25 = £20,868.75, with the balance due on the forfeited shares again transferred to **forfeited shares** column. This is also a form of suspense account, used until the shares are eventually issued.

Spreadsheet 17.7a Share issue including forfeiture (formulae)

	A	B	C	D	E	F	G	H	I	J
				Cash	Application & Allotment	Share Capital	Share Premium	Forfeited Shares	Call	
8	Opening Balance Sheet			-F8		-100000				
10	Application for Allotment									
11	105000	.75		A11*B11	-D11					
13	Share Applications Returned									
14	5000	.75		-A14*B14	-D14					
16	Due on Application & Allot.									
17	80000	.7			A17*B17	-E17				
19	Share Premium									
20	A17	.5			A20*B20		-E20			
22	Forfeited Shares									
23	500	B17				A23*B23		-F23		
25	Cash Received									
26	SUM(E7:E25)	A26/A20		A26-(A23*B26)	-D26					
28	Balance Transferred				-A26-E26			-E28		
30	Call Received									
31	A20-A23	.30		A31*B31					-D31	
33	Transferred to Share Capital					-I33			-I31	
35	Cash Paid for Shares									
36	A23	1.35		A36*B36				-D36		
38	Transferred to Share Capital					-H38		A36		
40	Balance to Share Premium						-H40	-SUM(H8:H38)		
42	Closing Balance Sheet			SUM(D8:D40)	SUM(E8:E40)	SUM(F8:F40)	SUM(G8:G40)	SUM(H8:H40)	SUM(I8:I40)	SUM(D42:I42)

Table 17.3 *Account to be paid by allotted shareholders*

On application	75p due	
On allotment	45p due	
	£1.20	due per share
	× 80,000	shares
	£96,000	total due from shares
Paid on application	£75,000	(i.e. 100,000 × 75p)
	£21,000	remaining from shares

So in November the company's call is due, i.e. $(80{,}000 - 500) \times 30p = £23{,}850$. This is first recorded in a **call** account before being transferred to **share capital**.

The forfeited shares are finally issued in December with cash recorded accordingly, with a double entry in the suspense account. The shares are then issued and the balance on the forfeited shares account is transferred to **share premium**.

The final balance sheet is the acid test, and as we can see share capital has risen by £80,000 and share premium by £40,000 plus the profit on the forfeited shares, £394. The spreadsheet has been formatted to **integers** in the spreadsheet columns to enhance presentation.

There are other ways of issuing shares; one such example is that of a rights issue. Suppose the company decides to raise its £4,000 not by issuing bonds but by a rights issue, asking its existing shareholders to subscribe for new shares at £5 each when the current ex-rights market price is £8 per share. See Spreadsheet 17.8 for accounting entries. The nominal value per share is £1.

Spreadsheet 17.8 Accounting for a rights issue

	A		B		C		D		E		F		G		H	
1																
2																
3					Other				Share				Share			
4					Assets		Bank		Capital		P & L		Premium			
5																
6	Pre-Rights B.S.				1500		1500		-2000		-1000		0			0
7																
8	Share Capital						800		-800							
9																
10	Share Premium						3200						-3200			
11					-----		-----		-----		-----		-----			
12	Closing B.S.				1500		5500		-2800		-1000		-3200			0

	A		B		C		D		E		F		G	
1														
2														
3					Other				Share				Share	
4					Assets		Bank		Capital		P & L		Premium	
5														
6	Pre-Rights B.S.				1500		1500		-2000		-1000		0	
7														
8	Share Capital						-E8		-4000/5					
9														
10	Share Premium						-G10						-2000/5*8	
11					-----		-----		-----		-----		-----	
12	Closing B.S.				SUM(C6:C10)		SUM(D6:D10)		SUM(E6:E10)		SUM(F6:F10)		SUM(G6:G10)	

£800-worth of new ordinary shares are issued if all rights are exercised and since £4,000 cash is received, £3,200 share premium is created.

If the company decided to issue the £4,000 by a placing at £8 per share, their current market price, Spreadsheet 17.9 shows the necessary accounting entries. It is assumed that £8 is paid as one amount.

A bonus issue raises no cash, it only involves a transfer from reserves to share capital. If the company, after the placing, decides to reduce its share premium by issuing one ordinary share for each one held, the results are shown in Spreadsheet 17.10.

As can be seen, share capital increases to £5,000 and share premium reduces to £1,000. The share price immediately falls to half its pre-bonus price.

The Companies Act 1985 allows companies to purchase their own shares. Let us consider an example. PRS Ltd has 1,200,000 ordinary £1 shares in issued, fully paid and originally issued at £1.15 per share. The company decides to redeem 400,000 of these shares at a premium of 40p per share. This is to be financed by

Spreadsheet 17.9 Placing shares at market price

	A		B		C		D		E		F		G		H	
1																
2																
3					Other				Share				Share			
4					Assets		Bank		Capital		P & L		Premium			
5																
6	Pre-Rights B.S.				1500		1500		−2000		−1000			0		0
7																
8	Share Capital						500		−500							
9																
10	Share Premium						3500						−3500			
11					----		----		----		----		----			
12	Closing B.S.				1500		5500		−2500		−1000		−3500			0

	A		B		C		D		E		F		G		H	
1																
2																
3					Other				Share				Share			
4					Assets		Bank		Capital		P & L		Premium			
5																
6	Pre-Rights B.S.		1500		1500		−2000		−1000		0		SUM(C6:66)			
7																
8	Share Capital				4000/8		−D8									
9																
10	Share Premium				D8*(8−1)						−D10					
11					----		----		----		----		----			
12	Closing B.S.		SUM(C6:C10)		SUM(D6:D10)		SUM(E6:E10)		SUM(F6:F10)		SUM(G6:G10)		SUM(C12:G12)			

Spreadsheet 17.10   Accounting for bonus issues

	A	B	C	D	E	F	G	H
1								
2								
3			Other		Share		Share	
4			Assets	Bank	Capital	P & L	Premium	
5								
6	Pre-Rights B.S.		1500	1500	-2000	-1000	0	0
7								
8	Share Capital			500	-500			
9								
10	Share Premium			3500			-3500	
11				---				
12	Post-Rights B.S.		1500	5500	-2500	-1000	-3500	0
13								
14	Bonus Issue				-2500		2500	
15				---				
16	Closing B.S.		1500	5500	-5000	-1000	-1000	0

	A	B	C	D	E	F	G	H
1								
2								
3			Other		Share		Share	
4			Assets	Bank	Capital	P & L	Premium	
5								
6	Pre-Rights B.S.	1500	1500	-2000	-1000	0	SUM(C6:G6)	
7								
8	Share Capital		4000/8	-D8				
9								
10	Share Premium		D8*(8-1)			-D10		
11				--				
12	Post-Rights B.S.	SUM(C6:C10)	SUM(D6:D10)	SUM(E6:E10)	SUM(F6:F10)	SUM(G6:G10)	SUM(C12:G12)	
13								
14	Bonus Issue			E12		-E14		
15				--				
16	Closing B.S.	SUM(C12:C14)	SUM(D12:D14)	SUM(E12:E14)	SUM(F12:F14)	SUM(G12:G14)	SUM(C16:G16)	

issuing 200,000 preference shares of £1 at a premium of 20p per share. The balance on the profit and loss account was £500,000.

Spreadsheet 17.11 shows the relevant accounting entries. The issue of the new preference shares is straightforward: 200,000 shares are issued at £1.20 per share so £240,000 is raised of which £40,000 is share premium. £400,000 ordinary shares are redeemed (hence the £400,000 debit entry in ordinary shares) at a premium of 20p per share, so that total cash needed is £480,000, hence the £480,000 credit entry in the **bank** column. The company would like to record all the remaining £80,000 debit to share premium as its uses are limited (i.e. it cannot be used to pay dividends as the profit and loss account can).

Spreadsheet 17.11 Purchase of shares

	Ordinary Shares	Share Premium	P & L	Preference Shares	Bank	C.R.R.F.	Other Assets
Opening B.S.	-1200000	-240000	-500000				1940000
Issue Pref. Shares				-200000	200000		
Premium on P.S.		-40000			40000		
Redemption of Ordinary Shares	400000				-400000		
Premium on O.S.		60000			-60000		
Balance o/s			20000		-20000		
Transfer to C.R.R.F.			160000			-160000	
Closing B.S.	-800000	-220000	-320000	-200000	-240000	-160000	1940000

	Ordinary Shares	Share Premium	P & L	Preference Shares	Bank	C.R.R.F.	Other Assets
Opening B.S.	-1200000	C6*.2	-500000				-SUM(C6:H6)
Issue Pref. Shares				-200000	-F8		
Premium on P.S.		F8*.2			-D10		
Redemption of Ordinary Shares	400000				-C13		
Premium on O.S.		C13*.15			-D15		
Balance o/s			C13*.05		-E17		
Transfer to C.R.R.F.			C13-G8-G10			-E19	
Closing B.S.	SUM(C6:C19)	SUM(D6:D19)	SUM(E6:E19)	SUM(F6:F19)	SUM(G6:G19)	SUM(H6:H19)	SUM(I6:I19)

However, company law restricts this set-off to the lesser of:

a. the balance on the **share premium** column following the new issue (i.e. 240,000 + 40,000 = £280,000);

b. the premium raised on the original issue of share now being redeemed (i.e. 400,000 × 0.15p = £60,000).

Therefore, in this example, only £60,000 can be debited to the **share premium** column; the remaining £20,000 has to be recorded in the profit and loss column.

Finally, for creditor protection, the amount of the redemption not backed by the new issue must be taken to a non-distributable reserve called the 'capital redemption fund'. This amount is:

	£
Nominal value of ordinary shares redeemed	400,000
less proceeds of replacement shares	240,000
	£160,000

17.3.9 Preference shares

The issue and redemption of preference shares is accounted for in similar ways to ordinary shares.

CHECKLIST _____

Having completed Chapter 17, you should be able to:

■ describe the various sources of finance available to companies;
■ be aware of the suitability of each source in different circumstances, helping the company to minimise its financing charges;
■ record the transactions necessary to account for financing transactions.

Workshop 17.1: Sources of finance

Telebuster plc has authorised and issued share capital of £200,000, consisting of 200,000 fully paid up ordinary shares of £1 each. On 2 June 19X9, the authorised share capital was increased to £400,000 and 160,000 £1 shares were offered to the public at £1.50 each, i.e. a premium of 50p a share. The terms of the offer were that 75p was payable on application, with a further 45p payable when the shares were allotted. The 75p due on application included the share premium. The final 30p a share was due on 2 November 19X9.

The offer finished on 16 June 19X9, and 210,000 applications were received. Of these, 10,000 were returned, leaving the balance to be allocated among the shares available on a *pro rata* basis.

Of the successful applicants, one for 1,000 shares was declared forfeited. These shares were reissued at £1.35 on 3 December 19X9. The call due on 2 November 19X9 was paid by the other shareholders.

Workshop guide

1. Firstly, enumerate the necessary transcations, so that you have a clear picture in your own mind of what is required. This is based on the example in the text so it should still be fresh in your mind.

2. Use the short cut of assuming that net assets consist of cash. We are not concerned with the whole balance sheet, just the extracts relating to share issue.

3. The company receives $210,000 \times 75p = £157,500$, with 10,000 applications returned, i.e. $10,000 \times 75p = £7,500$. The entries in the **cash** column are matched by entries in the **application and allotment** column.

4. From the application and allotment account come two amounts relating to share capital, $160,000 \times 70p = £112,000$ and share premium $160,000 \times 50p = £80,000$. The debit balance on the application and allotment account, £42,000, represents the total amount owed by the purchasers of the shares at this stage.

   This is to be gained from the sale of just 160,000 shares as the issue has been over-subscribed. Therefore for each ten shares applied for, the applicant will only receive eight. This means that for each share now allotted the applicant has to pay $42,000/160,000 = 26.25p$.

5. One applicant has forfeited his 1,000 shares so $1,000 \times 70p = £700$ is debited from the share capital account and placed into forfeited shares.

6. In November the company's call is due, i.e. $(160,000 - 1,000) \times 30p = £47,700$. This is recorded in the call account before being transferred to share capital.

7. The forfeited shares are issued in December and the balance on the forfeited shares account is transferred to **share premium.**

Spreadsheet 17.12a   Workshop 17.1: Telebuster – solution

	A	B	C	D Cash	E Application & Allotment	F Share Capital	G Share Premium	H Forfeited Shares	I Call	J
1										
2										
3										
4										
5										
6										
7										
8	Opening Balance Sheet			200000		-200000				
9										
10	Appication for Allotment									
11		210000	.75	157500	-157500					
12										
13	Share Applications Returned									
14		10000	.75	-7500	7500					
15										
16	Due on Application & Allot.									
17		160000	.7		112000	-112000				
18										
19	Share Premium									
20		160000	.5			80000	-80000			
21										
22	Forfeited Shares									
23		1000	.7			700		-700		
24										
25	Cash Received									
26		42000	.2625	41738	-41738					
27										
28	Balance Transferred				-263			263		
29										
30	Call Received									
31		159000	.3	47700					-47700	
32										
33	Transferred to Share Capital					-47700			47700	
34										
35	Cash Paid for Shares									
36		1000	1.35	1350				-1350		
37										
38	Transferred to Share Capital					-1000		1000		
39										
40	Balance to Share Premium						-788	788		
41										
42	Closing Balance Sheet			440788	0	-360000	-80788	0	0	0

Spreadsheet 17.12b Workshop 17.1: Telebuster – formulae

	A	B	C	D Cash	E Application & Allotment	F Share Capital	G Share Premium	H Forfeited Shares	I Call	J
8	Opening Balance Sheet			-F8		-200000				
10	Appication for Allotment									
11	210000	.75		A11*B11	-D11					
13	Share Applications Returned									
14	10000	.75		-A14*B14	-D14					
16	Due on Application & Allot.									
17	160000	.7			A17*B17	-E17				
19	Share Premium									
20	A17	.5			A20*B20		-E20			
22	Forfeited Shares									
23	1000	B17				A23*B23		-F23		
25	Cash Received									
26	SUM(E7:E A26/A20			A26-(A23*B26	-D26					
28	Balance Transferred				-A26-E26			-E28		
30	Call Received									
31	A20-A23	.30		A31*B31					-D31	
33	Transferred to Share Capital					-I33			-I31	
35	Cash Paid for Shares									
36	A23	1.35		A36*B36				-D36		
38	Transferred to Share Capital					-H38		A36		
40	Balance to Share Premium						-H40	-SUM(H8:H38)		
42	Closing Balance Sheet			SUM(D8:D40)	SUM(E8:E40)	SUM(F8:F40)	SUM(G8:G40)	SUM(H8:H40)	SUM(I8:I40)	SUM(D42:I42)

'What if?' problems

1. What if the shares were issued at premium of 75p? Which transactions would be affected?

2. If no shares were returned, what would be the balance due to be allocated among shareholders? How much would they each have to pay *pro rata*?

3. What would happen if the shares that were forfeited could not be reissued?

Answers

1. Change cell B20 to **.75**. This will affect cash received (row 26), the balance transferred (row 28) and the balance to **Share Premium** (row 40).

2. Balance to be shared amongst shareholders would be zero. The shareholders would have to pay 26.25p per share *pro rata*.

3. The amount would be written off against the share premium account.

Selected questions and exercises

Question 17.1
Applications were invited by the directors of Patricia plc for 150,000 of its £1 ordinary shares at £1.15 per share payable as follows:

On application	75p per share
On allotment (including the premium of 15p per share)	20p per share
On first and final call	20p per share

Applications were received for 180,000 shares and it was decided to deal with these as follows:

1. To refuse allotment to applicants for 8,000 shares.
2. To give full allotment to applicants for 22,000 shares.
3. To allot the remainder of the available shares pro rata among the other applicants.
4. To utilise the surplus received on applications in part payments of amounts due on allotment.

An applicant to whom 400 shares had been allotted, failed to pay the amount due on the first and final call and his shares were declared forfeited. These shares were re-issued as fully paid at 90p per share.

You are required to write up the necessary ledger accounts, including the cash book, to show how the transactions mentioned would be recorded in the company's books.

No solution provided

18 Taxation in company financial statements

AIMS OF CHAPTER _____

- to introduce you to some of the major elements of taxation in company accounts;
- to explain the major features of VAT, corporation tax, advanced corporation tax and income tax and how to account for these taxes in company accounts;
- to outline the need for deferred taxation, how it is calculated and how it affects company accounts.

18.1 Introduction

When you look at the published financial statements of companies you are likely to find many balances and descriptions relating to taxation. This proliferation of tax entries is often responsible for preventing someone with a good understanding of financial accounting making sense of company financial statements. Therefore the aim of this chapter is to explain those taxation elements which are most likely to be found in company financial statements. We will look at value added tax, corporation tax, advanced corporation tax, income tax and deferred tax.

Before proceeding it is important to bear in mind that we are not primarily concerned with how tax is calculated, which is a topic in its own right. What we are concerned with is how tax appears in company financial statements; in order to understand this we do, however, require some basic knowledge of how tax is calculated. This basic knowledge of how tax (no attempt is made to cover all eventualities) is calculated will be introduced when needed. The major points are introduced in the main body of the chapter, with the more detailed points (indicated here by superscript numbers) appearing at the end of the chapter as notes (see Section 18.9).

18.2 Valued added tax

Some goods and services are liable to VAT which is added to their selling price.[1] For example, if goods costing £100 are subject to 15 per cent VAT (the current rate) the selling price is shown in Table 18.1.

VAT is a tax borne by the final consumer; however, it is levied on all sales, even those intermediate sales, as the goods and services pass through manufacturer, wholesaler and retailer. Therefore these intermediate organisations are in the position of paying VAT on their purchases, which they can claim back, and collecting VAT on their sales, which they pay over to the Customs and Excise authorities.[2]

An example of how to account for these payments and receipts of VAT should make this clear. Suppose a company buys £100,000-worth of goods on which it pays £15,000 of VAT and sells £140,000-worth of goods on which it charges £21,000 of VAT. (Do not always expect the VAT to be exactly 15 per cent of either sales or purchases as some goods and services are exempt VAT or zero rated.) Spreadsheet 18.1 shows the accounting entries to record these transactions.

Purchases are recorded by debiting the **profit and loss** column and crediting **creditors**. The VAT on purchases is recorded by debiting a **VAT** column to reflect that the Customs and Excise authorities owe the company this VAT (i.e. a debtor) and a credit to the **creditors** column as the company is responsible for paying the VAT to the supplier just as much as they are for paying him for the cost of the purchase. Sales are recorded by debiting a **debtors** column and crediting the **profit and loss** column. VAT on sales is recorded as a debit to the **debtors** column as the debtor must pay the VAT to the company and as a credit to the **VAT** column as the company is responsible for paying the VAT to the Customs and Excise authorities.

As can be seen, there is no VAT in the **profit and loss** column, as the company is merely a collecting agent for the Customs and Excise and does not incur the tax. The only VAT figure which is entered in the balance sheet is the VAT creditor. The company must pay the Customs and Excise £6,000 of VAT by the due date or it may incur interest or penalties.[3]

If the VAT on purchases exceeds the VAT on sales the company would have a VAT debtor balance which it would claim back from the Customs and Excise. Try

Table 18.1 *VAT as a percentage of the cost of goods*

	£s
Goods cost	100
VAT at 15%	15
Selling price	£115

Spreadsheet 18.1 VAT owing to Customs and Excise

	A	B	C	D	E	F	G
1							
2							
3	Description			Profit	V.A.T.	Creditors	Debtors
4				and			
5				Loss			
6							
7	Purchases			100000		-100000	
8							
9	V.A.T. on purchase				15000	-15000	
10							
11	Sales			-140000			140000
12							
13	V.A.T. on sales				-21000		21000
14							
15	------						
16	Balances			-40000	-6000	-115000	161000
17	======						

changing the purchase figure to £160,000 and the VAT on these purchases to £24,000 to see how a VAT debtor can arise. Spreadsheet 18.2 shows this situation. Statement of standard accounting practice 5 discusses accounting for VAT.

18.3 Corporation tax (CT)

Companies are required to pay CT as a percentage of their taxable profits.[4] The current rate of corporation tax is 35 per cent. Taxable profit is the profit figure

Spreadsheet 18.2 VAT owed by Customs and Excise

	A	B	C	D	E	F	G
1							
2							
3	Description			Profit	V.A.T.	Creditors	Debtors
4				and			
5				Loss			
6							
7	Purchases			160000		-160000	
8							
9	V.A.T. on purchase				24000	-24000	
10							
11	Sales			-140000			140000
12							
13	V.A.T. on sales				-21000		21000
14							
15	------						
16	Balances			20000	3000	-184000	161000
17	======						

calculated from a series of rules laid down by Acts of Parliament, court cases and the Inland Revenue. As these rules are often different from the accounting polices used by the company in working out its accounting profit, the taxable profit and accounting profit are likely to be different figures. The reasons for the Inland Revenue using a different profit figure to that found in the accounts are that different companies use different accounting policies and there would be a strong temptation for a company to select those accounting policies which produced a low profit figure (such as high rates of depreciation) to reduce their tax bill. There are also some items such as entertaining expenses that are politically unacceptable as a deduction in determining taxable profit.

The accounting entry to record CT is to debit the **profit and loss** column (as CT is an appropriation of profit) and credit a **CT liability** column (as CT will have to be paid over to the Inland Revene in the future). Spreadsheet 18.3 shows the transaction to record a CT charge of £35,000, in row 9.

CT has to be paid between nine and twenty-one months after the company's year end.[5] If CT is payable less than twelve months after the year end then the liability is current. If the CT has to be paid more than twelve months after the year end, the liability is long term.

Spreadsheet 18.3 shows an adjustment necessary to correct last year's CT, as the liability originally provided in the accounts was found to be £1,000 too much. An adjustment of this sort is usually necessary each year if the accounts are prepared soon after the year end and before the company has finalised the exact

Spreadsheet 18.3   Adjusting last year's CT

	A	B	C	D	E	F	G	H
1								
2								
3	Description			Profit	C.T.	C.T. Liability	Bank	Capital
4				and	Expense	Current		
5				Loss				
6								
7	Opening Balances			−50000		−10000	70000	−10000
8								
9	This years tax				35000	−35000		
10								
11	Adjustment of last year's C.T.				−1000	1000		
12								
13	Payment of last year's					9000	−9000	
14	but ones tax							
15	--							
16	Sub-totals			−50000	34000	−35000	61000	−10000
17								
18	Transfer of C.T. expense to			34000	−34000			
19	Profit and Loss							
20	--							
21	Closing Balances			−16000	0	−35000	61000	−10000
22	==							

amount of CT it is required to pay over to the Inland Revenue. Therefore this year's CT is only an estimated figure, so it is adjusted in the following year when the exact figure is determined. To be on the cautious side (remember the prudence concept), this year's CT is slightly over-estimated so the adjustment is invariably a reduction. This is the case in our example as the agreed CT is £9,000 so the liability is reduced by £1,000 (the debit) and the **CT expense** column is credited. It can be argued that the adjustment relates to last year, so should not be taken to the **CT expense** column since this is reducing this year's CT figure; however, the adjustment is usually not material in amount and is expected to re-occur every year and so cannot be classified as a prior year adjustment, under the definition laid down in Statement of Standard Accounting Practice Number 6 (see Chapter 19).

Spreadsheet 18.4 shows how CT is recorded in the accounts when it is payable more than twelve months after the year end. The opening balance sheet shows two liabilities for CT: a current liability of £5,000 being 'last-year-but-one's' CT and a long-term liability of £10,000 being last year's CT. This year's CT is £35,000; it is recorded in the spreadsheet by debiting the *profit and loss* column and crediting the long-term liability for CT as it will not have to be paid in the next year. The adjustment of last year's CT, from its estimated figure to its actual figure, is

Spreadsheet 18.4   CT payable more than twelve months after year end

	A	B	C	D	E	F	G	H	I	J
1										
2										
3	Description			Profit	C.T.	C.T.	Liability		Bank	Capital
4				and	Expense	Current	Long			
5				Loss			Term			
6										
7	Opening Balances			-50000		-5000	-10000		75000	-10000
8										
9	This years tax				35000		-35000			
10										
11	Adjustment of last year's C.T.				-1000		1000			
12										
13	Transfer of last year's					-9000	9000			
14	tax from L.T. to current									
15										
16	Payment of last year's					5000			-5000	
17	but ones tax									
18										
19	---									
20	Closing Balances			-50000	34000	-9000	-35000		70000	-10000
21										
22	Transfer of C.T. expense to			34000	-34000					
23	Profit and Loss									
24	---									
25	Closing Balances			-16000	0	-9000	-35000		70000	-10000	0
26	===									

£1,000. Last year's tax now recorded at £9,000 will have to be paid next year so it is transferred from a long-term to a current **CT liability** column. 'Last-year-but-one's' CT is now due and paid over to the Inland Revenue. The closing balance sheet shows two CT liabilities: this year's CT as a long-term liability and last year's CT as a current liability.

18.4 Advanced corporation tax

When companies distribute profits by way of dividend they are required to pay over to the Inland Revenue an amount of this year's CT in advance of its due date. The logic behind this advanced corporation tax (ACT) payment rule is to encourage companies to keep their profits rather than distributing them to their shareholders (who will fritter them away on good living!).

ACT has to be paid over to the Inland Revenue within fourteen days of the end of the calendar quarter in which the dividend is paid.

The amount of ACT payable is calculated as follows:

$$\frac{\text{Basic rate of income tax}}{(100 - \text{Basic rate of income tax})} * \text{Dividend}$$

Currently the basic rate of income tax is 25 per cent so 25/75 is multiplied by the amount of the dividend payment.

Any CT paid[6] is set off against the CT in respect of the year in which the dividend is paid.[7] The remaining net sum of CT is called mainstream CT (MCT).

An example should make this clear. Suppose a company makes a taxable and an accounting profit of £800,000, pays an interim dividend of £25,000 (six months before the year end) and proposes a final dividend of £50,000. The current rate of CT is 35 per cent and the basic rate of income tax is 25 per cent. The company has only one asset, cash of £850,000. Spreadsheet 18.5 shows how we record the ACT on these dividends.

The dividends are recorded as usual by debiting the **profit and loss** column and crediting a **dividends liability** column. Once a dividend has been recorded we must calculate and record the associated ACT. The ACT on the dividends is calculated as follows:

Interim dividend: £25,000*25/(100 − 25) = £ 8,333
Final dividend: £50,000*25/(100 − 25) = £16,667

We record ACT by opening up an **asset** and a **liability** column for ACT called **ACT recoverable** and **ACT payable** and recording the calculated amount as a debit in **ACT recoverable** and as a credit in **ACT payable**. When the ACT is paid we debit the **ACT payable** column to extinguish the liability and credit the **bank**

Spreadsheet 18.5 ACT on dividends paid

	A	B	C	D	E	F	G	H	I
3	Description	C.T. Expense	C.T. Liability	Profit & Loss	Dividend Liab.	A.C.T. Recover.	A.C.T. Payable	Bank	Capital
6	Opening Balances			-800000				850000	-50000
8	C.T. for this year	280000	-280000						
10	Interim Dividend			25000	-25000				
12	A.C.T. on interim dividend					8333	-8333		
14	Payment of Interim Dividend				25000			-25000	
16	Payment of A.C.T.						8333	-8333	
18	Off-set of A.C.T. against		8333			-8333			
19	C.T. Liability								
21	Final Dividend			50000	-50000				
23	A.C.T. on Final Dividend					18493	-18493		
25	Sub-totals	280000	-271667	-725000	-50000	18493	-18493	816667	-50000
27	Transfer of C.T. to Profit	-280000		280000					
28	and Loss								
30	Closing Balances	0	-271667	-445000	-50000	18493	-18493	816667	-50000

Table 18.2 *The balance sheet with ACT recorded*

	£	£
Current assets:		
ACT recoverable		16,667
bank		816,667
		833,334
Less current liabilities:		
CT liability	271,667	
dividend	50,000	
ACT payable	16,667	
		338,334
		£495,000
		£
Capital		50,000
Profit and loss		445,000
		£495,000

column. Once it is paid we can utilise the ACT recoverable by off-setting it against the CT liability; in this example the CT liability reduces to £271,667 (i.e. 280,000 − 8,333); this is called the mainstream CT liability. The ACT on the final dividend cannot yet be setoff against CT as the dividend has not yet been paid. The balance sheet will look as shown in Table 18.2.

As can be seen there is a current asset, ACT recoverable of £16,667 and a current liability ACT payable of the same amount.

18.5 The imputation system

Let us look at the dividend from the shareholders' point of view. They receive a cheque from the company which they bank. As far as they are concerned this represents income after income tax (IT) has been deducted at the basic rate. So they not only receive a dividend payment but also a tax credit. Let us consider an example; suppose a shareholder receives a cheque for £10 as a dividend. This is called the 'net dividend'. The tax credit is calculated as follows:

$$£10 * \frac{\text{the basic rate of IT}}{(100 - \text{the basic rate of IT})}$$

$$£10 * 25/(100 - 25) = £3.33$$

Therefore the gross dividend is £13.33.

If the shareholder pays IT at the basic rate then he has no further commitments to the Inland Revenue. If he does not pay IT he can reclaim the tax credit of £3.33. If he pays IT at a higher rate he must make up the difference.

Statement of standard accounting practice 8 deals with the imputation system of taxation.

18.6 Income tax

Companies issue interest-paying debentures which are bought by investors. The Inland Revenue requires companies to hold back income tax at the basic rate and only pay the debenture holder's interest net of tax. This income tax collected on behalf of the debenture holder is then paid to the Inland Revenue within fourteen days after the end of the calendar quarter in which the interest is paid, in a similar way to the payment of ACT.

Companies may themselves purchase debentures in other companies. If this is so, they will receive interest net of income tax at the basic rate. Since companies do not pay IT they can off-set this IT against any IT they withhold on their own debentures. If they have no debentures in issue they may set it off against their CT at the end of the year, or if there is no CT they may reclaim it. An example should clarify the situation. Suppose a company has an issue £500,000 10 per cent debentures and owns £300,000 15 per cent debentures in another company. Assume debenture interest is paid and received twice a year in two equal installments, one payment half-way through the year and the other at the year end.

Spreadsheet 18.6 shows how we record these interest payments together with their IT implications. Total gross interest due by the company to the debenture holders is £50,000 (i.e. £500,000 * 10 per cent), split into two monthly payments of £25,000. The amount actually received by them in each installment is £18,750 (i.e. £50,000 * 0.5 * 75/100) which is net of income tax at the basic rate; this is debited to the **profit and loss** column as it is an expense of the company and credited to an **interest-payable** column as it represents a liability of the new company. The balance of the half-year's interest payment is the IT of £6,250 (withheld from the debenture holders) which is similarly debited to the **profit and loss** column; its credit is recorded in an **IT** column as it is owed to the Inland Revenue.

Spreadsheet 18.6 The effect of debenture interest

	A		B		C		D		E		F		G		H	
1																
2																
3	Description						Profit		Interest		I.T.		Interest		Bank	
4							and		Payable				Rec'able			
5							Loss									
6																
7	Interest Payable						18750		-18750							
8																
9	I.T. on Interest Payable						6250				-6250					
10																
11	Interest Receivable						-16875						16875			
12																
13	I.T. on Interest Receivable						-5625				5625					
14																
15	Payment of Interest								18750						-18750	
16																
17	Receipt of Interest												-16875		16875	
18							------		------		------		------		------	
19	Sub-total						2500		0		-625		0		-1875	
20																
21	Payment of I.T.										625				-625	
22																
23	Interest Payable						18750		-18750							
24																
25	I.T. on Interest Payable						6250				-6250					
26																
27	Interest Receivable						-16875						16875			
28																
29	I.T. on Interest Receivable						-5625				5625					
30																
31							------		------		------		------		------	
32	Closing Balances						5000		-18750		-625		16875		-2500	
33							======		======		======		======		======	

Table 18.3 *Closing balance sheet extracts prior to payment and receipt of interest*

	£s
Current assets:	
interest receivable	16,875
Current liabilities:	
interest payable	18,750
IT payable	625

Gross interest receivable by the company is £45,000 (i.e. 30,000 * 15 per cent), made up of two parts: one part receivable from the company which has the debentures of £16,875 which is credited to the **profit and loss** column, as it is income for the company, and debited to an **interest receivable** column as it is still owed. The second part of £5,625 is the part owed by the Inland Revenue; it is credited to the **profit and loss** column as it is income and debited to the **IT** column as it is a debtor. Interest is then paid and received. The spreadsheet is then sub-totalled to calculate the net payment; which is then paid over to the Inland Revenue.

The interest payable and receivable for the second half of the year is then recorded, together with its IT components. The columns are summed to show the balances owed and owing at the year end. Extracts from the closing balance sheet just before the payment and receipt of interest are as shown in Table 18.3. If, however, we consider another company which has £300,000 10 per cent debentures in issue and owns £500,000 15 per cent debentures in another company (this is the reverse of the above example), the IT position would be as shown in Table 18.4. In the case of a nil CT liability, the balance sheet extract relating to the IT would be as follows:

	£s
Current assets	
IT receivable	1,250

Otherwise, if the company owed sufficient CT the figure of £1,250 would be netted off the mainstream CT liability.

Table 18.4   *Net IT recoverable calculation*

	Gross	IT	Net
Interest paid	45,000	11,250	33,750
Interest receivable	50,000	12,500	37,500
Net IT recoverable		1,250	

18.7 Deferred taxation

The logic of deferred taxation (DT) can be understood by considering the following example. Suppose a company purchases a machine which has an estimated useful life of ten years and costs £500,000. If we use straight-line depreciation the yearly depreciation charges to the profit and loss account are £50,000 p.a. for ten years. If we also suppose that profits derived from using that machine (before depreciation) are the same in each of the first three years of its use, say £700,000, then the profit after depreciation is £650,000 in each of these years. If the CT rate is 35 per cent then we might expect the CT charges to be £227,500 each year. This is not in fact the case as CT is calculated, as shown in Spreadsheet 18.7, as £201,250 in year 1, £212,188 in year 2 and £220,390 in year 3.

These differences arise since the Inland Revenue has its own way of calculating depreciation, called 'capital allowances'. The allowance given is 25 per cent of the machine's written-down value in each year. The written-down value in year 1 is £500,000 (i.e. its original cost), in year 2 it is £375,000 (i.e. its original cost less year 1's capital allowance) and in year 3 it is £281,250 (i.e. original cost less years 1 and 2's capital allowances). Therefore the capital allowances are as shown in Table 18.5. Taxable profits are calculated as profit before depreciation less capital allowances and it is these figures that are used to calculate CT by multiplying them by the current rate of CT. The CT for years 1 to 3 are £201,250, £212,188 and £220,390. The profit after tax for the three years is therefore £448,750 in year 1, £437,812 in year 2 and £429,610 in year 3.

It is this profit after tax figure that investors look at to see how their investment is progressing; in this example this leads them to believe that the company has had a better year 1 than year 2 and a better year 2 than year 3. Accountants are unhappy with this picture as they know (and you can see) all three years were equally successful (because the profit after depreciation is the same in each of the three years, £650,000). So they contend the profit after tax figure should be the same in each year. Adjustments are therefore made to the taxation figure in the profit and loss account to achieve this result. These adjustments are referred to as 'deferred tax'. Spreadsheet 18.8 shows what the profit and loss account would look like when the corporation tax charge has been adjusted to include a deferred tax element. The profit after tax figure is now the same in each of the three years (i.e. £422,500) and the accountant is happy as the signal to the investor is that the company has had three similar years.

The make-up of the adjusted CT charge is analysed in Note 1. It is composed of two elements, a CT part calculated as per the Inland Revenue rules and a deferred tax part calculated as shown in Note 2. This deferred tax element is calculated as the difference between the accountant's depreciation and the capital allowances multiplied by the rate of CT. These differences between accountants' depreciation and capital allowances are referred to as 'timing differences', as the capital allowances occur in a different accounting period than the accountant's depreciation. These timing differences reverse themselves over the life of the

Spreadsheet 18.7 Corporation tax and deferred tax

	A		B		C		D		E		F		G	
1														
2														
3	COST OF MACHINE								500000					
4	RATE OF CORPORATION TAX								35%					
5	RATE OF CAPITAL ALLOWANCES								25% reducing balance					
6	RATE OF DEPRECIATION								10% straight line					
7														
8														
9	Calculation of Corporation Tax													
10														
11									Year 1		Year 2		Year 3	
12														
13	Profit before Depreciation								700000		700000		700000	
14														
15	Less Capital allowances								-125000		-93750		-70313	
16									-------------------					
17	Taxable Profits								575000		606250		629687	
18									===================					
19														
20	Corporation Tax								201250		212188		220390	
21									===================					
22														
23									Year 1		Year 2		Year 3	
24														
25	Written Down Value of Machine								-500000		-375000		-281250	
26														
27	Capital Allowance								125000		93750		70313	
28									-------------------					
29	Writting Down Value b/f								-375000		-281250		-210937	
30									===================					
31														
32														
33														
34														
35	--													
36														
37	Profit and Loss Account - without Deferred tax													
38														
39									Year 1		Year 2		Year 3	
40														
41	Profit before depreciation								700000		700000		700000	
42														
43	Depreciation								-50000		-50000		-50000	
44									-------------------					
45	Profit after Depreciation								650000		650000		650000	
46														
47	Corporation tax								-201250		-212188		-220390	
48									-------------------					
49	Profit after Corporation Tax								448750		437812		429610	
50									===================					
51														
52														
53	--													

Table 18.5 *Capital allowances over three years*

Year	Written-down value	Capital allowance
1	500,000	500,000 * 25% = 125,000
2	375,000	375,000 * 25% = 93,750
3	281,250	281,250 * 25% = 70,313

Spreadsheet 18.8 Profit and loss account – with deferred tax

```
     |   A   ||   B   ||   C   ||   D   ||   E   ||   F   ||   G   |
75   Profit and Loss account  -  with Deferred tax
76
77                                           Year 1    Year 2    Year 3
78
79   Profit before Depreciation             700000    700000    700000
80
81   Depreciation                           -50000    -50000    -50000
82                                          ----------------------------
83   Profit after Depreciation              650000    650000    650000
84
85   Corporation Tax    (see Note 1)       -227500   -227500   -227499
86                                          ----------------------------
87   Profit after Tax                        422500    422500   422501*
88                                          ============================
89
90   Note 1    Analysis of Corporation Tax
91
92   Corporation Tax Charge                  201250    212188    220390
93
94   Deferred Tax        (see Note 2)         26250     15313      7109
95                                          ----------------------------
96   Corporation Tax                         227500    227500    227499
97                                          ============================
98
99   Note 2    Analysis of Deferred Tax
100
101  Depreciation                             50000     50000     50000
102
103  Capital Allowances                      125000     93750     70313
104                                         ----------------------------
105                                          -75000    -43750    -20313
106                                         ============================
107
108  Difference * Rate of C.T.               -26250    -15313     -7109
109                                         ============================
110
111
112  Note - Small Company Rates of C.T. have been ignored
```

*Ignore the £1 rounding difference.

machine (i.e. over its life the total depreciation equals the total capital allowances); this is shown in Spreadsheet 18.9.

It is important to realise that what give rise to deferred tax are expenses and revenues that pass through the profit and loss account in a different accounting period to when they pass through the 'taxable profits' computation. These are different from those differences that are permanent in nature, such as items of expenditure which are included in the profit and loss account but which are not deductable for tax purposes (e.g. most entertaining costs). These differences do not give rise to deferred tax as they have no direct effect on the amount of CT a company pays.

How do we record this deferred tax in the records. This is shown in Spreadsheet 18.10 for years 1 to 3 and the movements in the deferred tax accountant in years 1 to 10 are shown in Spreadsheet 18.11. A deferred tax provision account is opened and credited with the deferred tax charge. The debit

Spreadsheet 18.9 Depreciation and capital allowances compared

	A		B		C		D		E		F		G		H	
1																
2	Cost Of Asset		500000													
3																
4	Economic Life				10 years											
5																
6	Allowance Rate		25.00%													
7																
8	Tax Rate		35.00%													
9									Capital				Tax			
10	Year Depreciation				W.D.V.		Allowance		Difference		Implications					
11	----		---------		--------		---------		---------		---------					
12																
13	1		50000		500000		125000		75000		26250					
14	2		50000		375000		93750		43750		15313					
15	3		50000		281250		70313		20313		7109					
16	4		50000		210938		52734		2734		957					
17	5		50000		158203		39551		-10449		-3657					
18	6		50000		118652		29663		-20337		-7118					
19	7		50000		88989		22247		-27753		-9713					
20	8		50000		66742		16685		-33315		-11660					
21	9		50000		50056		12514		-37486		-13120					
22	10		50000	---> *	37542		37542		-12458		-4360					
23																
24	Rounding Errors										1					
25			---------		---------		-------		-------							
26			500000				500000		0		0					
27			========				========		======		======					
28																
29																
30	* This is the balancing figure at the end of the machine's life.															

Spreadsheet 18.10 Accounting for the deferred tax provision

	A	B	C	D	E	F	G	H
1							Profit	Deferred
2	Description			Capital	Bank	Machine	And	Tax
3							Loss	Provision
4								
5	Opening Balances			-1000000	1000000			
6								
7	Purchase Machine				-500000	500000		
8								
9	Depreciation					-50000	50000	
10								
11	Profit (assume all cash)				700000		-700000	
12								
13	Corporation Tax				-201250		201250	
14	(assume paid immediately)							
15								
16	Deferred Tax						26250	-26250
17	------							------
18	Closing Balances			-1000000	998750	450000	-422500	-26250
19	at end of Year 1							
20								
21	Transfer Profit to Capital			-422500			422500	
22	------							------
23	Opening Balances			-1422500	998750	450000	0	-26250
24	at beginning of Year 2							
25								
26	Depreciation					-50000	50000	
27								
28	Profit				700000		-700000	
29								
30	Corporation Tax				-212188		212188	
31								
32	Deferred Tax						15313	-15313
33	------							------
34	Closing Balances			-1422500	1486562	400000	-422499	-41563
35	at end of Year 2							
36								
37	Transfer Profit to Capital			-422499			422499	
38	------							------
39	Opening Balances			-1844999	1486562	400000	0	-41563
40	at beginning of Year 3							
41								
42	Depreciation					-50000	50000	
43								
44	Profit				700000		-700000	
45								
46	Corporation Tax				-220391		220391	
47								
48	Deferred Tax						7109	-7109
49	------							------
50	Sub-totals			-1844999	1966171	350000	-422500	-48672
51								
52	Transfer Profit to Capital			-422500			422500	
53								
54	------							------
55	Opening Balances			-2267499	1966171	350000	0	-48672
56	at beginning of Year 3							
57	======							======

Spreadsheet 18.11 Movements on deferred tax account

	A	B	C	D
1				
2				
3				
4	Description			Deferred
5				Tax
6				Provision
7				
8	Year 1			-26250
9	------------------------------------			
10	Balance at year end			-26250
11				
12	Year 2			-15313
13	------------------------------------			
14	Balance at year end			-41563
15				
16	Year 3			-7109
17	------------------------------------			
18	Balance at year end			-48672
19				
20	Year 4			-957
21	------------------------------------			
22	Balance at year end			-49629
23				
24	Year 5			3657
25	------------------------------------			
26	Balance at year end			-45972
27				
28	Year 6			7118
29	------------------------------------			
30	Balance at year end			-38854
31				
32	Year 7			9713
33	------------------------------------			
34	Balance at year end			-29141
35				
36	Year 8			11660
37	------------------------------------			
38	Balance at year end			-17481
39				
40	Year 9			13120
41	------------------------------------			
42	Balance at year end			-4361
43				
44	Year 10			4361
45	------------------------------------			
46	Balance at year end			0
47	====================================			

entry is recorded in the **profit and loss** column as it is an increase in the CT charge for the year. Similar transactions are used to record deferred tax in years 2 to 4 when the balance on the deferred tax account reaches £49,629. From year 5 onwards the entry is reversed with a credit entry recorded in the **profit and loss** column so reducing the CT charge and the debit entry in the **deferred tax** column using up the deferred tax provision. At the end of year 10 all the deferred tax provision has been used up and the machine fully written off.

Now you have understood the basic idea behind deferred tax, some other issues need to be considered.

Firstly, other timing differences (as well as differences between capital allowances and depreciation, which are called 'accelerated capital allowances') between expenses and revenues in the profit and loss account and their associated expenses and revenues in the taxation computation can give rise to deferred tax. Other examples of timing difference are:

a. interest charged to the profit and loss account on an accruals basis, but charged to the taxation computation on a paid basis;

b. royalties charged to the profit and loss account on an accruals basis, but charged to the taxation computation on a paid basis;

c. provisions for the repair and maintenance in the accounts, which are not allowable expenditure for tax purposes until paid;

d. general doubtful debt provisions are not allowable; debt write-offs are only allowable when specifically provided for;

e. provisions for plant reorganisations or closures are not allowable until the associated costs are incurred;

f. provisions for pension costs are not allowable until the associated costs are incurred;

g. interest or royalties receivable are not taxed until they are received.

Secondly, the revaluation of a fixed asset might give rise to deferred tax since when the asset is sold a profit might arise which is subject to tax. It might be considered misleading to leave the assets revaluation reserve at its full value so it is debited with the amount of deferred tax associated with the revaluation. However, if the proceeds of sale are intended to be used to buy a replacement asset then the Inland Revenue allows the company to claim 'rollover relief' and no CT is payable; therefore no deferred tax need be provided.

Thirdly, the statement of standard accounting practice which deals with deferred tax (SSAP 15) allows companies to make a partial provision for deferred tax rather than provide for the full amount. This was introduced since the deferred tax provision in companies accounts could get bigger and bigger if they purchased more and more fixed assets each year. This means that the deferred tax provision was unlikely to be used (i.e. reduced) in the foreseeable future. Therefore in the United Kingdom, companies are allowed not to provide only when it is reasonably certain that CT will not have to be paid; however, the balance is required to be disclosed as contingent liability.

Fourthly, statement of standard accounting practice 8 requires any ACT recoverable to be offset against the deferred tax provision. This is a use of ACT which cannot be used to reduce the amount of current CT because it has arisen from an as yet unpaid dividend, or maximum set-off has already taken place (i.e. 25 per cent).

18.8 A worked example

Now we have seen how to account for taxation we can attempt a worked example. The example attempted is Lawson Ltd which is shown in Figure 18.1. The answer in spreadsheet form is shown in Spreadsheets 18.12a and 18.12b.

Lawson plc has an issued share capital of £400,000 in fully paid 50 pence ordinary shares. At 31 December 1986 the following balances were included in the company's balance sheet:

	£
Value added tax (credit balance)	56,780
Agreed corporation tax liability on 1985 profits	25,700
Estimated corporation tax liability on 1986 profits	32,400
Deferred taxation account (credit balance)	54,000
Profit and loss account (credit balance)	96,750

(no dividend has been paid or proposed in respect of 1986)

The following information relates to the year ended 31 December 1987:

Corporation tax liability for 1985 settled in January.
An interim dividend of 2 pence per share paid in August.
Advanced corporation tax on interim dividend paid in October.
Corporation tax liability for 1986 agreed at £31,000.
Net profit for 1987 before tax calculated at £124,800.
Taxable profits for 1987 calculated at £110,000.
Directors propose a final dividend of 5 pence per share.
The deferred tax account to be increased by £5,000.
Value added tax on sales was £256,000, on purchases of £176,000, and £80,000 was paid over to the Customs and Excise Authorities during 1987.
The rate of corporation tax is 35 per cent and the rate of income tax 27 per cent.

You are required to:
1. Make all relevant accounting entries in an appropriate format to record the above balances and transactions in the company's records.
2. Show how the final balances would be included in the company's profit and loss account for the year ended 31 December 1987 and balance sheet as at that date.
3. Explain why a deferred taxation provision is required in the company's balance sheet.

Figure 18.1 Lawson plc

Spreadsheet 18.12a Lawson plc—solution

DESCRIPTION	Profit and Loss	VAT	Bank	CT Current	CT Long-Term	DT	ACT Pay.	ACT Recov.	CT Expense	Dividend
Opening Balances	-96750	-56780		-25700	-32400	-54000				
CT liability for 1985 settled			-25700	25700						
Interim dividend paid	16000		-16000							
ACT on interim dividend							-5917	5917		
ACT paid			-5917				5917			
ACT recoverable used					5917			-5917		
Agreement of 1986 CT liability					1400				-1400	
1987 profit Assumed all cash	-124800		124800							
1987 CT Charge					-38500				38500	
1986 CT charge				-31000	31000					
Final dividend	40000									-40000
ACT on final dividend							-14794	14794		
Increase in DT						-5000			5000	
VAT sales		-256000								
VAT purchases		176000								
VAT paid		80000	-80000							
Closing Balances	-165550	-56780	-2817	-31000	-32583	-59000	-14794	14794	42100	-40000

Spreadsheet 18.12b   Profit and loss account extracts – solution

	A		B		C		D		E		F	
48						PROFIT AND LOSS ACCOUNT EXTRACTS						
49												
50											£s	
51	NET PROFIT BEFORE TAX										124800	
52												
53	Taxation										42100	
54											---------	
55	NET PROFIT AFTER TAX										82700	
56												
57	Dividends											
58			Interim						16000				
59			Final						40000				
60									---------			
61											56000	
62											---------	
63	RETAINED PROFITS FOR THE YEAR										26700	
64												
65	RETAINED PROFITS FROM PREVIOUS YEARS										96750	
66											---------	
67	RETAINED PROFITS BROUGHT FORWARD										123450	
68											=========	
69												
70												
71						BALANCE SHEET EXTRACTS						
72												
73												
74	CURRENT ASSETS											
75												
76			ACT Recoverable								14794		
77												
78												
79	CURRENT LIABILITIES											
80												
81			VAT								56780		
82												
83			Bank								2817		
84												
85			CT								31000		
86												
87			ACT Payable								14794		
88												
89			Dividends								40000		
90												
91												
92	LONG TERM LIABILITIES											
93												
94			CT								32583		
95												
96			DT								59000		

18.9   Notes

1. Some products and services are exempt from VAT such as education and funerals. All other products and services are subject to VAT at two rates, zero and the standard rate of 15 per cent. An example of zero-rated goods is food.

2. Small businesses with turnover of under £22,100 are usually exempt from VAT, i.e. they do not charge VAT on their sales and cannot reclaim VAT on their purchases.

3. VAT is usually collected/recorded over a three-month period and then paid to the Customs and Excise within one month of the end of this period, together with a VAT return. The VAT return is a document in which the company records its sales, purchàses and VAT. The three months period can be:

    a.   31 March, 30 June, 30 September, 31 December;
    b.   30 April, 31 July, 31 October, 31 January;
    c.   31 May, 31 August, 30 November, 28 (29) February.

    A company must allocate one of these periods. The reason for the three groups is to spread the collecting work for the Customs and Excise Department over the year.

4. Previous rates of corporation tax are as follows:

    1973–83 52 per cent
    1983–4   50 per cent
    1984–5   45 per cent
    1985–6   40 per cent
    1986 →   35 per cent

    There is a lower rate of corporation tax for companies who make small profits. This rate is 25 per cent for profits under £150,000. Profits between £150,000 and £750,000 are charged corporation tax at a higher rate so that when profits of £750,000 are reached the overall rate becomes 35 per cent. We have ignored this complicating factor in our example to ease explanation.

5. Companies who commence business after March 1965 have to pay corporation tax nine months after their accounting year end. For companies who were in business prior to March 1965 (the date corporation tax was introduced) corporation tax was payable on 1 January of the financial year (1 April–31 March) following the financial year in which the company's accounting year ends. So for a company with an accounting year end on 1 April corporation tax was not due for twenty-one months. However, with effect from 16 March 1987 those companies with a payment period of more than nine months are having their payment periods gradually reduced to be in line with post-March 1965 companies.

6. The maximum amount of set-off is limited to 25 per cent of taxable profits. Any uncleared advanced corporation tax can be offset against corporation tax of the past six years or carried forward indefinitely, as recoverable ACT.

7. If there is no corporation tax available (or likely to be available) to set advanced corporation tax against, the advanced corporation tax becomes to all intents and purposes irrecoverable. Therefore the dividend which gave rise to the advanced corporation tax becomes expensive as its cost is the dividend plus the advanced corporation tax.

CHECKLIST

Having completed Chapter 18, you should be able to:

■ explain the major features of VAT, corporation tax, advanced corporation tax and income tax and be able to account for these taxes in company accounts;

■ outline the need for deferred taxation and show how it affects company accounts.

Workshop 18.1: Taxation in company accounts

Dennis Terry plc is a car manufacturer, with an issued share capital of 600,000 £1 fully paid ordinary shares. As at 31 December 19x6, the balance sheet contained the balances shown in Table 18.6. As yet, no dividend has been paid or proposed for 19x6.

Table 18.6   *Details of the accounts of Dennis Terry plc*

	£
Profit and loss account	104,560 Cr
VAT	65,780 Cr
Current corporation tax liability	34,700 Cr
Long-term corporation tax liability	45,800 Cr
Deferred taxation account	64,000 Cr

You have the following information upon which to act:

1. The corporation tax is paid at the start of the year.

2. An interim dividend of 5p per share is paid half-way through the year, with the associated advanced corporation tax liability.

3. The liability for corporation tax for the year is assessed as £42,700. This is based on pre-tax profits of £137,600, of which only £122,000 is taxable.

4. The final dividend proposed by the directors is 7p per share.

5. The deferred tax account is to be increased by £7,000.

6. The VAT on sales amounted to £279,000, while the VAT on purchases came to £195,000. Payment to the authorities was only £84,000.

7. Tax rates applicable are: corporation tax 35 per cent and income tax 27 per cent.

You are asked to account for the above transactions, preparing an extract from the final accounts at the year end.

Workshop guide

1. The opening balances are input in row 7. There is no balancing cell as only extracts are requested.

2. The corporation tax liability for the year is settled in row 9, using the cell reference $-G7$ to create the payment, and the contents of cell F9 to generate the double entry.

3. The payment of dividends is recorded in row 11, with the ACT liability and payment in rows 13 and 15. Cell J13 is used to assess this liability.

4. The assessed corporation tax liability for 19x6 is then charged as an expense after allowing for any ACT recoverable.

5. The profit for the current year is entered along with any corporation tax thereon (see row 24). This year's corporation tax charge is therefore current.

6. The ACT on the final dividend is calculated in J30, with only the VAT entries remaining to complete the transactions.

Profit and loss account extracts

		£
Net profit before tax		137,600
Taxation		45,900
Net profit after tax		91,700
Dividends		
Interim	30,000	
Final	42,000	
		72,000
Retained profits for the year		19,700
Retained profits from previous years		104,560
Retained profits brought forward		124,260

Balance sheet extracts

Current assets	
ACT recoverable	15,534
Current liabilities	
VAT	65,780
Bank	22,195
CT	42,000
ACT payable	15,534
Dividends	42,000
Long-term liabilities	
CT	31,605
DT	71,000

Figure 18.2   Dennis Terry plc

Selected questions and exercises

Question 18.1

Humpledink Ltd, with an issued share capital of £250,000 in shares of £1 each, makes up its accounts to 31 December of each year, and its corporation tax is normally payable on 1 January next but one. On 1 January 1975, the liabilities for corporation tax are as follows:

year ended 31 December 1973 £52,000 (agreed with Inland Revenue)
year ended 31 December 1974 £60,000 (estimated on the profits of the year)

and there is a recoverable amount of ACT of £34,541, of which £16,071 is in respect of dividends paid in the year ended 31 December 1973.

During the year ended 31 December 1975, the liability in respect of the year ended 31 December 1973 is paid on the due date, and the liability in respect of the year ended 31 December 1974 is agreed at £57,500; the assessment notice was issued on 1 July 1975.

Spreadsheet 18.13a   Workshop 18.1: Dennis Terry plc – solution

	A	B	C	D	E	F	G	H	I	J	K
	DESCRIPTION	Profit and Loss	VAT	Bank	CT Current	CT Long-Term	DT	ACT Pay.	ACT Recov.	CT Expense	Dividend
7	Opening Balances	-104560	-65780		-34700	-45800	-64000				
9	CT liability for 19_5 settled			-34700	34700						
11	Interim dividend paid	30000		-30000							
13	ACT on interim dividend							-11095	11095		
15	ACT paid			-11095				11095			
17	ACT recoverable used					11095			-11095		
19	Agreement of 19_6 CT liability					3800				-3800	
21	19_7 profit	-137600		137600							
22	Assumed all cash										
24	19_7 CT Charge					-42700				42700	
26	19_6 CT charge				-42000	42000					
28	Final dividend	42000									-42000
30	ACT on final dividend							-15534	15534		
32	Increase in DT						-7000			7000	
34	VAT sales		-279000								
36	VAT purchases		195000								
38	VAT paid		84000	-84000							
44	Closing Balances	-170160	-65780	-22195	-42000	-31605	-71000	-15534	15534	45900	-42000

Spreadsheet 18.13b   Workshop 18.1: Dennis Terry plc – formulae

	A	B	C	D	E	F	G
1							
2							
3							
4	DESCRIPTION			Profit	VAT	Bank	CT
5				and Loss			Current
6							
7	Opening Balances			-104560	-65780		-34700
8							
9	CT liability for 19_5 settled					-69	-67
10							
11	Interim dividend paid			-F11		-.05*600000	
12							
13	ACT on interim dividend						
14							
15	ACT paid					-J15	
16							
17	ACT recoverable used						
18							
19	Agreement of 19_6 CT liability						
20							
21	19_7 profit			-137600		-D21	
22	Assumed all cash						
23							
24	19_7 CT Charge						
25							
26	19_6 CT charge						-H26
27							
28	Final dividend			.07*600000			
29							
30	ACT on final dividend						
31							
32	Increase in DT						
33							
34	VAT sales				-279000		
35							
36	VAT purchases				195000		
37							
38	VAT paid				-E34-E36	-E38	
39							
40							
41							
42							
43	--------			--------	--------	--------	--------
44	Closing Balances			SUM(D7:D42)	SUM(E7:E42)	SUM(F7:F42)	SUM(G7:G42)
45	--------			--------	--------	--------	--------

:	H	::	I	::	J	::	K	::	L	::	M	:

H	I	J	K	L	M
CT Long-Term	DT	ACT Pay.	ACT Recov.	CT Expense	Dividend
-45800	-64000				
		INT(27/73*F11)	-J13		
		-J13			
-K17			-K13		
-H7-42000				-H19	
-L24				0.35*122000	
-(H19+H7)					
					-D28
		INT(27/73*M28)	-J30		
	-L32			7000	

```
-----------------------------------------------------------------------
SUM(H7:H42)   SUM(I7:I42)  SUM(J7:J42)   SUM(K7:K42)  SUM(L7:L42)  SUM(M7:M42)
-----------------------------------------------------------------------
```

An interim dividend of 5p share is paid on 30 June 1975, and the directors propose that a final dividend of 10p per share, making 15p for the year, be paid.

The company has adopted the principle of deferred taxation, and at 1 January 1975, there is a credit balance of £26,500 in the deferred tax account. The liability for corporation tax based on the profits of the year ended 31 December 1975 is estimated to be £75,000 but, substituting accounting depreciation for legal capital allowance, this is increased to £79,500.

Note: ACT is to be calculated at 35/65ths.

Assuming that the profit for the year ended 31 December 1975 before taxation amounted to £150,000, and that the balance brought forward from the previous year was £120,000; you are required to:

a.   prepare the corporation tax account and deferred taxation account from the information given;
b.   prepare the profit and loss account for the year ended 31 December 1975;
c.   show the treatment of the appropriate items in the balance sheet prepared as of 31 December 1975.

Solution on page 553.   *Source: ACCA*

Question 18.2
Corax Ltd has an issued capital of £330,000 in fully paid 50p ordinary shares. At 31 December 1976 the balances shown in Table 18.7 were included in the company's balance sheet.

Table 18.7   *Details of the accounts of Corax Limited*

	£
Agreed corporation tax liability on 1975 profits	16,300
Estimated corporation tax liability on 1976 profits	5,000
Deferred taxation account	29,400
Profit and loss account (credit)	43,000
(No dividends had been paid or proposed in respect of 1976)	

The following information relates to the year ended 31 December 1977:

a.   corporation tax liability for 1975 settled (January);
b.   interim dividend of 2p per share paid (August);
c.   advanced corporation tax on interim dividend paid (October);
d.   corporation tax liability for 1976 agreed at £3,800 (December);
e.   net profit for 1977 before tax calculated at £88,800;
f.   corporation tax based on the 1977 profits estimated at £36,000;
g.   directors proposed a final dividend of 5p per share;

h. a transfer to the deferred taxation account of £7,000 for 1977 is to be made in respect of capital allowances in excess of depreciation charges.

Make all relevant entries in the ledger accounts (except cash and share capital) and complete the profit and loss account for 1977. Show how the final balances would be included in the balance sheet at 31 December 1977. (Assume that the basic rate of income tax is 34 per cent.)

Solution on page 554.

Source: ACCA

19 | *Accounting standards*

AIMS OF CHAPTER ────────────────────────────────

■ to examine the need for accounting standards, and the standard setting process;

■ to discuss SSAPs not covered in other chapters of the book, highlighting the accounting implications.

19.1 The need for accounting standards

A number of accounting scandals occurred in the late 1960s as a result of misleading reported profit figures. One such scandal occurred in 1967 when GEC announced its intentions to take over AEI. The directors of AEI attempted to prevent this takeover by informing their shareholders that a profit of £10m was anticipated for the next year. This profit figure was checked by a firm of accountants. GEC were, however, successful in their bid and duly took over AEI. The actual results for AEI were, in fact, a loss of £4.5m. This discrepancy between the anticipated profit and actual profit was analysed as follows:

	£m
Matters of fact	5
Matters of judgement	9.5
	14.5

It was the large matter of judgement difference of £9.5m that concerned the financial press. How could accountants be so far out?

This case clearly showed that there was a problem. How were the accountancy bodies to react? They seemed to have two choices.

1. The development of a financial accounting theory based upon a well-researched conceptual framework. This would involve agreement about the

nature and uses of financial statements, which clearly does not exist. This type of development is probably best left to the scientists. In any event the costs of such fundamental research would be prohibitive.

2. A piecemeal tackling of individual problems as they arise. This approach was the one adopted by the UK accounting profession, who formed the Accounting Standards Committee (ASC) who were required to issue statements of standard accounting practice (SSAPs). An SSAP explains a method of tackling a specific accounting problem which has been chosen as the only one acceptable to the accounting bodies. The advantages of SSAPs are as follows:

    a. they give clear guidance to accountants who are faced with the problem of how to account for contentious items;
    b. they therefore lead to a consistent approach and allow different companies' accounts to be comparable as well as a single company's accounts over a number of years;
    c. as standards are well researched and thought out the quality of accounts is improved;
    d. they provide users of accounts with additional information so enabling more informed decisions to be made;
    e. they help prevent deliberate manipulation of figures by unscrupulous accountants and directors.

19.2 The standard setting process

Figure 19.1 outlines the standard setting process.

The following points should be noted:

1. If the exposure draft (ED) is heavily criticised a new ED is produced rather than enforce the SSAP.

Accounting problem
Problem examined by the ASC
Exposure draft issued
(ED)
Comments on ED received and reviewed
by ASC
Statement of Standard Accounting Practice
produced based on a revised ED in light
of comments

Figure 19.1   Illustration of the standard setting process

2. If SSAPs are subsequently found to be unacceptable they are withdrawn. This explains the missing numbers in their sequence (e.g. SSAP 7 and 11).

SSAPs have to be followed by all companies unless they are specifically excluded. For example, SSAP 10 is not mandatory for companies with a turnover of under £10,000 and SSAP 3 is only applicable to companies whose shares are listed on the stock exchange. Accountants who are members of a professional body have to produce financial statements which comply with the standards and members acting as an auditor have to ensure they are complied with. Non-compliance can lead to disciplinary proceedings for misconduct.

19.3   Individual accounting standards

Now we have outlined the need for accounting standards and the standard setting process, we will examine some of the individual accounting standards issued to date. Some SSAPs are discussed in other chapters, so they will be omitted from this chapter (see Figure 19.2). In addition, all SSAPs which deal with group financial statements will be omitted, as they are outside the coverage of this text.

SSAP 2	Disclosure of accounting policies	Chapter 9
SSAP 5	Accounting for VAT	Chapter 18
SSAP 7	Current purchasing power	Chapter 24
SSAP 8	The treatment of taxation under the imputation system	Chapter 18
SSAP 9	Stocks	Chapter 16
SSAP 10	Statement of source and application of funds	Chapter 21
SSAP 11	Accounting for deferred tax (superceded by SSAP 15)	Chapter 18
SSAP 12	Accounting for depreciation	Chapter 7
SSAP 15	Accounting for deferred tax	Chapter 18
SSAP 16	Current cost accounting	Chapter 24

SSAPs not covered in this text–concerned with group accounts
SSAP 1	Accounting for the results of associated companies	
SSAP 14	Group accounts	
SSAP 20	Foreign currency translation	
SSAP 22	Accounting for good will	
SSAP 23	Accounting for acquisitions and mergers	

Figure 19.2   SSAPs not discussed in Chapter 19

19.4 SSAP 3 – earnings per share

Companies whose shares are traded on a stock exchange are required to calculate and show an earnings per share (EPS) figure in their financial statements for both the current and the previous year. The need for the inclusion of such a statistic arose from its use by investors and their financial advisors as a guide (together with the company's share price) to the company's investment potential.

The standard indicates how the EPS should be calculated, so that different companies' EPSs can be consistently compared and the same company's EPS can be compared from one year to the next. The formula is simply to divide the net profit by the number of shares in issue.

But what profit figure? This was defined as profit after tax, after preference dividend, but before extraordinary items. Tax and preference dividends are deducted, as they reduce the profit available to the ordinary shareholder. The logic for not adjusting the profit figure for extraordinary items is explained when SSAP 6 is discussed later in this chapter.

What number of shares is used in the formula? The number of ordinary shares ranking for dividends is used, as the statistic is used by ordinary shareholders and their advisors. Complications can arise if a share issue is made during the year, in which case a weighted average is used. If a bonus issue is made, the year-end number of shares in issue is used to calculate this year's EPS. A rights issue is treated as a combination of both an issue at full price and a bonus issue.

19.5 SSAP 4 – accounting for government grants

This standard details how government grants received by companies are to be accounted for. It distinguishes two types of grant: firstly, revenue-based grants which are grants received by companies to reduce the cost of revenue expenditure incurred – such grants should be credited to the profit and loss account in the period in which the revenue expenditure was charged; secondly, capital-based grants, which are received by the company to help towards the cost of fixed asset purchases. The standard identifies the accruals concept as requiring this revenue to be taken to the profit and loss account over the useful life of the fixed asset. This can be done in two ways:

1. By reducing the cost of the fixed asset by the amount of the grant and depreciating the net cost.

2. By recording the grant as a deferred credit balance which is taken to the profit and loss account over the life of the asset.

Spreadsheet 19.1 Accounting for government grants: method 1

	A	B	C	D Fixed Asset	E Cash	F Profit & Loss
1						
2						
3				Fixed		Profit
4				Asset	Cash	& Loss
5						
6	Purchase of Fixed Asset			9000	-9000	
7						
8	Receipt of Grant			-4500	4500	
9						
10	Depreciation			-1500		1500
11						
12				----------------------------		
13	Balance Sheet as at 31-12-88			3000	-4500	1500
14						
15	Depreciation			-1500		1500
16						
17				----------------------------		
18	Balance Sheet as at 31-12-89			1500	-4500	3000
19						
20	Depreciation			-1500		1500
21						
22				----------------------------		
23	Balance Sheet as at 31-12-90			0	-4500	4500

	A	B	C	D Fixed Asset	E Cash	F Profit & Loss
1						
2						
3				Fixed		Profit
4				Asset	Cash	& Loss
5						
6	Purchase of Fixed Asset			9000	-D6	
7						
8	Receipt of Grant			-4500	-D8	
9						
10	Depreciation			-D6/6		-D10
11						
12				---		
13	Balance Sheet as at 31-12-88			SUM(D6:D11)	SUM(E6:E11)	SUM(F6:F11)
14						
15	Depreciation			-D6/6		-D10
16						
17				---		
18	Balance Sheet as at 31-12-89			SUM(D13:D16)	SUM(E13:E16)	SUM(F13:F16)
19						
20	Depreciation			-D6/6		-D10
21						
22				---		
23	Balance Sheet as at 31-12-90			SUM(D18:D21)	SUM(E18:E21)	SUM(F18:F21)

Spreadsheet 19.2 Accounting for government grants: method 2

	A	B	C	D	E	F	G
1							
2							
3				Fixed		Profit	Deferred
4				Asset	Cash	& Loss	Credit
5							
6	Purchase of Fixed Asset			9000	-9000		
7							
8	Receipt of Grant				4500		-4500
9							
10	Depreciation			-3000		3000	
11							
12	Grant to P & L					-1500	1500
13							
14				---------------------------------------			
15	Balance Sheet as at 31-12-88			6000	-4500	1500	-3000
16							
17	Depreciation			-3000		3000	
18							
19	Grant to P & L					-1500	1500
20							
21				---------------------------------------			
22	Balance Sheet as at 31-12-89			3000	-4500	3000	-1500
23							
24	Depreciation			-3000		3000	
25							
26	Grant to P & L					-1500	1500
27							
28				---------------------------------------			
29	Balance Sheet as at 31-12-90			0	-4500	4500	0

	A	B	C	D	E	F	G
1							
2							
3				Fixed		Profit	Deferred
4				Asset	Cash	& Loss	Credit
5							
6	Purchase of Fixed Asset		9000	-D6			
7							
8	Receipt of Grant			4500		-E8	
9							
10	Depreciation		-D6/3		-D10		
11							
12	Grant to P & L				-G12	-G8/3	
13							
14				---			
15	Balance Sheet as at 31-12-88		SUM(D6:D13)	SUM(E6:E13)	SUM(F6:F13)	SUM(G6:G13)	
16							
17	Depreciation		D10		-D10		
18							
19	Grant to P & L				-G12	-G8/3	
20							
21				---			
22	Balance Sheet as at 31-12-89		SUM(D15:D20)	SUM(E15:E20)	SUM(F15:F20)	SUM(G15:G20)	
23							
24	Depreciation		D10		-D10		
25							
26	Grant to P & L				-G12	-G8/3	
27							
28				---			
29	Balance Sheet as at 31-12-90		SUM(D22:D27)	SUM(E22:E27)	SUM(F22:F27)	SUM(G22:G27)	

A simple example will show how each method works. Suppose a firm buys a fixed asset which cost £9,000 on 1 January 1988. It is to be depreciated using the straight-line method over three years, when its scrap value is estimated to be nil. The company receives a capital grant of £4,500 on 30 June 1987 to aid with the purchase cost.

Spreadsheets 19.1 and 19.2 show how we account for the fixed asset.

As can be seen, both methods produce the same effect upon profit. Method 1 takes a net depreciation of £1,500 to the profit and loss account each year, while method 2 takes £3,000 depreciation to the profit and loss account each year. The balance sheet shows more detail in method 2 as the unused portion of the grant is shown rather than being netted off against the cost of the fixed asset.

19.6   SSAP 6 – extraordinary and exceptional items

Extraordinary items are defined as 'material items which derive from events or transactions that fall outside the ordinary activities of the company and which are therefore expected not to recur frequently or regularly'. Exceptional items are defined as 'material items which derive from events or transactions that fall within the ordinary activities of the company'.

The way a transaction is classified will depend upon the company's situation, as the same transaction may be extraordinary for one company and exceptional for another. For example, the material profit on the sale of an office block may be exceptional for a property company, but extraordinary for a manufacturing company.

The standard explains how extraordinary and exceptional items should be accounted for. Exceptional items, since arising in the ordinary course of business, should be accounted for before arriving at the profit (or loss) on ordinary activities. As they are material a note is required describing them as exceptional, together with a description of how they arose. Extraordinary items, since arising outside the ordinary course of business, should be accounted for after profit on ordinary activities and after taxation. As they are material, a note is required describing the items as extraordinary, together with a description of how they arose, together with details of any tax incurred as a result of the extraordinary items.

19.7   SSAP 6 – prior year adjustments

Prior year adjustments are defined as 'those material adjustments applicable to prior years arising from changes in accounting policies or from the correction of fundamental errors'. They must be material, so that the previous year's accounts need adjusting to show a true and fair view. An example might be the omission of a large sale or the introduction of a new SSAP.

The standard specifically excludes 'corrections and adjustment which are the natural result of estimates inherent in accounting'. For example, the CT charge for the year has to be estimated at the year end since it has not yet been agreed with the Inland Revenue. During the following year the correct amount is agreed and the liability corrected through this year's CT charge, rather than adjusting last year's profit.

Prior year adjustments are accounted for by restating the prior year's financial statements, which appear as comparative figures in this year's financial statements, and adjusting the opening balance on retained profits.

19.8   SSAP 9 – long-term contract work in progress

SSAP 9 is in essence two accounting standards in one. Firstly, accounting for stock, which is discussed in Chapter 9, and secondly, accounting for long-term contract work in progress which is now discussed.

Many businesses such as construction companies are involved in single contracts that can last for a number of years. Using normal accounting rules, no profit would be taken on such a contract until it had been completed. This treatment is considered unfair as only the year in which the contract is completed is allocated any profit. SSAP 9 considers it much fairer to allocate some profit for the contract in the years in which the contract is in progress. Therefore, attributable profit is added to the costs to date for its balance sheet value.

However, this recognition of profit during the life of the contract presents the accountant with a number of problems which SSAP 9 seeks to clear up. Firstly, how much profit should be taken up at any time? The standard requires this profit to reflect the proportion of work carried out to date. This is usually determined by obtaining a certificate of work done from a qualified architect or surveyor. For example, if the contract is worth £10,000 to the company and it has incurred £5,000 costs to date with a further £3,000 estimated costs to completion, the contract profit is estimated as shown in Table 19.1.

The amount of this profit which can be taken can be calculated, see Figure 19.3.

Table 19.1   *Illustration of contract profit*

	£
Contract price	10,000
less costs incurred to date	(5,000)
less estimated costs to completion	(3,000)
Contract profit	£ 2,000

Contract profits × Amount of contract completed

$$2,000 \times \frac{5,000}{5,000 + 3,000} = £1,250$$

Figure 19.3   Calculation of contract profit

Therefore the contract would be valued at:

	£s
Costs incurred	5,000
Profits attributable	1,250
	£6,250

The second problem is what happens if the company expects to make a loss on the contract? In this case the prudence concept comes into play and the full expected loss must be taken as soon as it is recognised. The contract is therefore valued at net realisable value. Let us extend our example to show how to account for an expected loss, by changing the estimated costs to completion to £6,000. Therefore the estimated loss is as shown below:

	£s
Contract price	10,000
less costs to date	(5,000)
less estimated costs to completion	(6,000)
	£(1,000)

		£s
Costs incurred		5,000
less estimated loss		(1,000)
		4,000
less progress payments:		
	Received	(2,000)
	Receivable	(500)
		£1,500

Figure 19.4   Valuation of contract

The contract would be valued at:

	£s
Costs incurred to date	5,000
less estimated loss	(1,000)
	£ 4,000

Long-term work in progress usually involves progress payments which are advanced payments received (or receivable) by the company against the contract price. SSAP 9 requires these progress payments to be deducted from the contract value.

So if in our example the company had received £2,000 and was owed £500 in progress payments the contract would be valued as shown in Figure 19.4.

19.9   SSAP 13 – research and development expenditure

SSAP 13 deals with research and development expenditure incurred by the company. It attempts to provide a set of rules which should be used by companies when determining how much of these costs can be carried forward (to be offset against future revenues), and how much to write off immediately (against current revenues). The standard was issued largely in response to the crash of Rolls Royce, which incurred a considerable amount of research and development expenditure when developing a new aero-engine. However, the aero-engine project did not generate sufficient income and Rolls Royce went into liquidation. The way the research and development expenditure was accounted for was severely criticised as Rolls Royce carried it forward rather than writing it off. Research and development expenditure is categorised as follows:

1. Pure research – original research undertaken in order to gain new scientific or technical knowledge and understanding; not directed towards any specific practical aim or application.

2. Applied research – original research in order to gain new scientific or technical knowledge directed at a specific practical aim or objective.

3. Development – the use of 1 and 2 to produce a new or substantially improved material, device, product, process, etc., prior to commercial production.

The general rule in accounting for research and development expenditure is to write it off in the year it is incurred (i.e. prudence overriding matching). However, there is an exception for development expenditure if it fulfils certain criteria:

a. there must be a clearly defined project;

b. expenditure on the project must be separately identifiable;

c.   the outcome of the project has been assessed with reasonable certainty so we know it is technically feasible, commercially viable and acceptable to the public (i.e. it does not cause pollution, etc.);

d.   expected revenues/costs are available;

e.   the business must have sufficient resources to see the development through;

f.   once written off it can not be reinstated.

If all six criteria are met it can be carried forward and depreciated over the project's life once production starts. The standard goes on to state how it should be disclosed. Deferred development expenditure has to be shown separately and accounting policy stated. Also the amount of research and development expenditure written off in the profit and loss account has to be separately disclosed.

19.10   SSAP 17 – post balance sheet events

1.   Adjusting events – events after the balance sheet date which provide additional evidence of conditions existing at the balance sheet date, e.g. errors/fraud committed before the balance sheet date, subsequent deterioration of sale price of an item sold pre-year end.

2.   Non-adjusting events – events after the balance sheet date with no relation to events pre-balance sheet date, e.g. factory damaged by lightning. The exception to 2 is where a going concern is threatened, leading to the accounts being adjusted. See Figure 19.5 for a discussion of the going concern concept.

In drawing up the accounts of a business, the accountant makes the assumption that the business is likely to continue for a reasonable length of time in the future. It is said that the business is assumed to be a 'going concern', i.e. both likely and able to stay in business into the next accounting period. This has implications for the way certain items are treated by the accountant.

For example, the business may have bought a new piece of equipment which it expects to last for 10 years, so the accountant depreciates it over the expected lifespan. If the business ceased to exist tomorrow the item of machinery would have to be sold at a second-hand value which may be much less than the net book value calculated by the accountant. The accountant's NBV is not incorrect, as he assumed that the asset would be of value to the business for 10 years and allocated its cost accordingly. He did not value the asset at what it could be sold for, as the assumption that the business was a going concern led him to his accounting treatment of the asset.

Figure 19.5   The going concern concept

19.11 SSAP 18 – contingencies

SSAP 18 defines contingencies as 'a condition which exists at the balance sheet date where the outcome will be confirmed only on the occurrence/non-occurrence of future event(s). This can be a gain or a loss.' It indicates how to account for contingencies (see Table 19.2).

Table 19.2 *Illustration of contingency calculations*

Likelihood of occurrence	Loss	Gain
Probable	Accrue	Disclose by note
Possible	Disclose by note	Ignore
Remote	Ignore	Ignore

19.12 SSAP 21 – leases and hire purchase

The volume of assets leased expanded rapidly in the 1970s and early 1980s due to generous tax allowances.[1] There was, therefore, a need to consider the way companies accounted for assets acquired by way of a lease. SSAP 21 provides accountants with a standard accounting treatment.

The standard categorises leases as either finance leases or operating leases. Finance leases are those leases which substantially transfer all the risks and rewards of ownership to the leasee (the company who has use of the asset). These leases cannot be cancelled and the leasee has to maintain the asset. The (present) value of the sum of the rental payments must at least exceed the cost of the asset to the leasor (the company who buys the asset). Therefore, the leasee treats the asset in the same way as it would do if it purchased the asset, the only difference being it does not legally own the asset; legal title is vested in the leasor.

Operating leases are all other leases. They tend to be of shorter duration than finance leases so the (present) value of the lease payments tends to be less than the original cost of the asset. The lease agreements are often able to be cancelled by either party and the leasor is often responsible for the maintenance of the asset.

The accounting procedures for operating leases present no real problems. The leasee charges the rental payments to his profit and loss account (i.e. debit **profit and loss** and credit **bank** or **creditors**). The leasor records the leased asset as a fixed asset and depreciates it over its economic useful life; rental payments are recorded as income in the profit and loss account in the period to which they relate and any maintenance costs as an expense in the profit and loss account in the period in which they are incurred.

Accounting for finance leases is not so simple. We will firstly consider the position of the leasee. The standard requires assets acquired by finance leases to be included as fixed assets, even though the leasee does not legally own these assets. The reason is largely one of consistency. It takes the view that the leasee has full use of these assets in substantially the same way as if it owned the assets. The leasor treats the leasee as a debtor in their accounts.

19.13   SSAP 24 – accounting for pension costs

Many companies operate private pension schemes for their employees. These schemes require companies as well as their employees to contribute into the scheme; these employer contributions are costs which need to be charged in their profit and loss account. SSAP 24 outlines how these charges are to be made. The accruals concept is used, as the standard requires these costs to be charged to the profit and loss account over the period during which he receives benefit from the employees services. This can present some very difficult accounting problems which however are considered to be outside the scope of an introductory text.

19.14   Note

1. The Inland Revenue allowed companies to offset the full cost of plant and machinery purchased during the year against their taxable profits and so reduce the amount of corporation tax payable. These 100 per cent 'first year allowances' were in effect free depreciation. However, many manufacturing companies were making losses and could not use these allowances as they were not paying any corporation tax, even though they were replacing their plant and machinery. Finance companies and banks were, however, making taxable profits. Therefore it was tax efficient for these financial companies to purchase and lease plant and machinery to manufacturing companies and so obtain the capital allowances and reduce their corporation tax bill. These tax savings were then passed on to manufacturing companies through lower rental payments.

    In recent years the level of capital allowances has been reduced to 25 per cent p.a. and the rate of corporation tax to 35 per cent p.a., so these tax savings are not so attractive. However, companies still use many leased assets aquired under the old rates and leasing has become an accepted way of aquiring assets; therefore we still need to examine the way we account for leased assets.

CHECKLIST _____

Having completed Chapter 19, you should be able to:

■ explain the need for accounting standards;
■ outline the standard setting process;
■ understand the main contents of SSAPs 3, 4, 6, 9, 13, 17, 18, and 21;
■ highlight the accounting implications of the main SSAPs.

Selected questions and exercises

Question 19.1

It is generally agreed that, unless otherwise stated, financial statements will observe the following conventions:

a. going concern:
b. accruals:
c. consistency:
d. prudence.

Explain each of the above conventions giving examples of how each is observed in conventional financial statements.

No solution provided.   *Source: AAT, Basic Accounting, June 1988.*

Question 19.2

Outline the specific disclosure requirements contained in each of the following statements of standard accounting practice:

a. SSAP 2: disclosure of accounting policies;
b. SSAP 9: stocks and work in progress;
c. SSAP 12: accounting for depreciation;
d. SSAP 13: accounting for research and development.

No solution provided.   *Source: AAT, Financial Accounting, June 1988.*

Question 19.3

Following high rates of inflation in the 1970s, some accounting theorists lost faith in historical cost accounting resulting in the issue, in March 1980, of the accounting standard on current cost accounting, SSAP 16.

1. Outline the main shortcomings of accounts prepared under the historical cost convention.
2. Discuss the ways in which the adjustments recommended by SSAP 16 and ED 35 endeavour to solve these problems, and their effectiveness in doing so.

No solution provided.

Question 19.4

a. SSAP 13, accounting for research and development, can be said to be a logical application of the principles established by the accruals concept and the prudence concept, namely that costs be matched with associated revenue and expected losses be written off in the period in which they arise.

Discuss the ways in which recommendations of SSAP 13 effectively satisfy the above fundamental accounting concepts.

b. Keep Afloat plc is a company engaged in the design and manufacture of sailing boats. On 1 January 1984, it set up a development unit for the creation of a new type of multi-hulled sailing boat using revolutionary new materials. Involved was the purchase of new premises at a cost of £30,000 and new equipment costing £15,000. Annual expenditure on salaries, materials and overheads is estimated at £80,000.

It is hoped that a prototype will evolve from the work within two years which would enable commercial production to be possible within three years.

Recommend appropriate accounting treatment for the development expenditure, giving reasons for your answer.

c. To what extent should events occurring shortly after a company's year end influence the financial statements for the period just ended? Illustrate your answer by referring to the information in part b and the following possible events occurring in early 1985.

1. The company's premises and equipment are completely destroyed by fire. Although the premises are insured the equipment is not.
2. The government announces that it is prepared to fund up to 25 per cent of the total cost of research projects in your area and that the funding will be backdated to expenditure since 1 January 1984. It is expected that your project will qualify.

No solution provided.

Question 19.5

a. (i) Explain the nature of the four fundamental accounting concepts, as defined in statement of standard accounting practice 2.

(ii) Explain the nature of accounting bases and accounting policies, as defined in statement of standard accounting practice 2.

b. 'Stocks should be valued at the lower of cost and net realisable value'. Statement of standard accounting practice 9.

Explain how this statement relates to the four fundamental accounting concepts you have explained part a above.

No solution provided.

Question 19.6

Mike and Jean Oldwell established Beta Computers Limited on 1 April 1984 with £30,000 invested in the company as share capital. The major features of the first year of trading are presented below.

1. Twenty micro-computer systems had been acquired during the year, fifteen systems had been sold and two were used to develop and maintain software packages. The systems had cost £800 each and were sold for £1,400 each.

2. One hundred floppy disks, costing £1.50 each, had been acquired. Forty of these had been sold for £3.50 each, and twenty had been used for software development by the owners.
3. When the business started, the company acquired the exclusive rights to a number of software packages, the consideration being £10,000. Each software package was sold for £500, and fifteen such sales had been made. It is anticipated that at least forty more sales could be made.
4. During the first year £5,000 has been spent on developing a new software package. This is to be launched in July 1985. The Oldwells consider sales prospects for this new product to be reasonable.

At the end of the first year the replacement cost of the micro-computer systems is £700 each, and the systems have an estimated useful life of four years with no salvage value at the end of this period.

You are required to give the Oldwells specific advice on the accounting principles and the alternatives that exist in relation to the matters contained in 1 to 4 above when producing the profit and loss account for the year ended 31 March 1985 and the balance sheet as at that date. While wishing to present a true and fair view of the company's affairs, they wish to present a successful company in order to raise additional finance.

No solution provided. *Source: JMB, GCE A Level, June 1985.*

Question 19.7
The ledgers of Gamma plc have been closed for the year ending 31 March 1986, and the following items have been referred to the directors by the company accountant and all are considered to be of material significance.

1. A government grant of £265,000 for a new factory has been approved and, although the funds have not been received, the project was completed during the financial year. The new factory is to be depreciated over fifteen years.
2. Theta Limited, which owes Gamma plc £138,000 at 31 March 1986, has gone into receivership and it is forecast that the unsecured creditors of Theta Limited are likely, in due course, to receive approximately 25 pence in the pound.
3. During the stocktaking it was found that, of the total stock of £835,000, approximately £93,000 of stock was missing and had been misappropriated. A further £50,000 of stock was estimated to be obsolete, with very little likelihood of resale.
4. The directors have received a professional valuation of the company's properties valuing them at £2,850,000 as against the cost of £1,935,000 which is recorded in the accounts.

5. Due to unusual market conditions, Gamma plc has managed to negotiate the sale of an existing contract with Sigma Limited to Alpha plc for £385,000, with no costs to be borne by Gamma plc.

You are required:

a. to advise the directors how each item should be treated in the company's audited accounts;
b. to explain any alternative treatments and refer to statements of standard accounting practice where appropriate.

No solution provided.   *Source: JMB, GCE A Level, June 1986.*

Question 19.8

a. The Accounting Standards Committee has produced its statement of standard accounting practice 18, *Accounting for contingencies.*

1. What is a contingency?
2. What are the alternative accounting treatments for contingencies?
3. Explain how the alternative accounting treatments are determined?

b. The Delta Company manufacturers and sells a fluorescent thermostat. The financial year end was 31 March 1986. How should the following items be dealt with in the accounts for the year ended 31 March 1986?

1. A competitor has started producing a similar product which, it is believed, is in breach of a patent owned by Delta. On 25 February 1986 the company commenced legal proceedings. These are progressing slowly, but the company's lawyers believe that there is a 70 per cent chance that within twelve months the company could receive damages in the region of £250,000.
2. A customer has also commenced legal proceedings against Delta for damages based on a claim that the thermostat has caused ill health due to radiation. The company's lawyers believe that the £500,000 claim for damages has only a 30 per cent chance of success. At 31 March 1986 correspondence between the two parties was at a preliminary stage.

No solution provided.   *Source: JMB, GCE A Level, June 1985.*

Question 19.9

a. You are required to arrange the balances in Table 19.3 in a format that would be acceptable for publication in the audited accounts of Sigma Signs plc. The balances relate to the year ended 31 December 1985.
b. Explain the logic of the presentation that you have used in presenting the accounts of Sigma Signs plc.

Table 19.3 *Details of the accounts of Sigma Signs plc*

	£000s	
	Dr.	Cr
Interest receivable		1,200
Cost of sales	12,362	
Distributive costs	893	
Administrative expenses	1,121	
Interest payable	960	
Turnover		18,326
Taxation on profit on ordinary activities	870	
Extraordinary loss (net of taxation)	738	
Proposed ordinary dividend	1,200	

No solution provided.   *Source: JMB, GCE A Level, June 1986.*

Question 19.10

Celltech Limited is involved in the development and manufacture of high-technology electrical and electronic products. You are involved in the production of the financial accounts for the year ended 31 March 1985, and have ascertained the following facts and estimates.

1. The company has incurred expenditure of £230,000 during the year on a project which is concerned with developing new forms of energy storage. The project is continuing, but no conclusive results have been obtained.
2. £180,000 has been spent on updating an existing product which is selling well. The management has high expectations for the sales of the updated product. It is expected to have a life of five years. Sales are also expected to grow over the next five years.
3. £120,000 has been spent during the year on developing a new electronic device. Manufacture is due to commence in August 1986. The managers are confident that the product will sell as long as a number of persistent technical problems can be overcome.

You are required to advise the directors of the company how these items should be treated in the accounts. Make reference, where appropriate, to any relevant statements of standard accounting practice.

No solution provided.   *Source: JMB, GCE A Level, June 1988.*

Question 19.11

In preparing the accounts of your company, you are faced with the following problems.

1. The company's long-term prospects are not good.
2. Some very reliable customers have placed several large orders which could be very profitable. These are not recorded in the sales ledger.

3. The company accounts end in March, but the electricity bill is due in April.
4. One of the owners of the company used drawings to invest in some stocks and shares.
5. All the fixed assets of the company are worth a lot more than their original purchase price.
6. During the year, the company purchased £50-worth of calculator batteries; these had all been issued but all the calculators were working and the batteries had not gone flat.
7. Due to the company's poor profit margins, the owners believe that a better result could be obtained if a LIFO stock valuation method was adopted, instead of the present FIFO method.
8. One of the debtors, who owes the company a lot of money, is rumoured to be going into liquidation.
9. The company owns some shares which the accountant thinks are worthless.
10. Despite these problems, the company has very good industrial relations with the workforce which the accountant thinks should be reflected in the accounts.

You are required to examine the accounting convention the accountant should follow in dealing with each of the above problems.

No solution provided.

20 | *Final accounts of companies*

- to introduce students to the legally prescribed format for published company accounts;
- to outline some of the advantages and disadvantages of standardised formats;
- to prepare company accounts in the legally prescribed format from a list of transactions and/or balances.

20.1 Introduction

The Companies Act 1985 (schedule 4) lays down the format to be used when preparing published company accounts. Published accounts are those accounts sent to:

a. shareholders who are the owners of the company and require information on the performance of the company during the year;

b. the Registrar of Companies, who is responsible for enforcing the statutory provisions relating to companies.

It is important to understand that the company can adopt any type of format it wants when preparing accounts for its own internal use by directors and managers; the prescribed formats are only necessary for the above-mentioned parties.

The advantages to be gained from such standardisation include:

a. comparability of the accounts of a single company over a number of years;

b. comparability of the accounts of different companies.

As we will see in Chapter 22, standardised formats are invaluable when we have to analyse company accounts.

The Companies Act 1985 gives companies the choice of four alternative formats for the profit and loss account and two for the balance sheet. Two of the profit and loss account formats and one of the balance sheet formats are horizontal in style like a T account, with two balancing sets of figures side-by-side. The other two profit and loss account and balance sheet formats have a familiar vertical layout similar to the formats used so far in this text. Since the horizontal formats are generally considered to be old-fashioned and not used by many companies today, we will direct our attention upon the vertical formats.

20.2   Profit and loss account layouts

The two profit and loss account layouts are shown in Figure 20.1. Layout 1, which is suitable for trading companies, is shown in Figure 20.1a and layout 2, which is suitable for manufacturing companies, in Figure 20.1b. The difference between the two layouts lies in the way expenditure is analysed; layout 1 analyses expenses by

Notes	Profit and loss account for the year ended 31 December 1988	£
	See Section 20.4.1	
1.	TURNOVER	X
2.	Cost of sales	(X)
	Gross profit	X
2.	Distribution costs	(X)
2.	Administrative expenses	(X)
		X
	Other operating income	X
	OPERATING PROFIT	X
3.	Income from other fixed asset investments	X
	Other interest receivable	X
		X
4.	Interest payable	(X)
5.	PROFIT ON ORDINARY ACTIVITIES BEFORE TAXATION	X
6.	Tax on profit on ordinary activities	(X)
	Profit on ordinary activities after taxation	X
7.	Extraordinary item, less taxation	(X)
	PROFIT FOR THE FINANCIAL YEAR	X
	DIVIDENDS	(X)
8.	TRANSFERS TO RESERVES	X

Figure 20.1a   Layout 1

Profit and Loss Account
for the year ended 31 December 1988

Notes
See Section 20.4.1   £

1.	TURNOVER	X
	Change in stocks of finished goods and work in progress	X
	Own work capitalised	X
		X
	Raw materials and consumables	(X)
		X
2.	Staff costs	(X)
2.	Depreciation	(X)
2.	Other operating charges	(X)
	OPERATING PROFIT	X
3.	Income from other fixed asset investments	X
	Other interest receivable and similar income	X
4.	Interest payable and other similar charges	(X)
5.	PROFIT ON ORDINARY ACTIVITIES BEFORE TAXATION	X
6.	TAX on profit on ordinary activities	(X)
	Profit on ordinary activities after taxation	X
7.	Extraordinary items, less taxation	(X)
	PROFIT FOR THE FINANCIAL YEAR	X
	DIVIDENDS	(X)
8.	TRANSFERS TO RESERVES	X

Figure 20.1b   Layout 2

type of operation (e.g. distribution costs, administration expenses, etc.) and layout
2 by type of expenditure (e.g. raw materials, staff costs, depreciation, etc.).

20.3   Balance sheet layouts

The balance sheet layout is shown in Figure 20.2. After your first review of these
accounts you may be slightly confused on a number of points. Firstly, the
language used may be strange – we will describe the meaning of the wording used
in the next part of this chapter. Secondly, you may also be surprised to see such an
abbreviated amount of information shown, compared to the more detailed
accounts you have been used to preparing. For example, in the balance sheet only
one figure is shown for tangible fixed assets and one for creditors payable within
one year (i.e. current liabilities). More detail is shown in a series of notes which
form part of the accounts and are described below.

```
                          Balance sheet
                      as at 31 December 1988

Notes                                                          £     £
1.        FIXED ASSETS
2.        Intangible assets                                          X
3.        Tangible assets                                           X
4.        Investments                                               X
5.        CURRENT ASSETS
6.        Stocks                                              X
7.        Debtors                                             X
4.        Investments                                         X
          Cash at bank and in hand                            X
                                                             ───
                                                              X
8.        CREDITORS: amounts falling due within one year    (X)
          NET CURRENT ASSETS                                         X
          TOTAL ASSETS LESS CURRENT LIABILITIES                     X
8.        CREDITORS: amounts falling due after more than one year  X
9.        PROVISIONS FOR LIABILITIES AND CHARGES            X
                                                                   (X)
                                                                   £X

          CAPITAL AND RESERVES
10.       Called up share capital                                   X
9.        Share premium account                                    X
9.        Revaluation reserve                                      X
9.        Other reserves                                           X
9.  ·     Profit and loss account                                  X
                                                                   £X
```

Figure 20.2   Layout

20.4   Notes to the accounts

In order to provide more detailed information concerning the figures in the accounts, notes are provided. These notes are cross-referenced to the relevant figure in the accounts. This practice saves cluttering up the accounts with unnecessary detail and enables us to see the important total figures.

The most popular notes are as follows.

20.4.1   Profit and loss account notes

1.   This is the analysis of turnover by different class business and geographical area (if material). It can be omitted if the directors consider its disclosure would damage the company's interests; if such an option is taken the company must state the reason for non-disclosure.

2. The following expenditures included in cost of sales, distribution costs and administrative expenses need to be disclosed:
   a. depreciation on tangible assets;
   b. diminution in the value of intangible assets;
   c. the employees' aggregate remuneration and social security and pension costs; also the average number of employees during the year needs to be disclosed, together with a split of employee numbers between categories of the business and the number of employees whose emoluments fall within bands of £5,000;
   d. the following details of directors' emoluments:
      (i) aggregate emoluments,
      (ii) aggregate pensions,
      (iii) aggregate compensation paid for loss of office;
        plus the split of three above sums into amounts receivable for services as directors and sums receivable for other offices.
        If aggregate emoluments exceed £40,000 (exclusive of pension contributions and emoluments of directors whose duties were mainly outside the United Kingdom), the following details are also required:
      (i) the chairman's emolument,
      (ii) the highest paid director's emolument,
      (iii) the number of directors whose emoluments fall within bands of £5,000,
      (iv) the amount of emoluments waived and number of directors involved;
   e. amounts charged for the hire of plant and machinery;
   f. the auditor's remuneration;
   g. details of any exceptional items.

3. Income from investments in shares and debentures in other companies and rents from land if material must be disclosed. The amount of income from listed investments needs to be disclosed separately.

4. Details of interest charged on bank loans and overdrafts and interest on other loans (both split between those repayable within five years and those repayable after five years) need to be disclosed.

5. Analysis of pre-tax profit or loss by different class of business, using the same classification as that used for turnover.

6. Taxation charged and basis of calculation (see Chapter 18).

7. Details of any extraordinary items (see Chapter 19).

8. Any amounts set aside for the redemption of share capital and loans must be disclosed (see Chapter 17).

20.4.2 Balance sheet notes

1. For each fixed asset class of item the following information is required:
   a. the aggregate purchase price (or production cost or other valuation) as at the beginning and end of the year, together with the acquisitions, disposals or transfers of assets during the year and any revaluations;
   b. the cumulative provision for depreciation (or diminution in value) as at the beginning and end of the year, together with the annual depreciation charge, depreciation on disposals and any other adjustments to the depreciation provision;
   c. if any fixed assets are revalued, the year in which the valuation was made must be shown. If an asset is revalued during the year the names or qualifications of the valuers must be stated together with the bases of valuation.

2. Intangible assets can comprise:
   a. development costs. The reasons for capitalising development costs and the period of write-off have to be disclosed;
   b. concessions, patents, licences, trade marks and similar rights purchased or created by the company;
   c. goodwill arising on the acquisition of companies. This goodwill represents the excess of the purchase price paid for the company over and above its balance sheet valuation. An understanding of consolidated accounts is required to throughly understand goodwill; this is outside the scope of this text. If goodwill is written off the period of write-off must be disclosed, together with the reasons for choosing that period;
   d. payments on account; see below for explanation.

3. Tangible assets must be split into the component categories, such as land and buildings, plant and machinery, fixtures, fittings, tools, equipment, payments on account and assets in the process of construction. For land and buildings the split between freehold, long leasehold and short leasehold must be shown.

4. For investments in other companies the following must be shown:
   a. analysis of investments listed on the Stock Exchange and others;
   b. the market value of listed investments;
   c. if over 10 per cent of the shares of the company are owned or if the investment exceeds 10 per cent of its own assets then the name, country of incorporation if outside Great Britain or country of registration if different from the company are required to be disclosed;
   d. if more than 20 per cent or 50 per cent of a company's share capital is owned other disclosure rules apply, which are outside the scope of this text. They are the topic of SSAP 1.

5. Current assets are to be shown at the lower of cost and net realisable value.

6. Stocks can be analysed into:
    a. raw materials and consumables;
    b. work in progress;
    c. finished goods and goods for resale;
    d. payments on account.

Stocks are discussed in Chapter 8 and long-term work in progress payments on account in Chapter 19.

7. Debtors can be analysed into:
    a. trade debtors;
    b. other debtors;
    c. called up share capital not paid. This is described in Chapter 17;
    d. prepayments and accrued income.

Debtors included in current assets must be those falling due for settlement within one year.

The details of loans to directors (or persons connected with directors such as members of their family), employees and other officers of the company have to be disclosed; these details include such information as the individual concerned, the amount of the loan, the terms and interest. Such loans can be included as either current or fixed assets depending upon when they are due to be repaid.

8. Creditors falling due within one year and after one year must be shown under different balance sheet headings. Creditors can be analysed into:
    a. debenture loans;
    b. bank loans and overdrafts;
    c. payments received on account. See Chapter 19 for an explanation of payments on account for long-term contract work in progress. If the progress payments exceed the contract work paid for, the excess is shown here;
    d. trade creditors;
    e. bills of exchange payable. See Chapter 17;
    f. other creditors, including taxation and social security;
    g. accruals and deferred income.

If any category of creditor has been secured on assets of the company, details of this security must be disclosed. This means that if the company failed to pay such a creditor, they are legally entitled to sell the asset; in this way the asset gives them security for their debt.

The terms of repayment of any loan must be disclosed:
(i) the dates of repayment;
(ii) the rate of interest;
(iii) the conversion terms if applicable (see Chapter 17 for explanations of convertible loans);
(iv) details of redeemable debentures which the company has the power to reissue (see Chapter 17);
(v) if any of the loans are held in trust on behalf of the company the amount so held must be disclosed.

If any debentures have been issued during the year the reason for the loan, the class of debentures issued and the consideration received must be stated.

Details of loans made to employees to enable them to purchase the company's shares require disclosure.

The amounts of any dividends owing must be stated. If fixed cumulative dividends are in arrears the amount of arrears and period of arrears must be disclosed.

9. For each reserve and provision; a company must disclose:
    a. the purpose of the reserve or provision;
    b. its opening and closing balance;
    c. transfers to and from reserves and provisions;
    d. source and application of each transfer;
    e. taxation treatment of transfers to and from revaluation reserves.

The amount of any provision for taxation has to be disclosed.

The actual or estimated amount and legal nature of any contingent liability has to be disclosed. For any capital expenditures, the amount contracted for but not yet provided, and the amount authorised but no yet contracted for, has to be disclosed.

Pension commitments for which provision has been made and those for which no provision has been made are required to be disclosed.

Details of any other financial commitment not provided for require disclosure.

10. Authorised share capital, together with the number, nominal value and amount called up of shares alloted require disclosure.

The details of redeemable shares (i.e. earliest and latest redemption date, the premium payable upon redemption, if any, and whether redemption is compulsory or optional) require disclosure. The classes and reasons of shares allotted during the current year, together with the number, nominal value and consideration recieved for each class of shares allotted require disclosure.

20.4.3 General notes

1. A statement of accounting policies which has been used to prepare the accounts must be included. This is also a requirement of SSAP 2.

2. The basis of translating transactions denominated in foriegn currencies is required.

3. All items included in the notes to the accounts should be accompanied with the corresponding amount of the preceeding year.

4. Details of any capitalised interest should be enclosed. This can arise if a company borrows money to finance the production of an asset and includes the interest payable on the loan in with the cost of the asset to be included in the balance sheet.

5. The breakdown of aggregate amounts must be included in the accounts, if such a breakdown is required by the Companies Act (see Sections 20.2 and 20.3 above).

6. Where an asset is included in the balance sheet at a valuation other than cost the basis of valuation and historic cost must be stated. See Chapter 24 for an analysis of these alternative valuation methods.

20.5 Small and medium-sized companies

The above accounts are known as 'full accounts' and have to be produced by all companies for their members. However, small and medium-sized companies are allowed to reduce the amount of information they disclose in the accounts they submit to the Registrar of Companies. These accounts are called 'modified' accounts.

The company must satisfy at least two of the criteria as shown in Table 20.1 for the current and the preceding year if it is able to take advantage of the reduced disclosure requirements.

Table 20.1 *Reduced disclosure criteria*

	Medium-sized companies	Small companies
Turnover for the year	Not to exceed £5.75m	Not to exceed £1.4m
Balance sheet assets	Not to exceed £2.8m	Not to exceed £0.7m
Average number of employees per week	Not to exceed 250	Not to exceed 50

20.6   Abridged accounts

If a company publishes its accounts in newspapers it can restrict the amount of information disclosed; such accounts are called 'abridged' accounts. However, a statement must accompany the abridged accounts stating the following:

1.   The accounts are not full accounts.
2.   Full accounts are filed with the Registrar of Companies.
3.   An auditor has reported on the full accounts and whether their report was qualified. See Chapter 25 for discussion of the audit process.

20.7   Directors' report

The Companies Act 1985 requires directors of companies to prepare a directors' report and stipulates its minimum contents. The contents represent a mixture of information considered important for shareholders, who have entrusted the directors to look after their company.

The minimum contents of the directors' report are as follows:

1.   The principal activities of the company, together with any significant changes in these activities during the year.

2.   A fair review of the development of the business of the company during the year and its year-end position.

3.   Details of post balance sheet events (see Chapter 19).

4.   Indications of any significant future developments in the business of the company.

5.   Indications of research and development activities of the company.

6.   Details of significant changes in fixed assets during the year.

7.   Details of the market value of land and buildings, if significantly different from their balance sheet values.

8.   Amounts of recommended dividends.

9.   Any dividends waived. This is a Stock Exchange listing requirement.

10.   Amounts transferred to reserves.

11.   Details of charitable and political contributions, if in excess of £200.

12. Names of all directors during the year.

13. The number and nominal value of shares and debentures owned by directors at the beginning (or at date of appointment) and end of the year. If this information is provided as a note to the accounts there is no need to repeat it in the directors' report.

14. The number and nominal value of its own shares purchased by the company (see Chapter 17) or, together with the purchase price, reasons for purchase and the percentage of issued share capital these purchased shares represent.

15. Details of the company's shares acquired by the company (or its nominee with financial assistance from the company) and any shares subject to charges and liens, i.e. outstanding debt.

16. A statement describing steps taken by the company to involve employees in the company's affairs. This is a requirement of the 1982 Employment Act.

20.8 Chairman's statement

Companies with a Stock Exchange listing invariably prepare a statement by the chairman. This statement is not required by the Companies Act. Companies usually include a significant amount of detailed information in this statement, such as information on:

a. sales and customers;

b. new product developments;

c. purchases and suppliers;

d. directors;

e. employees;

f. important financial statistics (e.g. earnings per share);

g. significant purchases and disposals of assets;

h. dividends;

i. the economic and political environment in which the company has, and will be, operating;

j. the future.

As the information contained in the chairman's statement is based upon the personal opinion of the chairman, future-orientated, provided on a voluntary basis and unaudited (see Chapter 25), there is a temptation for it to concentrate upon information favourable to the company and exclude or explain away information unfavourable to the company. However, such a biased view must be tempered to ensure the picture painted is consistent with the information contained in the accounts.

20.9 A worked example

Now let us consider an example. A list of balances and transactions for Jennings plc is shown in Figure 20.3. We are required to prepare a set of accounts which conform to The Companies Act 1985 format, together with suitable notes. These published accounts are shown in Figure 20.4.

CHECKLIST _____

Having completed Chapter 20, you should be able to:

■ outline the legally prescribed format for published company accounts;

■ outline some of the advantages and disadvantages of standardised formats;

■ prepare company accounts in the legally prescribed format from a list of transactions and/or balances.

Jennings plc has the following totals in its records from which you are required to prepare a balance sheet and trading and profit and loss account for the year ended 31 December 1988.

	£ Debit	£ Credit
Sales		11,660,656
Sales returns	112,658	
Carriage outwards	92,778	
Discounts allowed	106,380	
Purchases	5,974,840	
Purchase returns		112,702
Carriage inwards	71,800	
Discounts received		49,360
Opening stock	1,302,400	

Share capital £1 shares		6,000,000
Share premium account		400,000
Revaluation reserve		200,000
General reserve		58,648
Profit and loss account		1,127,784
Interim dividend	136,000	
Bank overdraft		112,960
Bad debts	25,460	
Doubtful debt provision		91,660
Rent payable	253,000	
Rent receivable		90,000
Commission receivable		47,400
Insurance	90,000	
Land	5,092,800	
Motor vans	912,600	
Machinery	3,093,560	
Provisions for depreciation as at 1 January 1991		
Motor vans		51,200
Machinery		265,280
Profit on sale of motor car		11,360
Selling expenses	912,720	
Office expenses	491,590	
Wages and salaries	1,309,300	
Creditors		895,836
Debtors	2,685,600	
Cash	11,360	
Loan		1,500,000
	22,674,846	22,674,846

The following notes are relevant:

	£
1. Closing stock was	
Raw materials	492,980
Work in progress	270,960
Finished goods	731,680
2. Rent payable accrued was	90,744
3. Insurance prepaid	30,000
4. Wages and salaries accrued	30,940
5. Commission due	13,400
6. Rent received overpaid	9,000
7. Provision for doubtful debts to be increased to	130,000

8. Motor vans are to be depreciated using the straight method at a rate of 25 per cent p.a. on cost. A full year's depreciation is to be charged in the year of purchase and not in the year of sale.

8. Machinery is to be depreciated using the reducing balance method at a rate of 10 per cent p.a. A full year's depreciation is to be charged in the year of purchase and not in the year of sale.

9. Corporation tax on profits is 35 per cent.

10. The final dividend is to be 15 pence per share.

11. Transfer to General Reserve £200,000

12. No provisions for the audit fee has been made. The audit fee is estimated at £20,000

Figure 20.3   Jennings plc

Notes		£s
a.	TURNOVER	11,547,998
b.	Cost of sales	5,740,718
	Gross profit	5,807,280
c.	Distribution costs	1,069,298
d.	Administrative expenses	2,872,932
		1,865,050
e.	Other operating income	202,520
		2,067,570
	Income from other fixed asset investments	
	Other interest receivable	
		2,067,570
f.	Interest payable	180,000
	PROFIT ON ORDINARY ACTIVITIES BEFORE TAXATION	1,887,570
g.	Tax on profit on ordinary activities	660,650
	Profit on ordinary activities after taxation	1,226,921
h.	Extraordinary item, less taxation	
	PROFIT FOR THE FINANCIAL YEAR	1,226,921
i.	DIVIDENDS	1,036,000
p.	TRANSFERS TO RESERVES	190,921

Figure 20.4a Jennings plc – profit and loss account for the year ended 31 December 1988

Notes		£	£
	FIXED ASSETS		
	Intangible assets		
j.	Tangible assets		8,271,502
	Investments		
			8,271,502
	CURRENT ASSETS		
k.	Stocks	1,495,620	
l.	Debtors	2,599,000	
	Investments		
	Cash at bank and in hand	11,360	
		4,105,980	
	CREDITORS: amounts falling due		
m.	within one year	2,900,130	
	NET CURRENT ASSETS		1,205,851
	TOTAL ASSETS LESS CURRENT LIABILITIES		9,477,353
	CREDITORS: amounts falling		
	due after more than one		
n.	year	1,500,000	
	PROVISIONS FOR LIABILITIES AND CHARGES		
			1,500,000
			7,977,353
	CAPITAL AND RESERVES		
o.	Called up share capital		6,000,000
	Share premium account		400,000
	Revaluation reserve		200,000
p.	Other reserves		258,648
p.	Profit and loss account		1,118,705
			7,977,353

Figure 20.4b Jennings plc – balance sheet as at 31 December 1988

a.	Sales			11,660,656
	Less sales returns			112,658
	Turnover			11,547,998
b.	Opening stock			1,302,400
	Purchases			5,974,840
	Carriage inwards			71,800
	Less purchase returns			−112,702
				7,236,338
	Less closing stock			1,495,620
	Cost of sales			5,740,718
c.	Carriage outwards			92,778
	Selling expences			912,720
	Bad debts			25,460
	Change in doubtful debt provision			38,340
	Distribution costs			1,069,298
d.	Rent			343,744
	Insurance			60,000
	Office expences			491,590
	Wages and salaries			1,340,240
	Discounts allowed			106,380
	Audit fee			20,000
	Depreciation:			
	Motor vans		228,150	
	Machinery		282,828	
				510,978
	Administration expenses			2,872,932
e.	Discounts received			49,360
	Rent receivable		90,000	
	Less prepayment		9,000	
				81,000
	Commission receivable		47,400	
	Add accrual		13,400	
				60,800
	Profit on sale of van			11,360
	Other operating income			202,520
f.	Interest payable			
	12 per cent debentures			180,000
g.	Taxation			
	Corporation tax: 35 per cent of profits			660,650
h.	Extraordinary item			
	none			
i.	Interim dividend			136,000
	Final dividend			900,000
				1,036,000

j. Tangible fixed assets

	Cost	Depreciation	NBV
Land	5,092,800		5,092,800
Machinery	3,093,560	548,108	2,545,452
Motor vans	912,600	279,350	633,250
	9,098,960	827,458	8,271,502

k.	Raw materials	492,980	
	Work in progress	270,960	
	Finished goods	731,680	
		1,495,620	
1.	Trade debtors	2,555,600	
	Prepaid expenses	30,000	
	Accrued income	13,400	
	Debtors	2,599,000	
m.	Trade creditors	895,836	
	Accrued expenses	121,684	
	Prepaid revenue	9,000	
	Corporation tax	660,650	
	Debenture interest	180,000	
	Dividend	900,000	
	Audit fee	20,000	
	Bank overdraft	112,960	
		2,900,130	
n.	12 per cent debentures	1,500,000	
o.	Authorised share capital		
	8,000,000 1 shares	8,000,000	
	Issued and fully paid share capital		
	6,000,000 1 shares	6,000,000	

		Profit and loss	General Reserve
p.	Balance as at 1 January 1988	1,127,784	58,648
	Profit for year	190,921	
	Transfer to general reserve	−200,000	200,000
	Balance as at 31 December 1988	1,118,705	258,648

Figure 20.4c Notes to Jennings plc

Selected questions and exercises

Question 20.1

The trial balance in Table 20.2 has been extracted from the books of account of Greet plc as at 31 March 1988.

Additional information:

1. Stock at 31 March 1988 was valued at £150,000.
2. The items in Table 20.3 (*inter alia*) are already included in the balances listed in Table 20.2.
3. The following rates of taxation are to be assumed: corporation tax, 35 per cent; income tax, 27 per cent.

Table 20.2 *Details of the accounts of Greet plc*

	Dr. £000	Cr. £000
Administrative expenses	210	
Called up share capital (ordinary shares of £1 fully paid)		600
Debtors	470	
Cash at bank and in hand	40	
Corporation tax (overprovision in 1987)		25
Deferred taxation (at 1 April 1987)		180
Distribution costs	420	
Extraordinary item		60
Fixed asset investments	560	
Franked investment income (amount received)		73
Plant and machinery:		
at cost	750	
accumulated depreciation (at 31 March 1988)		220
Profit and loss (at 1 April 1987)		182
Purchases	960	
Stock (at 1 April 1987)	140	
Trade creditors		260
Turnover		1,950
	£3,550	£3,550

Table 20.3 *Distribution costs and administrative expenses*

	Distribution costs £000	Administrative expenses £000
Depreciation (for the year to 31 March 1988)	27	5
Hire of plant and machinery	20	15
Auditors' remuneration	—	30
Directors' emoluments	—	45

4. The corporation tax charge based on the profits for the year is estimated to be £52,000.
5. A transfer of £16,000 is to be made to the credit of the deferred taxation account.
6. The extraordinary item relates to the profit made on the disposal of a factory in Belgium following the closure of the company's entire operations in that country. The corporation tax payable on the extraordinary item is estimated to be £20,000.
7. The company's authorised share capital consists of 1,000,000 ordinary shares of £1 each.
8. A final ordinary dividend of 30p per share is proposed.
9. There were no purchases or disposals of fixed assets during the year.

10. The market value of the fixed assets investments as at 31 March 1988 was £580,000. There were no purchases or sales of such investments during the year.

Insofar as the information permits, prepare the company's published profit loss account for the year to 31 March 1988 and a balance sheet as at that date in accordance with the Companies Act 1985 and with related statements of standard accounting practice.

Relevant notes to the profit and loss account and balance sheet and detailed workings should be submitted with your answer, but a statement of the company's accounting policies is not required.

Solution in pages 555-7.   *Source: AAT, Financial Accounting, June 1988.*

Question 20.2

Bustle Ltd, a retailer of high-class ladies' dresses, has the items shown in Table 20.4 among its trial balance entries at 31 December 1986.

Table 20.4   *Details of the accounts of Bustle Limited*

	Dr £000	Cr £000
Interim dividend paid	3	
Purchases and sales	210	290
Stock 1 January 1986	40	
Advertising	7	
General distribution costs	12	
Agents' commission	3	
General administration costs	15	
Audit fee	4	
Van running expenses	8	
Accounting office costs	6	
Bad debt	5	
Loss on shoes division closure	13	
Share capital in 10p shares		50

Notes:

1. Stock at 31 December 1986 was valued at £60,000.
2. The van is used to take dresses to customers' homes.
3. The bad debt was caused by the bankruptcy of a customer.
4. The van running expenses include licence fees for the year ending 30 June 1987 of £2,000.
5. Advertising includes the cost (£3,000) of a series of advertisements in a monthly magazine running from November 1986 to April 1987 inclusive.
6. The shoe sales division, which had been a significant part of the business, was closed down because it had become unprofitable.
7. Tax on ordinary activities is expected to be £12,000.
8. A final dividend of 1p a share is proposed.

Prepare the profit and loss account in format 1 of the Companies Act 1985. You should omit lines in which no amount for Bustle would appear, but include line 14.

No solution provided.   *Source: RSA, Accounting, II, June 1987.*

Question 20.3

The balances extracted from the books of Arthur plc, at 30 June 1988, the firm's year end, were as shown in Table 20.5.

Table 20.5 *Details of the accounts of Arthur plc*

	£000s
Ordinary shares, £1 each	300
6 per cent preference shares £1 each	100
Capital redemption reserve	60
Share premium account	240
Revaluation reserve	300
8 per cent debentures (secured on freehold property)	200
Profit and loss account – credit balance 31 July 1987	120
Freehold property – cost £720,000, revalued 31 June 1988	960
Depreciation provision account – freehold property	160
Plant, machinery and equipment – cost £160,000 revalued 31 June 1988	220
Depreciation provision account – plant, etc.	80
Creditors	260
Debtors	280
Bank – debit balance	40
Sales	1,300
Stock at 1 July 1987	240
Purchases	920
Employees' salaries and wages	244
Directors' salaries	80
General business expenses	84
Debenture interest	8
Bad debts	8
Preference dividend paid	6
Ordinary dividend – interim paid	30

The following additional information is also available: authorised capital – 400,000 ordinary shares of £1 each, and 200,000 6 per cent preference shares of £1 each; debenture interest is payable half-yearly on 1 January and 1 July.
Stock at 30 June 1988 is valued at £500,000.

You are required to make the following provisions:

1. Bad debt at 5 per cent of debtors
2. Audit and accountancy fees, £6,000
3. Salesmen's commission, £4,000

4. Depreciation:
    a. plant, machinery and equipment is £23,000.
    b. freehold property has an estimated useful life of another forty years. The straight-line method is to be used;
    c. depreciation on fixed assets is based on the year-end valuation.

A final dividend of 10 pence per share is proposed on the ordinary shares.
    Corporation tax based on the year's profit is estimated at £50,000.
    You are required to prepare trading, profit and loss and appropriation accounts for the year ended 30 June 1988, and a balance sheet as at that date for presentation to the members.

Solution on pages 557–61.

Question 20.4
As Chief Accountant of Hebden plc, a small retailing chain, you are required to prepare the final accounts for the year ended 30 September 1988 for approval by the directors on 1 December 1988. Most of the adjustments necessary to complete the accounting information have been included in the figures for the latest trial balance. This is as follows:

Trial balance for year ending 30 September 1988
(balances extracted from accounts at 27 November 1988)

	Dr	Cr
	£'000	£'000
Ordinary shares of £1		1,000
Share premium account		25
8 per cent convertible debentures		500
Fixed assets of cost		
Land and building	1,200	
Motor vehicles	245	
Provision for depreciation at 30 September 1988		
Land and buildings		40
Motor vehicles		25
Distribution costs	690	
Administrative expenses	360	
Investments	190	
Loan interest paid	20	
Corporation tax 1986/7		90
Sales		3,600
Purchases	2,200	
Stock at 1 October 1987	270	
Debtors	600	

	Dr	Cr.
Creditors		420
Interest on investments		21
Profit and loss account balance at		
1 October 1987		379
Cash	70	
Suspense account	255	
	6,100	6,100

The following have not been taken into account

(i) The directors of Bigwoods plc have decided to reflect the market value of land and buildings in the accounts. The market value at 30 September 1988 is estimated by Messrs Smith and Harris, local valuers, at £1,800,000, of which £1,000,000 is for the land. In the past depreciation has been charged only on buildings (estimated cost £400,000). The directors see no reason to change their estimates of the useful life of these assets. 90 per cent of the land and buildings are used for distributive purposes, the rest for administrative use.

(ii) The corporation tax charges for 1987/8 have been calculated at £290,000. The corporation tax liability for 1986/7 has been agreed at £102,00, the provision made in the 1986/7 accounts was £90,000.

(iii) Stock was valued at 30 September 1988 at £290,000. On 3 October 1988 £50,000 worth of stock was destroyed in a fire.

(iv) The market value of the investments at 30 September 1988 is £209,000. They are all 'listed investments'.

(v) On 1 March 1988 an offer was made to holders of the 8 per cent convertible debentures of conversion to ordinary shares at 80 ordinary shares for each £100 debenture held or repayment at £102. By 31 March 1988 half of the debenture holders have opted for conversion and half for repayment. The money paid to the debenture holders was debited to a suspense account. No other entries have yet been made to record these matters.

(vi) Yesterday, news was received that a firm owing Hebden plc £240,000 was going into liquidation. No further information is available. £200,000 of the debt is for goods delivered in 1987/8.

(vii) You are to recommend an ordinary share dividend for the year ended 30 September 1988 and use this in preparing the accounts. A competitor has recently announced a distribution of 25p per £1 share.

Required

a. Prepare the final accounts of Hebden plc for submission to the directors, these should consist of:

(i) the profit and loss account for the year ended 30 September 1988; and

(ii) the balance sheet at 30 September 1988.

b.   Prepare a draft memorandum to the finance director justifying your recommended dividend.

Notes:

Your answers should be in accordance with current legislation and SSAP's. You should produce clear working papers showing how you have treated items (i) to (vii) in the accounts and citing the authorities invoked.

Assume corporation tax rate of 35 per cent. Ignore ACT and Deferred Tax.

Solution on pages 561–4.

Part D

Interpretation and comparison of financial statements

21 Funds flow statements

- to introduce students to some of the limitations of the profit and loss account in assessing financial performance;
- to develop the student's understanding of the concept of funds flow, starting with cash flow statements;
- to expand this understanding to more complex statements involving working capital movements;
- to develop the student's skill in the preparation and basic interpretation of statements of sources and applications of funds.

21.1 Introduction

Businesses can be put into liquidation or receivership, with their owners and creditors losing much or all of their stake in the business, even where business make a healthy profit. How can this be? The answer to this question is that profit and having sufficient money in the bank or in hand are two very different things. Profits can be made by the business selling its goods and services to customers. However, the firm's bank balance only increases when the customer pays for these goods and services. These two transactions (i.e. selling goods and services and receiving payment) can occur at different points in time. If the businessman allows customers too much credit then the businessperson may find that there are insufficient funds to pay the creditors, who may not be willing to wait for settlement of their debts. It is very tempting for a business to 'over sell' or 'over trade' if its market is buoyant, as expansion is seen as the road to success. In fact, when some debtors do pay up, these receipts are often used to purchase new fixed assets and stocks to meet the increasing demand for output. These decisions can lead to liquidity problems, as the business is left with insufficient liquid resources to pay its creditors.

411

Trading, profit and loss account
for the year ended 31 December 1988

	£000	£000
Sales		1,900
Less purchases	805	
Stock as at 31 December 1987	391	
	1,196	
Stock as at 31 December 1988	478	
Cost of goods sold		718
GROSS PROFIT		1,182
Less expenses (cash)	695	
Depreciation	50	
Loss on sale of plant	5	
	750	
NET PROFIT		432
Taxation		145
		287
Dividends proposed		50
Retained profit		£237

Balance sheet as at 31 December

	1988				1987	
	£000	£000	£000	£000	£000	£000
Ordinary shares @ £1			560			430
Profit and loss account			577			340
Loan – 10 per cent p.a.			—			200
			£1,137			£970

Represented by:
Fixed assets:

	Cost	Depreciation	NBV	Cost	Depreciation	NBV
Land	300	—	300	250	—	250
Plant and machinery	360	210	150	285	170	115
	660	210	450	535	170	365

Current assets:

	1988		1987	
Stocks		478		391
Trade investments		180		420
Debtors		190		118
Cash and bank balances		226		300
		1,074		1,229

Less current liabilities:

Trade creditors	192		349	
Taxation	145		195	
Proposed dividend	50		80	
	387		624	
		687		605
		£1,137		£970

Figure 21.1   Cathays Park Limited

How can the accountant help businesses to recognise that they have liquidity problems?

The trading, profit and loss account is of little use as it is designed to show how the profit for the year was arrived at; as we have already seen, profit is often no guide to a business's liquidity situation. The balance sheet is of more help as it shows the amount of current/liquid assets and liabilities at any point in time. However, it does not explain how these amounts come into being. It is this process of liquid asset generation and current liability usage which we are interested in. Therefore we need to prepare statements designed to highlight the way liquid resources are being obtained and used. This chapter examines three such statements: the cash flow statement, the working capital flow of funds statement and the source and application of funds statement.

In order to show how each of these statements are interrelated, the same illustrative example will be used to explain each statement. This example is shown in Figure 21.1.

We are presented with the balance sheets at the beginning and end of the year together with the trading, profit and loss account for the year under consideration, that is, the year ended 31 December 1988.

21.2 The cash flow statement

The cash flow statement is designed to show the movements into and out of bank and cash. In order to obtain this information, it is necessary to reconstruct the **bank** and **cash** columns of our spreadsheet. This is done for Cathays Park Ltd in Spreadsheet 21.1, together with all the other transactions undertaken by the business during the year.

The spreadsheet is constructed by recording the opening balance sheet figures along the top row of the spreadsheet and the closing balance sheet figures along the bottom row. The profit and loss account entries are recorded as the link between the opening and closing profit and loss balance together with their corresponding double entry. Finally, accounting logic is used to record the missing transactions.

Once the complete spreadsheet has been constructed, the cash flow statement can be written out; it is made up solely from the entries in the **bank** and **cash** column together with their related explanation. (The cash flow statement for Cathays Park Ltd is shown in Figure 21.2.)

Inflows are separately listed from outflows for ease of reading. There has been a net outflow of cash of £74, as shown by the difference between the opening position of £300 and the closing figure of £226. This has arisen due to inflows amounting to £2,204 while outflows amount to £2,278. We would need the previous year's cash flow statements or cash flow statements from a similar business to help explain which inflows are too small and/or which outflows are too large. By identifying such weaknesses the specific liquidity problems can be highlighted and action taken to rectify them.

21.3   Working capital flow of funds statements

The cash flow statement is useful but does not show the complete liquidity position. It is naïve to concentrate solely upon a business's bank or cash resources when other assets and liabilities are important in any assessment of its liquidity position. For instance, a business may generate a surplus of cash when its liquidity position deteriorates since other liquid assets such as stock and debtors may be falling or only increasing at a slow rate, while creditors are rising to an uncontrollable level. The business can be in liquidation or receivership even though its cash and bank balances are increasing. Therefore, we must widen our horizons and look at how other current assets and liabilities are derived.

It is generally accepted that current assets and liabilities which are worthy of examination comprise stocks, debtors (including prepayments), cash and bank and creditors (including accruals). These assets and liabilities are commonly referred to as working capital.

Working capital represents the life blood of a firm, in that the organisation under consideration is in the business of selling the goods and services which it holds as stocks. These sales generate debtors which, when collected, are used to pay the supplier of the materials and labour used to make the goods and services sold. Working capital is often referred to as circulating capital to indicate this process is continual. Figure 21.3 shows a useful diagram explaining this movement in working capital.

We can use the analogy of a tank of water to understand the fund concept. Suppose our tank does not contain *water*, but *money* instead – in the form of cash, bank and money tied up in stock, debtors and creditors. At the beginning of the year it will read a certain level. During the year, funds will flow into the tank from sales, sales of fixed assets, and so on, while outflows will reduce its level. Examples of outflows are expenses and payments of tax. By the end of the year the level of the tank will be the result of its start position and these inflows and outflows. Figure 21.4 represents what the funds flow statement attempts to show.

It should be noted that all other current asset and liability accounts have been left out of our definition of working capital. For example, trade investments are not included as the holding of investment is considered to be outside the normal business of the organisation. Therefore the inclusion of trade investments in working capital would probably complicate the liquidity picture rather than illuminate it. Of course, if the normal business of the organisation was to buy and sell investments (such as investment companies) then we should include it in our definition of working capital. Taxation and dividends are also excluded as they represent allocations of profit and are not part of the day-to-day operations of the business.

Now we have defined working capital as a collection of the stock, debtors, bank and cash and creditor accounts we can start to explain the funds flow concept. As the terms imply, we are attempting to produce a statement which lists the inflows and outflows to and from a fund. The fund is our working capital accounts

Spreadsheet 21.1 Building up the cash flow statement

```
! A !! B !! C!! D !! E !! F !! G !! H !!I!! J !! K !! L !! M !!N!! O !! P !!Q!
```

Row	Account Title	Ordin. Shares (B)	P & L Account (C)	Loan 10%p.a. (D)	Land at cost (E)	Pl't & M. at cost (F)	Pl't & M. Dep'n (G)	Stock (H)	Trade Invests (I)	Debtors (J)	Cash & Bank (K)	Trade Creds. (L)	Tax (M)	Proposed Divs. (N)	Sale of F. Assets (O)	(P)
1																
2																
3																
7	Narrative															
9	Op. Balance Sheet	−430	−340	−200	250	285	−170	391	420	118	300	−349	−195	−80	0	0
11	Sales		−1900							1900						
13	Purchases							805				−805				
15	Expenses		695									−695				
17	Depreciation		50				−50									
19	Loss on Sale of Plant		5												−5	
20	Write out asset at cost					−21									21	
21	Write out dep'n on Asset						10								−10	
22	Therefore cash rec'd										6				−6	
24	Tax		145										−145			
26	Dividend		50											−50		
28	Issue of Shares	−130									130					
30	Repayment of Loan			200							−200					
32	Purchase of Land				50						−50					
34	Purchase of P & M					96					−96					
36	Cost of Goods Sold		718					−718								
38	Sale of Investments								−240		240					
40	Receipts from Debtors									−1828	1828					
42	Payments to Creditors										−962	962				
44	Tax Paid										−195		195			
46	Dividends Paid										−80			80		
49	Cl. Balance Sheet	−560	−577	0	300	360	−210	478	180	190	226	−192	−145	−50	0	0

(*continued*)

Spreadsheet 21.1 (*Continued*)

Row	A	B	C	D	E	F	G	H
1								
2								
3								
4			Ordinary	P & L	Loan	Land	Pl't & M.	Pl't & M.
5	Account Title--->		Shares	Account	10%p.a.		at cost	Dep'n
6								
7	Narrative							
8								
9	Op. Balance Sheet		-430	-340	-200	250	285	-170
10								
11	Sales			-1900				
12								
13	Purchases							
14								
15	Expenses			695				
16								
17	Depreciation			50				-D17
18								
19	Loss on Sale of Plant			5				
20	Write out asset at cost						-P20	
21	Write out dep'n on Asset							-P21
22	Therefore cash rec'd							
23								
24	Tax			145				
25								
26	Dividend			50				
27								
28	Issue of Shares		C49-C9					
29								
30	Repayment of Loan				E49-E9			
31								
32	Purchase of Land					F49-F9		
33								
34	Purchase of P & M.						G49-G20-G69	
35								
36	Cost of Goods Sold			-136				
37								
38	Sale of Investments							
39								
40	Receipts from Debtors							
41								
42	Payments to Creditors							
43								
44	Tax Paid							
45								
46	Dividends Paid							
47								
48	--							
49	Cl. Balance Sheet		-560	SUM(D6:D47)	0	300	360	-210

: I	:: J	:: K	:: L	:: M	:: N	:: O	:: P	:: Q :
Stock	Trade Invests.	Debtors	Cash & Bank	Trade Creds.	Taxation	Proposed Divs.	Sale of F. Assets	
391	420	118	300	-349	-195	-80	0	SUM(C9:P9)
		-D11						
805				-I13				
			-D15					
							-D19	
							21	
							-10	
			-P22				-SUM(P19:P21)	
				-D24				
					-D26			
			-C28					
			-E30					
			-F32					
			-G34					
I49-I13-I9								
	J49-J9		-J38					
		K49-K11-	-K40					
			-M42	M49-M13-M9				
			-N44		N49-N24-N9			
			-O46			O49-O26-O9		
478	180	190	SUM(L6:L47)	-192	-145	-50	SUM(P6:P47)	SUM(C49:P49)

Cash flow statement for the year ended 31 December, 1988

	£	£
INFLOWS:		
Receipts from sales		1,828
Sale of trade investments		240
Receipts on sale of plant		6
Issue of shares		130
		2,204
OUTFLOWS:		
Payment for purchases	962	
Expenses	695	
Taxation	195	
Dividends	80	
Repayment of loan	200	
Purchase of land	50	
Purchase of P & M	96	
		2,278
Decrease in cash/bank		(£ 74)

Figure 21.2   Cash flow statement

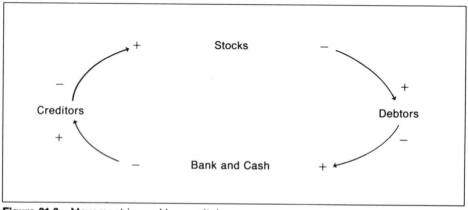

Figure 21.3   Movement in working capital

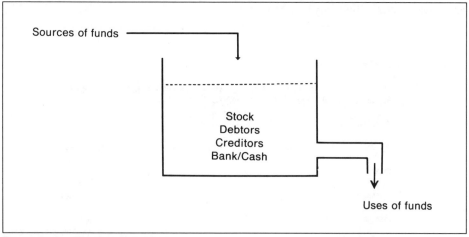

Figure 21.4 The flow of funds

grouped together. So the opening balance on the fund Cathays Park Ltd is the sum of the relevant accounts (see Table 21.1) and the closing balance on the fund is as shown in Table 21.2.

The fund has risen during the year by £242 (see Figure 21.4). How has this arisen? The answer lies in the spreadsheet (see Spreadsheet 21.1).

A change in the fund arises when one side of a transaction is recorded in any one of the fund accounts and the other side of the entry is in a non-fund account. For example, the first transaction recorded in the spreadsheet is the sales of £1,900. One side of this transaction is to the **debtors** column (i.e. a fund account), while the other is to the **profit and loss** column (i.e. a non-fund account). Another

Table 21.1 *Opening balance on the fund Cathays Park Limited*

	£s
Stock	391
Debtors	118
Bank and cash	300
Creditors	(349)
	£460

Table 21.2 *Closing balance on the fund Cathays Park Limited*

Stock	478
Debtors	190
Bank and cash	226
Creditors	(192)
	£702

Spreadsheet 21.2 The funds flow column

	A	B	C	D	E	F	G	H	I
1									
2	Working Capital Funds ---->								*
3									
4		Ordinary	P & L	Loan	Land	Pl't & M.	Pl't & M.	Stock	
5	Account Title--->	Shares	Account	10%p.a.		at cost	Dep'n		
6									
7	Narrative								
8									
9	Op. Balance Sheet	-430	-340	-200	250	285	-170	391	
10									
11	Sales		-1900						
12									
13	Purchases							805	
14									
15	Expenses		695						
16									
17	Depreciation		50				-50		
18									
19	Loss on Sale of Plant		5						
20	Write out asset at cost					-21			
21	Write out dep'n on Asset						10		
22	Therefore cash rec'd								
23									
24	Tax		145						
25									
26	Dividend		50						
27									
28	Issue of Shares	-130							
29									
30	Repayment of Loan			200					
31									
32	Purchase of Land				50				
33									
34	Purchase of P & M.					96			
35									
36	Cost of Goods Sold		718					-718	
37									
38	Sale of Investments								
39									
40	Receipts from Debtors								
41									
42	Payments to Creditors								
43									
44	Tax Paid								
45									
46	Dividends Paid								
47									
48		----------	----------	----------	----------	----------	----------	----------	
49	Cl. Balance Sheet	-560	-577	0	300	360	-210	478	

	J	K	L	M	N	O	P	Q	R
	Trade Invests.	Debtors	Cash & Bank	Trade Creds.	Taxation	Proposed Divs.	Sale of F. Assets		Funds Flow
	420	118	300	-349	-195	-80	0	0	460
		1900							1900
				-805					
			-695						-695
							-5		
							21		
							-10		
			6				-6		6
					-145				
						-50			
			130						130
			-200						-200
			-50						-50
			-96						-96
									-718
	-240		240						240
		-1828	1828						
			-962	962					
			-195		195				-195
			-80			80			-80
	180	190	226	-192	-145	-50	0	0	702

(*continued*)

Spreadsheet 21.2 (*Continued*)

```
    :  A  ::  B  ::  C  ::  D  ::  E  ::  F  ::  G  ::  H  ::  I  ::  J  :
 1
 2  Working Capital Funds ---->                                        *
 3
```

Row / Account Title --->	Ordinary Shares	P & L Account	Loan 10%p.a.	Land	Pl't & M. at cost	Pl't & M. Dep'n	Stock	Trade Invests.
7 Narrative								
9 Op. Balance Sheet	-430	-340	-200	250	285	-170	391	420
11 Sales		-1900						
13 Purchases							805	
15 Expenses		695						
17 Depreciation		50				-D17		
19 Loss on Sale of Plant		5						
20 Write out asset at cost					-P20			
21 Write out dep'n on Asset						-P21		
22 Therefore cash rec'd								
24 Tax		145						
26 Dividend		50						
28 Issue of Shares	C49-C9							
30 Repayment of Loan			E49-E9					
32 Purchase of Land				F49-F9				
34 Purchase of P & M.					G49-G20-G9			
36 Cost of Goods Sold		-I36					I49-I13-I9	
38 Sale of Investments								J49-J9
40 Receipts from Debtors								
42 Payments to Creditors								
44 Tax Paid								
46 Dividends Paid								
49 Cl. Balance Sheet	-560	SUM(D6:D47) 0	300	360		-210	478	180

K	L	M	N	O	P	Q	R
*	*	*					
Debtors	Cash & Bank	Trade Creds.	Taxation	Proposed Divs.	Sale of F, Assets		Funds Flow
118	300	-349	-195	-80	0	SUM(C9:P9)	I9+K9+L9+M9
-D11							I11+K11+L11+M11
		-I13					
	-D15						I15+K15+L15+M15
					-D19		
					21		
					-10		
	-P22				-SUM(P19:P21)		I22+K22+L22+M22
			-D24				
				-D26			
	-C28						I28+K28+L28+M28
	-E30						I30+K30+L30+M30
	-F32						I32+K32+L32+M32
	-G34						I34+K34+L34+M34
							I36+K36+L36+M36
	-J38						I38+K38+L38+M38
K49-K11-	-K40						
	-M42	M49-M13- M9					
	-N44		N49-N24-N9				I44+K44+L44+M44
	-O46			O49-O26-O9			I46+K46+L46+M46
190	SUM(L6:L47)	-192	-145	-50	SUM(P6:P47)	SUM(C49:P49)	I49+K49+L49+M49

example of such a transaction is the expenses of £695. One side of the transaction is to **fund** column, **cash** and **bank**, while the other is to the profit and loss account, a non-fund account.

We can let the spreadsheet identify these funds flow entries by summing the **fund** columns into a newly created column entitled **funds flow items**. This is shown in Spreadsheet 21.2.

Let us for a few minutes think about those transactions which do not affect our fund. They can be of two kinds.

1.   Firstly, transactions that have both entries outside the fund. An example is depreciation, which has a negative (i.e. credit) entry in the **depreciation provision** column and a positive (i.e. debit) entry in the **profit and loss account** column. This is why depreciation does not lead to a flow of funds. Another example is the profit made on the sale of a fixed asset; its double entry is a negative entry to the **profit and loss account** column and a positive entry to a **sale of fixed asset** column.

Cathays Park Ltd
Flow of funds statement for the year ended
31 December 1988

	£	£
INFLOWS:		
Share issue		130
Funds generated from operations:		
Sales	1,900	
less COGS	(718)	
less expenses	(695)	
		487
Proceeds of sale of FA		6
Sale of investments		240
		863
OUTFLOWS:		
Taxation	195	
Dividends	80	
Repayments of debentures	200	
Purchase of land	50	
Purchase of P & M	96	
		621
Net change in working capital		£242
(i.e. £702 − £460)		

Figure 21.5   Cathays Park Limited

2. Accordingly, transactions which have both entries in **fund** columns, for example purchases, lead to an increase in **stocks** and **creditors**; since both these columns are part of the fund they net off. Another example is the **receipts from debtors** which produce a decrease in **debtors** and an increase in **bank** and/or **cash**.

The working capital flow of funds statement for Cathays Park Ltd is shown in Figure 21.5.

Inflows and outflows are grouped together as in the cash flow statement for ease of reading. Also the operating changes are collected (i.e. sales £1,900, less cost of goods sold £718, less expenses £695) to show the net movement from the business's operations as this is considered to be useful for control purposes.

21.4 Source and application of funds statement

Statement of Standard Accounting Practice Number 10 requires all companies with a turnover of £25,000 per annum or more, to produce a statement of source and application of funds. The method of presentation is left to the discretion of the individual company; however it provides an illustrative example in an accompanying appendix which many companies adopt. It is this layout that we will use.

A statement of source and application of funds is, in conception, the same as a working capital flow of funds statement. The only differences are in presentation. Figure 21.6 shows such a statement for Cathays Park Ltd.

It is convenient to think of the statement as being composed of three parts, as indicated in Figure 21.6. Part 1 provides a reconciliation between the profit before tax (a figure required to be disclosed by SSAP 10) and the 'total generated from operations'. The latter figure represents the working capital part of the profit before tax. It is derived in the statement by adding back/taking away those expenses or revenues that do not involve a movement in funds. The depreciation charge for the year and loss or profit on the sale of a fixed asset are two of the most common non-fund flow adjustments (as explained in Section 21.3). It can alternatively be derived (as in the working capital fund flow statement) by deducting the funds flow expenses from the funds flow revenues (Table 21.3).

Part 2 of the statement is identical to the working capital flow of funds statement. Part 3 lists the net changes in the **fund** columns: **stocks, debtors,** and **bank and cash** and **creditors**. The net change in **bank and cash** is highlighted as this is one of the most liquid assets. The reasons for including Part 3 (which is a SSAP 10 requirement) seems to have its roots in the accountant's desire to see before him two lists of figures having the same total!

Cathays Park Ltd
Statement of source and application of funds
for the year ended 31 December 1988

	£	£
Part 1 Sources of funds:		
Profit before tax		432
Adjustments for items not involving the movement of funds:		
Depreciation	50	
Loss on sale of plant	5	
		55
Total funds generated from operations		487
Part 2 Funds from other sources:		
Issue of shares from other sources	130	
Proceeds of sale of P & M	6	
Proceeds of sale of investments	240	
		376
		863
Application of funds:		
Tax paid	195	
Dividends paid	80	
Loans repaid	200	
Purchase of land	50	
Purchase of P & M	96	
		621
		£242
Part 3 Increase/decrease in working capital:		
Increase in stock		87
Increase in debtors		72
Decrease in creditors		157
		316
Decrease in cash and bank		(74)
		£242

Figure 21.6   Cathays Park Limited

Table 21.3   *Calculation of funds generated from operations*

	£	£
Sales		1,900
Less cost of goods sold	718	
expenses	895	
		1,413
Total generated from operations		£ 487

CHECKLIST _____

Having completed Chapter 21, you should be able to:

- express the limitations of the profit and loss account in assessing the liquidity position of the business;
- prepare a cash flow statement for the business;
- prepare and interpret a working capital flow of funds statement and a statement of source and application of funds.

_____

Workshop 21.1: Funds flow statements – Pontypandy Ltd

From the profit and loss account and balance sheets (Figure 21.7), prepare a sources and applications of funds statement in accordance with SSAP 10.

Workshop guide

1. The first stage is to place the opening balance sheet at the top of the spreadsheet as in row 9 of the solution. Cell Q9 is used to ensure that all entries sum to zero and no transcription errors have occurred.

2. From the profit and loss account reconstruct the accounting entries that were made to create it, e.g. the **sales** must have come from **debtors**, the **purchases** from the **stock** column, etc.

3. The sale of plant requires some explanation. The profit on the sale came from the disposal account and is reconstructed. This account also contained entries for the writing out of the asset and any accumulated depreciation to date. The balancing entry on the disposal account must therefore be the cash received for the sale. This is calculated in cell O22 and equates to £25,000.

4. At this stage the known figures from the closing balance sheet are entered in row 47. Do not enter the figures for **profit, depreciation provision, cash and bank** or **disposal account**, as we will sum the columns to check the closing balances.

5. The missing entries needed to make the remaining columns balance are then deduced. For example, the ordinary shares have risen from £500,000 to £600,000, therefore the difference between these figures is entered in cell C28 with the corresponding double entry to the **cash and bank** column.

6. All remaining entries are deduced in much the same manner. Some columns, however, such as **debtors**, will have entries other than opening and closing

Trading, profit and loss account for the year ended 31 December, 19X8.

	£000	£000
Sales		2,400
Less purchases	1,800	
Stock as at 31 December 1987	300	
	2,100	
Stock as at 31 December 1988	450	
Cost of goods sold		1,650
GROSS PROFIT		750
Less expenses (cash)	400	
Depreciation	125	
Profit on sale of plant	(20)	
		505
NET PROFIT		245
Taxation		60
		185
Dividends proposed		65
Retained profit		£120

The plant sold cost £70,000 when purchased and depreciation of £65,000 had been provided on the asset at the time of its disposal.

Balance sheet as at 31 December 19X8

	19x8				19x7	
	£000	£000	£000	£000	£000	£000
Ordinary shares @ £1		600				500
Profit and loss account		380				260
Loan		100				—
		£1,080				£760

Represented by:
Fixed assets:

	Cost	Depreciation	NBV	Cost	Depreciation	NBV
Land	540	—	540	340	—	340
Plant and machinery	170	180	435	290	120	170
	1,250	180	1,070	630	120	510

Current assets:

Stocks	450	300
Debtors	95	70
Cash and bank balances	—	60
	545	430

Less current liabilities:

Trade creditors	320		30
Overdarft	90		—
Taxation	60		90
Proposed dividend	65		60
	535		180
		10		250
		£1,080		£760

Figure 21.7　Pontypandy Limited

balances to account for. The same logic is used, i.e. the entry needed to make the column sum to the closing figure is inserted and the double entry completed.

7. The **funds flow** column (column Q) is then derived by summing the **working capital** columns of **stock**, **debtors**, **cash and bank**, and **trade creditors**. In this example the columns were arranged adjacent to one another to allow the **sum** command to be utilised. If this is not the case, individual column additions may be necessary, as in the example in the chapter. However, once the relative cell references for one row are established, the formula can be copied to the remaining rows in the column.

8. All that remains is to present the information in good format. The solution is given in Spreadsheet 21.3, and Figure 21.8.

'What if?' problems

1. What if the company issued £200,000 shares, making the closing balance £700,000? What would be the effect on the cash balance? How does this affect the funds flow statement (e.g. do sources or applications rise)?

2. What if the company had spent only £190,000 on new plant? How would this affect the funds flow statement (i.e. does it affect profit or other sources, or does it alter applications)? How does the statement still remain in balance?

3. It could be argued that the company has sought to expand its asset base through short-term finance rather than long-term (i.e. it has reduced working capital to buy plant and land). Examine the effects of increasing the share issue and the loan on the cash balance. How could any cash balance be used to affect the other working capital balances?

4. If the company had chosen to increase this year's dividends, would this affect the sources and applications of funds statement?

5. If the asset sold had been fully depreciated, with the receipt remaining unchanged, which figures in the source and applications of funds statement will alter?

Answers

1. Cash balance changes to £10,000; the sources of funds increase.
2. Application will fall by £3,000; working capital alters.
3. The cash and loan balance will be increased and hence increase working capital.
4. No, as dividends are not *paid* until next year.
5. Profit or loss on disposal.

Spreadsheet 21.3a   Workshop 21.1: Pontypandy Ltd – solution

	A	B	C	D	E	F	G	H
1								
2	Working Capital Funds ---->							
3								
4			Ordinary	P & L	Loan	Land	Pl't & M.	Pl't & M.
5	Account Title--->		Shares	Account	10%p.a.		at cost	Dep'n
6								
7	Narrative							
8								
9	Op. Balance Sheet		-500	-260	0	340	290	-120
10								
11	Sales			-2400				
12								
13	Purchases							
14								
15	Expenses			400				
16								
17	Depreciation			125				-125
18								
19	Profit on Sale of Plant			-20				
20	Write out asset at cost						-70	
21	Write out dep'n on Asset							65
22	Therefore cash rec'd							
23								
24	Tax			60				
25								
26	Dividend			65				
27								
28	Issue of Shares		-100					
29								
30	Take up of Loan				-100			
31								
32	Purchase of Land					200		
33								
34	Purchase of P & M.						490	
35								
36	Cost of Goods Sold			1650				
37								
38	Receipts from Debtors							
39								
40	Payments to Creditors							
41								
42	Tax Paid							
43								
44	Dividends Paid							
45								
46			----------	----------	----------	----------	----------	----------
47	Cl. Balance Sheet		-600	-380	-100	540	710	-180

I	J	K	L	M	N	O	P	Q
Stock	Debtors	Cash & Bank	Trade Creds.	Taxation	Proposed Divs.	Sale of F. Assets		Funds Flow
300	70	60	-30	-90	-60	0	0	400
	2400							2400
1800			-1800					
		-400						-400
						20		
						70		
						-65		
		25				-25		25
				-60				
					-65			
		100						100
		100						100
		-200						-200
		-490						-490
-1650								-1650
	-2375	2375						
		-1510	1510					
		-90		90				-90
		-60			60			-60
450	95	-90	-320	-60	-65	0	0	135

(*continued*)

Spreadsheet 21.3b   Workshop 21.1: Pontypandy Ltd – formulae

	A	B	C	D	E	F	G	H	I
2	Working Capital Funds ---->								*
4		Ordinary		P & L	Loan	Land	Pl't & M.	Pl't & M.	Stock
5	Account Title--->	Shares		Account	10%p.a.		at cost	Dep'n	
7	Narrative								
9	Op. Balance Sheet	-500		-260	0	340	290	-120	300
11	Sales			-2400					
13	Purchases								1800
15	Expenses			400					
17	Depreciation			125				-D17	
19	Profit on Sale of Plant			-20					
20	Write out asset at cost						-020		
21	Write out dep'n on Asset							-021	
22	Therefore cash rec'd								
24	Tax			60					
26	Dividend			65					
28	Issue of Shares	C47-C9							
30	Take up of Loan				E47-E9				
32	Purchase of Land					F47-F9			
34	Purchase of P & M.						647-620-69		
36	Cost of Goods Sold			-136					147-113-19
38	Receipts from Debtors								
40	Payments to Creditors								
42	Tax Paid								
44	Dividends Paid								
46	--								
47	Cl. Balance Sheet	-600		SUM(D6:D45)	-100	540	710	SUM(H6:H45)	450

! J ::	K ::	L ::	M ::	N ::	O ::	P ::	Q !
*	*	*					
Debtors	Cash & Bank	Trade Creds.	Taxation	Proposed Divs.	Sale of F. Assets		Funds Flow
70	60	-30	-90	-60	0	SUM(C9:09)	SUM(I9:L9)
-D11							SUM(I11:L11)
		-I13					
	-D15						SUM(I15:L15)
					-D19		
					70		
					-65		
	-022				-SUM(019:021)		SUM(I22:L22)
			-D24				
				-D26			
	-C28						SUM(I28:L28)
	-E30						SUM(I30:L30)
	-F32						SUM(I32:L32)
	-G34						SUM(I34:L34)
							SUM(I36:L36)
J47-J11-	-J38						
	-L40	L47-L13-L9					
	-M42		M47-M24-M9				SUM(I42:L42)
	-N44			N47-N26-N9			SUM(I44:L44)
95	SUM(K6:K45)	-320	-60	-65	SUM(06:045)	SUM(C47:047)	SUM(I47:L47)

Cash flow statement for the year ended 31 December, 19X8

	£	£
INFLOWS		
Receipts from debtors		2,375
Loan		100
Receipts on sale of plant		25
Issue of shares		100
		2,600
OUTFLOWS:		
Payments for purchases	1,510	
Expenses	400	
Taxation	90	
Dividends	60	
Purchase of land	200	
Purchase of P & M	490	
		2,750
Decrease in cash/bank		(£ 150)

Flow of funds statement for the year ended 31 December 19x8

		£	£
INFLOWS:			
Share issue			100
Funds generated from operations:			
Sales	2,400		
less COGS	(1,650)		
less expenses	(400)		
			350
Proceeds of sale of FA			25
Loan			100
			575
OUTFLOWS:			
Taxation		90	
Dividends		60	
Purchase of land		200	
Purchase of P & M		490	
			840
Net change in working capital (i.e. £135 − £400)			£(265)

Statement of source and application of funds for the year ended 31 December 19x8

	£	£
Sources of funds:		
Profit before tax		245
Adjustments for items not		
involving the movement of		
funds:		
Depreciation	125	
Profit on sale of plant	(20)	
		105
Total funds generated from operations		350

Funds from other sources:			
Issue of shares for cash		100	
Proceeds of sale of P & M		25	
Loan		100	
			225
			575
Application of funds:			
Tax paid		90	
Dividends paid		60	
Purchase of land		200	
Purchase of P & M		490	
			840
			£(265)
Increase/decrease in working capital:			
Increase in stocks			150
Increase in debtors			25
Increase in creditors			(290)
			(115)
Decrease in cash and bank			(150)
			£(265)

Figure 21.8 Pontypandy Limited

Selected questions and exercises

Question 21.1

The balance sheet of Kershaw and Russon plc and the corresponding figures for the previous year are shown in Table 21.4.

One of the directors is rather puzzled that despite an apparently profitable year, a share issue, and the sale of an asset, the bank balance has deteriorated until it is now in overdraft. To assist the director to understand what has happened, you are required to:

1. Calculate the net trading profit for the year.
2. Draw up a cash flow statement to explain the changes in the bank balance during the year.
3. Prepare a sources and application of funds statement for the year showing working capital movements.

Note: £3,800 was received for the fixed asset which was sold during the year. At 1 April 1987 £2,000 depreciation had been written off this asset.

Solution on pages 565–6.

Source: RSA, Accounting II, March 1987.

Table 21.4 *Details of the accounts of Kershaw and Russon plc*

Kershaw and Russon plc
Balance sheet as at 31 March 1988

1987				1988
£				£
258,000	Fixed assets (at cost)			288,000
30,000	Additions (at cost)			14,000
288,000				302,000
—	Sales (at cost)			6,000
288,000				296,000
28,000	Less depreciation			38,000
260,000				258,000
	Current assets			
27,000		stock in hand	50,000	
18,000		debtors	45,000	
15,000	60,000	bank	—	95,000
	320,000			353,000

Financed by:				
£				£
200,000		Issued share capital		225,000
85,000		Profit and loss account		102,000
285,000				327,000
		Current liabilities		
20,000		creditors		6,000
15,000		proposed dividends		10,000
—		bank overdraft		10,000
320,000				353,000

Question 21.2

You have been appointed the accountant of a local business located in Cardiff. The summarised financial statements are shown in Table 21.5

Notes:
1. There were no purchases of motor vehicles during the year.
2. The debentures were paid off on 1 January 1987. You are required to prepare a source and application of funds statement, for the year end 31 December 1987.

Table 21.5 *Details of the accounts of Fast Limited*

Fast Ltd
Balance sheet as at 31 December 1987

1986 £000		£000 Cost	£000 Depreciation	£000
	Fixed assets			
160	land	200	—	200
130*	motor vehicles	140	55	85
290				285
	Current assets			
255	stock		276	
143	debtors		164	
20	bank		—	
708			440	
	Current liabilities			
(57)	creditors	93		
(61)	taxation	21		
(30)	dividends	10		
—	bank	7	131	309
£560	Net assets			£594
	Financed by:			
345	share capital (£1 ordinary shares)			450
115	profit and loss account			119
—	general reserve			25
100	10 per cent debentures			—
£560				£594

* Made up of cost £180,000 less depreciation £50,000

Trading and profit and loss account
for the year ended 31 December 1987

1986 £000		£000	£000
500	Sales		500
325	Less cost of sales		366
175	Gross profit		134
(63)	Less expenses (all cash)	59	
(30)	Depreciation	25	
			84
82			50
—	Add profit on sale of motor vehicles		10
£82	Net profit		£ 60

No solution provided.

Question 21.3

Pentost plc is a well-established company in the manufacture and sale of metal products. The information in Table 21.6 is obtained from the company's financial records.

Table 21.6 *Details of the accounts of Pentost plc*

Balance sheet at 30 June

	1985 £	1985 £	1986 £	1986 £
Fixed assets at cost		637,100		767,300
Less depreciation		297,500		321,400
		339,600		445,900
Trade investments at cost		106,000		106,000
Current assets:				
stock and work in progress	230,200		260,100	
trade debtors and prepayments	135,800		196,400	
bank balance	—		9,300	
	366,000		465,800	
Less current liabilities:				
trade creditors and accruals	96,800		101,700	
taxation due: 31 March 1986	63,800		—	
31 March 1987	—		61,000	
dividend payable	60,000		66,000	
bank overdraft	71,000		—	
	291,600		228,700	
Net current assets		74,400		273,100
		£520,000		£789,000
		£		£
Financed by:				
ordinary share capital				
(ordinary shares of £1 each)		200,000		220,000
share premium account		—		30,000
reserves		320,000		339,000
		520,000		589,000
15 per cent debenture		—		200,000
		£520,000		£789,000

Profit and loss accounts, year ended 30 June

	1985 £	1985 £	1986 £	1986 £
Operating profit		160,500		176,000
Less finance charges: bank interest		9,200		—
debenture interest		—		30,000
Net profit before taxation		151,300		146,000
Less taxation		63,800		61,000
Profit after taxation		87,500		85,000
Less dividend proposed		60,000		66,000
Retained profit for the year		£27,500		£19,000

Notes:
1. On 31 January 1986 a rights issue was made of one ordinary share for every ten ordinary shares currently held. For the purpose of this issue the ordinary shares were valued at £2.50 each.
2. The debenture is secured on the company's freehold property which is included among fixed assets in the balance sheet shown above.
3. During the year ended 30 June 1986 the company disposed of fixed assets, which cost £65,200 some years' ago for £17,900. A loss of £9,600 arising on disposal has been deducted in arriving at the operating profit for the year.

You are required to prepare the following.

1. The statement of source and application of funds of Pentost plc for the year ended 30 June 1986 in accordance with the provisions contained in SSAP 10, entitled 'Statements of source and application of funds'.
2. An examination of the respective positions of Pentost plc at 30 June 1985 and 30 June 1986 and a discussion of the financial developments which have occurred during the intervening period. The financial statement prepared under 1 and the relevant accounting ratios should be used to support your analysis.

Ignore advance corporation tax.

No solution provided.

22 | *Interpretation of financial statements: the use of ratios*

AIMS OF CHAPTER _____

- to introduce students to the concept of ratios;
- to present the main ratios used in financial analysis, together with their interpretation;
- to place caveats on the use of certain ratios, and on the reliance on ratios as the sole weapon in the accountant's interpretive armoury.

22.1 Introduction

It is often necessary to interpret a set of financial statements in order to identify the strengths and weaknesses of a company and highlight any underlying trends in its operations. For instance, shareholders and investment analysts require this information to make investment decisions and bank managers need to decide whether to make loans to a company. A useful method of interpreting company financial statements is the use of ratio analysis. This chapter will discuss the use of ratio analysis. The various ratios will be described and a worked example used to show their application. Finally the problems of using ratios will be discussed.

22.2 What is a ratio?

A ratio is the arithmetic relationship between two figures in a set of financial statements. It can be presented in a number of forms. Firstly as a percentage, where one figure is divided by another and multiplied by 100. Secondly as a fraction, where one figure is divided by another. Thirdly as a period of time, where one figure is divided by another and multiplied by a time period (usually a month or a year). Finally as a proportion, by setting one figure to 1 showing the other figure as its relative value to 1.

Liquidity ratios

1. Debtor collection period (in months)

$$\frac{\text{Trade debtors}}{\text{Sales}} * 12$$

2. Creditor payment period (in months)

$$\frac{\text{Trade creditors}}{\text{Purchases}} * 12$$

3. Stock turnover period (in months)

$$\frac{\text{Stocks}}{\text{Cost of sales}} * 12$$

4. Current ratio

$$\frac{\text{Current assets}}{\text{Current liabilities}} : 1$$

5. Quick ratio

$$\frac{\text{Current assets} - \text{Stocks}}{\text{Current liabilities}} : 1$$

Profitability ratios

6. Return on capital employed

   Overall ROCE

$$\frac{\text{Net profit} + \text{Loan interest}}{\text{Share Capital} + \text{Reserves} + \text{Loans}}$$

   Shareholders' ROCE

$$\frac{\text{Net profit}}{\text{Share capital} + \text{Reserves}}$$

7. Gearing *

$$\frac{\text{Loans}}{\text{Share capital} + \text{Reserves} + \text{Loans}}$$

8. Asset turnover

$$\frac{\text{Sales}}{\text{Net assets}}$$

9. Net profit margin

$$\frac{\text{Net profit}}{\text{Sales}} * 100$$

10. Gross profit margin

$$\frac{\text{Gross profit}}{\text{Sales}} * 100$$

Long-term growth ratios

11. P/E ratio

$$\frac{\text{Current share price}}{\text{Earnings per share}}$$

12. Dividend yield

$$\frac{\text{Dividends per share}}{\text{Current share price}} * 100$$

13. Dividend cover

$$\frac{\text{Net profit}}{\text{Dividends}}$$

* An alternative measure of gearing (called 'leverage' in North America) is:

$$\frac{\text{Loans}}{\text{Share capital and reserves}}$$

This measure can range from zero to infinity, while the gearing measure in 7 above can range from zero to one. The later measure has been chosen as we find it easier to interpret a smaller, distinct range.

Figure 22.1 Commonly used ratios

The particular form of presentation chosen for any relationship examined is the one which the analyst can best interpret. For instance, some people prefer to look at time periods while others prefer percentages.

It is mathematically possible to calculate a very large number of ratios from any given set of financial statements. However, experience has shown that certain ratios are most meaningful. There ratios are listed in Figure 22.1. It should be mentioned that the choice of ratios is a personal one and inevitably other financial accounting textbooks will include additional ratios and omit some of those in Figure 22.1.

The ratios in Figure 22.1 are classified according to the particular aspect of the business to which they are addressed. Firstly, the ratios which measure how liquid or financially stable a company is are considered; these ratios are concerned with the short-term problem of predicting whether a company can pay its debts in the next few months. Secondly, ratios which measure profitability or efficiency are considered, and finally ratios which attempt to measure long-term growth prospects are considered. Each set of ratios will be considered in turn.

22.3   Liquidity ratios

The first three ratios are all concerned with a period of time. The debtors collection period shows how quickly a company is collecting its debts from its customers; the creditors payment period shows how quickly the company is paying its suppliers; the stock turnover ratio shows how quickly a company is turning over its stock.

The optimum period of time for all three ratios is largely dependent upon the type of business the company operates in. For example, in the retail trade settlement is usually on receipt of the goods, while in the wholesale trade it is usual to find a one or two month settlement period. Since an individual company (unless it is in a monopoly position) will find it hard to change these generally accepted terms of trade, it will have to take them as given and measure its actual results against this criteria.

What can be done to improve a company's liquidity?

If the debtors collection period is significantly in excess of the industry standard, it should review its credit control procedures. Maybe the collection system could be improved by giving discounts for early settlement or preparing detailed age analyses of debts and putting increasing pressure (in the form of visits, letters or telephone calls) on late payers. Of course, if the debtors collection period is less than the industry standard, little attention is needed, other than to carry on the good work and be alert so as to take advantage of any further methods which may reduce the collection period even further.

If the creditors payment period is in excess of the industry standard, this means the company is extracting longer credit from its suppliers, which on the face of it seems a good thing. However, the company should be careful not to get a reputation as a slow payer and find itself on a 'stop list' (a list kept by suppliers of customers they will only do business with if goods are paid for upon collection). Delays in payment may put key suppliers out of business and take away a valuable source of supply. This is especially significant for small firms with limited sources of finance. If the creditors payment period is less than the industry standard, the company is probably paying its debts too quickly and would be advised to keep the money in its bank account available for internal use or interest earning until the required settlement date. Early payment may be intentional to curry favour with suppliers or to take advantage of discounts.

If the stock turnover period is too high it indicates that too much money is being tied up in stocks, which could be released into other areas of the business to earn a higher return. Also the costs of holding stock, such as those of warehousing, damage, deterioration and obsolesence, could be saved. Against these costs are the savings to be made (usually in the form of trade discounts or lower prices) by ordering in large quantities. If the stock turnover period is below the industry standard there is the danger of losing sales due to 'stock outs'.

All three ratios are subject to seasonal trends, which can distort the ratios. For example, if most sales are made immediately before the company's year end, the debtors collection period will be unrepresentative of the normal collection period applying to the rest of the year. The creditors payment and stock turnover periods can be similarly affected.

The inclusion of a few large balances with either longer or shorter turnover periods than the other balances can also distort these ratios. For example, foreign customers often receive longer credit periods than domestic customers, so a significant amount of export sales can increase the debtors collection period.

Two other liquidity ratios, the current ratio and the quick ratio, are also useful indicators of a company's liquidity position. The current ratio measures the excess (or deficency) of current assets compared to current liabilities. This is a useful piece of information as current liabilties will be paid from current assets. Tradition stipulates a level of 2:1 to be adequate, but the above discussion indicates that this is unlikely to be the case for many industries. If this ratio is too low the company may not be able to meet its debts as they fall due for payment. If it is too high the company is probably using its resources inefficiently and could free some cash, debtors or stock balances to earn higher rates of return elsewhere in the business.

The quick ratio is the same as the current ratio except that the stock figure is excluded from current assets. The reason for excluding stocks is that in many industries it cannot be quickly turned into cash, so it is inappropriate to rely upon it to meet the settlement of current liabilities. Tradition suggests it should be 1:1. However, the relevance of this is again dubious when the debtor and creditor periods are significantly different.

22.4 Profitability ratios

The first profitability ratio considered is return on capital employed. It measures the return earned by using the resources invested in the business. It comes in two forms, firstly a shareholders version and secondly an overall version. The difference between the two is the inclusion of long-term loan interest in the numerator and the long-term loan in the denominator of the overall version and their exclusion from the shareholders version. The particular version chosen depends upon the information needs of the analyst. If return on equity is required the shareholders version is used. If the overall company's return is required (as it may well be by the company's management who are interested in the overall return they have achieved using all the long-term funds they have been entrusted with), the overall version is used.

These ratios are useful as they provide a return figure which can be compared with the return offered by other investments, such as interest on building society accounts or the return from another business. However, in any comparison the risks of the investment should be taken into account. For example, an investment in a building society account is very secure while an investment in a small business carries much more risk. It will be up to the analyst to weigh up these returns with some assessment of the risk involved and it would not be illogical to favour an investment with a lower return if this return was guaranteed when compared with a higher return from a riskier investment. In recent years the subject of business finance, which deals with the choice between two investments, has been developed; a knowledge of the investors' attitude to risk and return (often measured by indifference curves) is required to enable a choice to be made.

The risk associated with an investment in a company can be thought of as being composed of two elements: business risk and financial risk. The former has to be left to the analyst's subjective judgement to assess (e.g. what type of business is the company operating in, one with well-established products or one with new and largely untried products?). However, the financial risk can be measured to some extent by the gearing ratio, which shows the proportion of long-term debt in a company's overall capital structure.

The optimum level of gearing has been extensively discussed in the business finance literature. There seem to be arguments for having some debt in a company's capital structure to take advantage of this relatively cheap form of finance (interest charges are allowable against tax). However, too much debt creates problems for companies when their profits are low, as this debt interest has to be met regardless of profit levels. If it cannot be met the debt holders can force the company into liquidation.

In order to explain a company's return on capital employed it is useful to split it up into two components: the net profit margin and the asset turnover ratio.

When multiplied together they equate to the overall capital employed ratio:

$$\frac{\text{Sales}}{\text{Capital employed}} * \frac{\text{Net profit}}{\text{Sales}} = \frac{\text{Net profit}}{\text{Capital employed}}$$

The asset turnover ratio measures the efficiency with which assets are used within the business. The optimum level of asset turnover varies among industries, with some industries (e.g. manufacturing industries) requiring a greater investment in assets than other industries (e.g. service industries). This ratio can itself be split into a fixed assets turnover ratio (i.e. sales/fixed assets), which is a measure of how efficiently a company is using its fixed assets to generate sales; and a net current assets turnover ratio (i.e. sales/net current assets), which is a measure of how efficiently a company is using its current assets to generate sales.

The net profit margin expresses how much profit is being made on sales, that is, how much net profit is being made per £1 of sales. The higher the net profit margin the better, subject to the long-term aim of satisfying customer needs with quality products. So a large net profit margin in the short term may not be advisable if quality is being sacrificed and will lead to falling sales in the future.

The final profitability ratio considered is the gross profit margin, which is similar to the net profit margin but replaces net profit with gross profit, so excluding overheads as they do not vary with sales. It shows approximately how much extra profit could be earned if sales were expanded from their current level. The optimum level varies between industries but it should be as high as possible, subject to the same quality constraint that the net profit margin was subjected to.

22.5 Long-term growth ratios

The first ratio which attempts to measure a company's long-term growth prospects is the price/earnings ratio (usually abbreviated to the P/E ratio). It takes as its input data the earnings per share figure from the company's last available set of financial statements (an accounting standards – SSAP 3 – disclosure requirement of all companies whose shares are traded on a stock exchange), and its current share price. Since only companies who have their shares traded on a stock market will have a share price, its applicability is so restricted. The P/E ratio tells how many times the company's current earnings an investor is willing to pay for the share. This multiple of current earnings is popular with investment analysts since it uses published information and changes as the share price moves, reflecting moods of optimism and pessimism in the company's and market's future.

The dividend yield measures the dividend per share as a percentage of its share price and is a useful predictor of incoming cash flows from holding the company's shares, if the company pursues a consistent dividend policy. This ratio does not attempt to measure any change in the value of the company due to retaining rather than distributing its earnings.

Finally, the dividend cover is included since it shows the percentage of profits paid out as dividends. It provides a useful indication of how much profit is being retained for future growth. Investors who want a regular payout of most of the company's profits should invest in companies with high dividend yields and low dividend cover. Investors who want to invest for future growth should invest in companies with high dividend cover and low dividend yields.

22.6. An example using ratio analysis

Now the ratios in Figure 22.1 have been explained, we are in a position to analyse, using ratio analysis, a set of company financial statements. However, one particular ratio on its own does not tell us very much about a company. Two or more ratios are needed to form any significant opinions. In Figure 22.2, the financial statements of two companies are shown. Their ratios are calculated in Figure 22.3 and a report interpreting these ratios is shown in Figure 22.4.

Such a comparison of two or more companies is called a 'cross-sectional' or 'interfirm' study. An alternative would have been the analysis of the financial statements of one company over a number of periods; this is called a 'time series or intertemporal study'.

22.7   Problems encountered in ratio analysis

Ratio analysis is not without its problems. Some of these problems are listed below.

1.   Ratios can be distorted or window dressed; for instance the quick ratio can be improved by selling stock at large discounts for cash, just before the year end.

2.   When comparing two companies with different year ends the underlying trends in the economy may have changed in the period between the end of one company's year end and the other company's year end; so it can appear that one company is doing better than the other when this may well not be the case.

3.   Low profits or even losses can result in very large, very small or even negative ratios which have profit as an input figure.

4.   The accounting policies used to prepare financial statements are often arbitrary, such as the depreciation policy chosen. So different companies will use different accounting policies, rendering comparison difficult. However, SSAP 2 ensures companies are consistent in their use of accounting policies from year to year; so this problem should be confined to cross-sectional studies.

The financial statements for two companies are as follows:
Balance sheet as at 31 December 1988

	Ellis plc		Jenkins plc	
	£	£	£	£
Fixed assets				
Cost	255,000		127,500	
Depreciation	85,000		42,500	
		170,000		85,000
Current assets				
Stock	242,250		127,500	
Trade debtors	93,500		85,000	
Bank and cash	46,750		42,500	
	382,500		255,000	
Current liabilitites				
Trade creditors	127,500		127,500	
		255,000		127,500
Net assets		425,000		212,500
		£s		£s
Financed by:				
Share capital (nominal value £1)		340,000		170,000
Reserves		63,750		21,250
7 per cent loan		21,250		21,250
		425,000		212,500

Trading and profit and loss account for the year ended 31 December 1988

	Ellis plc		Jenkins plc	
	£	£	£	£
Sales		680,000		510,000
Less cost of sales				
Opening stock	165,750		85,000	
Purchases	484,500		361,250	
	650,250		446,250	
Closing stock	242,250		127,500	
		408,000		318,750
GROSS PROFIT		272,000		191,250
Less overheads		238,000		165,750
NET PROFIT		34,000		25,500
Less dividends		25,500		8,500
		8,500		17,000
Add reserves from previous years		12,750		4,250
Reserves as per balance sheet		21,250		21,250
Earning per share		10p.		15p.
Current share price		£2.00		£4.50

You are required to calculate the ratios you find most useful to analyse the financial statements of Ellis plc and Jenkins plc, and prepare a report analysing the ratios you have calculated.

Figure 22.2 An inter-company comparison

Ellis plc

Liquidity ratios

1. Debtor collection period

$$\frac{93,500}{680,000} * 12 = 1.65 \text{ months}$$

2. Creditor payment period

$$\frac{127,500}{484,500} * 12 = 3.16 \text{ months}$$

3. Stock turnover period

$$\frac{165,750 + 242,250}{2 * 408,000} * 12 = 6 \text{ months}$$

4. Current ratio

$$\frac{382,500}{127,500} : 1 = 3:1$$

5. Quick ratio

$$\frac{382,500 - 242,250}{127,500} : 1 = 1.1:1$$

Profitability ratios

6. Return on capital employed

Overall ROCE

$$\frac{34,000 + (0.07 * 63,750)}{425,000} * 100 = 9\%$$

Shareholder ROCE

$$\frac{34,000}{340,000 + 63,750} * 100 = 8.4\%$$

Jenkins plc

Liquidity ratios

1. Debtor collection period

$$\frac{85,000}{510,000} * 12 = 2 \text{ months}$$

2. Creditor payment period

$$\frac{127,500}{361,250} * 12 = 4.24 \text{ months}$$

3. Stock turnover period

$$\frac{85,000 + 127,500}{2 * 318,750} * 12 = 4 \text{ months}$$

4. Current ratio

$$\frac{255,000}{127,500} : 1 = 2:1$$

5. Quick ratio

$$\frac{255,000 - 127,500}{127,500} : 1 = 1:1$$

Profitability ratios

6. Return on capital employed

Overall ROCE

$$\frac{25,500 + (0.07 * 21,250)}{212,500} * 100 = 12.7\%$$

Shareholder ROCE

$$\frac{25,500}{170,000 + 21,250} * 100 = 13.3\%$$

7. Gearing

$$\frac{63,750}{425,000} * 100 = 15\%$$

$$\frac{21,250}{212,500} * 100 = 10\%$$

8. Net asset turnover

$$\frac{680,000}{425,000} = 1.6 \text{ times}$$

$$\frac{510,000}{212,500} = 2.4 \text{ times}$$

9. Net profit margin

$$\frac{34,000}{680,000} * 100 = 5\%$$

$$\frac{25,500}{510,000} * 100 = 5\%$$

10. Gross profit margin

$$\frac{272,000}{680,000} * 100 = 40\%$$

$$\frac{191,250}{510,000} * 100 = 37.5\%$$

Long-term growth ratios

11. P/E ratio

$$\frac{2.00}{0.10} = 20$$

$$\frac{4.50}{0.15} = 30$$

12. Dividend yield

$$\frac{25,500}{340,000 * 2.00} * 100 = 3.75\%$$

$$\frac{8,500}{170,000 * 4.50} * 100 = 1.11\%$$

13. Dividend cover

$$\frac{34,000}{25,500} = 1.33\%$$

$$\frac{25,500}{8,500} = 3\%$$

Figure 22.3 Calculation of ratios for Ellis Limited and Jenkins Limited

A. Liquidity

Ellis plc collects its debts in a shorter time period than Jenkins plc (1.65 months compared with 2 months). However, Jenkins plc takes longer to pay its creditors (4.24 months compared with 3.16 months). Both companies collect their debts at a faster rate than they take to pay their creditors. Ellis plc has a net positive working capital period (i.e. creditor payment period less debtor collection period) of 1.51 months and Jenkins a positive working capital period of 2.24 months. Jenkins may find it takes so long to pay its creditors it will find itself on suppliers' stop lists.

Jenkins plc turns over its stock in 2/3rds the time Ellis plc takes, thus freeing resources to be used elsewhere in the business. This difference in stocking policy produces a higher current ratio for Ellis plc (3:1 compared with 2:1). The question is raised that Ellis plc might look at its stocking policy, if indeed it has one. Once stock is removed from the current ratio the quick ratio produced is similar for both companies (1.1:1 compared with 1:1).

B. Profitability

The return on capital employed for Ellis plc is approximately 9 per cent compared with a rate of approximately 13 per cent for Jenkins plc, indicating Jenkins plc is more efficient in its use of resources and is probably a better investment. This comparative advantage in return is explained by a more efficient use of its asssets (it turns its assets over 2.4 times a year compared with 1.6 times for Ellis plc). There is no difference in their net profit margins. Ellis plc should consider employing its assets more efficiently.

Ellis plc, however, has a higher gross profit margin than Jenkins plc (40 per cent compared with 37.5 per cent). This indicates that there may be some room to increase the control over its overheads.

The levels of gearing are quite low for both companies: 15 per cent for Ellis plc and 10 per cent for Jenkins plc; so no great financial risk is expected, since interest payments are well covered by profits. Maybe there is some room to increase the element of debt in both companies' capital structures?

C. Growth prospects

Jenkins plc has a higher P/E ratio than Ellis plc, indicating the market considers Jenkins plc to have more growth potential than Ellis plc and/or a less risky investment. However, Ellis plc's dividend yield is higher (3.75 per cent compared with 1.11 per cent), so it is distributing relatively more of its profits than Jenkins plc. This is also reflected in a lower dividend cover (1.3 compared with 3).

Figure 22.4   Report on the financial performance of Ellis Limited and Jenkins Limited

5. Many published financial statements are the consolidated results (i.e. the summation of the balance sheets and profit and loss accounts) of many different businesses in a group. Therefore any ratio only shows the net position of the group; the results of individual firms within the group are hidden.

6. It is uncommon for companies to adjust their financial statements to take account of price and price level changes (i.e. inflation). Since the figures in the financial statements are affected by price changes in different ways, ratios can be distorted. For example, when prices are rising, the profit figure tends to be overstated, as historic costs rather than higher current costs are matched with current revenues, and capital employed understated, as the historic cost of assets is used rather than their higher current cost. Therefore the return on capital employed ratio becomes doubly overstated:

In conclusion, ratios are a useful tool with which to analyse a set of financial statements. However, they are only one such tool available to accountants (others include source and application of funds statements, see Chapter 10; value added statements, see Chapter 23; and inflation-adjusted accounts, see Chapter 24) and, as we have seen above, ratios are not without their limitations.

CHECKLIST

Having completed Chapter 22, you should be able to:

- calculate suitable ratios from financial statements;
- describe the meaning of these ratios;
- analyse the liquidity, profitability and long-term growth potential of a company from these ratios;
- discuss the limitations of ratio analysis.

Workshop 22.1: Ratio analysis – Pontypandy plc

From the Pontypandy – spreadsheet (Spreadsheet 22.1) (this spreadsheet has already been used to produce a statement of source and application of funds statement in Workshop 21) calculate the ratios needed to analyse the change in the company's position and results over the year.

Spreadsheet 22.1   Workshop 22.1: Working capital funds

	A	B	C	D	E	F	G	H	I	J	K
1											
2	Working Capital Funds ---->								‡	‡	‡
3											
4		Ordinary	P & L	Loan		Land	Pl't & M.	Pl't & M.	Stock	Debtors	Cash &
5	Account Title--->	Shares	Account	10%p.a.		at cost	Dep'n				Bank
6											
7	Narrative										
8											
9	Op. Balance Sheet	-500.00	-260.00	.00		340.00	290.00	-120.00	300.00	70.00	60.00
10											
11	Sales		-2400.00							2400.00	
12											
13	Purchases								1800.00		
14											
15	Expenses		400.00								-400.00
16											
17	Depreciation		125.00					-125.00			
18											
19	Profit on Sale of Plant		-20.00								
20	Write out asset at cost						-70.00				
21	Write out dep'n on Asset							65.00			
22	Therefore cash rec'd										25.00
23											
24	Tax		60.00								
25											
26	Dividend		65.00								
27											
28	Issue of Shares	-100.00									100.00
29											
30	Take up of Loan			-100.00							100.00
31											
32	Purchase of Land					200.00					-200.00
33											
34	Purchase of P & M.						490.00				-490.00
35											
36	Cost of Goods Sold		1650.00						-1650.00		
37											
38	Receipts from Debtors									-2375.00	2375.00
39											
40	Payments to Creditors										-1510.00
41											
42	Tax Paid										-90.00
43											
44	Dividends Paid										-60.00
45											
46											
47	Cl. Balance Sheet	-600.00	-380.00	-100.00		540.00	710.00	-180.00	450.00	95.00	-90.00
48											

49				
50				
51	LIQUIDITY RATIOS	19-8	19-7	PROFITABILITY RATIOS
52				
53	Debtor's Collection Period	.48 months	.42 months	Overall Return on Capital Employed
54				
55	Creditor's Payment Period	2.13 months	.26 months	Shareholder's Return on Capital Employed
56				
57	Stock Turnover Period	3.27 months	2.48 months	Gearing
58				
59	Current Ratio	1.33 times	14.33 times	Net Asset Turnover
60				
61	Quick Ratio	.23 times	4.33 times	Net Profit Margin
62				
63				Gross Profit Margin

! L !!	M !!	N !!	N !!	O !!	P !!	Q !!	R !!	S !!	T !!	U !!	V !!	W !

‡

Trade Creds.	Taxation	Proposed Divs.	Sale of F. Assets		Funds Flow							
-30.00	-90.00	-60.00	.00	.00	400.00							

OTHER INFORMATION TO CALCULATE RATIOS

						Description	Value
					2400.00		
-1800.00						Previous Year's Sales	2000.00
					-400.00	Previous Year's Purchases	1400.00
						Previous Year's Cost of Sales	1450.00
			20.00			Previous Year's Net Profit	150.00
			70.00				
			-65.00			Previous Year's Loan Interest	.00
			-25.00		25.00		
						Previous Year's Gross Profit	550.00
	-60.00					Previous Year's Dividends	30.00
		-65.00				Previous Year's Share Price	6.00
					100.00		
						This Year's Share Price	7.50
					100.00		
						This Year's Net Profit	245.00
					-200.00		
						This Year's Gross Profit	750.00
					-490.00		
					-1650.00		
1510.00							
	90.00				-90.00		
		60.00			-60.00		
----------------	----------------				----------------		
-320.00	-60.00	-65.00	.00	.00	135.00		
================	================				================		

19-8	19-7	LONG TERM GROWTH RATIOS	19-8	19-7
.23 %	.20 %	Price / Earnings Ratio	18.37 times	20.00 times
.25 %	.20 %	Dividend Yield	26.53 %	20.00 %
.09 %	.00 %	Dividend Cover	3.77 times	5.00 times
2.22 times	2.63 times			
10.21 %	7.50 %			
31.25 %	27.50 %			

Workshop guide

1. The three sets of ratios explained in the chapter have been calculated to show the company's liquidity and profitability positions and its long-term growth prospects. These ratios, together with the original spreadsheet, are shown below. In addition some previous years' figures are shown, together with the company's share prices.

2. The ratios are calculated by taking the appropriate cell references from elsewhere in the spreadsheet. For example, the debtors' collection period as at 31 December 1988 is calculated by taking the debtors figure from cell **J47** and dividing it by the sales figure from **J11**; the result is multiplied by 12 to turn it into a monthly figure.

3. Ratios for both 1988 and 1987 are calculated so that we can make comparisons.

4. Liquidity position: the debtors collection period remains quite small, at just less than half a month, while the creditors payment period has increased substantially, from about a week to over two months. Is the company taking advantage of extended credit terms from suppliers or having difficulty paying them? There may be a danger of suppliers withholding supplies. The stock turnover period increased by almost a month as a result of an increase in stock holdings; the company may have expanded its product range to meet increased customer demand but should ensure it is not tying up too many funds which could otherwise earn a more profitable return elsewhere in the business. The current ratio has fallen significantly, from a very high figure of 14.33 to 1.33. The main reasons for this change are the change in the bank position from positive to overdraft and the large increase in creditors. The company should ensure it can pay these creditors as their debts fall due for payment. To this end the quick ratio has been calculated, which takes the most illiquid current asset of stock; it shows a significant fall from 4.33 to 0.23. Only 23 per cent of creditors (including the bank) can be paid out of debtors; this may be a worrying position.

    This liquidity analysis is supplemented by reviewing the statement of source and application of funds statement as shown in the previous chapter's workshop. This shows a net application of funds of £265. The main reason for this net application is the large purchases of land and plant and machinery; it looks as though the company is expanding, as the sales of fixed assets are small (£25) and the depreciation charge (a measure of the wearing out or use of fixed assets) only £125. This has been financed from four main areas:
    a. funds generated from operations of £350;
    b. issuing shares, so increasing capital by £100;
    c. raising long-term loans of £100;
    d. an increase in creditors and the bank overdraft.

5. Profitability position: the return achieved by the company on its capital employed has increased from 20 per cent to 23 per cent. This is as a result of an increase in the net profit margin by almost 3 per cent; that is, an extra £3 profit is made on each £100 sale. The net asset turnover ratio has fallen from 2.63 to 2.22, so preventing the full impact of the increased net profit margin being reflected in the return on capital employed ratio. The company has taken on £100 of long-term loans (at the end of the year, as there is no interest charge in the spreadsheet) so increasing the financial risk as measured by the gearing ratio; however, 9 per cent should not prove too detrimental. The gross profit ratio has also increased, indicating the company is trading (i.e. buying and selling) more efficiently.

6. Long-term growth prospects: the price earnings ratio has fallen from twenty times net profit to 18.37 times net profit. This is due to the increase in net profit outstripping the increase in the company's share price. The market may be taking into consideration the deterioration in the liquidity position which the above analysis seemed to indicate. The dividend yield has increased due to the significant increase in this year's dividend (£65) compared with last year's (£30). The dividend cover, while reduced from five times net profits to 3.77 times, is still well covered.

'What if?' problems

1. What if the company issued £200,000 shares, making the closing balance £700,000? Which ratios would change and by how much? What effect would this have on your assessment of the company's liquidity and profitability?

2. What if the company issued £200,000 loans, making the closing balance £200,000? Which ratios would change and by how much? What effect would this have on your assessment of the company's liquidity and profitability?

3. What if the company had only spent £190,000 on new plant? Which ratios would change and by how much? What effect would this have on your assessment of the company's liquidity and profitability?

4. If the company had chosen to double this year's dividend which ratios would change and by how much? What effect would this have on your assessment of the company's liquidity, profitability and long-term growth prospects?

5. If the company's share price at 31 December 1988 had been (a) £5 or (b) £10 instead of £7.50 how would this have affected your analysis?

Answers

1. Ratios: ROCE 21 per cent (1988).
    Shareholders ROCE 23 per cent (1988).
    Gearing 8 per cent (1988).
    Net asset turnover, 2.03 times (1988).
    P/E ratio 21.43 (1988).

    The company has a slightly larger capital base and is making the same profit. The effect is therefore marginal.

2. Ratios: ROCE, 21 per cent.
    Gearing, 17 per cent.
    NAT, 2.03.

    The effect is to increase the company's gearing marginally.

3. There are no changes at ratios calculated. However, some analysts prefer a fixed asset turnover ratio instead of a net asset turnover, in which case this would alter.

4. Ratios (all 1988):
    ROCE, 24 per cent; shareholders ROCE, 27 per cent.
    Gearing, 10 per cent; net asset turnover, 2.36 times.
    Dividend yield, 53.06 per cent; dividend cover, 1.88 times.

    Profitability ratio changes are explained by the reduction in capital employed. The higher dividend has led to an increase in yield and a reduction in cover.

5(a). P/E is 12.24 times; (b) 24.49 times.

Selected questions and exercises

Question 22.1

Table 22.1 gives some of the financial statistics for Eunice plc.

Table 22.1   *Details of the accounts of Eunice plc*

	1986 £000	1987 £000	1988 £000
Sales	7,000.00	9,500.00	11,000.00
Gross profit	2,200.00	1,600.00	3,200.00
Net profit	600.00	500.00	1,000.00
Shareholders' equity	6,000.00	7,500.00	10,000.00
Long-term loans	.00	1,500.00	5,000.00
Number of employees	25.00	30.00	44.00

You are required to prepare a report for a potential investor in Eunice plc, which includes the following.

1. Calculation of the following ratios for each year:
   a. the gross margin;
   b. the net margin;
   c. return on capital employed;
   d. net asset turnover;
   e. gearing;
   f. net profit per employee.
2. Comments on the profitability of the company given the above information and the ratios you have calculated.
3. An outline of any further information you would require in order to provide the investor with more relevant information. For each suggestion say (briefly) how it could be used.

Solution on page 567.

Question 22.2
Table 22.2 gives some of the financial statistics for The Playfull Toy Company plc. The company did not have any cash balances during this period.

Table 22.2 *Details of the accounts of The Playfull Toy Company plc*

	£000s			
	1983	1984	1985	1986
Sales	33,400	38,800	43,200	42,000
Net profit (loss) before taxation	4,050	2,700	1,520	(2,100)
Stocks	12,300	14,800	16,400	19,200
Debtors	8,900	8,400	10,500	11,100
Bank overdraft	2,400	6,700	10,600	23,100
Creditors	8,200	8,100	9,300	11,100

You are required to prepare a report which includes the following.

1. Calculation of the following ratios for each year:
   a. the net margin;
   b. the current ratio;
   c. the acid-test ratio;
   d. the debtors days' ratio.
2. Comments on the financial state of the company, given the above information and the ratios you have calculated.
3. An explanation, in principle, based upon the ratios that you have calculated, of what courses of action you would advise the management of Playfull Toys to take.

No solution provided.   *Sources: JMB, GCE A Level, June 1987.*

Question 22.3
The accounts of Turk Ltd and Jack Ltd (both wholesale wine merchants) for the year ended 31 March 1986 are as shown in Table 22.3.

Table 22.3   *Details of the accounts of Turk Limited and Jack Limited*

Profit and loss	Turk		Jack	
Sales		50,000		100,000
Opening stock	10,000		12,000	
Purchases	35,000		77,000	
	45,000		89,000	
Closing stock	10,000	35,000	15,000	74,000
Gross profit	15,000		26,000	
Expenses		11,000		17,000
Net profit	4,000		9,000	
Proposed dividends:				
ordinary		2,000		6,000
preference		1,000		—
		1,000		3,000

Balance sheets	Turk		Jack	
Fixed assets (NBV):				
buildings	7,000		11,000	
fixtures	1,500	8,500	4,000	15,000
Current assets:				
stock	10,000		15,000	
debtors	9,500		15,000	
bank	5,500		—	
	25,000		30,000	
Current liabilities:				
creditors	4,000		10,000	
bank	—		500	
dividends	3,000		6,000	
Net current assets		18,000		13,500
		26,500		28,500

	Turk	Jack
Share capital £1.00 ordinary	5,000	10,000
Debentures 10%	10,000	—
Reserves	7,500	14,000
Profit and loss account	4,000	4,500
	26,500	28,500

Prepare a report for the directors of Turk Ltd in which you compare the position and performance of the two companies. (Use approximately ten ratios in your analysis.) Suggest ways in which Turk's position and performance may be improved.

No solution provided.

Question 22.4

Table 22.4 gives summarised accounting statements for years 11 and 12 which relate to Lakeland Ltd.

Table 22.4   *Details of the accounts of Lakeland Limited*

| | *Profit and loss accounts* | | | |
| | Year 11 | | Year 12 | |
	£000	£000	£000	£000
Sales		430		662
Cost of sales		253		384
Gross profit		177		278
Profit on sale of plant and machinery		—		3
		177		281
Depreciation of plant and machinery	27		43	
Interest on debentures	8		8	
Other expenses	107	142	164	215
		35		66
Proposed dividend		14		24
		21		42
Retained profits brought forward		36		57
Retained profits carried forward		57		99
	Balance sheets			
Freehold property at cost		150		150
Plant and machinery at cost	204		232	
less depreciation	85	119	81	151
Stocks		77		82
Debtors		105		78
Bank		14		3
		465		464
Ordinary share capital		175		225
Share premium		25		35
Retained profits		57		99
8 per cent debentures		100		—
Trade creditors		94		81
Proposed dividend		14		24
		465		464

During year 12; plant and machinery originally costing £83,000, was sold and some replacement machinery was purchased; the dividend for year 11 was paid; the debentures were redeemed at par; and further ordinary shares were issued.

Stock at the beginning of year 11 was £88,000.

1. Prepare a statement of Lakeland Ltd's source and application of funds for year 12, in good style.
2. Calculate each of the following for years 11 and 12:
    a. working capital ratio;
    b. acid-test (liquid) ratio;

    c. debtors collection period (expressed in months);

    d. rate of stock turnover.

    Note: all calculations should be to the nearest two decimal places.

3. Select any one of your answers to part 2 above, and briefly comment on the significance of your results.

No solution provided.　　　　　　　　　　*Source: LCCI, Accounting, November 1987.*

Question 22.5

You are presented with information for three quite separate and independent companies (see Table 22.5).

Table 22.5　*Details of the accounts of Chan plc, Ling plc and Wong plc*

Summarised balance sheets at 31 March 1987

	Chan plc £000	Ling plc £000	Wong plc £000
Total assets less current liabilities	600	600	700
Creditors: amounts falling due after more than one year 10% debenture stock	—	—	(100)
	£600	£600	£600
Capital and reserves:			
called up share capital			
ordinary shares of £1 each	500	300	200
10% cumulative preference shares			
of £1 each	—	200	300
profit and loss account	100	100	100
	£600	£600	£600

Additional information:

1. The operating profit before interest and tax for the year 31 March 1988 earned by each of the three companies was £300,000.

2. The effective rate of corporation tax for all three companies for the year to 31 March 1988 is 30 per cent. This rate is to be used in calculating each company's tax payable on ordinary profit.

3. An ordinary dividend of 20p for the year to 31 March 1988 is proposed by all three companies, and any preference dividends are to be provided for.

4. The market prices per ordinary share at 31 March 1988 were as follows: Chan plc, £8.40; Ling plc, £9.50; Wong plc, £10.38.

5. There were no changes in the share capital structure or in long-term loans of any of the companies during the year to 31 March 1988.

1. Insofar as the information permits, prepare the profit and loss account for each of the three companies (in columnar format) for the year to 31 March 1988 (formal notes to the accounts are not required).

2. Calculate the following accounting ratios for each company:
   a. earnings per share;
   b. price earnings;
   c. gearing (taken as total borrowings – preference share capital and long term loans – to ordinary shareholders' funds).
3. Using the gearing ratios calculated in answering part 2 of the question, briefly examine the importance of gearing if you were thinking of investing in some ordinary shares in one of the three companies, assuming that the profits of the three companies were fluctuating.

Solutions on pages 567–9. *Source: AAT, Financial Accounting, June 1988.*

Question 22.6

The trading stock of Joan Street, retailer, has been reduced during the year ended 31 March 1988 by £6,000 from its commencing figure of £21,000.

A number of financial ratios and related statistics have been compiled relating to the business of Joan Street for the year ended 31 March 1988; these are shown in Table 22.6 alongside comparative figures for a number of retailers who are members of the trader association to which Joan Street belongs.

Table 22.6   *Details of the accounts of Joan Street*

	Joan Street %	Trade association %
Net profit / Net capital employed	15	16
Net profit / Sales	9	8
Sales / Net capital employed	$166\frac{2}{3}$	200
Fixed assets / Sales	45	35
Working capital ratio: current assets / current liabilities	400	$287\frac{1}{2}$
Acid-test ratio: bank + debtors / current liabilities	$233\frac{1}{3}$	$187\frac{1}{2}$
Gross profit / Sales	25	26
Debtor collection period: debtors × 365 / sales	$36\frac{1}{2}$ days	$32\frac{17}{20}$ days
Stock turnover (based on average stock for the year and sales)	10 times	8 times

Joan Street has supplied all the capital for her business and has had no drawings from the business during the year ended 31 March 1988.

1. Prepare the trading and profit and loss account for the year ended 31 March 1988 and balance sheet of Joan Street as at that date in as much detail as possible.
2. Identify two aspects of Joan Street's results for the year ended 31 March 1988 which compare favourably with the trade association's figures and identify two aspects which compare unfavourably.
3. Outline two drawbacks of the type of comparison used in this question.

No solution provided.   *Source: AAT*

23 | *The corporate report and value added statements*

AIMS OF CHAPTER _____

- to introduce the student to the contents of the corporate report;
- to identify the users of financial information and their information requirements;
- to examine the nature of value added statements and their preparation.

23.1 Introduction

Up to now we have been assuming that only shareholders require information about corporate enterprises. This is largely the approach adopted by the Companies Act and the accountancy profession. However, it is not difficult to think of other sectors who require corporate information, such as employees and creditors. Employees depend upon the company for their salaries and creditors for payment for goods and services supplied to the company. This chapter will introduce the idea that there are other potential users of corporate information.

23.2 The corporate report

In 1975 the Accounting Standards Committee issued a discussion paper entitled *The corporate report*, which attempted to answer the question, '*who* should report *what* to *whom*?'. We will consider each of the three elements to this question.

1. The corporate report saw no real problems in *who* should report. Those entities that command sufficient resources to impinge materiality upon a user group (see 2 below) should report. The concept of materiality is used to indicate that organisations over a certain size, or of particular importance, are the important criteria. The organisation uses resources supplied by one or

more of the user groups, so this custodian role renders it responsible and hence the necessity to report on how these resources are used.

2. The corporate report identifies seven user groups, all potentially having a reasonable right to information from the reporting organisation. The seven user groups are as follows:

  a. existing and potential shareholders;
  b. existing and potential loan creditors;

Users	*Information needs*
Existing and potential shareholders	Shareholders require information to assist them in their decision to buy, sell or hold shares. This included: —evaluating the company's (and management's) performance, —assessing whether objectives have been met; —assessing stability and liquidity of the company; —the company's ability to raise short- and long-term finance; —estimating growth prospects and future dividends; —comparing the company over a period of time and with other organisations; —ascertaining the ownership and control of the company.
Existing and potential loan creditors	—loan creditors require information to enable assessment of the company's ability to repay loans and interest. Their information needs are similar to shareholders, with an emphasis on short- and long-term liquidity.
Existing, potential and past employees	—employees require information to assess the security and prospects of employment and information to assist with pay negotiations. Special employee reports may serve their needs better than annual reports.
Customers, suppliers, competitors and other business contract groups	—customers need information on price and continuation of supply. Suppliers need information on the company's ability to pay for goods supplied and continuation of demand. Competitors need information on all aspect of the company, but the provision of this information must be restricted due to confidentiality.
Government (including the tax authorities, the Department of Trade and Industry)	—the government needs information to ensure compliance with tax regulations and company law.
The public (including tax payers, consumers and environmental societies and pressure groups)	—the public is a diverse group whose information needs spring from their own particular interests in the company.

Figure 23.1 Users of financial statements and their information needs

c. existing, potential and past employees;
d. analysts and advisers;
e. customers, suppliers, competitors and other business contact groups;
f. government (including the tax authorities, local authorities, the Department of Trade and Industry);
g. the public (including taxpayers, consumers and environmental societies and pressure groups).

3. Figure 23.1 summarises the information needs of each user group.

The corporate report required that this information should be:

relevant
understandable
reliable (e.g. complete and objective)
timely
comparable.

However, it was recognised that the above must be limited by the practical considerations of cost and confidentiality. In a cost-free world, corporate reports would be produced for each user group and each component of a single group. The costs of such an undertaking can be prohibitive. Therefore companies often limit themselves to reporting solely to shareholders. However, some companies prepare employee reports, as they take the view that their employees have a reasonable need for information as their livelihood is often dependent upon their wages or salary.

The corporate report identified a statement which is of general use to most of the user groups – the value added statement. We will now examine this general purpose statement.

23.3 The value added statement (VAS)

The VAS is based upon an economic concept of measuring the value added to goods and services the company buys. This concept can be easily understood by referring to the diagram in Figure 23.2.

How do we go about constructing a value added statement? We will prepare a VAS for Tonic plc whose profit and loss account appears in Figure 23.3. The VAS is based upon the same information used to prepare the profit and loss account, i.e. the **profit and loss** column of the spreadsheet, as it is just another way of explaining how capital has changed over a period of time. The VAS for Tonic plc is shown in Figure 23.4.

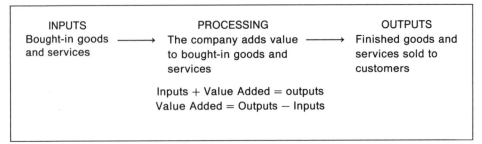

INPUTS
Bought-in goods ⟶
and services

PROCESSING
The company adds value ⟶
to bought-in goods and
services

OUTPUTS
Finished goods and
services sold to
customers

Inputs + Value Added = outputs
Value Added = Outputs − Inputs

Figure 23.2   Diagram to show a systems approach to value added

As we can see, the VAS is in two reconciling parts. Firstly, a top half in which the value added is calculated (i.e. outputs less inputs or sales less bought-in goods and services). Secondly, an analysis of how this value added has been distributed among the various user groups. Percentages are included to provide a more immediate picture of how one user group has fared relative to the other user groups.

Before considering the usefulness of the VAS it is worth considering how depreciation was classified. Depreciation is part of value added since it was not considered to be part of brought-in goods and services. The logic for this accepted treatment of depreciation is dubious, as depreciation is an allocation of the cost of fixed assets used up in the process of production.

	£000s	£000
Sales		5,000
Less: Cost of sales		
Wages	2,000	
Materials	1,500	
Overheads*	750	
		4,250
PROFIT BEFORE TAX		750
Less: tax		250
PROFIT AFTER TAX		500
Less: interest		200
PROFIT AFTER INTEREST		300
Less: dividends payable		200
RETAINED PROFITS		£ 100

* Includes £300,000 for depreciation

Figure 23.3   Profit and loss for Tonic plc for the year ending 31 December 1989

	£000s	£000s	%
Calculation of value added:			
Sales		5,000	
Less: bought-in goods and services*		1,950	
		£3,050	
Distribution of value added:			
To employees		2,000	66
To providers of capital			
interest on loans	200		
dividends	200		
		400	13
To government		250	8
Retained in business for:			
Depreciation	300		
Retained profits	100		
		400	13
		£3,050	100
	£000s		
* Materials	1,500		
Overheads (net)	450		
	1,950		

Figure 23.4   Value added statement for Tonic plc for the year ended 31 December 1989

The production of a VAS has a number of advantages:

1. It redirects the users' attention from profit (only directly relevant to share-holders) to value added (directly relevant to all users). This is supposed to increase the team approach, i.e. all users working together to increase value added.

2. It shows both the absolute and relative (i.e. percentage) return of value added to each user group. The employees can clearly see how much value they receive in their pay packets; shareholders can see how much return they are earning; the government how much taxes it is collecting and how much value added is being retained by the company for future expansion.

3. Management performance will be measured at least in part by how well it manages value added as well as profit.

CHECKLIST _____

Having completed Chapter 23, you should be able to:

■ describe the contents of the corporate report;

■ identify the users of financial information and their information requirements;

■ prepare value added statements and be able to analyse them.

_____

Workshop 23.1: Value added statements

Refer to Chapter 20 on the final accounts of companies and look at the profit and
loss account of Jennings plc, given in Figure 20.4a. This workshop asks you to
redraft this account as a value added statement. Use the other information in
Figure 20.3 to help you.

Workshop guide

1. The first figure that can be placed in the value added statement is sales or
    turnover, which can be taken from the profit and loss account, i.e.
    £11,547,998.

2. The figure of bought-in goods and services cannot be disaggregated until we
    have calculated an amount of distributed value to employees and retained in
    the business for depreciation.

3. The employees have been paid £1,309,300, but are owed £30,940. Therefore
    included in the costs of the company will be £1,340,240 employee earnings.

4. The motor vehicles are valued at £912,600 and have been depreciated on a
    reducing balance of 25 per cent. As there was £51,200 accumulated deprecia-
    tion in the trial balance, the charge to this year's accounts is $(1,309,300 -
    51,200)*.25 = £215,350$. The charge for machinery depreciation for the period
    is calculated in the same manner $(3,093,560 - 265,280)*.10 = £282,828$. This
    gives a total depreciation charge for the period of £498,178.

5. Knowing these two figures for depreciation and employee earnings, we are
    able to compute the amount of bought-in goods and services as the total
    expenses for the period less the isolated amounts (see Table 23.1).

6. All the information is now available for a value added statement to be
    presented. The answer is given in Figure 23.5.

Table 23.1 *Computation of amount of bought-in goods and services*

	£
Sales	11,547,998
Cost of sales	5,740,718
Distribution costs	1,069,298
Administration expenses	2,872,932
Other income	(202,520)
Less:	
employees' earnings	(1,340,240)
depreciation	(498,178)
Bought-in goods and services	7,642,010

	£000s	£000s	%
Calculation of value added:			
Sales		11,548	
Less: bought-in goods and services		7,642	
		£3,906	
Distribution of value added:			
To employees		1,340	34
To providers of capital			
Interest on loans	180		
Dividends	1,036		
		1,216	31
To government		661	17
Retained in business for:			
Depreciation	498		
Retained profits	191		
		689	18
		£3,906	100

Figure 23.5 Value added statement for Jennings plc

'What if?' problems

As this is not a spreadsheet exercise, this section will confine itself to asking a few questions designed to make you follow the consequences of changing certain figures.

1. If the employees earned more, who would get less – the providers of capital, the government, or both?

2. If the government increased the rate of corporation tax, would this put pressure on the wages of the workers or the dividends to shareholders, or both?

3. What if the workers were more productive and efficient – would their share of the value added rise or fall as a result of the decrease in bought-in goods and services?

Answers

1. The company would make less profit so the government would charge less tax. The company's dividend policy would also alter if profits fell dramatically.

2. Both.

3. Greater efficiency will increase the profits made and can be used when negotiating wage claims.

Selected questions and exercises

Question 23.1

The balances shown in Table 23.2 have been extracted from the books of the company for the year ended 30 June 1979.

Table 23.2   *Balances for year ended 30 June 1979*

	£000
Customs and excise duties (included in the turnover)	160.4
Depreciation charge for the year	13.5
Dividends to ordinary shareholders	6.7
Interest on borrowed money	7.3
Investment income received	6.2
Minority interests in subsidiaries (including dividends 2.5 payable by the subsidiaries)	4.0
Profit retained	16.5
Purchases of plant	120.4
Raw materials and bought-in services used	325.1
Stock and work-in-progress at 30 June 1979	62.7
Turnover (excluding value added tax)	642.7
United Kingdom and overseas corporation tax	15.4
Wages, salaries and retirement benefits	100.0

You are required to:
a. prepare a value added statement for the year ended 30 June 1979, selecting the appropriate items from the list of balances;
b. state the purpose(s) of the value added statement now being presented by many public companies.

No solution provided.

Question 23.2

Table 23.3 is a draft income statement for LM Ltd for the period t_1 to t_2. Prepare a net value added statement for that period using the data provided.

Table 23.3 *Draft income statement for L M Limited*

LM Ltd

Income statement for the period t_2 to t_2

	£
Turnover	204,000
Change in stocks t_1 to t_2	7,000
Purchase of goods	(134,000)
Wages	(26,000)
Depreciation of: motor vehicles	(7,000)
plant	(14,000)
Other business overheads	(7,000)
Income before taxation	23,000
Tax on income	(11,000)
Income after taxation	12,000
Dividends proposed on: preference capital	(700)
ordinary capital	(3,500)
Transfers to reserve	(2,000)
Retained income	5,800

No solution provided.

Question 23.3

1. You are required to describe your understanding of the term 'value added' as used in accounting.
2. Using the following summarised information prepare:
   a. a conventional profit statement of a company;
   b. a value added statement.

Summarised information for XYZ Ltd in respect of the year ended 31 December 1979 is shown in Table 23.4.

Table 23.4 *Details of the accounts of X YZ Limited*

	£000
Salaries and wages	200
Purchased materials used in production	300
Sales	740
Corporation tax on the profit for the year	60
Dividend proposed	24
Services purchased	60
Depreciation of fixed assets	40
Loan interest paid and payable	20

3. There is an alternative view on the treatment of depreciation in value added statements. What is this view and how would it affect the answer you have produced in answer to question 2b.
4. What advantages are claimed for including a value added statement in a company's corporate report?

No solution provided.

24 || *Introduction to inflation accounting*

AIMS OF CHAPTER _____

- to examine the imperfections of historic cost accounting;
- to calculate the effect different rates of inflation have on assets;
- to outline some of the alternative accounting systems which attempt to cope with changing prices;
- to apply the principles of these alternative accounting systems to accounts.

24.1 Problems of historic cost accounting

The problems of historic cost accounting will be discussed under two headings: those which do not relate to changing prices and those which do relate to changing prices

24.1.1 Problems not related to changing prices

A major advantage claimed of historic cost accounting is that it is based upon objective criteria (i.e. a clearly defined set of rules), so can be carried out by an accounts clerk who only has to follow the rules to calculate the profit. However, these foundations are anything but objective, as the determination of provisions (depreciation, stock, bad debts and general provisions), accruals and prepayments depends upon the subjective judgement of the person preparing the financial statements.

Let us consider the case of depreciation. Two firms may purchase an identical fixed asset which they plan to use in exactly the same way, but choose to depreciate it over different time periods. For example, one firm may use an estimated life of ten years, while another firm may use an estimated life of twenty years. The former will therefore charge a greater depreciation expense to its profit

473

and loss account over the first ten year period; if the firms are otherwise identical, it will report a lower profit figure. Of course the situation will reverse between ten and twenty years. The reason for these differences is the subjective choice of accounting policy.

Therefore two individuals provided with the same data concerning a company's affairs can come up with two different profit figures, neither profit figure being incorrect.

A second claimed advantage of historic cost accounts is that profits are only recognised upon realisation; this is problematic as one can conceive of profits being reasonably certain upon production, such as the case of a manufacturer in a sellers' market or of profits not being reasonably certain upon the occurrence of a credit sale. This is the case if there is doubt as to whether the debtor will pay.

These problems can be traced to the system of historic cost accounting not being a coherent system at all, only a set of practices which evolved over seven centuries and were only clearly formulated in the past fifty years. Many of these practices were in fact developed before economists adequately defined income and value.

24.1.2   Problems relating to changing prices

The foundation of historic cost accounting rests upon many accounting concepts, two of which are cost and realisation (discussed in Chapter 4). The cost concept leads to assets beings recorded at their purchase or historic cost when they are acquired by the organisation, while the realisation concept keeps the assets at this historic cost (regardless of changes in their market price or the general price level) until the assets are realised. At realisation (this is usually when the assets are sold or used up in the production process), historic costs are matched with the revenue they generate and the difference taken to the profit and loss account.

It is the strict adherence of historic cost accounting to these two fundamental concepts that leads to many of the problems of historic cost accounting. It is these problems we will now examine, since they will direct us towards their solution which we will look at in the next section.

In recent years the spearhead of the attack upon historic cost accounting is that price and price level changes are ignored. Price level changes are changes in the general level of prices (i.e. inflation and deflation), usually measured by a price index such as the Retail Price Index, while price changes are changes in the specific prices (up or down) of costs (e.g. purchases) and sales. It is interesting to note that when historic cost accounting was clearly formulated in the 1920s and 1930s prices were generally stable, or even falling slightly; therefore price changes were not considered to be a serious problem. The fact that historic cost accounting refuses to take notice of these prices and price level changes has led to several problems in recent years, when prices have risen sharply.

These problems can be summarised as follows:

1. Profits tend to be overstated when prices rise as historic costs are matched with current revenues (current costs can be significantly higher than historic costs during times of inflation). Let us look at an example to illustrate this problem. Suppose a business buys an item of stock for £20 and sells it in one month's time at £25. The historic cost profit is clearly £5. However, if the item of stock cost £21 to replace (in a month's time when the sale is made) the real profit is only £4 as the business has to replace the item of stock to put itself back in the same position as it was before it made the sale (i.e. possess one item of stock). The £4 can be thought of as a current cost profit, as it is a profit figure derived under the assumption that the business is going to replace the item of stock sold.

2. Asset values tend to be understated due to the realisation concept not recognising value changes until realisation. Suppose a business bought some land for £25,000 ten years ago, which costs £100,000 to replace today. The land will still be recorded at its original purchase price of £25,000 in the balance sheet, while its real value is £100,000. Therefore two identical firms can have vastly different asset values simply because one firm has held its assets for a number of years and the other firm has recently replaced or purchased its assets.

3. Since asset values are understated so is capital employed and when combined with the first problem of profits being overstated, the resultant 'return on capital employed' ratio is doubly overstated. This ratio was discussed in Chapter 22, where it was found to be much used by investors in making their investment decisions, so its overstatement could well lead to incorrect investment decisions for the investor and a misallocation of resources for the economy as a whole (as prices of different items increase at different rates).

4. No distinction is made between holding gains and current operating profit. This distinction can be seen by referring back to the example used to illustrate problem 1 above. The historic cost profit was £5 and the current cost profit was £4. The difference of £1 between these two profit figures is called a 'holding gain' as it arose from the item of stock being held by the business for one month when its price increased from £20 to £21.

   Therefore the historic cost profit can be thought of as being composed of two components: a current cost profit and a holding gain. Such a distinction is important, as these may well have arisen from different situations; holding gains from holding assets while their prices rise between purchase and realisation and current operating profit due to good trading decisions. Shareholders may need to know the management's ability at each which is not possible if they are not shown separately. In fact, holding gains are consumed into current operating profit, so making the latter look larger than it really is.

5. It should be remembered that even small rates of inflation can lead to large changes in prices over time; for instance a rate of 3.5 per cent p.a. can lead to a doubling of the price level in just over twenty years. Suppose a business owns an asset which cost £1,000 twenty years ago and has increased in price at the rate of 3.5 per cent p.a. See Figure 24.1 for a demonstration of the effect of inflation.

6. Historic cost accounting has been criticised for having an inadequate capital maintenance base. The base is measured in terms of the amount of money invested in the firm by its owners. As time proceeds, the amount of goods and services this fixed amount of money can buy reduces (as we saw above), so forcing the firm to reduce its operations if more capital is not invested. Since it is this capital which the creditors of the company have recourse to in the event of the company ceasing to trade, creditor protection can become a serious problem.

    When all the above imperfections of historic cost accounting are taken into consideration, it is not surprising that many accounting academics and practitioners have researched into alternative systems of accounting put forward as solutions to these problems. They are called 'current value systems', as they replace historic cost values by current values. It is to these alternative systems we will now turn.

Let us use the spreadsheet to examine some of the effects of inflation. The formula needed to calculate the price rise is given by:

Inflated price = price now $(1 + i)^n$
(price then)

where: i = the rate of inflation
n = the number of years

The rate of inflation is usually expressed as a percentage, so in the equation a rate of inflation of 10 per cent is 10/100 or 0.10.

The way inflation works is that it compounds price rises. If prices rise by 10 per cent each year then in 10 years prices have not risen by 100 per cent but by 259 per cent!

How can this be? Let's work out this example. A price rise of 10 per cent will increase the price of an asset costing £100 by £10. In the second year the asset would start the year costing £110 and end the year costing £121, i.e. £110 × 10% = £11, plus the £110 original price. This is how the equation builds up:

£100 $(1 + 0.10)^2$ = £121
Uplift factor

Try putting the equation into practice on your spreadsheets as in Spreadsheet 24.1 (the formula back up is given in Spreadsheet 24.2).

Experimenting with the rate, we can try firstly inserting a rate of 28 per cent. This was the rate of inflation in the mid-1970s in Great Britain. Look at the result. You should have a difference in price of £138,380, which would distort the asset's price in the balance sheet enormously. Try a few of your own 'what if' statements, e.g. what about a negative rate of increase, i.e. deflation, or imagine the problems of some South American countries where inflation rate can be 200 per cent per annum! (You may need to format column D to a larger cell width for this one.)

However, inflation rates, as you are aware, do not remain constant. They vary even within the year in question. So how do we calculate just how much prices have been affected?

One method is to use an index. This entails finding the price of an asset in the past and comparing it with the asset's price at the present time. For example, the price of a car in January 19x5 was £6,000 and in January 19x9 the price had risen to £7,500. We apply an index value to the January 19x5 price of 100. This 100 does not represent any particular monetary value, but merely relates to the car's price at that point in time. By January 19x9, the car is now priced at £7,500, an increase in price of 25 per cent over the three-year period. Therefore, the index for the car has risen to 125 (i.e. 125/100 = 1.25). It does not matter if this rate of increase was constant or not, it is the index that calculates the effect of inflation.

Year	Price	Index	Inflation during year
19X5	6,000	100	—
19X6	6,300	105	$105/100 - 1 = 5\%$
19X7	6,600	110	$110/105 - 1 = 4.7619\%$
19X8	6,900	115	$115/110 - 1 = 4.545\%$
19X9	7,500	130	$130/115 - 1 = 13.0435$
			$= \underline{27.3504}$

Inflation can be deduced between any two periods by using the index.

The rise between 19x5 and 19x7 was $(110/100 - 1) = 10$ per cent or $(1.05 \times 1.047619) - 1 = 10$ per cent. The rise between 19x5 and 19x8 was $(115/100 - 1) = 15$ per cent or $(1.05 \times 1.047619 \times 1.04545) - 1 = 15$ per cent.

As you can see, it is far easier to use an index to calculate the effects of inflation, rather than using the varying inflation rates.

This method relates to a specific asset. We measure the general effect of inflation using the retail price index. This relates to the price paid for a 'basket of goods' at various points in time. The 'basket' includes items not found in supermarkets such as interest payments, with the aim of being able to establish the effect of the rise in prices of a number of commonly purchased goods and services on the average member of the community. No-one actually 'buys' the exact 'basket', but it does give a general indication of the effect of inflation.

There are specific indices for types of assets or for types of industries that operate on the same principle, e.g. there is a Health Service Price Index which health authorities use to monitor, and account for, the effects of inflation on the goods and services they use. It's not a good idea for them to use the Retail Price Index as it would not contain the effects of increasing drug prices, for example, which may be very significant from the health authority's point of view.

Figure 24.1 The effects of inflation

Spreadsheet 24.1   The effects of inflation

	A	B	C	D	E	G
1						
2		THE EFFECTS OF INFLATION				
3						
4						
5		RATE OF INFLATION			3.50% PER ANNUM	
6						
7		NUMBER OF YEARS			20	
8						
9		UPLIFT FACTOR			1.99 = $(1+i)^n$	
10						
11		PRICE NOW			1000	
12						
13		PRICE THEN			1990	
14						
15		DIFFERENCE IN PRICE			990	
16						
17						
18						
19						
20						

D9 $ Form=$((1+D5/100)^{D7})$
Width: 16   Memory: 256   Last Col/Row:E15   ? for HELP
   1>

F1=Help F2=Cancel F9=Plot F10=View

Spreadsheet 24.2   The effects of inflation

	A	B	C	D	E	G
1						
2		THE EFFECTS OF INFLATION				
3						
4						
5		RATE OF INFLATION		3.5	% PER ANNUM	
6						
7		NUMBER OF YEARS		20		
8						
9		UPLIFT FACTOR		$((1+D5/100)^{D7})$ = $(1+i)^n$		
10						
11		PRICE NOW		1000		
12						
13		PRICE THEN		D11*D9		
14						
15		DIFFERENCE IN PRICE	D13-D11			
16						
17						
18						
19						
20						

D9 $ Form=$((1+D5/100)^{D7})$
Width: 16   Memory: 256   Last Col/Row:E15   ? for HELP
   1>
F1=Help F2=Cancel F9=Plot F10=View

24.2 Systems of current value accounting

Before we look at these current value systems it should be pointed out that many companies do not employ the pure historic cost concept. They accept that the assets most likely to be undervalued are fixed assets, whose life extends over many years. Therefore, companies often revalue these assets, taking the revaluation surplus to an asset revaluation reserve rather than the profit and loss account to reflect the situation that the increase in value is not a trading profit. However, there is no rule to say companies have to revalue assets every so many years, so they tend to revalue when it suits them to do so (it is often undertaken as a window-dressing exercise by a company before it goes to the market for finance).

The systems of current accounting can be split into those that attempt to deal with changes in the general price level and those that deal with changes in the prices of assets owned by the business. The former systems are called 'current purchasing power' accounting systems and the latter 'current value' accounting systems.

24.2.1 Current purchasing power accounting systems

Current purchasing power (CPP) accounting measures the assets and liabilities, revenues and expenses of a firm in units of constant purchasing power; that is, in units (usually pounds sterling) of currency at some common date. Let us look at an example to see how the system works. Suppose a business owns a machine which cost £1,000 ten years ago when the General Price Index was 100. If the General Price Index now stands at 250, the current purchasing power of this asset is £2,500 (i.e. the historic cost of the asset multiplied by the current General Price Index, divided by the General Price Index at the date the asset was acquired).

The system depends upon the use of some general index, such as the Retail Price Index or General Price Index.

The capital maintenance properties of CPP accounting are that CPP income is only arrived at after maintaining last year's assets at opening year prices, multiplied by the increase in the general index during the year. This can be contrasted with historic cost accounting which arrives at income after maintaining last year's assets at last year's prices, the price movements for the year being ignored.

24.2.2 Current value accounting systems

Current value accounting (CVA) values the firm's assets at some current value. Three current values (CVs) can be distinguished.

1. Current replacement cost (CRC), which represents today's cost of replacing an asset, that is, its current buying price.

2. Current net realisable value (CNRV), which represents the amount of money raised by selling the asset, less any costs of sale. The difference between CRC and CNRV is due to market imperfections.

3. Present value (PV) is the discounted value of the future net cash flows generated by the asset in its present use.

Let us look at an example of how to value an asset using present values. Suppose a business buys in a machine for £150, which it expects to generate (net) revenues in its first year of £100 and £200 in its second year of use. If the machine is worthless at the end of its second year, the rate of interest is 10 per cent p.a. and the (net) revenues arise at the end of the years, the machine has a present value of:

$$\frac{100}{(1 + 0.10)} + \frac{200}{(1 + 0.10)^2} = £256$$

The basic differences between the three systems of CVA can be seen by examining the capital maintenance concepts underlying each alternative.

Current replacement cost income is the increase in the firm's CRC of its assets after maintaining its productive capacity. The productive capacity to be maintained is measured in terms of its opening physical assets at their end-of-year replacement (buying) prices. Note that the holding gains are part of capital to be maintained if the firm is to stay in the same line of business at its current level of operations and not part of current cost operating profit.

Current net realisable value accounting values assets at their selling price less any costs of sale, in the ordinary course of business. So capital to be maintained represents opening assets valued at their opening selling values; hence there is no need to restate the opening assets at end-of-year selling values.

Present value income is the increase in the PV of the firm of the closing net assets over the opening net assets (assuming no dividends paid out or capital injected during the year). So the capital to be maintained represents the PV of net income generated from the opening net assets at the beginning of the year. It is important to note that the capital maintenance concept is incorporated into each investment decision the firm undertakes, as the NPV of the investment must be positive if the investment is to be accepted; that is, the present value of inflows must exceed the present value of outflows (the capital maintenance/investment in the project).

It is possible to combine any of the current valuation systems as an alternative system to historic cost accounting. One such system was recommended by the Accounting Standards Committee in its statement of Standard Accounting Practice 16, whose main underlying base is a combination of CPP and CRC. The idea is to capture the capital maintenance criteria of both systems, that is, to maintain the firm's physical assets, plus the general purchasing power of its net monetary assets. A similar system has been recommended by the FASB in the United States, FASB number 33.

24.3 Current accounting financial statements

Now it is appropriate to see how we can prepare a set of current value accounting statements. We will restrict our coverage to CPP and CRC financial statements.

Figure 24.2 describes the transactions of a business (and additional information) which we are going to use to prepare current value financial statements. However, before we see how to prepare the current value financial statements, we need to prepare the historic cost financial statements. These historic cost financial statements are shown in Spreadsheet 24.3. An historic cost profit of £86,000 has been earned during the year.

Now we will turn to the preparation of CPP financial statements. These statements are shown in Spreadsheet 24.4, see also Spreadsheet 24.5.

It is important to understand the distinction between monetary and non-monetary items or columns. Monetary columns are those columns which contain items whose value is fixed by contract, such as **debtors**, **creditors**, **loans** and **cash**. Let us examine these columns to clarify what we mean.

If you buy goods (i.e. **creditor**) or raise a loan you will be contractually committed to pay the agreed amount when it becomes due; you will not pay an additional amount to compensate the lender for any inflation between the date of the originating transaction and the settlement date. Therefore you will gain as you are repaying your debts in money of lesser value.

Current plc starts trading on 1 January 1988. During the year to 31 December 1988, the following transactions take place:

		£s
1 January 1988	Equity capital raised in cash	100,000
1 January 1988	Purchase machine for cash	40,000
1 January 1988	Purchase stock of 30,000 units for cash	60,000
1 July 1988	Sold 30,000 units of stock for cash	150,000
1 July 1988	Purchased 30,000 units of stock for cash	90,000

The general price index was 100 on 1 January, 120 on 1 July and 130 on 31 December. The 30,000 items of stock purchased on 1 July were still in stock at 31 December, when it would cost £120,000 to replace. The machine is expected to have a useful life of 10 years and no scrap value; it is to be depreciated using the straight-line method; it would cost £44,000 to replace on 31 December.

You are required to prepare a profit and loss account for the year ended 31 December 1988 and a balance sheet on that date using:

1. Historic cost accounting.
2. Current purchasing power accounting.
3. Replacement cost accounting.

Figure 24.2 A question to illustrate how to prepare current value financial statements

Spreadsheet 24.3 Historic cost spreadsheet

	A	B	C	D	E	F	G	H	I	J	K
4	Date	Description		Capital	Cash		Machine	Stock	P + L A/C		
6	1 Jan.	Equity Capital in Cash		-100000	100000						
8	1 Jan.	Purchase Machine for Cash			-40000		40000				
10	1 Jan.	Purchase stock for cash			-60000			60000			
12	1 July	Sale for Cash			150000				-150000		
14	1 July	Cost of Sale					-60000	60000			
16	1 July	Purchase Stock for Cash			-90000			90000			
18	31 Dec.	Depreciation					-4000		4000		
20	31 Dec.	Balance Sheet		-100000	60000		36000	90000	-86000		

Historical Cost Balance Sheet
as at 31 December 1988

	£s	£s
Fixed Assets		
Machinery		36000
Current Assets		
Stock	90000	
Debtors	0	
Cash	60000	

	150000	
Less: Current Liabilites		
Creditors	0	

Net Current Assets		150000

NET ASSETS		186000
		=========

Financed by: £s

Share Capital	100000
Profit and Loss Account	86000

	186000
	=========

Historical Cost Profit & Loss A/c
for the year ended 31 December 1988

	£s
Sales	150000
Less: Cost of Sales	60000

Gross Profit	90000
Less: Expenses	
Depreciation	4000

Net Profit	86000
	=========

Spreadsheet 24.4 Current purchasing power

	A ::	B :: C :: D :: E :: F :: G :: H :: I :: J :

```
     :  A  ::   B   ::  C  ::   D   ::  E  ::   F   ::   G   ::   H   ::   I   ::  J  :
1
2    HISTORICAL COST
3
4    Date      Description              Capital  Cash    Machine  Stock    P + L A/C
5
6    1 Jan.    Equity Capital in Cash    -100000  100000
7
8    1 Jan.    Purchase Machine for Cash         -40000   40000
9
10   1 Jan.    Purchase stock for cash           -60000            60000
11
12   1 July    Sale for Cash                     150000                     -150000
13
14   1 July    Cost of Sale                                       -60000    60000
15
16   1 July    Purchase Stock for Cash           -90000            90000
17
18   31 Dec.   Depreciation                               -4000              4000
19
20   ------------------------------------------------------------------------------
21
22   31 Dec.   Balance Sheet            -100000  60000    36000    90000   -86000
23
24
25
26
27   General Price Indexes:     1 Jan.   1 July   31 Dec.
28
29                                100      120      130
30
31   CPP UPLIFT FACTOR            1.30     1.08     1.00
32
33
34   CURRENT PURCHASING POWER
35
36   Date      Description              Capital  Cash    Machine  Stock    P + L A/C  Monetary
37                                                                                    Item
38   1 Jan.    Equity Capital in Cash    -100000  100000
39             cpp adj: 100(130/100-1)   -30000                                        30000
40   1 Jan.    Purchase Machine for Cash         -40000   40000
41             cpp adj: 40(130/100-1)                     12000                        -12000
42   1 Jan.    Purchase stock for cash           -60000            60000
43             cpp adj: 60(130/100-1)                              18000               -18000
44   1 July    Sale for Cash                     150000                     -150000
45             cpp:adj. 150(130/120-1)                                      -12500     12500
46   1 July    Cost of Sale                                       -60000    60000
47             cpp adj.:60(130/120-1)                             -18000    18000
48   1 July    Purchase Stock for Cash           -90000            90000
49             cpp adj. 90(130/120-1)                              7500                -7500
50   31 Dec.   Depreciation                               -4000              4000
51             cpp adj: 4(130/100-1)                      -1200              1200
52   ------------------------------------------------------------------------------
53
54   31 Dec.   Balance Sheet            -130000  60000    46800    97500   -79300      5000
55
56             Transfer of M.I.                                              5000      -5000
57   ------------------------------------------------------------------------------
58
59   31 Dec.   Balance Sheet            -130000  60000    46800    97500   -74300         0
60   ==============================================================================
```

If you sell goods (i.e. **debtors**) on credit, your customer should pay you the contracted amount when the debt becomes due; he will not pay you an additional amount to compensate you for any inflation between the date of the sale and the settlement date. Therefore you will lose out. Cash is of course a monetary item whose purchasing power falls during inflation, so holders of cash lose out.

Non-monetary columns contain transactions whose value is assumed to keep pace with inflation, so no gain or loss will result. Examples of non-monetary columns are **fixed assets, stock** and **equity**.

Now we can distinguish whether a column is monetary or non-monetary, we can identify three types of transaction as follows:

1. One which has both entries in monetary columns.

2. One which has both entries in non-monetary columns.

3. One which has one entry in a monetary column and one entry in a non-monetary column.

Transaction type 1 has two entries whose values are fixed in money terms, so the amounts recorded are identical with those recorded in historic cost accounting. Transaction type 2 has two entries whose values are assumed to keep pace with inflation, so the CPP value of both entries is uplifted by the amount of inflation which has occurred since the transaction took place. Since we are concerned with general inflation, a general price index is used. We can define the CPP adjustment as shown in Figure 24.3.

Transaction type 3 has one monetary and one non-monetary entry. The monetary entry's value is the same as its historic cost equivalent, while the non-monetary entry is uplifted by the above formula.

Where does the uplift get recorded? We open up a new column called **monetary items** and record the uplift generated as a result of transaction type 3 in that column. If the entry to the monetary item column is positive, it represents a loss (i.e. the firm is holding monetary assets), and if the entry is negative it represents a gain (i.e. the firm is holding monetary liabilities).

Now let's go through the transactions making the CCP adjustments as necessary:

1. Equity capital was introduced on 1 January, so the CPP adjustment is:

$$£100,000*[(130/100) - 1] = £30,000$$

$$\text{Transaction HC value} * \left(\left(\frac{\text{general price index at date the transaction occurred}}{\text{general price index at the year end}} \right) - 1 \right)$$

Figure 24.3 Holding gains

An additional £30,000 is recorded in the **capital** column (a non-monetary column) and the corresponding entry is recorded in the new column called **monetary items**, as this is a type 3 transaction. It could not be recorded as an increase in cash, as cash is a monetary item whose value is fixed irrespective of changes in the price level. Therefore the debit of £30,000 represents a loss on holding equity capital as cash for the year. The total of the **monetary item** column is eventually taken to the profit and loss account.

2. The same procedure is used to record the purchase of the machine and the stock on 1 January.

3. On 1 July the company sells for £150,000 cash the stock it purchased on 1 January. The CCP uplift on sales is therefore from the date the sale occurred (i.e. 1 July) to the year end (i.e. 31 December). It is calculated as follows:

$$£15,000*[(130/120) - 1] = £12,500$$

This amount is recorded in the **profit and loss** column (a non-monetary column) as a negative figure, with the corresponding entry recorded in the **monetary items** column as a debit. It is entered as a positive figure in the **monetary items** column as it represents the loss incurred in holding £150,000 cash from 1 July to 31 December, during inflationary times.

4. The cost of goods sold CPP adjusted represents the uplift required to clear out the uplifted value of stock from the **stock** column into the **profit and loss account** column. It is a type 2 transaction, so there is no entry recorded in the **monetary item** column.

5. On 1 July more stock is purchased for cash and remains unsold at the year end. Since the CPP value of this stock rises to £97,500, an adjustment of £7,500 is required to uplift this stock by £7,500, hence a positive entry is placed in the **stock** column. The corresponding entry is recorded in the **monetary item** column as the stock was purchased for cash; this is to reflect the situation that the company has gained £7,500 because it held stock (a non-monetary asset whose value is assumed to keep pace with general inflation) rather than cash (a monetary asset whose value does not keep pace with general inflation).

6. The CPP value of the machine has been increased so its depreciation charge also need to be increased. The depreciation CPP adjustment is:

$$£1,200 = £4,000*[(130/100) - 1]$$

There is a good argument to use the 1 July price index instead of the 1 January price index since depreciation is incurred over the whole year, so if the rate of price increases is reasonably constant during the year then the half-year index will be appropriate.

7. Since the CPP depreciation adjustment is a type 2 transaction there is no monetary item entry. The credit is recorded in the **machine** column and the debit in the **profit and loss account** column.

8. Finally all the columns are totalled and the **monetary items** total is transferred to the **profit and loss account** column. It is a debit balance of £5,000, representing a net loss due to £60,000 cash being held between 1 July and 31 December, that is, the 1 July sales of £150,000 less the 1 July purchases of £90,000. The monetary item adjustment can be calculated as follows:

$$£5,000 = £60,000*[(130/120) - 1]$$

See the **cash** column to prove this for yourself. There was no cash balance held between 1 January and 1 July, so no loss or profit arose on monetary items during this period.

The CPP profit figure is £74,300, compared with the historic cost profit figure of £55,600; the difference is due to general inflation.

The balance sheet figures are all different, except for cash, which is the only monetary item whose value is fixed irrespective of changes in the general price level. All the other balances are non-monetary items whose values are assumed under CPP accounting to vary directly with changes in the general price level.

Now we will turn our attention to the preparation of CCAs. The workings are shown in Spreadsheet 24.6, together with the CC financial statements. The objective of the exercise is to record transactions at their current cost, that is, the amount of funds it would cost the firm to replace the assets, either:

a. at the date they were sold (e.g. stock) or used in production (e.g. fixed assets); or

b. at the year end.

Let us apply this logic to our current company's 1988 transactions:

1. The equity capital of £100,000 is the cash invested in the business by the owners; since it is an investment in cash there is no CCA adjustment, as cash has the same value when it is used or unused (i.e. at the year end) as when it was acquired by the company. Therefore any transactions involving cash do not require a CCA adjustment.

2. The machine costs £44,000 to replace at the year end, so an additional £4,000 is required in the **machine** column to raise its recorded value to its CC. The corresponding entry is recorded in a **holding gains** column to reflect the gain accruing to the company from holding the machine for the entire year.

3. the stock purchased on 1 January for £60,000 is sold on 1 July when it would cost the company £90,000 to replace. Therefore the **stock** column requires £30,000 uplift to ensure the stock is recorded at £90,000, its current cost. The corresponding entry is recorded in the **holding gains** column for the same

Spreadsheet 24.5 Current purchasing power statements

	A		B		C		D		E		F		G		H		I		J		K	
61																						
62																						
63																						
64			CPP Balance Sheet												CPP Profit and Loss Account							
65			as at 31 December 1988												for the year ended 31 December 1988							
66																						
67									£s		£s										£s	
68			Fixed Assets																			
69																						
70			Machinery								46800				Sales						162500	
71																						
72			Current Assets												Less: Cost of Sales						78000	
73																					---------	
74			Stock						97500						Gross Profit						84500	
75			Debtors						0													
76			Cash						60000						Less: Expenses							
77									---------													
78									157500						Depreciation						5200	
79																					---------	
80			Less: Current Liabilites																		79300	
81																						
82			Creditors						0						Monetary Items						5000	
83									---------												---------	
84			Net Current Assets								157500				Net Profit						74300	
85											---------										=========	
86			NET ASSETS								204300											
87											=========											
88																						
89			Financed by:						£s													
90																						
91			Share Capital						130000													
92																						
93			Profit and Loss Account						74300													
94																						
95									---------													
96									204300													
97									=========													

reason as the machine uplift was recorded as a holding gain; that is, it represents the gain accruing to the company from holding the stock from acquisition to sale/use.

4. On 1 July this stock is sold for £150,000; since the £150,000 represents the current value of the sale no CC ajustment is required. Also the stock has already been recorded at its CC in the **stock** column so we take out of that column £90,000 into the **profit and loss** column to account for the current cost of the stock sold.

5. On 1 July another purchase of stock is made for £90,000. This stock remains unsold at the year end so we are required to record it at its current cost (which is £120,000) at that date. Therefore an extra £30,000 is added to the **stock** column, reflecting this new replacement cost. A corresponding £30,000 is recorded as a holding gain.

6. The final transaction to examine is depreciation. Since one-tenth of the machine has been used up during the year, the CC depreciation is £4,400. The uplift of £400 is deducted from the **machine** column and a corresponding amount recorded as a profit and loss charge.

7. The spreadsheet is summed to derive the balance sheet at 31 December. The profit figure is £55,600, compared with the historic cost profit of £86,000. The reduction is due to the increased cost of replacing stock (£30,000) and the part of the machine used (£400). The balance sheet records assets at replacement cost. The stock is therefore valued at £90,000 and the machine at £39,600. Cash is still at £60,000 and capital still at £100,000, as their historic and current costs are by definition identical.

The holding gains reserve of £64,000 is created to house the increase in asset values during the year. It can be analysed into its realised and unrealised components (Figure 24.4).

Realised holding gains are those that relate to stock sold and machinery used, that is, those transactions which have passed through the profit and loss account. Unrealised holding gains are those amounts which represent the increase in asset values of those assets held at the year end, that is, the unsold stock and the unused machinery.

	£	£
Realised		
Stock	30,000	
Machine	400	
		30,400
Unrealised		
Stock	30,000	
Machine	3,600	
		33,600
		64,000

Figure 24.4   Realised and unrealised components

Spreadsheet 24.6 Current cost accounting

	A	B	C	D	E	F	G	H	I	J
1										
2										
3										
4	Date	Description			Capital	Cash	Machine	Stock	P + L A/C	Holding
5										Gains
6	1 Jan.	Equity Capital in Cash			-100000	100000				
7										
8	1 Jan.	Purchase Machine for Cash				-40000	40000			
9		cc adj:					4000			-4000
10	1 Jan.	Purchase stock for cash				-60000		60000		
11										
12	1 July	Sale for Cash				150000			-150000	
13										
14	1 July	Cost of Sale						-60000	60000	
15		cc adj:						30000	-30000	
16	1 July	Purchase Stock for Cash				-90000		90000		
17		cc adj:						30000		-30000
18	31 Dec.	Depreciation					-4000		4000	
19		cc adj:					-400		400	
20	------	------	------	------	------	------	------	------	------	------
21										
22		31 Dec. Balance Sheet			-100000	60000	39600	120000	-55600	-64000

	A	B	C	D	E	F	G	H	I	J
1										
2										
3										
4	Date	Description			Capital	Cash	Machine	Stock	P + L A/C	Holding
5										Gains
6	1 Jan.	Equity Capital in Cash			-F6	100000				
7										
8	1 Jan.	Purchase Machine for Cash				-40000	-F8			
9		cc adj:					4000			-G9
10	1 Jan.	Purchase stock for cash				-60000		-F10		
11										
12	1 July	Sale for Cash				150000			-F12	
13										
14	1 July	Cost of Sale						-60000	-H14	
15		cc adj:						30000	-I15	
16	1 July	Purchase Stock for Cash				-90000		-F16		
17		cc adj:						30000		-H17
18	31 Dec.	Depreciation					-4000		-G18	
19		cc adj:					-400		-G19	
20	------	------	------	------	------	------	------	------	------	------
21										
22		31 Dec. Balance Sheet			SUM(E6:E19)	SUM(F6:F19)	SUM(G6:G19)	SUM(H6:H19)	SUM(I6:I19)	SUM(J6:J19)

Spreadsheet 24.7 Worksho, 24.1: Current cost profit and loss accounts and balance sheet

	A		B		C		D		E		F		G		H		I		J		K	
26			CCA Balance Sheet												CCA Profit and Loss Account							
27			as at 31 December 1988												for the year ended 31 December 1988							
28																						
29									£s		£s										£s	
30			Fixed Assets																			
31																						
32			Machinery								39600				Sales						150000	
33																						
34			Current Assets												Less: Cost of Sales						90000	
35																					---------	
36			Stock						120000						Gross Profit						60000	
37			Debtors						0													
38			Cash						60000						Less: Expenses							
39									---------													
40									180000						Depreciation						4400	
41																					---------	
42			Less: Current Liabilites												Net Profit						55600	
43																					=========	
44			Creditors						0													
45									---------													
46			Net Current Assets								180000											
47											---------											
48			NET ASSETS								219600											
49											=========											
50																						
51			Financed by:								£s											
52																						
53			Share Capital								100000											
54																						
55			Profit and Loss Account								55600											
56																						
57			Holding Gains								64000											
58																						
59											---------											
60											219600											
61											=========											

CHECKLIST

Having completed Chapter 24, you should be able to:

■ discuss the imperfections of historic cost accounting;

■ calculate the effect different rates of inflation have on assets;

■ outline some of the alternative accounting systems which attempt to cope with changing prices;

■ apply the principles of two alternative accounting systems so as to produce accounts adjusted for price changes.

Workshop 24.1: inflation accounting

One of the most significant advantages of using the spreadsheet approach is the ability to handle 'what if?' questions, once a working model has been constructed. We will ask a series of such questions in this workshop, which relates to examples in the chapter.

1. What if there was no inflation during the year?

2. What if the inflation rate was 4 per cent per annum?

3. What if there was 30 per cent deflation?

4. What if there was 100 per cent inflation?

5. What if the machine would cost £80,000 to replace at the year end?

6. What if the stock held at the year end would cost £180,000 to replace at the year end?

7. What if the machine would cost £20,000 to replace at the year end?

8. What if the stock held at the year end would cost £45,000 to replace at the year end?

You are required to adjust your spreadsheet models to reflect the above conditions and discuss the effect on the company's financial position and trading performance.

Answers

The results of situations 1, 2, 3 and 4 can be summarised as shown in Table 24.1.
Situations 1, 2, 3 and 4 only affect CPP accounts as the general level of prices are being changed.

Table 24.1   *CPP adjustment*

The situation would be as follows:

	Historic cost	30% inflation	(1) 0% inflation	(2) 4% inflation	(3) 30% deflation	(4) 100% inflation
Net worth	186	204	186	189	164	252
Net profit	86	74	86	85	94	52

Situations 1, 2, 3 and 4 have no effect on replacement cost accounting as the system ignores changes in the general rate of inflation; it is designed only to reflect changes in the replacement cost of those specific assets held by the company during the year.

1. The higher the inflation rate, the higher the reported net worth of the company. Any deflation decreases the reported net worth of the company. However, the net worth does not rise by the same percentage as the rate of inflation since:
   a. only the non-monetary assets are uplifted by the inflation rate; monetary assets remain at their historic cost valuation. Therefore the larger the percentage of net assets held in monetary form, the less the net worth of the company will increase as a result of a given rate of inflation.
   b. non-monetary assets are only uplifted by the amount of inflation which has taken place from their date of acquisition to the accounting year end. For example, the stock held at the year end was purchased on 1 July, so it is only uplifted by inflation which occurred in the second half of the year.

2. The reported net profit falls as the inflation rate increases (and increases as a result of any deflation). However, the percentage fall in net profit is not as large as the rate of inflation due to:
   a. sales being uplifted by the amount of inflation which has occurred between the date of sale and the accounting year end, while costs of sales are uplifted by the amount of inflation which has occurred between the date the stock was purchased and the year end (which is almost certainly a longer time period)
   b. the monetary adjustment.

Situations 5, 6, 7, and 8 have no effect on the CPP accounts as the system is only designed to reflect changes in the general rate of inflation. That is, it ignores specific changes in asset values.

The results of situations 5, 6, 7 and 8 are summarised in Table 24.2

Table 24.2   *CCA net worth and net profit summary*

The situation would be as follows:

	Historic cost	CCA as per question	(5)	(6)	(7)	(8)
Net worth (£'000s)	186	219.6	252	279.6	196.2	144.6
Net profit (£'000s)	86	55.6	52	55.6	56.2	55.6

1. If the machine doubles in value by the year end, the net worth of the company increases by £32,400. It does not increase by the full amount of the value change or holding gain (i.e. £36,000 = £40,000 less £4,000) as the depreciation

adjustment increases by £3,600 to reflect some consumption of this increased cost. Hence the fall in net profit from £55,600 to £52,000.

2. If the value of stock doubles by the year end the results are explained in a similar way to 1 above. However, the company's net worth and holding gain increase by the full amount of the value change (i.e. £60,000 = £90,000 − £30,000) as none of this cost has been used up by the year end.

3. If the value of the machine halves, the net worth of the company falls as do the holding gains (if there were no other holding gains available for off-set there would be a holding loss).

4. If the value of stock fell, the net worth and holding gains fall by the amount of this value decrease.

Selected questions and exercises

Question 24.1
A machine cost £30,000 on 1 January 1980. The General Price Index was 100 on 1 January 1980. The rate of inflation was 18 per cent per annum.

1. What is the current cost of the machine on 31 December 1990?
2. What is the current value of the machine if the rate of inflation was 15 per cent?
3. What is the current value of the machine if the rate of inflation was 5 per cent?
4. What is the current value of the machine if the rate of inflation was −5 per cent?
5. What is the current value of the machine if the rate of inflation was 10 per cent between 1 January 1980 and 13 December 1985 and 15 per cent between 1 January 1985 and 31 December 1990?

No solution provided.

Question 24.2
Sally plc starts trading on 1 January 1988. During the year to 31 December 1988, the transactions shown in Table 24.3 take place.

Table 24.3 *Details of the accounts of Sally plc*

		£
1 January 1988	Equity capital raised in cash	600,000
1 January 1988	Purchased machine for cash	140,000
1 January 1988	Purchased stock of 60,000 units for cash	430,000
1 July 1988	Sold 60,000 units of stock for cash	750,000
1 July 1988	Purchased 60,000 units of stock for cash	500,000

The general price index was 100 on 1 January, 150 on 1 July and 180 on 31 December. The 60,000 items of stock purchased on 1 July were still in stock at 31 December, when they would cost £800,000 to replace. The machine is expected to have a useful life of five years and no scrap value; it is to be depreciated using the straight-line method; it would cost £200,000 to replace on 31 December.

You are required to prepare a profit and loss account for the year ended 31 December 1988 and a balance sheet on that date using the following methods:

a. historic cost accounting;
b. current purchasing power accounting;
c. replacement cost accounting.

No solution provided.

25 || *Auditing*

Students of financial accounting are often required to have a basic understanding of the related subject of auditing. This chapter will aim to provide such an understanding. Firstly, the nature of auditing will be discussed. Secondly, the stages of an audit will be outlined.

25.1 What is an audit?

An audit has been defined as:

> The INDEPENDENT examination of, and expression of OPINION on, the financial statements of an enterprise by an APPOINTED auditor in pursuance of that appointment and in compliance with any relevant STATUTORY obligation.
>
> The responsibility for the preparation of the financial statements and the presentation of the information therein rests with the management, the auditor's responsibility is to REPORT on the financial statements as presented by management.
>
> Source: The Auditing Standards Committee (this is a committee composed of representatives of the accounting professional institutes that deal with

auditing and publish auditing standards in much the same way as the Accounting Standards Committee deals with accounting and publishes accounting standards).

This definition, like many other definitions, when read on its own does not tell us very much.[1] We need to highlight and discuss the important words to see what they mean in an auditing context.

1. Independent examination. The auditor's job is to examine the financial statements of an organisation so that they can be relied upon by certain interested people who need to make important decisions concerning the organisation. If this examination is to be most useful it must be carried out by a person independent of the organisation (which includes the accountants who prepare the financial statements), who has no vested interest in the financial statements showing a false position.

What does independence mean? Independence means not depending upon others for one's opinion and making one's own decisions. So if the financial statements do not show a true and fair (see Section 2 for a discussion of this phrase) representation of the events which occurred during the year, the auditor can be relied upon to report this.

How can auditors prove they are independent? This is not as easy as it may seem, as independence is, above all, a state of mind. Therefore, in order to gain the confidence of the users of financial statements, the auditors must make sure they are seen to be independent. This may be achieved by ensuring that the following conditions are maintained.

a. Capital is not owned by, or loans made to, the organisation. If the auditors own capital in the organisation, they will probably have a vested interest in ensuring the financial statements show a high profit and if loans are made, a vested interest in the statement showing a sound liquidity position.

b. The fees receivable for carrying out the audit are based upon the amount and difficulty of the work done. Therefore their remuneration is objectively determined and can be accounted for and they cannot be accused of receiving payments for concealing important information.

c. The auditors do not prepare the financial statements, since if they did they would have a vested interest in covering up any mistakes and reduce the likelihood of spotting errors.

d. In fact, the auditors should not have any other financial relationship with the organisation, which may compromise their position. For example, carrying out tax or consultancy work for their clients or accepting a loan.

e. The fees receivable from one client should not make up an unduly large part of the auditor's total income, as this would put considerable pressure on the auditor. They would not want to upset the client by giving an unfavourable opinion and run the risk of losing the appointment.

f.   Personal relationships between client and auditor can put pressure on the auditor to avoid submitting an unfavourable opinion. Therefore the client and auditor should not be members of the same family or close friends. This latter point does present problems as a close relationship is required between auditor and client in order for the auditor to obtain all the information and explanations needed for an opinion on the financial statements to be formed.

g.   The auditor requires some protection from being removed from office by the client if an unfavourable opinion is given.

2.   Expression of an opinion. For companies, the auditor has to decide whether their financial statements show a true and fair view and report this to the members of the companies. For a discussion of the meaning of true and fair to see Figure 25.1. Also, the report must state whether the financial statements comply with the requirements of the Companies Act.

The Companies Act also requires the auditors to include in their report details concerning the following, if they are not satisfied that:

a.   proper accounting records have been kept;

b.   proper returns from branches (if the organisation has any) not visited by the auditor have been made;

c.   the balance sheet and profit and loss account are in agreement with the records;

d.   all information and explanations required for the purpose of the audit have been received.

If the company fails to follow the requirements of any of the SSAPs the auditors are required to note this omission in their report.

The auditor is also under some obligation to detect errors and fraud. If these errors and frauds are so significant that they prevent the financial statements showing a true and fair view then the auditor is under a statutory obligation to report these problems. However, even if they are not so significant, and they only come across them in the course of their work, they should still be brought to the attention of the organisation's management, usually by way of a written letter (this is referred to as 'the management letter' or 'letter of weakness').

3.   Statutory obligation. The Companies Act 1985 requires all limited companies to be audited annually. This has been a requirement since 1844. This came into being as a check on directors who were often under pressure to present an optimistic picture of the state of the company's affairs to the shareholders.

There are many advantages to be gained from having financial statements audited:

a.   the audited financial statements can be relied upon by the owners of the organisation. This reduces the possibility for disputes between providers of capital;

The Companies Act does not define the terms 'true' and 'fair', so it is up to the auditor to interpret its meaning. They do so with reference to the following criteria:

1. Materiality – it is accepted that the auditor cannot examine every single transaction undertaken by the organisation during the year, since to do so would lead to ridiculously large audit fees. Therefore the auditor examines (hopefully representative) samples of transactions and from the results of these samples draws conclusions about the overall financial statements. This approach is acceptable to users of financial statements as it is generally accepted that they are only interested in material errors, that is, errors which would lead them to make different decisions. For example, if a shareholder was considering whether to sell his shares in a company he may look to the company's financial statements for assistance. If the profit figure was large he may decide to keep his shares. It may later transpire that this profit figure is materially overstated due to an undetected error, not found by the auditor. In this case the shareholder may have a case to sue the auditor. On the other hand if the error was not significant, in that the shareholder would have kept the shares even if the financial statements had reported the adjusted (and lower) profit figure, he would not have a good case against the auditor.

   If no material errors are found, then the audit report is termed 'clean'. If material errors are found during the course of the audit and the financial statements not adjusted, the audit report is termed 'qualified', as it contains a description of the error together with details of how it would affect the financial statements.
2. Generally accepted accounting principles are used to prepare the financial statements. These principles should be consistently applied, appropriate to the needs of the organisation and stated along with the financial statements.
3. SSAPs should be consistently applied.
4. The organisation should keep proper accounting records which fully explain the transactions which have occurred during the year. The financial statements should be prepared from these accounting records.
5. Company financial statements need to conform to the prescribed layout requirements of the Companies Act.
6. The descriptions in the financial statements should not be misleading or ambiguous.
7. All relevant information is disclosed.

Figure 25.1   True and fair view

    b.   the Inland Revenue will place more reliance upon audited financial statements;

    c.   it will be easier for organisations to raise loans, for example from banks;

    d.   the auditors can provide useful advice on how to administer the organisation, as a result of their experience of many different types of business.

It can be seen that many of these advantages are just as applicable to other forms of organisations as well as limited companies (e.g. sole traders, partnerships, clubs and societies and public sector organisations). For example, in the case of partnerships, when a new partner is admitted an audited set of accounts is useful to determine capital and profit splits. Therefore it is not unusual to find the financial statements of organisations other than limited companies being subject to audits.

The audit so far described is often referred to as an 'external' audit as the auditor is not an employee of the company. This term is used to distinguish the role from that of the 'internal' auditor, who is an employee of the company. An internal auditor is employed to examine the economy, efficiency and effectiveness of the organisation's systems of internal control. See Figure 25.2 for an outline of the role of the internal auditor.

The managers are responsible for preparing the financial statements. They may require help in this task if the organisation is small and does not employ an accountant. The financial statements are prepared for the owners of the organisation – this is the idea of accountability we met in Chapter 1. The owners appoint managers to run their organisation and auditors who make an independent examination of the financial statements (i.e. the audit).

If the financial statements are found not to be true and fair and the organisation suffers loss, then the shareholders have redress against both the managers and the auditors. As the auditors are likely to be the wealthier of the two, the shareholders are likely to concentrate their actions against the auditors. The auditors are contractually bound to 'exercise a reasonable standard of care' in carrying out their work. If such standards of care are not exercised, they will be responsible for any resultant loss.

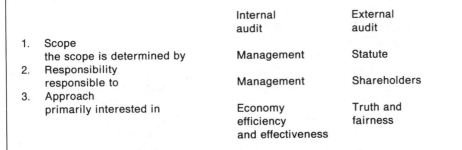

The internal auditor is primarily concerned with:

1. Economy – this ensures that purchases of goods and services (including labour) are made at the lowest cost and adequate quality.
2. Efficiency – this ensures maximum output is achived from a given level of purchases (or a given level of output is achieved from minimum purchases).
3. Effectiveness – this ensures the organisation is meeting its objectives. They could be profit maximisation, customer service, product quality, etc.

The major differences between the internal and external auditor are:

		Internal audit	External audit
1.	Scope the scope is determined by	Management	Statute
2.	Responsibility responsible to	Management	Shareholders
3.	Approach primarily interested in	Economy efficiency and effectiveness	Truth and fairness

Figure 25.2 The internal auditor

25.2   Stages of an audit

In order to understand what a statutory audit entails it is useful to outline the stages of an audit. These stages are as follows.

1. Appointment. It is necessary to ensure that the auditor is properly appointed. The members of a company appoint an auditor to hold office until the next annual general meeting. The directors are empowered to fill any temporary vacancy should it arise (e.g. due to the death of the auditor). The auditor should obtain the previous client's permission to contact the previous auditor, to ask if there are any reasons the appointment should not be undertaken. The auditor must ensure that the client is clear about the terms of reference for the audit work; this is usually done through a letter of engagement, detailing the terms of the work and the basis upon which the auditor's fee is to be costed.

2. Planning. Like any other major piece of work the audit must be planned. This involves estimating the type, difficulty and time the work will take to complete and allocating staff of suitable levels of training and experience to the tasks. Once the initial plan has been drawn up, it is necessary to monitor the progress of the work continually and adjust the plan as necessary. The plan is likely to involve a number of visits to the client during the year; probably an initial interim visit and a final visit after the year end once the financial statements have been prepared.

3. Ascertain the accounting system. The auditor needs to collect and record details of the client's accounting system through observing how the system works and discussions with client empolyees. Diagrams are used to record the systems. Walk-through tests are undertaken which involve following individual transactions through the system to confirm that the system as recorded is correct.

4. Evaluate the accounting system. The auditor then evaluates the recorded accounting system to see if it can be relied upon to produce accurate accounting records. This is done by highlighting important internal controls. If adequate controls are in place tests are carried out to ensure they have been working properly throughout the year; these tests are referred to as 'compliance tests'.

5. Substantive tests. These are then carried out to obtain direct evidence of the accuracy, completeness and validity of the transactions and balances contained in the accounting records. These tests can be either 'vouching' or 'verification' tests. Vouching tests involve checking transactions recorded in the records back to their underlying documentation (i.e. tests to see if the recorded transactions are not overstated) and checking from the underlying documentation forward to the recorded transactions (i.e. tests to see if the

recorded transactions are understated). See Chapter 11 for descriptions of the underlying documentation used by businesses to support transactions. Verification tests are used by the auditor to check that assets and liabilities exist as described by the balances in the accounting records.

It will be necessary to check that there are not arithmetic errors in the accounting records.

6. Management letter. It is good audit practice to prepare a letter for the management of the organisation which details any weaknessess found during the evaluation of the accounting system and substantive testing stages of the audit. The weaknesses are noted together with descriptions of the risks involved and the auditor's recommendations for countering the weaknessess.

7. Checking financial statements. Once the auditor is satisfied that there are no material errors (or all material errors have been corrected) in the accounting records, the closing balances are agreed to the financial statements to ensure they have been correctly extracted.

8. Checking disclosure requirements. It is necessary to ensure the financial statements of limited companies comply with the relevant disclosure requirements:

Companies Act layouts: see Chapter 20;
SSAPs: see Chapter 19;
Stock Exchange disclosure requirements if the company is listed;
Any other relevant disclosure requirements.

These tasks are usually done with the use of checklists.

9. Analytical review. The auditor has now satisfied himself that the individual balances in the financial statements contain no material errors; now it is necessary to ensure that these figures fit together to make some accounting sense. It is this review that enables the auditor to stand back from the detail he has been concerned with to date and review the overall picture presented to the users of the financial statements.

The comparison of this year's figures with their corresponding preceding years' amounts is useful as it can reveal significant changes which require explanation. Ratio analysis (see Chapter 22) can also be employed to highlight significant changes. The client's senior management should be able to provide satisfactory explanations to the auditor's questions.

10. Formulate the final audit opinion. It is now time for the auditor to formulate his opinion as to whether the financial statements show a true and fair view and sign the audit report. The auditor should have obtained sufficient evidence in order to form such an opinion. Inevitably the decision will not always be clear cut, in which case the auditor will have to use his skill, experience and judgement to come to a decision.

25.3 Examples of audit reports

1. An unqualified audit report
   AUDITOR'S REPORT TO THE MEMBERS OF...
   We have audited the financial statements on pages ... to ... in accordance with approved auditing standards.

   In our opinion the financial statements give a true and fair view of the state of the company's affairs at 31 December 19 ... and of its profit/loss and source and application of funds for the year then ended and comply with the Companies Act 1985.

2. Qualified audit report
   An audit report can be qualified for all kinds of reasons, of which the following is an example. Here the audit report is qualified since there is doubt as to the company's continued survival.

   AUDITOR'S REPORT TO THE MEMBERS OF...
   We have audited the financial statements on pages ... to ... in accordance with approved auditing standards.

   As stated in note ..., the company is currently negotiating long-term facilities to replace the loan of £... which becomes repayable on ... (a date early in the next financial year); continuation of the company's activities is dependent upon a successful outcome to these negotiations. The financial statements have been drawn up on a going concern basis which assumes that adequate facilities will be obtained.

   Subject to a satisfactory outcome of the negotiations referred to above, in our opinion the financial statements give a true and fair view of the state of the company's affairs at 31 December 19 ... and of its profit/loss and source and application of funds for the year then ended and comply with the Companies Act 1985.

For detailed descriptions of qualified audit reports see the auditing standard on audit reports.

25.4 Notes

1. The major problem with constructing definitions is to ensure they are broad enough to contain an adequate description of the concept they are attempting to define while not being so broad that they could include other concepts.

This is just about an impossible task, as different people have different ideas as to what is being defined, so inevitably when a definition is decided upon by a committee it becomes a compromise between these two aims.

CHECKLIST

Having completed Chapter 25, you should be able to:

- understand the meaning of the term 'audit';
- appreciate what is meant by 'independence' and why this is important;
- describe the contents of a typical audit report;
- exhibit an awareness of the role of the internal auditor;
- identify the stages of an audit.

Selected questions and exercises

Question 25.1

1. What is an audit and what advantages do companies derive from audits?
2. Explain what you understand by the term 'internal control'.
3. Give five examples of internal control with which you are familiar.

No solution provided.

Questions 25.2

1. G. Fallon's book-keeper is unable to balance his accounts. With the help of his accountant he discovers the following items which enable him to balance:
   a. Discount of £70 has been received but not yet posted to the nominal ledger.
   b. In the closing stock sheets, 400 items have been entered at £15 per 10 instead of £15 per 100.
   c. The sales day book sub-total of £1,784 has been carried forward as £1,874.
   d. An item of machinery costing £9,120 has been incorrectly entered into goods for resale. Normal depreciation is 10 per cent on original cost.
   e. Insurance premiums paid include £138 for next year.
   f. An invoice of £320 for fuel relates to deliveries after the end of the accounting period.
   g. An invoice of £18 has been correctly entered in the day book, but posted to the ledger as £81.

You are required to indicate:

  (i) the effect on the profit;
  (ii) the effect on the relevant balance sheet items;
  (iii) the original difference.

2.   Outline the types of error which may affect a true and fair view being shown in the financial statements.

3.   Which internal controls would obviate these errors?

No solution provided.

Part E

Solutions to selected questions and exercises

Solution to Question 3.1

	A	C	D	E	F	G	H	I
		Cash	Capital	Bank	Motor Van	Stock	Creditors	Loan: J.Smith
6	Starting the business	2000	-2000					
8	Deposit Cash in Bank	-1500		1500				
10	Purchase of Goods (Cash)	-450				450		
12	Loan: J.Smith			1000				-1000
14	Purchase of Goods (Credit)					500	·500	
17	Total (or Balance Sheet)	50	-2000	2500	0	950	-500	-1000

Solution to Question 3.2

	A	C	D	E	F	G	H	I
		Cash	Capital	Bank	Stock	Van Sales Ltd	S.Jones	Motor Van
6	Starting the business	10000	-10000					
8	Deposit Cash in Bank	-4000		4000				
10	Purchase of Goods (Credit)				5000		-5000	
12	Motor Van (Credit)					-5000		5000
14	Purchase of Goods (Cash)	-500			500			
16	Pay Creditor			-3000			3000	
18	Total (or Balance Sheet)	5500	-10000	1000	5500	-5000	-2000	5000

Solution to Question 3.3

	A	C	D	E	F	G	H	I	J
		Cash	Capital	Bank	Stock	Grumpits	I.C.I	Vehicles	Loan
6	Starting the business	250000	-250000						
8	Deposit Cash in Bank	-200000		200000					
10	Purchase of Goods (Credit)				200000	-200000			
12	Motor Vehicles (Credit)						-105000	105000	
14	Motor Vehicles (Cash)	-40000						40000	
16	Loan			100000					-100000
18	Pay Creditor			-180000			180000		
20	Total (or Balance Sheet)	10000	-250000	120000	200000	-105000	-20000	145000	-100000

508 Solutions to questions and exercises

Solution to Question 4.3

	A	B	C	D	E	F	G	H	I	J
1										
2										
3	Description	Cash	Capital	Bank	Stock	T.Run	D.Opal	G.Lime	Van	
4										
5	Start buisiness	12,500	-12,500							
6										
7	Opened bank a/c	-10,000		10,000						
8										
9	Purchases				900	-900				
10					5,600		-5,600			
11					4,500			-4,500		
12										
13	Bought Van								8,790	
14										
15	Sale									
16										
17	Cost of Sale				-3,000					
18										
19	Sale	12,000								
20										
21	Cost of Sale				-8,000					
22										
23	Equipment	-5,431								
24										
25	Loan	10,000								
26										
27	Purchases				4,320		-4,320			
28					3,579			-3,579		
29					5,600					
30										
31	Purchases	-4,376			4,376					
32										
33	Rent	-450								
34										
35	Sales									
36										
37										
38										
39	Cost of Sales				-15,000					
40										
41	Receipt			5,000						
42										
43	Payments			-900		900				
44				-5,000			5,000			
45				-4,250				4,250		
46										
47	Payment			-8,790						
48										
49	Receipts			4,400						
50				11,000						
51										
52	Machine									
53	---------									
54	Balance Sheet	14,243	-12,500	11,460	2,875	0	-4,920	-3,829	8,790	
55	=========									

	K	L	M	N	O	P	Q	R	S	T	U
	T.Cooke	F.Smith	Profit	Equipment	Loan	K.Star	G.William	H.Herbert	Machine	K.Kelly	
	-8,790										
		5,600	-5,600								
			3,000								
			-12,000								
			8,000								
				5,431							
					-10,000						
						-5,600					
			450								
		4,500	-4,500								
			-12,980				12,980				
			-13,000					13,000			
			15,000								
		-5,000									
	8,790										
		-4,400									
							-11,000				
									4,500	-4,500	
	0	700	-21,630	5,431	-10,000	-5,600	1,980	13,000	4,500	-4,500	0

(continued)

Solution to Question 4.3 (Continued)

```
Balance Sheet as at ......              £         £

Fixed Assets
  Machine                                      4,500
  Equipment                                    5,431
  Van                                          8,790
                                             ----------
                                               18,721

Current Assets
  Stock                                2,875
  Debtors                             15,680
  Bank                                11,460
  Cash                                14,243
                                     ----------
                                       44,258
Less Current Liabilities
  Creditors                           18,849
                                     ----------
                                               25,409

Loan                                           10,000
                                             ----------
                                               34,130
                                             ==========
Financed by:

Capital                                        12,500

Profit                                         21,630
                                             ----------
                                               34,130
                                             ==========
```

```
Creditors            £          Debtors              £
-----------                     --------

D.Opal            4,920         F.Smith             700
G.Lime            3,829         G.Williams        1,980
K.Star            5,600         H.Herbert        13,000
K.Kelly           4,500
                ----------                       ----------
                  18,849                           15,680
                ==========                       ==========
```

```
Trading and Profit and Loss Account
for the year ended ......                      £

Sales                                          48,080

Less Cost of Sales                             26,000
                                             ----------
GROSS PROFIT                                   22,080

Rent                                              450
                                             ----------
NET PROFIT                                     21,630
                                             ==========
```

Solution to Question 5.1

	A	B	C	D	E	F	G	H	I	J
1										
2										
3										
4	Description			Bank	Rent	Profit	Rates	Petrol	Electricity	
5										
6	(i) Rent paid			-884	884					
7										
8	Rent used				-663	663				
9										
10	(ii) Rates paid			-2400			2400			
11										
12	Rates used					1840	-1840			
13										
14	(iii) Petrol expenses			-567				567		
15										
16	Petrol used					806		-806		
17										
18	(iv) Electricity paid			-4400					4400	
19										
20	Electricity used					4800			-4800	
21										
22	Balance Sheet			-8251	221	8109	560	-239	-400	
23										

Solution to Question 5.2

	A	B	C	D	E	F	G	H	I	J	K
1											
2											
3	Description			Bank	Rent	Profit	Rates	Petrol	Electric	Rent Rec.	Commission
4											
5	Opening Balance Sheet			-8251	221	8109	560	-239	-400		
6											
7	(i) Rent paid			-946	946						
8											
9	Rent used				-931	931					
10											
11	(ii) Rates paid			-2600			2600				
12											
13	Rates used					3560	-3560				
14											
15	(iii) Petrol expenses			-683				683			
16											
17	Petrol used					576		-576			
18											
19	(iv) Electricity paid			-4200					4200		
20											
21	Elecricity used					3240			-3240		
22											
23	(v) Rent received			1500						-1500	
24											
25	Rent revenue					-1200				1200	
26											
27	(vi) Commission received			540							-540
28											
29	Commission revenue					-885					885
30											
31	Balance Sheet			-14640	237	14331	-400	-132	560	-300	345
32											

Solution to Question 5.3

Eric Fluffy
Trading and Profit and loss Account
for the year ended 31/12/91.

	£s	£s
Sales		21456
Less Cost of Sales:		
Opening Stock	2392	
Purchases	12418	
	14810	
Closing Stock	2460	
		12350
GROSS PROFIT		9106
Add, Rent Receivable 6800-124		6676
Commission Receivable 56+68		124
Less, Rent Payable 4600+560	5160	
Insurance 1206-120	1086	
Selling Expenses	450	
Office Expenses	760	
Wages and Salaries 352+240	592	
	8048	
NET PROFIT		7858
		=========

Eric Fluffy
Balance Sheet as at 31/12/91.

	£s	£s	£s
Fixed Assets			
Land			16390
Motor Van			5600
			21990
Current Assets			
Stock		2460	
Debtors		4580	
Prepayments Expenses		120	
Accrued Revenues		68	
Cash		45	
		7273	
Current Liabilities			
Creditors	3480		
Accrued Expenses	800		
Prepaid Revenue	124		
Bank Overdraft	3291		
		7695	
Net Current Liabilities			-422
Loan			7560
			14008
			=========
Financed by:			
Capital as at 1/1/91			8600
Add Profit for year			7858
			16458
Less Drawings			2450
			14008
			=========

Solution to Question 6.1

	A	B	C	D	E	F	G
1							
2							
3							
4	Description			Profit	Debtors	Cash	Provision
5							
6	Y/E 31/12/89						
7							
8	Sales			-113890	113890		
9							
10	Receipts				-109654	109654	
11							
12	Bad debts			450	-450		
13							
14	Provision			560			-560
15	---						
16	Balance sheet			-112880	3786	109654	-560
17							
18	Y/E 31/12/90						
19							
20	Sales			-134800	134800		
21							
22	Receipts				-129786	129786	
23							
24	Bad debts			1769	-1769		
25							
26	Written-off debt pays			-65		65	
27	---						
28	Sub-totals			-245976	7031	239505	-560
29							
30	Provision			-208.45			208.45
31	---						
32	Balance sheet			-246184.	7031	239505	-351.55
33							
34	Y/E 31/12/91						
35							
36	Sales			-167439	167439		
37							
38	Receipts				-159879	159879	
39							
40	Bad debts			3673	-3673		
41	--						
42	Sub-totals			-409950.	10918	399384	-351.55
43							
44	Provision			194.35			-194.35
45	--						
46	Balance sheet			-409756.	10918	399384	-545.9
47	==						

Solution to Question 6.2

```
                Hywel Williams
         Trading and Profit and loss Account
            for the year ended 31/12/91.
                                    £s            £s
Sales                                         150,192
Less Cost of Sales:
   Opening Stock                    16,744
   Purchases                        86,926
                                   ---------
                                   103,670
   Closing Stock                    17,220
                                   ---------
                                                 86,450
                                               ---------
GROSS PROFIT                                     63,742
Add, Rent Receivable       47600-868            46,732
     Commission Receivable 392+476                 868
Less, Rent Payable         32200+392   36,120
      Insurance            8442-840     7,602
      Selling Expenses                  3,150
      Office Expenses                   5,320
      Wages and Salaries   2464+1680    4,144
      Bad Debts                          568
      Change in Doubtful debt            758
            Provision2450-1692
                                      ---------
                                                 57,662
                                               ---------
NET PROFIT                                       53,680
                                               =========
Balance Sheet as at 31/12/91.
                             £s        £s         £s
Fixed Assets
   Land                                         114,730
   Motor Van                                     39,200
                                               ---------
Current Assets                                  153,930
   Stock                              17,220
   Debtors                 31,492
   Less Provision           2,450
                          ---------
                                      29,042
   Prepayments Expenses                  840
   Accrued Revenues                      476
   Cash                                  315
                                      ---------
                                      47,893
Current Liabilities
   Creditors               24,360
   Accrued Expenses3920+1680 5,600
   Prepaid Revenue            868
   Bank Overdraft          23,037
                          ---------
                                      53,865
                                      ---------
Net Current Liabilities                          -5,972
Loan                                             51,228
                                               ---------
                                                 96,730
                                               =========
Financed by:
Capital as at 1/1/91                             60,200
Add Profit for year                              53,680
                                               ---------
                                                113,880
Less Drawings                                    17,150
                                               ---------
                                                 96,730
                                               =========
```

Solution to Question 7.1

	A	B	C	D	E	F	G
				Machine	Provision for Depreciation	Profit and Loss	Net Asset Inc. Cash
7	Year ended 31/12/89						
9	Purchase of Machine			1300			-1300
11	Depreciation Expense				-65	65	
13	Closing Balance Sheet			1300	-65	65	-1300
15	Year ended 31/12/90						
17	Purchase of Machines			18000			-18000
19	Depreciation Expense:						
20	1989 Purchases				-130	130	
21	1990 Purchases				-1350	1350	
24	Closing Balance Sheet			19300	-1545	1545	-19300
26	Year ended 31/12/91						
28	Purchase of Machines:						
29	1/2/91			5000			-5000
30	1/8/91			13000			-13000
32	Depreciation Expense:						
33	1989 Purchases				-130	130	
34	1990 Purchases				-1800	1800	
35	1991 Purchases:						
36	1/2/91				-458	458	
37	1/8/91				-542	542	
39	Closing Balance Sheet			57900	-6085	6085	-57900
41	Year ending 31/12/92						
43	Depreciation Expense:						
44	1989 Purchases				-130	130	
45	1990 Purchases				-1800	1800	
46	1991 Purchases:						
47	1/2/91				-500	500	
48	1/8/91				-1300	1300	
50	Closing Balance Sheet			57900	-9815	9815	-57900

Solution to Question 7.3

	A	B	C	D	E	F	G	H	I
1									
2									
3									
4				Machine	Provision	Profit	Net Assets		Sale of
5					for	and	Inc. Cash		Machine
6					Depreciation	Loss			
7									
8									
9	Opening Balance Sheet			53600	-9060	9060	-53600		
10									
11									
12	Depreciation Expense:								
13		1989 Purchase			-120	120			
14		1990 Purchase			-800	800			
15		1991 Purchase:							
16			1/2/91		-500	500			
17			1/8/91		-1300	1300			
18									
19	Sale of Machine:								
20		Cost		-16000					16000
21		Depreciation			5200				-5200
22		Proceeds					8000		-8000
23		Loss				2800			-2800
24									
25	Closing Balance Sheet			37600	-6580	14580	-45600		0
26									

Solution to Question 7.5

	A		B		C		D		E		F		G

(i) Straight-Line Basis

Description		Printer	Prov. for Dep,n	Bank	Profit and Loss
Purchased Printer		1,800		-1,800	
Depreciation			-450		450
Balance Sheet as at 31/12/-9		1,800	-450	-1,800	450
Depreciation			-450		450
Balance Sheet as at 31/12/-9		1,800	-900	-1,800	900
Depreciation			-450		450
Balance Sheet as at 31/12/-9		1,800	-1,350	-1,800	1,350
Depreciation			-450		450
Balance Sheet as at 31/12/-9		1,800	-1,800	-1,800	1,800

(ii) Diminishing Balance Method

Description		Printer	Prov. for Dep,n	Bank	Profit and Loss
Purchased Printer		1,800		-1,800	
Depreciation			-1,080		1,080
Balance Sheet as at 31/12/-9		1,800	-1,080	-1,800	1,080
Depreciation			-432		432
Balance Sheet as at 31/12/-9		1,800	-1,512	-1,800	1,512
Depreciation			-173		173
Balance Sheet as at 31/12/-9		1,800	-1,685	-1,800	1,685
Depreciation			-69*		69
Balance Sheet as at 31/12/-9		1,800	-1,754	-1,800	1,754

* As can be seen this method does not enable the provision to
  equate to the printer's cost

(continued)

Solution to Question 7.5 (Continued)

	A		B		C		D		E		F		G		H	

```
 57  (iii) Sum of Output Method
 58
 59  This is a new method not covered in the text. It was included to
 60  see if you could work it out for yourself.
 61
 62  Description                        Printer  Prov.    Bank      Profit
 63                                              for                and
 64                                              Dep,n              Loss
 65
 66  Purchased Printer                   1,800          -1,800
 67
 68  Depreciation                                        -350                  350
 69  ------------------------------------------------------------------------
 70  Balance Sheet as at 31/12/-9        1,800  - 350   -1,800                 350
 71
 72  Depreciation                                        -450                  450
 73  ------------------------------------------------------------------------
 74  Balance Sheet as at 31/12/-9        1,800  - 800   -1,800                 800
 75
 76  Depreciation                                        -450                  450
 77  ------------------------------------------------------------------------
 78  Balance Sheet as at 31/12/-9        1,800  -1,250  -1,800               1,250
 79
 80  Depreciation                                        -550                  550
 81  ------------------------------------------------------------------------
 82  Balance Sheet as at 31/12/-9        1,800  -1,800  -1,800               1,800
 83  ========================================================================
 84
 85
 86  Sale of Printer
 87
 88  Description                        Printer  Prov.    Bank      Profit  Sale of
 89                                              for                and     Printer
 90                                              Dep,n              Loss
 91
 92  Balance Sheet as at 31/12/-9        1,800  -1,685  -1,800     1,685
 93
 94  Cost                               -1,800                                      1,800
 95
 96  Depreciation                                1,685                             -1,685
 97
 98  Proceeds                                              200                      -200
 99  ------------------------------------------------------------------------
100  Totals                                  0       0   -1,600     1,685           -85
101
102  Profit on Sale                                                  -85            85
103  ------------------------------------------------------------------------
104  Balance Sheet                           0       0   -1,600     1,600             0
105  ========================================================================
```

Solution to Question 8.1

a.

Stores ledger records

Weighted average method

Date	Receipts Quantity	Receipts Price £	Issues Quantity	Issues Price £	Balance Quantity	Balance Price £	Stock Value £
Opening					100	39	3,900
May	100	41			200	40	8,000
June	200	50			400	45	18,000
July			250	45	150	45	6,750
August	400	51.875			550	50	27,500
September			350	50	200	50	10,000
October			100	50	100	50	5,000

FIFO method

Date	Receipts Quantity	Receipts Price £	Issues Quantity	Issues Price £	Balance Quantity	Balance Price £	Stock Value £
Opening					100	39	3,900
May	100	41			{100 / 100	39 / 41	8,000
June	200	50			{100 / 100 / 200	39 / 41 / 50	18,000
July			250	{100 @ 39 / 100 @ 41 / 50 @ 50	150	50	7,500
August	400	51.875			{150 / 400	50 / 51.875	28,250
September			350	{150 @ 50 / 200 @ 51.875	200	51.875	10,375
October			100	51.875	100	51.875	5187.5

(*continued*)

Solution to Question 8.1 (Continued)

LIFO method

Date	Receipts Quantity	Receipts Price £	Issues Quantity	Issues Price £	Balance Quantity	Balance Price £	Stock value £
Opening					100	39	3,900
May	100	41			{ 100	39	
					{ 100	41	8,000
June	200	50			⌈ 100	39	
					{ 100	41	
					⌊ 200	50	18,000
July			250	{ 200 @ 50	⌈ 100	39	
				{ 50 @ 41			
					⌊ 50	41	5,950
August	400	51.875			⌈ 100	39	
					{ 50	41	
					⌊ 400	51.875	26,700
September			350	51.875	⌈ 100	39	
					{ 50	41	
					⌊ 50	51.875	8,543.75
October			100	{ 50 @ 51.875	100	39	3,900
				{ 50 @ 41			

b.   Trading accounts for the period

		Weighted Average £	FIFO £	LIFO £
Sales				
Sales		47,900	47,900	47,900
	£			
Opening Stock	3,900			
+ Purchases	34,850	⎛38,750⎞	⎛38,750 ⎞	⎛38,750⎞
− Closing Stock		⎝ 5,000⎠	⎝ 5,187.5⎠	⎝ 3,900⎠
= Cost of Sales		33,750	33,562.5	34,850
= GROSS PROFIT		£14,150	£14,337.5	£13,050

c. In this example, with rising purchase prices, the most realistic profit will be found when the costs of material charged relate most closely to current prices. The method which does this is the LIFO system. See Chapter 24 for a rationale.

Solution to Question 8.5

J.Turner

Manufacturing, Trading and Profit and Loss Account
for the year ended 31 December 1987.

	£s	£s
Stock of raw materials at 31/12/86		12,000
Purchases		97,000
		109,000
Stock of raw materials at 31/12/87		9,000
Cost of raw materials consumed		100,000
Direct labour		30,000
PRIME COST		130,000
Less Factory Overhead Expenses:		
Indirect Labour	10,000	
Rates	2,400	
Plant Maintenance	5,000	
Power	3,500	
Depreciation on Plant and Machinery	6,500	
		27,400
		157,400
Work in Progress at 31/12/86		4,000
		161,400
Work in Progress at 31/12/87		4,600
PRODUCTION COST OF GOODS CONPLETED		156,800
Sales		240,000
Less Cost of Goods Sold:		
Finished Goods at 31/12/86	15,000	
Production Cost of Goods Completed	156,800	
	171,800	
Finished Goods at 31/12/87	13,500	
		158,300
GROSS PROFIT		81,700
Less Administrative Expenses:		
Wages	10,000	
Office Expenses	5,000	
Rates	1,600	
Power	1,500	
Depreciation on Fittings and Fixture	1,000	
	19,100	
Less Selling and Distribution Expenses:		
Wages	10,000	
Selling and Distribution Costs	6,500	
	16,500	
		35,600
NET PROFIT		46,100

(*continued*)

Solution to Question 8.5 (Continued)

J.Turner

Balance Sheet as at 31 December 1987.

Fixed Assets

	£s	£s	£s
	Cost	Dep'n	
Land and Buildings	110,000		110,000
Plant and Machinery	50,000	30,500	19,500
Fixtures and Fittings	12,000	9,000	3,000
	172,000	39,500	132,500

Current Assets
Stocks:

Finished Goods	13,500		
Work in Progress	4,600		
Raw Materials	9,000		
		27,100	
Debtors		22,000	
Bank		3,500	
		52,600	

Less Current Liabilities

Creditors	16,000		
Wages Accrued	6,000		
		22,000	

WORKING CAPITAL   30,600

                                                   163,100

Financed by:

Capital   140,000
                                                    46,100

                                                   186,100
Drawings   23,000

CAPITAL EMPLOYED   163,100

Solution to Question 9.2

Edward Peter
Trading and Profit and Loss Account
for the year ended 31 December 1991

	£s	£s	£s
Sales less returns			576,862
Less cost of sales:			
Opening stock		64,584	
Purchases less returns		324,521	
Carriage Inwards		25	
		389,130	
Closing Stock		66,420	
			322,710
GROSS PROFIT			254,152
Add rent receivable			180,252
Commission receivable			3,348
Profit on sale of van			680
Discounts received			13,420
Less rent payable		139,320	
Insurance		29,322	
Selling expenses		12,150	
Office expenses		20,520	
Wages and salaries		15,984	
Bad debts		568	
Change in doubtful debt provision		758	
Depreciation charge:			
Machinery	3,173		
Motor vans	37,800		
		40,973	
Discounts allowed		4,500	
Carriage outwards		12,359	
			276,454
NET PROFIT BEFORE TAXATION			175,398
Less taxation			61,389
NET PROFIT AFTER TAXATION			114,009

(*continued*)

Solution to Question 9.2 (Continued)

Edward Peter
Balance sheet as at 31 December 1991

	£s	£s	£s
Fixed assets			
	Cost	Depreciation	
Land	442,530		442,530
Machinery	56,320	27,765	28,555
Motor van	151,200	94,780	56,420
	650,050	122,545	527,505
Current assets			
Stock		66,420	
Debtors	203,984		
Less provision	2,450		
		201,534	
Prepayments expenses		3,240	
Accrued revenues		1,836	
Cash		1,215	
		274,245	
Current liabilities			
Creditors	93,960		
Taxation	61,389		
Accrued expenses	21,600		
Prepaid revenue	3,348		
Bank overdraft	88,857		
		269,154	
Net current liabilities			5,091
Loan			252,537
			280,059
Financed by:			
Capital as at 1 January 1991			232,200
Add profit for year			114,009
			346,209
Less drawings			66,150
			280,059

Solution to Question 9.3

1. The faults in the final accounts are as follows.
    a. There are three mistakes in the title to the profit and loss account:
        (i) the name of the business should be: **Astra Grocers** (proprietor Hickson Blunt) or: **Astra Grocers**
        (ii) the statement should be labelled: *Trading and Profit and Loss Account*
        (iii) the time period should be labelled: *for the year ended 31 May 1988*
    b. There are no currency signs (£) anywhere in the statements.
    c. Returns outwards should be deducted from purchases, not added to sales.
    d. Rents received should be shown separately as 'other income' and not included in gross profit.
    e. The stocks figures in cost of sales have been reversed. Opening stock should have been labelled 'at 1 June 1987' not '31 May 1987'.

Solution to Question 9.3 (Continued)

f. Return inwards should be deducted from sales and not added to purchases.

g. Discounts received should not be included as part of cost of sales but should be separately included under 'other income'.

h. 'Drawings' is not an operating expense and should have been deducted from the opening balance on capital plus net profit in the balance sheet.

i. The balance sheet has been labelled wrongly–it should be *Balance Sheet as at 31 May 1988*

j. Stock is not a fixed asset–it should be included as a current asset.

k. The order of current assets is wrong–trade debtors should be listed before cash on hand.

l. Accrued expenses are not current assets and should be shown among current liabilities.

m. Similarly, the bank overdraft is not a current asset and should be shown in current liabilities.

n. Prepaid expenses is not a current liability. This heading should be shown in current assets between trade debtors and cash on hand.

o. Net profit has been calculated erroneously by adding operating expenses to gross profit.

p. Working capital has been calculated by adding current assets and current liabilities. This is wrong–working capital is the difference between current assets and current liabilities.

2. Revised calculation of profit:

Astra Grocers
(proprietor Hickson Blunt)
Trading and Profit and Loss Account
for the year ended 31 May 1988

			£
Sales			127,000
Less: Returns inwards			2,140
			124,860
Less: Cost of Goods sold			
Stock at 1 June 1987		6,780	
Purchases	111,090		
Less: Returns outwards	3,600		
		107,490	
		114,270	
Less: Stock at 31 May 1988		7,450	
			106,820
GROSS PROFIT			18,040
Add: OTHER INCOME			
Discounts received		11,800	
Rents received		2,500	
			14,300
			32,340
Less: OPERATING EXPENSES			
Selling and distribution		11,800	
Administration		4,670	
			16,470
NET PROFIT			15,870

Solution to Question 9.4

A.   Purchase of stock costing £5,000 on credit.
B.   Purchase of new equipment costing £10,000. This is partly financed by a loan of £7,000 with the remaining £3,000 being paid in cash.
C.   Sold stocks which had cost £2,000 for £3,000 which is received by cheque. The resulting profit of £1,000 is credited to capital.
D.   Payment of accrued expenses by cheque £4,000.
E.   Receive by cheque £11,000 from credit customers.
F.   Payment by cheque of an expense/expenses of £4,000 of which £1,000 is prepaid at the time of payment.
G.   Owner withdraws goods costing £1,000 for personal use–or stock losses of £1,000 recognised.
H.   Equipment with a net book value of £18,000 is sold for £15,000 which is received by cheque. The resultant loss of £3,000 is deducted from capital.
I.   Depreciation at 10 per cent reducing balance method is charged on fixed assets (i.e. buildings and equipment).
J.   A balance owing from a credit customer is offset against a balance due to a credit supplier, or vice versa. Presumably this is a case where both customer and supplier are the same business.
     Note: feasible alternative explanations will be accepted.

Solution to Question 9.5

1.   *Calculation of sales*

	£		£
Opening debtors b/f	35,780	Cash and cheques received	268,420
		Contras from creditors' ledger	3,000
		Discounts allowed	3,100
SALES	716,670	Cash sales	433,740
		Bad debts	2,080
		Returns inwards	5,560
		Closing debtors c/f	36,550
	752,450		752,450

2.   *Calculation of purchases*

	£		£
Cash and cheques paid	397,600	Opening Creditors b/f	44,210
Contras to debtors' ledger	3,000		
Discounts received	1,980		
Returns outwards	4,670	PURCHASES	406,150
Closing creditors c/f	43,110		
	450,360		450,360

Solution to Question 10.1

	Description	F & F	M.V.	Stock	Debtors	Bank & Cash	Sundry Creditors	Capital	Profit	Drawings	Suspense
8	From question	2800	4500	4250	1400	752	-1600	-11085	-7180	6400	-237
10	(1) Omitted rent and rates								100		-100
12	(2) Fitment incorrectly included	150							-150		
13	in purchases										
15	(3) Cash payment omitted from				-170						170
16	debtors										
18	(4) Wrong amount entered						36		-36		
20	(5) Credit entered as debit						-180				180
22	(6) Omitted petty cash					13					-13
24	(7) Sales Undercast				10				-10		
26	Corrected Balance Sheet	2950	4500	4250	1240	765	-1744	-11085	-7276	6400	0

Solution to Question 10.2

	A	B	C	D	E	F	G	H	I	J	K
1											
2											
3						Profit	Bank	Creditors	Debtors	Motor	Motor
4										Vehicles	Vehicles
5						-305660					Dep'n
6											Provision
7	Number	Description									
8											
9	1	Bank charges omitted from Cash Book				56	-56				
10											
11	2	Purchase Journal Overcast				-400		400			
12											
13	3	Sales Journal Undercast				-100			100		
14											
15	4	Incorrect amount entered in Purchase				-90		90			
16		Journal									
17											
18	5	Bad debt written off				88			-88		
19											
20	6	Expense posted as capital				550				-550	
21											
22	7	Overprovision of depreciation on 6				-55					55
23											
24						---------					
25		CORRECTED PROFIT FIGURE =				-305611					
26						=========					

Solution to Question 10.3

Thomas Smith

a.   *Corrected trial balance as at 31 March 1988*

	£	£
Stock in trade at 1 April 1987	10,700	
Discounts allowed	310	
Discounts received		450
Provision for doubtful debts		960
Purchases	94,000	
Purchases returns		1,400
Sales		132,100
Sales returns	1,100	
Freehold property: at cost	70,000	
provision for depreciation		3,500
Motor vehicles: at cost	15,000	
provision for depreciation		4,500
Capital: Thomas Smith		84.600
Balance at bank	7,100	
Trade debtors	11,300	
Trade creditors		7,600
Establishment and administrative expenditure	16,600	
Drawings	9,000	
	235,110	235,110

b.

	£	£
1988		
31 March Stock in trade	1,300	
To Capital: Thomas Smith		1,300
Being correction of stock valuation at		
1 April 1987 to £12,000		
31 March Trade creditors	210	
To Purchases returns	210	
Goods returned in December 1987 to J. Hardwell		
Limited now accepted as not of merchantable quality		
31 March Sales	1,000	
To Trade debtors		1,000
Being correction for free trade samples previously		
wrongly charged as sales to John Grey		
31 March Trade samples	1,000	
To Purchases		1,000
Being free trade samples sent to John Grey		
in February 1988		
31 March Repairs and renewals	150	
To Purchases		150
Being paint withdrawn from stock for		
decoration of stockroom walls		

Solution to Question 10.4

	A	B	C	D	E	F	G	H	I	J	K	L	M	N
1	.													
2														
3														
4	Description	Plant	Debtors	Stock	Bank	Capital	Profit	Loan	Creditors	Interest Accrued	Rent Accrued	Doubtful Debt	Drawings	
5														
6												Provision		
7														
8	As per question	6210	12200	8500	1000	-8140	-3470	-6000	-10300					
9														
10	1)Outstanding loan interest						180			-180				
11														
12	2)Overvalued stock			-240			240							
13														
14	3)Plant overvalued	-200					200							
15														
16	4)Rent due						300				-300			
17														
18	5)Bad debt		-150				150							
19	Provision						70					-70		
20														
21	6)Cost of sales omitted			-50			50							
22														
23	7)Bank charges omitted				-60		60							
24	Drawings omitted				-520									520
25	----													----
26	Corrected Balance	6010	12050	8210	420	-8140	-2220	-6000	-10300	-180	-300	-70	520	
27	====													====

Solution to Question 11.1

Purchase Day Book

Date	Details	£
1 January	AB	108
1 January	CD	250
1 January	EF	500
1 January	GH	650
31 January	*Total* to Purchases a/c	£1,508
	and Purchase ledger Control	

Returns Outwards Day Book

8 January	AB	58
8 January	GH	30
	Total to Returns Inwards a/c	£88
	and Purchase ledger Control	

Sales Day Book

10 January	XY	420
	VW	205
	RS	108
	CD	55
	TV	40
31 January	*Total* to Sales a/c	£828
	and Sales ledger Control	

Returns Inwards Day Book

		£
15 January	VW	5
31 January	*Total* to Return Inwards a/c	
	and Sales ledger Control	£5

Cash Book

	Discount Allowed	Bank		Discount Received	Bank
31 January XY		150	31 January CD	25	170
31 January VW	10	190	31 January AB	2	48
			31 January EF		100
			31 January Balance c/d		22
	10*	340		27*	340
1 February Balance b/d		22			

* Totals to Discount Allowed a/c and Sales ledger Control
    and Discount Received a/c Purchase ledger Control

(*continued*)

Solution to Question 11.1 (Continued)

Date	Journal	Dr.	Cr.
31 January	Purchase ledger CD	55	
	Sales ledger CD		55
	Control entry—CD, Ltd		
31 January	Bad Debts—Expenses	40	
	Sales ledger TV		40
	w/off of debt due to bankruptcy (TV)		

Purchases

31 January	Sundry Creditors	1508		

Returns Outwards

			31 January Sundry Creditors	88

Discounts Received

			31 January Sundry Creditors	27

IGNORE CONTROL ACCOUNTS IF NOT YET COVERED

Purchase ledger Control

31 January	Returns Outwards	88	31 January Goods	150
31 January	Discount Received	27		
31 January Bank		318		
31 January Control		55		
31 January	Balance c/d	1020		
		£1508		£1508
			1 February Balance b/d	1020

Sales ledger Control

31 January	Goods	828	31 January Returns Inwards	5
			31 January Bank	340
			31 January Discount Allowed	10
			31 January Control	55
			31 January Bad Debts	40
			31 January Balance c/d	378
		£828		£828

Solution to Question 11.1 (Continued)

Sales

				31 January	Sundry Debtors	828

Discount Allowed

31 January	Sundry Debtors	10		

Bad Debts

31 January	Sundry Debtors	40		

Returns Inwards

31 January	Sundry Debtors	5		

Trial Balance

	Dr.	Cr.
Bank	22	
Total Debtors	378	
Sales		828
Discount Allowed	10	
Bad Debts	40	
Returns Inwards	5	
Purchases	1508	
Returns Outwards		88
Discount Received		27
Creditors		1020
Totals	1963	1963

Purchase ledger

AB

8 January	Returns	58	1 January	Goods	108
31 January	Bank	48			
	Discount	2			
		£108			£108

CD

31 January	Bank	170	1 January	Goods	250
31 January	Discount	25			
31 January	Control—Sales ledger	55			
		£250			£250

(*continued*)

Solution to Question 11.1 (Continued)

EF

31 January	Bank	100	1 January	Goods	500
31 January	Balance c/d	400			
		£500			£500
			1 February	Balance b/d	400

GH

8 January	Returns	30	1 January	Goods	650
31 January	Balance c/d	620			
		£650			£650
			1 February	Balance b/d	620

Total Creditors per listing = £1,020

Sales Ledger

XY

10 January	Goods	420	31 January	Bank	150
			31 January	Balance c/d	270
		420			420
1 February	Balance b/d	270			

VW

10 January	Goods	205	15 January	Returns	5
			31 January	Discount	10
			31 January	Bank	190
		205			205

RS

10 January	Goods	108	31 January	Balance c/d	108
1 February	Balance b/d	108			

CD

10 January	Goods	55	31 January	Control—Paid ledger	55

TV

10 January	Goods	40	31 January	Bad Debts	40

Solution to Question 12.1

```
          |   A   ||   B   ||   C   ||   D   ||   E   ||   F   |
 1
 2
 3
 4    (i)Correction of Sales Control Account
 5
 6    Balance per question                        45124
 7
 8    (3)Bad debt                                  -100
 9    (4)Contra                                    -460
10    (5)Sales day book under-added                 200
11                                              ---------
12    Corrected Balance                           44764
13                                              =========
14
15    (ii)Correction of List of Sales Ledger Balances
16
17    Balance per question                        45560
18
19    (1)Sales invoice entered twice             -1316
20    (7)Ommitted balance                          520
21
22                                              ---------
23    Corrected Balance                           44764
24                                              =========
25
26    (iii)Correction of Creditor Control Account
27
28    Balance per question                        29461
29
30    (4)Contra                                    -460
31    (6)Purchase returns book over-added           20
32
33                                              ---------
34    Corrected Balance                           29021
35                                              =========
36
37    (iv)Correction of List of Purchase Ledger Balances
38
39    Balance per question                        28912
40
41    (2)List of balances undercast                100
42    (8)Transcription error                         9
43
44                                              ---------
45    Corrected Balance                           29021
46                                              =========
```

Solution to Question 12.2

(i)Control Account before correction

Description	Control Account
Creditor balances 1 April 1986	36846
Debtor balances 1 April 1986	-328
Discount received	-1957
Purchases	276220
Payments	-258972
Purchase returns	-3116
Cash refunds	262
Bills payable	-1118
Contras	-784
	47053
Debtor balances 31 March 1987	419
Balance as at 31 March 1987	47472

(ii) and (iii)Correction of Errors

Control Account

Balance as above	47472
Purchase Day Book undercast	200
Discounts received debited not credited	-274
Incorrectly entered in PR Day Book	100
	47498

List of balances reconciliation

Total of list	47332
Omitted balance	176
Omitted discount received	-28
Incorrect posting	18
As above	47498

Solution to Question 12.3

```
Bank Reconciliation Statement as at 28 January
                                        £          £
Balance as per Bank Account                     9479.25

Items in bank statement but not
in Cash Book:

Add,     Bank credit                             106.89
                                               ---------
                                                9586.14
Less,    Standing order             357.82
         Standing Order             156.95
         Bank Charges               101.78
                                   ----------
                                                 616.55
                                               ---------
Corrected Bank Account Balance                  8969.59

Items in Cash book but not
in Bank statement:

Add,     Unpresented cheques
              15373                  56.75
              15374                1360.09
              15369                4500.89
                                 ----------
                                                5917.73
                                               ---------
                                               14887.32

Less,    Unrecorded Lodgements                  4560.75
                                               ---------
Balance as per Bank statement                  10326.57
                                               =========


Reconciliation of Opening Balance

Balance per bank account                        9777.06

Add, Unpresented Cheques:
              15365                6741.94
              15366                  56.87
                                 ----------
                                                6798.81
                                               ---------
Balance per Bank Statement                     16575.87
                                               =========
```

538 Solutions to questions and exercises

Solution to Question 13.1

	A	B	C	D	E	F	G	H	I
1									
2									
3									
4	Description		Capital	Loan	Trade	Wages	F&F	F&F	
5					Creditors		Cost	Dep'n	
6									
7	Opening balances		−31000	−3300	−8000	−1500	27500	−16500	
8									
9	Rent								
10	Sale of Vehicle								
11	Other Receipts								
12									
13	Purchase of New Vehicle								
14	Purchase of New F&F						3400		
15	Wages					48000			
16	Stock Purchases				158000				
17	Rent/Rates								
18	Light/Heat								
19	Drawings								
20	Loan Interest								
21									
22	Sales								
23	Purchases				−158800				
24	Cost of Goods Sold								
25	Depreciation F&F							−6180	
26	Sale of Vehicle-cost								
27	Sale of Vehicle-dep'n								
28	Profit on Sale								
29	Depreciation Vehicles								
30	Rent/Rates								
31	Light/Heat								
32	Wages					−50000			
33	--------								
34	Closing Balance Sheet		−31000	−3300	−8800	−3500	30900	−22680	
35	========								

I	J	K	L	M	N	O	P	Q	R	S
	Vehicles Cost	Vehicles Dep'n	Stock	Debtors	Bank	P+L	Sale of Vehicle	Rent/ Rates	L/H	Drawings
	9000	-4000	22500	2600	2700					
					8000	-8000				
					5500		-5500			
				-241500	241500					
	14000				-14000					
					-3400					
					-48000					
					-158000					
					-12000			12000		
					-7000				7000	
					-14500					14500
					-561	561				
				238900		-238900				
			158800							
			-143340			143340				
						6180				
	-9000						9000			
		4000					-4000			
						-500	500			
		-2800				2800				
						9000		-9000		
						9000			-9000	
						50000				
	14000	-2800	37960	0	239	-26519	0	3000	-2000	14500

Solution to Question 13.2

	Deposits received from Customers	Deposits paid to Ferry Operators	Creditors	Camping Equip.	Deferred Expenses	Bank	Profit and Loss	Capital	Sources and Uses
Opening Balances	-200	110	-300	3000	60			-2670	-330
Deposits rec'd from customers	-2000					2000			0
Cash payments to ferry operators		710				-710			0
A + A Expenses					245	-245			0
Sales	1970						-1970		1970
Cost of Sales		-660					660		-660
Depreciation				-1000			1000		0
Purchases of Camping Equip.			-400	400					-400
Payments for Camping Equip.			660			-660			0
A + A Expenditure					-245		245		-245
Transfer profit to capital							65	-65	0
Closing Balance Sheet	-230	160	-40	2400	60	385	0	-2735	335

Solution to Question 13.3

	Stock	Trade Creditors	Other Creditors	F+F	Bank	Drawings	Debtors	Profit and Loss	Cash	F+F Dep'n	Capital
Opening Balances	2,540	-1,824	-78	1,000	-918						-720
Payments		33,442			-33,442						
Rent					-1,000			1,000			
General Expenses			2,872		-2,872						
Drawings					-696	696					
Receipts					39,024				-39,024		
Sales-Cash								-42,963	42,963		
Sales-Credit							660	-660			
Cost of sales	-32,942							32,942			
Purchases	33,234	-33,234									
Wages								1,788	-1,788		
Depreciation								100		-100	
Other Purchases			-2,920					2,920			
Cash to bank					2,151				-2,151		
Profit to capital								4,873			-4,873
Closing Balance Sheet	2,832	-1,616	-126	1,000	96	2,847	660	0	0	-100	-5,593

Solution to Question 14.1

	A	B	C	D	E	F	G	H	I	J	K	L	M	N
1														
2														
3														
4	Description	Bank	Premises	Equip.	Bar Stocks	Creditors for Stocks	Cash	Income and Expend.	Bar Account	Dep'n. of Equip.	Subs.	I&E
5														
6														
7														
8	Balances 1 January 1986	7200	60000	50000	8100	-6200						-119100
9														
10	Bank Transactions:												
11	Bar takings	84200							-84200			
12	Rents received	6400						-6400				
13	Subscriptions	7800									-7800	
14	Payments for bar	-56100				56100						
15	Rates	-3600						3600				
16	Equipment	-30400		30400								
17	Light & heat	-3800						3800				
18	Telephone	-1800						1800				
19	Gen. expences	-2900						2900				
20	Admin. salary	-9700						9700				
21														
22	Cash Transactions:												
23	Wages							-3120		3120			
24	Bar cash sales							3120		-3120			
25	Cash Payments						4900	-4900					
26	Bar cash sales							4900		-4900			
27	Depreciation								7500		-7500		
28	of equipment												
29														
30	Deduced entries:												
31	Bar purchases					60900	-60900						
32	Bar cost of sales					-60700				60700			
33	Subscriptions								-7750			7750	
34	Bar profit								-28400	28400			
35	Excess of I over E								13250				-13250
36														
37														
38	Balance Sheet	-2700	60000	80400	8300	-6100	0	0	0	-7500	-50	-132350
39														

(continued)

Solution to Question 14.1 (Continued)

Northminster Arts Centre

Income and Expenditure Account for the year ended 31 December 1986

	£s	£s
INCOME		
Subscriptions		7,750
Bar (see note 1 below)		28,400
Rents		6,400

		42,550
EXPENDITURE		
Rates	3,600	
Light and heat	3,800	
Telephone	1,800	
General expenses	2,900	
Admin. salary	9,700	
Depreciation of Equipment	7,500	
		29,300

		13,250
		=======

Northminster Arts Centre

Balance Sheet as at 31 December 1986

	£s	£s	£s
Fixed Assets			
	Cost	Dep'n	
Premises			60,000
Equipment	80,400	7,500	72,900

			132,900
Current Assets			
Bar Stocks		8,300	

		8,300	
Current Liabilities			
Bar creditors	6,100		
Bank Overdraft	2,700		
Subscriptions due	50		

		8,850	
Net current liabilities		-------	550

			132,350
			=======
			£s
Excess of Income over Expenditure			132,350
			=======

Solution to Question 14.1 (Continued)

Note (1)	£
Bar Account	

	£
Sales	92,220
Less Cost of sales	60,700

GROSS PROFIT	31,520
Less Wages	3,120

	28,400
	========

Solution to Question 14.2

	A		B		C		D		E		F		G		H		I		J		K		L	
1																								
2																								
3	Description		Subs.		Premises Cost		Premises Dep'n		F + F Cost		F + F Dep'n		Bank		I + E Year		I + E		Dance				
4																								
5																								
6	Opening Balances		1200		90000		-50000		20000		-14000		2000				-49200						
7																								
8	Subs. received		-34000										34000										
9	Dance Takings												15000						-15000				
10	Rates												-1200		1200								
11	General Expenses												-28000		28000								
12	Dance Expenses												-8000						8000				
13	-------																						
14	Sub-Totals		-32800		90000		-50000		20000		-14000		13800		29200		-49200		-7000				
15																								
16	Subscriptions		33700										-33700										
17	Depreciation - Premises						-4000						4000										
18	Depreciation - F + F										-2000		2000										
19	Dance Profit												-7000						7000				
20	Surplus of I over E for year												5500		-5500								
21	-------																						
22	Closing Balance Sheet		900		90000		-54000		20000		-16000		13800		0		-54700		0				
23	=====																						

(continued)

Solution to Question 14.2 (Continued)

```
Allied Bowls Club
Income and Expenditure Account
   for the year ended 31 December 1987
```

	£	£
INCOME		
Subscriptions		33,700
Dance Profit		7,000
		40,700
EXPENDITURE		
Rates	1,200	
General Expences	28,000	
Depreciation	6,000	
		35,200
Surplus of Income over Expenditure		5,500

```
Accummulated Fund as at 31 December 1987
```

Fixed Assets	Cost £	Dep'n £	NBV £
Premises	90,000	54,000	36,000
Fixtures and Fittings	20,000	16,000	4,000
			40,000
Current Assets			
Subscription Debtors		900	
Bank		13,800	
			14,700
			54,700
Accumulated Fund			54,700

Solution to Question 15.1

	A		B		C		D		E		F		G		H	
1																
2																
3										.6		.4					
4	Description				Capital		Capital		Current		Current		Profit		Other	
5					Angie		Ben		Angie		Ben		& Loss		Net	
6													App.		Assets	
7	Opening Balances				-50000		-40000								90000	
8																
9	Profit for year												-42000		42000	
10																
11	Salary										-1500		1500			
12																
13	Drawings								2000						-2000	
14									2000						-2000	
15									2000						-2000	
16									2000						-2000	
17																
18																
19	Drawings										1500				-1500	
20											1500				-1500	
21											1500				-1500	
22											1500				-1500	
23																
24	Interest on Drawings								180				-180			
25									120				-120			
26									60				-60			
27									0				0			
28																
29	Interest on Drawings										135		-135			
30											90		-90			
31											45		-45			
32											0		0			
33																
34	Interest on Capital								-6000				6000			
35																
36											-4800		4800			
37																
38	Sub Total				-50000		-40000		2360		-30		-30330		118000	
39																
40	Profit Share								-18198				18198			
41																
42	Profit Share										-12132		12132			
43																
44																
45	Balance Sheet				-50000		-40000		-15838		-12162		0		118000	
46																

Solution to Question 15.2

	A Description	D Tangible Fixed Assets	E Net Current Assets	F Capital Account PP	G Current a PP	H RR	I Net Profit 1st Half	J Net Profit 2nd Half	K Capital Account RR	L Goodwill	M Loan
7	Balance Sheet 31-4-88	100000	123000	-170000	-18000	3000	-19000	-19000			
9	Assets brought in	40000	11000						-60000	9000	
11	Writing-off Goodwill			5400					3600	-9000	
13	Loan			40000							-40000
15	Salaries					-8000	4000	4000			
17	Interest on capital				-4115	-1410	5525				
18					-3115	-1410		4525			
20	Loan interest				-2000			2000			
22	Sub-totals	140000	134000	-124600	-27230	-7820	-9475	-8475	-56400	0	-40000
24	Profit split										
25	1st half				-5685	-3790	9475				
26	2nd half				-4237.5	-4237.5		8475			
28	Balance Sheet	140000	134000	-124600	-37152.5	-15847.5	0	0	-56400	0	-40000

Solution to Question 15.2 (Continued)

	Description	Tangible Fixed Assets (D)	Net Current Assets (E)	Capital Account PP (F)	Current acco PP (G)	RR (H)	Net Profit 1st Half (I)	Net Profit 2nd Half (J)	Capital Account RR (K)	Goodwill (L)	Loan (M)
7	Balance Sheet 31-4	100000	123000	-170000	-18000	3000	-38000/2	-38000/2			
9	Assets brought in	40000	11000						-60000	-SUM(D9:K9)	
11	Writing-off Goodwill			-L11*3/5					-L11*2/5	-L9	
13	Loan			40000							-F13
15	Salaries					-SUM(I15:J1	4000	4000			
17	Interest on capital				(F7+F11)*.0	(K9+K11)*.0	-SUM(G17:H17)				
18					(F7+F13+F11)*.05/2	(K9+K11)*.05/2		-SUM(G18:H18)			
20	Loan interest				-J20			-M13*.1/2			
22	Sub-totals	SUM(D7:D20)	SUM(E7:E20)	SUM(F7:F20)	SUM(G7:G20)	SUM(H7:H20)	SUM(I7:I20)	SUM(J7:J20)	SUM(K7:K20)	SUM(L7:L20)	SUM(M7:M20)
24	Profit split										
25	1st half				I22*3/5	I22*2/5	-SUM(G25:H25)				
26	2nd half				J22*.5	J22/2		-SUM(G26:H26)				
28	Balance Sheet	SUM(D22:D26)	SUM(E22:E26)	SUM(F22:F26)	SUM(G22:G26)	SUM(H22:H26)	SUM(I22:I26)	SUM(J22:J26)	SUM(K22:K26)	SUM(L22:L26)	SUM(M22:M26)

548 Solutions to questions and exercises

Solution to Question 15.3

	A	B	C	D	E	F	G	H	I	J	K	L
1												
2				.67	.33							
3	Description			Capital Accounts		Creditors	Goodwill	Furniture	Debtors-------		Bank	Realisation
4				C	T				Leeds	M/CR		
5												
6	Balance Sheet			-50.000	-13.000	-11.000	10.000	9.000	10.000	5.000	40.000	
7												
8	Goodwill						-10.000					10.000
9	Goodwill revalued			7.000	5.000							-12.000
10	Furniture							-9.000				9.000
11	Furniture revalued			5.000	3.000							-8.000
12	Debtors								-10.000	-5.000		15.000
13	Debtors taken			9.200	4.600							-13.800
14	Creditors					11.000						-11.000
15	Creditors Taken			10.700								-10.700
16	Dissolution costs										-1.100	1.100
17	Redecoration costs			-2.500	-.700							3.200
18	--------											----
19	Sub-totals			-20.600	-1.100	.000	.000	.000	.000	.000	38.900	-17.200
20												
21	Realisation split			-11.467	-5.733							17.200
22												
23	Cash split			11.467	5.733							-17.200
24	=======											=======

Solution to Question 15.5

Amis, Lodge and Pym

1. a.   *Trading, profit and loss and profit and loss appropriation account*
for the year to 31 Mary 1988

	£	£	£
Sales			404,500
Less: Cost of goods sold:			
Opening stock		30,000	
Purchases	225,000		
Carriage inwards	4,000		
		229,000	
		259,000	
Less: Closing stock		35,000	
			224,000
GROSS PROFIT			180,500
Add: Incomes:			
Bank interest		750	
Discounts received		4,530	
			5,280
			185,780
Less: Expenses:			
Carriage outwards		12,000	
Depreciation:			
Motor vehicles [(£80 − 20) × 25%]	15,000		
Plant and machinery (£100 × 20%)	20,000		
		35,000	
Discounts allowed		10,000	
Increase in provision for bad and doubtful debts			
[(£14,300 × 5%) − 420]		295	
Office expenses (£30,400 + 405)		30,805	
Rent, rates, heat and light (£8,800 − 1,500)		7,300	
			95,400
NET PROFIT FOR THE YEAR			90,380
Add: Interest on drawings and current accounts:			
Amis		1,000	
Lodge		900	
Pym		720	
			2,620
			93,000
Less: Appropriations:			
Salary–Pym		13,000	
Interest on capital accounts:			
Amis	8,000		
Lodge	1,500		
Pym	500		
		10,000	
			23,000
			70,000
Balance of profit:			
Amis (5/10)		35,000	
Lodge (3/10)		21,000	
Pym (2/10)		14,000	
			70,000

(continued)

Solution to Question 15.5 (Continued)

b.   *Current accounts*

	Amis £	Lodge £	Pym £		Amis £	Lodge £	Pym £
Balances b/d	1,000	500	400	Salary	—	—	13,000
Drawings	25,000	22,000	15,000	Interest on			
Interest on				capital accounts	8,000	1,500	500
Drawings	1,000	900	720	Balance of			
Balances to				profit	35,000	21,000	14,000
Capital Accounts	16,000	—	11,380	Balance to			
				Capital Account	—	900	—
	£43,000	£23,400	£27,500		£43,000	£23,400	£27,500

2. a.   *Realisation account at 1 April 1988*

	£		£
Motor vehicles (Wkg 1)	10,000	Trade creditors (Wkg 5)	500
Plant and machinery (Wkg 3)	8,400	Stock (Wkg 6)	3,500
Trade debtors (Wkg 4)	600	Good will (Wkg 2)	35,000
Capital accounts:			
Amis (5/10)	10,000		
Lodge (3/10)	6,000		
Pym (2/10)	4,000		
	£39,000		£39,000

b.   *Bank account*

	£		£
1988		1988	
31 March Balance b/d	4,900	1 April Office expenses	405
1 April Trade debtors	12,985	Trade creditors	16,000
Rent returned	1,500	Balance to Amis	76,000
Fowles Ltd	63,500		
Cash contributed by			
partners (to Capital):			
Lodge	4,900		
Pym	4,620		
	£92,405		£92,405

c.   *Capital accounts*

	Amis £	Lodge £	Pym £		Amis £	Lodge £	F £
1 April 1988				1 April 1987			
Current	—	900	—	Balances b/d	80,000	15,000	5,000
account							
Motor vehicles	5,000	—	—	1 April 1988			
Shares	25,000	25,000	25,000	Current	16,000	—	11,380
				accounts			
Bank	76,000	—	—	Realisation			
				account	10,000	6,000	4,000
				Bank	—	4,900	4,620
	£106,000	£25,900	£25,000		£106,000	£25,900	£25,000

Solution to Question 16.1

```
              Julie Morse
    Trading and Profit and loss Account
     for the year ended 31/12/91.
```

	£s	£s
Sales less returns		2,915,566
Less Cost of Sales:		
Opening Stock	325,312	
Purchases less returns	1,678,083	
Carriage Inwards	25	
	2,003,420	
Closing Stock	334,560	
		1,668,860
GROSS PROFIT		1,246,706
Add, Rent Receivable		907,936
Commission Receivable		16,864
Profit on sale of van		680
Discounts Received		13,420
Less, Rent Payable	701,760	
Insurance	147,696	
Selling Expenses	61,200	
Office Expenses	103,360	
Wages and Salaries	80,512	
Bad Debts	568	
Change in Doubtful debt Provision	758	
Depreciation Charge:		
Machinery 3,173		
Motor Vans 190,400		
	193,573	
Discounts Allowed	4,500	
Carriage Outwards	12,359	
		1,306,286
PROFIT BEFORE TAXATION		879,320
Less Taxation		307,762
PROFIT AFTER TAXATION		571,558
Less Transfer to reserves		100,000
PROFITS AVAILABLE FOR DISTRIBUTION		471,558
Less Interim Dividend	53,000	
Final Dividend	175,440	
		228,440
		243,118

(*continued*)

Solution to Question 16.1 (Continued)

```
Julie Morse
Balance Sheet as at 31/12/91.
                                £s              £s              £s
Fixed Assets
                                Cost        Depreciation
    Land                      2,229,040                       2,229,040
    Machinery                    56,320         27,765           28,555
    Motor Van                  761,600         247,380          514,220
                              ----------      ----------      ----------
                              3,046,960        275,145        2,771,815
                              ==========      ==========      ==========
Current Assets
    Stock                                       334,560
    Debtors                     203,984
    Less Provision                2,450
                              ----------
                                                201,534
    Prepayments Expenses                          16,320
    Accrued Revenues                               9,248
    Cash                                           6,120
                                                ----------
                                                567,782
Current Liabilities
    Creditors                   193,080
    Taxation                    307,762
    Proposed Dividend           175,440
    Accrued Expences            108,800
    Prepaid Revenue              16,864
    Bank Overdraft              447,576
                              ----------
                                              1,249,522
                                              ----------
Net Current Liabilities                                        -681,740
Loan                                                            232,357
                                                               ----------
                                                              1,857,718
                                                              ==========
Financed by:
Share Capital £1 Shares                                       1,169,600
Reserves                                                       429,342
Profit and Loss Account                                        258,776
                                                               ----------
                                                              1,857,718
                                                              ==========
```

Solution to Question 18.1

	CT current	Liability Future	ACT Recoverable	ACT Payable	DT	Divided	P + L	CT P + L a/c
Balance b/d	(52,000)	(60,000)	34,541		(26,500)		(120,000)	
ACT Recoverable Recovered	16,071	18,470	(34,541)					
Payment of CT Cr Bank	35,929							
Adjustment of CT		2,500						(2,500)
Transfer to Current	(39,030)	39,030						
ACT on interim dividend 35/65 × 12,500			6,731	(6,731)				
ACT paid Cr Bank		6,731		6,731				
ACT offset			(6,731)					
			13,462					
ACT on final dividend 35/65 × 2,500				(13,462)				
CT on profits for year		(75,000)						75,000
Profit for year							(150,000)	
DT calculator 79,500 − 75,000 = 4,500					(4,500)			4,500
CT to P + L a/c							77,000	(77,000)
Dividends – interim – Bank Cr							12,500	
– final					(25,000)	25,000		
	(39,030)	(68,269)	13,462	(13,462)	(31,000)	(25,000)	(155,500)	—
Balance b/d								

offset in B/S

Solution to Question 18.2

	CT current	L-T	DT	P + L	ACT Recoverable	Pay	CT in P + L a/c	Dividends
Balance b/d	(16,300)	(5,000)	(29,400)	(43,000)				
CT 1975 paid Cr Bank	16,300							
Dividend – interim Cr Bank				13,200				
ACT on interim dividend 34/66 × 6,600					6,800	(6,800)		
ACT paid Cr Bank						6,800		
Agreement of CT inability		1,200					(1,200)	
Net profit for 1977				(88,800)				
CT		(36,000)					36,000	
Transfer of 1976 Profits to Current	(3,800)	3,800						
Final Dividend				33,000				(33,000)
ACT on final dividend 34/66 × 16,500					17,000	(17,000)		
DT			(7,000)				7,000	
ACT Recoverable on paid dividend of that against CT liability		6,800		41,800	(6,800)		(41,800)	
Balance b/d	(3,800)	(29,200)	(36,400)	(43,800)	17,000	(17,000)	NIL	(33,000)

offset in B/S

Solution to Question 20.1

1. **Greet plc**
Profit and loss account for the year to 31 March 1988

	Notes	£000
Turnover		1,950
Cost of sales (£140 + 960 − 150)	1	(950)
GROSS PROFIT		1,000
Distribution costs	1	(420)
Administrative expenses	1	(210)
OPERATING PROFIT		370
Non-operating income [£73 + (73 × 27/73)]	2	100
PROFIT ON ORDINARY ACTIVITIES BEFORE TAXATION		470
Tax on profit on ordinary activities		(70)
PROFIT ON ORDINARY ACTIVITIES AFTER TAXATION		400
Extraordinary item less taxation	4	40
PROFIT FOR THE FINANCIAL YEAR AVAILABLE FOR APPROPRIATION		440
Dividend	5	(300)
RETAINED PROFIT FOR THE YEAR		£140
Earnings per share	6	66.7p

Balance sheet as at 31 March 1988

	Notes	£000
FIXED ASSETS		
Tangible assets	7	530
Investments	8	560
		1,090
CURRENT ASSETS		
Stock		150
Debtors		470
Cash at bank and in hand		40
		660
CREDITORS: AMOUNTS FALLING DUE WITHIN ONE YEAR	9	(716)
NET CURRENT ASSETS		(56)
TOTAL ASSETS LESS CURRENT LIABILITIES		1,034
PROVISIONS FOR LIABILITIES AND CHARGES		
Taxation, including deferred taxation	10	(112)
		£922
CAPITAL AND RESERVES		
Called up share capital	11	600
Profit and loss account	12	322
		£922

These accounts were approved by the Board on 00 Month 1988

_____

_____ *Directors*

(*continued*)

Solution to Question 20.1 (Continued)

The attached notes form part of these accounts.

Notes to the accounts for the year to 31 March 1988

	£000
1. The following items have been charged in arriving at distribution costs and administrative expenses:	
Depreciation	32
Hire of plant and machinery	35
Auditors' remuneration	30
Directors' emoluments	45
2. Non-operating income:	
Listed fixed asset investments	100
3. Tax on profit on ordinary activities	
Made-up as follows:	
UK Corporation tax based on the profits for the year at a rate of 35 per cent	52
Overprovision for tax in the previous year	(25)
Tax credit on franked investment income (£73 × 27/73)	27
Increase in provision for deferred taxation	16
	70
4. Extraordinary item	
Profits deriving from events or transactions outside the normal activities of the company:	
Sale of Belgium factory	60
Taxation thereon	(20)
	40
5. Dividend	
Proposed final ordinary dividend of 50p per share	300
6. Earnings per share	
The calculation of earnings per ordinary share is based upon the number of ordinary shares in issue during the year (600,000) and on the profit for the year after taxation, but before the extraordinary item (£400,000)	66.7p
7. Tangible assets	
Plant and machinery:	
Cost at 31 March 1987	750
Aggregate depreciation at 31 March 1987	188
Provided during the year	32
	220
Net book value at 31 March 1988	530
8. Investments	
Investments include listed fixed asset investments at cost (market value at 31 March 1988, £580,000).	
There have been no movements during the year	560
9. Creditors: amounts falling due within one year	
Trade creditors	260
Other creditors including taxation and social security (£52 + 20) + (111 − 27)	156
Proposed dividend	300
	716

Solution to Question 20.1 (Continued)

10. Provisions for liabilities and charges
    Deferred taxation

At 31 March 1987	180
Provided during the year	16
	196
Recoverable advance corporation tax (111 − 27)	(84)
	112

11. Called up share capital

	Authorised	*Issued*
	£000	£000
Ordinary shares of £1 each	1,000	600

12. Profit and loss account

At 31 March 1987	182
Retained profit for the year	140
At 31 March 1988	322

Solution to Question 20.3

ARTHUR PLC

PROFIT AND LOSS ACCOUNT
for the year ended 30 June 1988

NOTES		£s
(a)	TURNOVER	1,300
(b)	Cost of Sales	660
	Gross Profit	640
(c)	Distribution costs	26
(d)	Administrative expenses	461
		153
(e)	Other operating income	0
		153
	Income from other fixed asset investments	
	Other interest receivable	
		153
(f)	Interest payable	16
	PROFIT ON ORDINARY ACTIVITIES BEFORE TAXATION	137
(g)	Tax on profit on ordinary activities	50
	Profit on ordinary activities after taxation	87
(h)	Extraordinary item, less taxation	
	PROFIT FOR THE FINANCIAL YEAR	87
(i)	DIVIDENDS	66
(p)	TRANSFERS TO RESERVES	21

(*continued*)

Solution to Question 20.3 (Continued)

ARTHUR PLC

BALANCE SHEET
as at 30 June 1988

NOTES		£s	£s
	FIXED ASSETS		
	Intangible assets		
(j)	Tangible assets		893
	Investments		
			893
	CURRENT ASSETS		
(k)	Stocks	500	
(l)	Debtors	266	
	Investments		
	Cash at bank and in hand	40	
		806	
	CREDITORS: Amounts falling due		
(m)	within one year	358	
	NET CURRENT ASSETS		448
	TOTAL ASSETS LESS CURRENT LIABILITIES		1,341
	CREDITORS: Amounts falling due after more than one		
(n)	year	200	
	PROVISIONS FOR LIABILITIES AND CHARGES		
			200
			1,141
	CAPITAL AND RESERVES		
(o)	Called up share capital		400
	Share premium account		240
	Capital Redemption Reserve		60
	Revaluation reserve		300
(p)	Other reserves		0
(p)	Profit and Loss Account		141
			1,141

Solution to Question 20.3 (Continued)

	NOTES		£s
(a)	Sales		1,300
	Less sales returns		0

	Turnover		1,300
			=========
(b)	Opening stock		240
	Purchases		920
	Carriage inwards		0
	Less purchase returns		0

			1,160
	Less closing stock		500

	Cost of sales		660
			=========
(c)	Carriage outwards		0
	Selling expenses		4
	Bad debts		8
	Change in doubtful debt provision		14

	Distribution costs		26
			=========
(d)	Rent		0
	Insurance		0
	General Business Expenses		84
	Wages and Salaries		324
	Discounts allowed		0
	Audit fee		6
	Depreciation:		
	FL&B	24	
	PME	23	

			47

	Administration expenses		461
			=========
(e)	Discounts received		0
	Rent receivable	0	
	Less prepayment	0	

			0
	Commission receivable	0	
	Add accrual	0	

			0
	Profit on sale of van		0

	Other operating income		0
			=========
(f)	Interest payable		
	8% Debentures		16
			=========

(continued)

Solution to Question 20.3 (Continued)

(g)	Taxation		
	Corporation tax: 35% of profits		50
			=========
(h)	Extraordinary Item		
(i)	Interim Dividend		
	Ordinary		30
	Preference		6
	Final Dividend		
	Ordinary		30
	Preference		0

			66
			=========

(j)   Tangible Fixed Assets

	Cost Revaluat.	Dep'n	NBV
Freehold Property	960	184	776
Machinery	220	103	117
	----	-----	---
	1,180	287	893
	=====================================

The Freehold property was revalued on 31.6.88
Its cost was £720,000
The Machinery was revalued on 31.6.88
Its cost was £160,000

(k)   Raw materials
         Work in progress
         Finished goods

                                                       500
                                                  =========

(l)	Trade debtors	280	
	Less Provision	14	

			266
	Prepaid expenses		0
	Accrued income		0

	Debtors		266
			=========

(m)	Trade creditors	260
	Accrued expenses	4
	Prepaid revenue	0
	Corporation tax	50
	Debentur interest	8
	Dividend	30
	Audit fee	6
	Bank overdraft	0

		358
		=========

Solution to Question 20.3 (Continued)

```
(n)      8% Debentures                                          200
                                                          =========
         The Debentures are secured on Freehold Property.

(o)      Authorised share capital
         400,000 Ordinary Shares at £1 each                    400

         200,000 6% Pref. Shares at £1 each                    200
                                                          ---------
                                                               600
                                                          =========

         Issued and fully paid share capital
         300,000 Ordinary Shares at £1 each                    300

         100,000 6% Pref. Shares at £1 each          1         100
                                                          ---------
                                                               400
                                                          =========

                                                       P & L

(p)      Balance as at 1 January 1988                          120
         Profit for year                                        21
                                                          ---------
         Balance as at 31 December 1988                        141
                                                          =========
```

Solution to Question 20.4

file hebden

HEBDEN plc

PROFIT AND LOSS ACCOUNT
for the year ended 30 September 1988

NOTES		s
(a)	TURNOVER	3600
(b)	Cost of Sales	2180
	Gross Profit	1420
(c)	Distribution costs	930
(d)	Administrative expenses	360
		130
(e)	Other operating income	0
		130
	Income from other fixed asset investments	21
	Other interest receivable	
		151
(f)	Interest payable	40
	PROFIT ON ORDINARY ACTIVITIES BEFORE TAXATION	111
(g)	Tax on profit on ordinary activities	302
	Profit on ordinary activities after taxation	−191

(*continued*)

Solution to Question 20.4 (Continued)

(h)	Extraordinary item, less taxation	
	PROFIT FOR THE FINANCIAL YEAR	−191
(i)	DIVIDENDS	250
(p)	TRANSFERS TO RESERVES	−441

Layout and notes

HEBDEN plc
BALANCE SHEET
as at 30th September 1988

NOTES		s	s
	FIXED ASSETS		
	Intangible assets		
(j)	Tangible assets		1980
(q)	investments		190
			2170
	CURRENT ASSETS		
(k)	Stocks	290	
(l)	Debtors	360	
	Investments		
	Cash at bank and in hand	70	
		720	
(m)	CREDITORS: Amounts falling due within one year	792	
	NET CURRENT ASSETS		−72
	TOTAL ASSETS LESS CURRENT LIABILITIES		2098
(n)	CREDITORS: Amounts falling due after more than one year	290	
	PROVISIONS FOR LIABILITIES AND CHARGES	—	
			290
			1080
	CAPITAL AND RESERVES		
(o)	Called up share capital		1200
(p)	Share premium account		70
	Capital Redemption Reserve		
(p)	Revaluation reserve		600
(p)	Other reserves		
(p)	Profit and Loss Account		−62
			1808

	13
	2
	15

(a)	Sales	3600
	Less sales returns	0
	Turnover	3600

Solution to Question 20.4 (Continued)

(b)	Opening stock		270
	Purchases		2200
	Carriage inwards		0
	Less purchase returns		0
			2470
	Less closing stock		290
	Cost of sales		2180
(c)	Carriage outwards		
	Selling expenses		690
	Bad debts		
	Change in doubtful debt provision		240
	Distribution costs		930
	Administration expenses		360
(e)	Other operating income		0
(f)	Interest payable		
	8 per cent Debentures		40
(g)	Taxation		
	Corporation tax: 35 per cent of profits		302
(h)	Extraordinary Item		
(i)	Interim Dividend		
	Ordinary		0
	Preference		0
	Final Dividend		
	Ordinary		250
	Preference		0
			250

(j) Tangible Fixed Assets

	Cost Revaluat.	Dep'n	NBV
Land	1000		1000
Buildings	800	40	760
Motor Vehicles	245	25	220
	2045	65	1980

The Land and Buildings were revalued on 30.9.88 by Messrs Smith and Harris, local valuers. Its cost had cost 800,000 and 400,000 respectively.

(k)	Raw materials	?
	Work in progress	?
	Finished goods	?
		290

On 3rd October 50,000 of this stock was destroyed by fire.

(l)	Trade debtors	600	
	Less Provision	240	
			360
	Prepaid expenses		0
	Accrued income		0
	Debtors		360

(*continued*)

Solution to Question 20.4 (Continued)

(m)

	Trade creditors	420
	Accrued expenses	0
	Prepaid revenue	0
	Corporation tax	102
	Debenture interest	20
	Dividend	250
	Audit fee	0
	Bank overdraft	0
		792
	Corporation Tax	290
(n)		290

The Debentures are secured on Freehold Property.

(o)

Authorised share capital	
1,200,000 Ordinary Shares at £1 each	1200
	1200
Issued and fully paid share capital	
1,200,000 Ordinary Shares at £1 each	1200
	1200

		P & L P & L	Share Premium	Revaluati Reserve
(p)	Balance as at 1 January 1988	379	25	
	Profit for year	−441		
	Redemption of debentures		− 45	
	Revaluation			600
	Balance as at 31 December 1988	− 62	70	600
(q)	Investments			
	Listed Investments			

Cost	190
Market Value	209

RECOMMENDED DIVIDEND

Too high as this year profits can not finance it. Who is the competitor. Problems of failing to meet investor expectations. One mark for each point.

Solution to Question 21.1

	Description	Fixed Assets Cost	Fixed Assets Dep'n	Stock	Debtors	Bank	Creditors	Dividend	Share Capital	P & L	Source & APP
8	Balance Sheet 31/3/87	288000	-28000	27000	18000	15000	-20000	-15000	-200000	-85000	40000
10	Fixed Asset Additions	14000				-14000					-14000
12	Fixed Asset Sales	-6000	2000			3800				200	3800
14	Depreciation		-12000							12000	0
16	Share Issue					25000			-25000		25000
18	Dividend Paid					-15000		15000			-15000
20	Dividend Proposed							-10000		10000	0
22	Change in debtors				27000	-27000					0
24	Change In Stock			23000		-23000					0
26	Change in Creditors					-14000	14000				0
28	Change in Profit					39200				-39200	39200
30											0
33	Balance Sheet 31/3/88	296000	-38000	50000	45000	-10000	-6000	-10000	-225000	-102000	79000

(a) Net Trading Profit

Net Trading Profit	39,200
Less Loss on sale of FA	200
Less Depreciation	12,000
	27,000
Less Dividends	10,000
Change in P & L Account	17,000

(continued)

Solution to Question 21.1 (Continued)

(b)Cash Flow Statement for the year ended 31 March 1988.

Bank balance at beginning of year   15,000

Additions:

Sale of Fixed Assets	3,800	
Share Issue	25,000	
Trading Profit	39,200	

		68,000

Deductions:

Purchase of Fixed Assets	14,000	
Dividend Paid	15,000	
Change in Debtors	27,000	
Change in Stock	23,000	
Change in Creditors	14,000	

		93,000

		-10,000
		========

(c)Statement of Source and Application of Funds
     for the year ended 31 March 1988.

	£s	£s
Trading Profit		27,000
Adjustment for those items which do not involve the flow of funds:		
Depreciation	12,000	
Loss on sale of Fixed Asset	200	

		12,200

Total Generated from Operations		39,200
Other Sources:		
Sale of Fixed Asset	3,800	
Share Issue	25,000	

		28,800

		68,000
Applications:		
Purchase of Fixed Assets	14,000	
Dividend Paid	15,000	

		29,000

		39,000
		========
Change in Stocks		23,000
Change in Debtors		27,000
Change in Creditors		14,000

		64,000
Movement in Net Liquid Funds:		
Change in Bank		-25,000

		39,000
		========

Solution to Question 22.1

1. Ratios

	1986.00	1987.00	1988.00
Gross Margin	31.43	16.84	29.09
Net margin	8.57	5.26	9.09
ROCE	10.00	6.67	10.00
Net asset turnover	1.17	1.06	0.73
Gearing	0.00	16.67	33.33
Net profit per employee	24.00	16.67	22.73

2. Comments

Sales expanding each year – signs of a slow off in this growth
Profit variable – through an upturn in 1988
Growth financed by an expansion in capital employed (both equit
Gearing climbing – could be risky
Profit margins variable – fall-off last year but appear to have
Better control of overheads in 1988 = highest net margin
ROCE at 10 per cent – acceptable return these days;
1987 fall due largely to poor margins
1988 recovery due to improved margins, but worrying decline
    in net asset turnover
profit per employee variable, and falling from its 1986 level

One mark for each clearly made point

3. Other information

Market values for assets and share price
Industry prospects
Statistics on other companies in this industry
LIQUIDITY INFORMATION
Quality of management
Quality of employees and training policy
Product profile

Solution to Question 22.5

Profit and loss accounts for the year to 31 March 1988

	Chan plc £000	Ling plc £000	Wong plc £000
1. Operating profit	300	300	300
Interest payable	—	—	(10)
PROFIT ON ORDINARY ACTIVITIES BEFORE TAX	300	300	290
Taxation (30 per cent)	(90)	(90)	(87)
PROFIT ON ORDINARY ACTIVITIES AFTER TAX	210	210	203
Dividends: Preference	—	(20)	(30)
Ordinary	(100)	(60)	(40)
	(100)	(80)	(70)
RETAINED PROFIT FOR THE YEAR	£110	£130	£133

(continued)

Solution to Question 22.5 (Continued)

		Chan plc	Ling plc	Wong plc
2. a. Earnings per share Net profit after tax and preference dividend Number of ordinary shares in issue	=	$\dfrac{210}{500}$	$\dfrac{210-20}{300}$	$\dfrac{203-30}{200}$
	=	42p	63.3p	86.5p
b. Price/earnings ratio Market price of ordinary shares Earnings per share	=	$\dfrac{840}{42}$	$\dfrac{950}{63.3}$	$\dfrac{1038}{86.5}$
	=	20	15	12

c. Gearing ratio

Chan plc $\quad=\quad$ Nil

$$\text{Ling plc} = \frac{200}{600} \times 100 \quad = \quad 33.3 \text{ per cent}$$

$$\text{Wong plc} = \frac{300 + 100}{700} \times 100 \quad = \quad 57.1 \text{ per cent}$$

3. A gearing ratio expresses the relationship that exists between total borrowings (that is, preference share capital and long-term loans), and the total amount of ordinary shareholders' funds. It should be noted that other definitions of gearing are possible and are sometimes used.

Any company with a gearing ratio of (say) 50 per cent would be considered to be high geared, while a company with a gearing ratio of (say) 20 per cent would be low geared.

Gearing is an important matter to consider when investing in ordinary shares in a particular company. A high geared company means that a high proportion of the company's earnings are committed to paying either interest on any debenture stock and/or dividends on any preference share capital before an ordinary dividend can be declared. If a company is low geared, then a high proportion of the company's earnings can be paid out as ordinary dividends.

Chan plc has not issued any long-term loans or any preference share capital. Gearing does not, therefore, apply to this company, and all of the earnings may be paid out to the ordinary shareholders.

Ling plc is a relatively low geared company. It has no debenture stock, and only a small proportion of its earnings are committed to paying its preference shareholders. The balance may then all be declared as an ordinary dividend.

Wong plc is an extremely high geared company. A high proportion of borrowings (in this case consisting of both debenture stock and preference share capital), means that a high proportion of its earnings has to be set aside for both its debenture holders and its preference shareholders before any ordinary dividend can be declared. As a result, if the profits of the company are low, no ordinary dividend may be payable.

If profits are rising a high geared company may not be a particularly risky company in which to purchase some ordinary shares, but the reverse may apply if profits are falling.

For the year to 31 March 1988. Chan, Ling and Wong's operating profit is identical. Wong is committed to paying interest on its debenture stock (which is allowable against tax), and both Ling and Wong have to pay a preference dividend (which is not allowable against tax).

In deciding whether to invest in any of the three companies, there are a great many other factors to be considered, including future prospects of all three companies. However, *ceteris paribus*, when profits are fluctuating an ordinary shareholder is more likely to receive a higher return by investing in Chan rather than by investing in either Ling or Wong.

Similarly, an ordinary shareholder can expect a higher return by investing in Ling rather than by investing in Wong.

Based on the limited amount of information given in question, therefore, an investor considering purchasing ordinary shares in only one of these three companies would be recommended to buy shares in Chan plc.

It should be noted that if profits were *increasing*, an investor would be recommended to buy shares first in Wong, then in Ling and finally in Chan. The earnings per share in both Ling and Wong are far higher than in Chan, so there is a much greater chance of an increase in the ordinary dividend, but this is not necessarily the case if profits are falling or fluctuating.

Index

abacus, 3
abridged accounts, 398
absolute performance measures, 116
absolute relationship, 13
accelerated capital allowances, 355
account, 188
account prompts, 197
accounting equation, 22
accounting for depreciation
  new method, 88
  old method, 88
accounting ledger systems, 184
accounting policies, 397, 474
accounting profits, 342
accounting software packages, 196
accounting standards, 368
Accounting Standards Committee *see* ASC
accounts clerk, 473
accounts for internal use, 389
accruals, 54
  concept, 355, 371
accrued expenses, 54
accrued revenues, 57
accumulated depreciation, 84
ACT, 344
  payable, 344
  recoverable, 344
adding machine, 3
adjusting events, 378
administration costs, 391
administration expenses, 106
Advanced Corporation Tax *see* ACT
advisers, 465
AEI, 368
age analysis of debtors, 70, 442
agents, 8
allocation, 107
allotment of shares, 316, 325
amortisation, 278
analysts, 465
analytical review, 501
annual general meeting, 307, 308

application and allotment column/account, 327
application for shares, 316, 325
applied research, 377
appointment of an auditor, 500
arbitrary, 446
articles of association, 306
articles of association–model set, 306
ASC, 369, 495
asset turnover ratio, 444
assets, 22
attributable profit, 375
audit, 9
  fees, 393, 496, 498, 500
  opinion, 497, 501
  report, 498, 502
auditing, 495
auditor, 9, 370
authorised share capital, 305, 327, 396
AVCO (average cost), 109

Babbage, Charles, 5
bad and doubtful debts (subscriptions), 246
bad debts, 70
balance sheet, 29
bank
  account, 29
  borrowing, 312, 318
  managers, 440
  reconciliation statement, 206
  statement, 206
bankruptcy, 220
basic rate of income tax, 344, 346
bills of exchange, 314, 320
binary notation, 5
bit, 5
blank, 14
bogus values, 197
bonus (script) issue, 317, 331
books of prime entry, 184
bought-in goods and services, 466
bounced cheques, 206
brand names, 273

Burroughs, William, 5
business
    contact groups, 465
    finance, 308, 444
    risk, 444
buying price, 479
byte, 5

calculator, 8
calls, 316, 325
capital, 22, 26, 149
    allowances, 314, 349
    based grants, 371
    employed, 475
    expenditure, 134, 396
    gains, 307, 316
    maintenance base, 476, 479, 480
Capital Redemption Reserve Fund (CRRF), 317, 334
capitalise, 246, 323
capitalised interest, 397
carriage inwards, 139
carriage outwards, 139
cash book, 187
cash discounts, 139, 185
cash flow problems, 220
cash flow statement, 241, 413
ccc, 305
cells, 11
chairman's remuneration, 393
chairman's statement, 399
changes in accounting policy, 374
charges (fixed and floating), 315
charitable contributions, 398
cheque stub, 187
circulating capital, 414
class of account, 168
clean audit report, 498, 502
clubs, 241
collecting agent, 340
columns, 11
commission, 320
Companies Act 1985, 304, 389, 497, 501
Companies Acts, 4
companies limited by guarantee, 305
comparability, 369
compensating error, 168
competitors, 465
compliance tests, 500
computerised accounting systems, 195
conceptual framework, 368
confidentiality, 465
consistency, 110
consolidated accounts, 394, 451
consolidating act, 305
construction companies, 375
contingencies, 379
contingent liability, 356, 396

control account ledger system, 192
control accounts, 191
control cell, 167
control, column, 167
control totals, 197
controls in computerised systems, 197
convertable debentures, 315
copy, 13
copy invoice, 185
corporate report, 463
Corporation Tax (CT), 341
Corporation Tax liability, 342
Corporation Tax payable, 342
cost accounting, 106
cost concept, 34, 474
cost of sales, 42
costs of dissolution, 282
CPP *see* current purchasing power
CRC *see* current replacement cost
credit, 23
    control, 442
creditor protection, 476
creditors, 34
creditors control account reconciliation statement, 203
creditors falling due
    after one year, 395
    within one year, 395
creditors ledger, 190
creditors' collection period, 442
creditors' information needs, 463
cross-sectional study, 446
CT *see* Corporation Tax
cumulative preference shares, 318
current
    assets, 149, 394
    cost, 271, 475
    cost profit, 475
    liabilities, 149
    operating profit, 475
    ratio, 443
    value systems, 476
current net realisable value (CNRV) accounting, 480
current purchasing power (CPP) accounting, 479
current replacement cost (CRC) accounting, 479
current value accounting (CVA), 479
custodian role, 464
customers, 465
Customs and Excise Authorities, 340
CVA *see* current value accounting

debenture interest, 346
Debenture Redemption Reserve, 325
debentures, 315, 346
debit, 23
debtors, 42, 395

debtors control account reconciliation statement, 201
debtors ledger, 190
Debtors' collection period, 442
deferred
 credit balance, 371
 revenue account, 246
 tax charge, 352
 tax provision, 352
deferred taxation (DT), 349
definitions, 503
deflation, 477
delete, 14
Department of Trade and Industry, 465
depreciation, 83, 473
 expense, 88
development, 377
 costs, 394
direct debits, 206
direct materials, 106
direct wages, 106
directors, 305, 399
directors'
 remuneration, 393
 report, 398
disciplinary proceedings, 370
discount house, 314, 321
discounts allowed, 139
discounts for early settlement, 313
discounts received, 139
dishonoured cheques, 206
disposal of fixed assets, 93
distribution expenditure/costs, 107, 391
dividend
 cover, 466
 policy, 308, 445
 waiver, 398
 yield, 445
dividends, 307, 316
division of accounts, 189
double entry, 23
doubtful debts, 70
drawings, 223
DT *see* deferred taxation
duality concept, 23
due date, 340
duties of directors, 306

earnings per share (EPS), 371, 445
economic life, 85
economic life of goodwill, 278
economists, 474
economy, 499
ED *see* exposure draft
edit, 14
effectiveness, 499
efficiency, 445, 499
electronic computer, 5

employee reports 465
employees, 465
employees'
 information needs, 463
 remuneration, 393
Employment Act (1982), 399
enforsed balancing, 197
enterprise agencies, 220
entertaining costs, 352
entity concept, 26
entrance fees, 246
environmental societies, 465
equity capital, 315, 325
errors, 165
 of addition, 167
 of commission, 168
 and fraud, 497
 not revealed by the spreadsheet, 168
 of ommission, 168
 of principle, 170
 revealed by the spreadsheet, 167
 of transcription, 167
exceptional items, 374, 393
exempt goods and services, 340, 359
expense, 133
export sale, 314, 443
exposure draft (ED), 369
external audit, 499
extraordinary items, 371, 393

factoring, 313, 318
FASB, 480
FIFO, 109
final audit visit, 500
final dividend, 308
finance lease, 315, 323, 379
financial accounting, 9
 theory, 368
financial manager, 311
financial risk, 444
finished goods, 108
first/initial record, 185
fixed asset register/ledger, 191
fixed asset replacement reserve, 307
fixed asset turnover ratio, 445
fixed assets, 83, 148, 394, 398
fixed price, 316
forfeited share, 328
foreign customers, 443
foreseeable future, 355
format of accounts, 141, 389, 390, 391
formulae, 13
fraction, 440
fraud and error, 3, 189, 192
free depreciation, 380
full accounts, 397
full product cost, 107
fund, 414

fundamental errors, 374
funds flow, 414
future orientated, 400

gearing ratio, 444
GEC, 368
general price index, 479
general reserve, 307
generally accepted accounting principles, 498
going concern concept, 378
goodwill, 394
government, 465
graph, 88
grid refrence, 11
gross amount, 187
gross dividend, 346
gross profit, 133
    margin, 445
group financial statements, 370
guaranteed, 313

health service price index, 477
heavy share price, 317
high street banks, 312
highest paid director's remuneration, 393
hire purchase, 314, 322
historic cost accounting, 473
historic cost convention, 9, 270
holding gains, 475, 480
    reserve, 488
    holding loss, 493
Hollerith, Herman, 5
horizontal presentation of accounts, 141
horizontal style, 390

IBM, 5, 6, 196
immaterial, 343
impersonal accounts, 190
imputation system of taxation, 346
in the post, 206
income, 223
    and expenditure account, 244
    tax, 223, 308, 346
incomplete records, 221
incorrect figure, 168
independence, 496
indirect materials, 106
inflation accounting, 451
information, 9
    technology, 6, 7
Inland Revenue, 342, 498
    rules, 349
input, 9
insert, 14
Institute of Chartered Accountants in England
    and Wales, 4, 6

insurance companies, 317
insurance scheme, 314
intangible assets, 394
integers, 330
inter-firm study, 446
inter-temporal study, 446
interest, 313
    on building society investments, 444
    rates, 313
interim audit visit, 500
interim dividend, 308
intermediate sales, 340
internal audit, 499
internal controls, 500
investment analysis, 440
investment decisions, 475
investments, 394
investors, 307
invoice, 185
irrecoverable VAT, 360
issued share capital, 327

joining fees, 246
journal entries, 170

Lascaux, 3
leasing, 314, 323, 379
ledger system, 185, 188
Leibniz, Gottfried von, 5
letter of engagement, 500
letter of weakness, 497
leverage, 441
liabilities, 22, 149
life membership, 246
LIFO, 109
limited liability companies, 304
limited partners, 260
liquidation, 304, 311, 313, 377, 411, 444
liquidity ratios, 442
loan, 34
    creditors, 464
    guarantee scheme, 313
loans to directors, 395
loans to employees, 396
local authorities, 465
lodgements, 206
long term
    finance, 312
    growth ratios, 445
    liabilities, 149
    loan, 315, 323
    project, 311
    work in progress, 375

mainstream corporation tax, 344
make or buy decision, 116
management accounting, 105
management letter, 497, 501

manufacturing, 105
  account, 116
  companies, 390
  cost, 106
market value of land and buildings, 398
market value of listed investments, 394
material errors, 498
material items, 374
materiality concept, 134, 463, 498
matrix, 11
medium companies, 397
members, 306
memorandum of association, 305
merchant bank, 317
micro-processor, 6
misallocation of resources, 475
missing entires, 222
modified accounts, 397
modular computerised systems, 196
monetary
  assets, 484
  column, 481
  gain, 484
  items, 481, 484
  liabilities, 484
  loss, 484
money measurement concept, 273
money of lesser value, 481
motor van, 33

nanoseconds, 9
net amount, 187
net book value, 84
net current asset turnover ratio, 445
net dividend, 346
net present value (NPV), 480
net profit, 133
  margin, 444, 445
net realisable value, 376
Neumann, John von, 5
nominal
  accounts, 191
  ledger, 191
  value, 316
non-adjusting events, 378
non-distributable reserve, 317
non-monetary items, 481
non-profit making organisations, 241
non-voting shares, 317
notes to accounts, 392
NRV (net realisable value), 113

objective criteria, 473
objectives of a company, 305
objectivity, 93
  concept, 112
one sided entry, 167
operating lease, 314, 379

optimum level of gearing, 444
options, 315
order of liquidity, 149
ordinary activities, 374
ordinary resolution, 306, 307
ordinary share capital, 315
ordering in large quantities, 443
over-subscription, 316
overdrafts, 312
overhead costs, 106
overstatement, 475, 500
overtrading, 411

Pacioli, Luca, 4, 7
paid basis, 355
par value, 327
partial provision for deferred tax, 355
participating preference shares, 318
Partnership Act
  1890, 260
  1907, 260
partnerships, 259
  admittance of a new partner, 275
  agreement, 260
  allocation of profits, 262
  capital column/account, 262
  change in profit sharing ratio, 275
  changes in partners, 270
  current column/account, 262
  dissolution, 278
  exit of a partner, 275
  Garner vs. Murray (1904), 282
  goodwill, 274
  interest on capital, 263
  interest on drawings, 265
  introduction of capital, 261
  new profit sharing ratio, 275
  profit and loss appropriation account, 267
  salaries, 265
  winding up, 278
Pascal, Blaise, 4
passwords, 197
penalties, 340
pension
  commitments, 396
  costs, 380
pension funds, 317
percentage, 440
period of time (ratios), 440
period statements, 147
permanent differences, 352
personal accounts, 189
physical assets, 480
piecemeal, 369
placing, 317, 331
planning an audit, 500
plc, 305

political contributions, 398
position statements, 147
post balance sheet events, 398
preference shares, 317, 332, 334
prepaid expenses, 56
prepaid revenues, 58
prepayments, 56
prescribed format, 389
present value (PV), 480
pressure groups, 465
price, 474
  accounting, 474
  changes, 474
price level
  accounting, 474
  changes, 474
price/earnings (PE ratio), 445
principle activities, 398
prime cost, 106
prior year adjustments, 374
private companies, 305
privatisation, 325
pro rata basis, 327
problems of historic cost accounts, 473
product cost, 106
production overheads, 106
productive capacity, 480
profit, 39
  and loss account, 133
  and loss appropriation account, 139, 306
  goal, 241
  -making activities within non-profit making
    organisations, 245
profitability ratios, 444
profits available for distribution, 308
progress payments, 377
proper accounting records, 497, 498
proportion, 440
prospectus, 316
provision for depreciation, 88
provision for doubtful debts, 70
provisions, 69, 396
prudence concept, 34, 59, 376
prudence overriding accruals, 377
public companies, 305
public issue, 316
published company accounts, 389
purchase invoice, 186
purchase ledger control account, 192
purchase of own shares, 317, 331, 399
purchase returns day book, 187
purchases, 33
pure research, 377

qualified audit report, 498, 502
quality, 445
quick ratio, 443

ratio analysis, 440, 501
raw material valuation, 109
raw materials, 108
re-occurring items, 343
real accounts, 190
realisation, 44, 474
  column/account, 278
realised holding gain, 488
receipts and payments account, 241
receivership, 411
recommended dividend, 398
reconciliation statements, 200
reconciling items, 200
recoverable VAT, 360
redeemable shares, 396
redemption of debentures, 323
reducing balance method of depreciation, 85
registered office, 305
Registrar of Companies, 389, 397
relative performance measures, 116
relative relationship, 13
remittance advice, 187
rent, 41
rental payments, 379
repayable on demand, 313
replicate, 13
repurchasing debentures, 315
research and development, 398
reserves, 396
residual value, 85
retail price index, 474, 477
retail trade, 442
retained profits, 316
return of value added, 467
return offered by other investments, 444
return on capital employed, 444, 451, 475
  overall version, 444
  shareholders' version, 444
returns
  inwards, 135, 186
  outwards, 135, 186
revaluation, 271, 355, 479
  reserve, 96, 479
revenue based grants, 371
revenue expenditure, 134
rights issue, 316, 330
risks of investments, 444
rollover relief, 355
Rolls Royce, 377
rows, 11

sale and lease back, 315
sale of fixed assets, 93
sales, 42
  day book, 185
  ledger control account, 192
  returns day book, 187
samples, 498

save, 16
scrap value, 85
screen prints, 14, 264
seasonal trends, 443
secured against fixed assets, 313
security, 395
segregation of duties, 192, 197
sellers market, 474
selling expenditure/costs, 107
selling price, 480
settlement discount, 442
  premium, 324
  price, 445
shareholders, 464
shoebox accounting, 220
short-term finance, 312
short-term loans, 312
single entry book-keeping, 220
sinking fund, 325
slow payer, 443
small companies, 397
societies, 241
software, 6
sole trader, 219
source and application of funds statement, 425
source document, 184
sources of finance, 311
special resolution, 306
specific index, 477
spreadsheet, 6, 7, 10
Statements of Standard Accounting Practice
    (SSAPs), 95, 369, 497, 498, 501
  1: associated companies, 370, 394
  2: accounting policies, 397
  3: earnings per share, 370, 371, 445
  4: accounting for government grants, 371
  5: accounting for VAT, 340
  6: extraordinary items and prior year adjust-
    ments, 343, 371, 374
  7: current purchasing power accounting, 479
  8: the imputation system of taxation, 346, 356
  9: stocks and work in progress, 112, 375
  10: source and application of funds, 370
  11: deferred tax (superceded by SSAP 15), 349
  12: accounting for depreciation, 95
  13: research and development, 377
  14: group accounts, 370
  15: deferred tax, 349
  16: current cost accounting, 480
  17: post balance sheet results, 378
  18: contingencies, 379
  19: investment properties, 95
  20: foreign currency translation, 370
  21: accounting for leases, 323, 379
  22: accounting for goodwill, 278, 370
  23: accounting for acquisitions and mergers,
    370
  24: accounting for pension costs, 380

stages of an audit, 500
standard setting process, 369
standardisation, 389
standing orders, 206
status line, 16
statutory obligations, 497
stock, 34, 395
Stock Exchange, 316, 370, 394
  listing requirements, 398, 501
Stock Market, 325
stock provision, 113
stock turnover period, 442, 443
stock valuation, 108
stock-outs, 443
stocking policy, 450
stocktaking procedures, 108
stop list, 313, 443
straight line method of depreciation, 84
striking price, 316
subjective judgement, 444
subjectivity, 93
subscriptions, 246
substantive tests, 500
suppliers, 465
surplus of expenditure over income, 245
surplus of income over expenditure, 245
suspense column, 170, 327
suspense account, 170
systems approach, 466

T account, 189, 390
Table A, 306
tangible assets, 394
Tax
  allowances, 379
  authorities, 465
  liability, 223
taxable profits, 341, 380
taxation in company accounts, 339
team approach, 467
tender, 316
time series study, 446
timing differences, 349
titles, 14
total accounts, 192
total cost of manufacture, 106
total creditors account, 192
total debtors account, 192
total reversal of a transaction (errors in ac-
    counts), 168
trade credit, 149, 313, 318
trade discount, 139, 185
trading account, 133
trading companies, 390
transactions recorded only once, 220
transfer to reserves, 307
transferable skills, 7
translating, 397

trial balance, 165
true and fair, 9, 375, 497, 498
turnover, 392
two credits/debits, 167
two sided accounts format, 141
type of expenditure, 391

UK accounting profession, 369
ultra-vires, 306
understatement, 475, 501
units of constant purchasing power, 479
unlimited companies, 305
unlimited liability, 260
unpresented cheques, 206
unrealised holding gain, 488
unrecorded lodgements, 206
user groups, 466

value added statements, 465
value added tax (VAT), 340
    column/account, 340
        return, 359

verification tests, 500, 501
vertical presentation of accounts, 141
vested interest, 496
voting rights, 306, 317
vouching tests, 500

wages, 42
walk-through tests, 500
warrants, 315
wealth, 24, 223
who should report what to whom, 463
wholesale trade, 442
winding up, 318
window dressing, 479
windows, 14
word processing, 6
work in progress, 108
    valuation, 110
working capital, 414
    period, 450

zero rated goods and services, 340, 359